Letter to my Descendants

by

Niels Aage Skov

In memory of Aage and Thies –
and all the others.

History with its flickering lamp
stumbles along the trail of the past,
trying to reconstruct its scenes,
to revive its echoes, and kindle
with pale gleam the passions
of former days.

Winston Churchill
in the Commons
November, 1940

Niels Aage Skov

Letter to my Descendants

Odense University Press 1997

© Niels Aage Skov and Odense University Press 1997
Printed by Special-Trykkeriet Viborg a-s, Denmark
Cover design by Klaus Bjergager (DesignCo)
ISBN 87-7838-329-3

The photo on the front cover of the book shows the author
as he had just become a US Army volunteer after his escape
from the Wansleben concentration camp, April 1945.

Odense University Press
Campusvej 55
5230 Odense M
Denmark

Phone +45 66 15 79 99
Fax +45 66 15 81 26
E-mail: press@forlag.ou.dk
Internet-location: http://www.ou.dk/press

Distribution in The United States and Canada:

International Specialized Book Services
5804 NE Hassalo Street
Portland, OR 97213-3644
USA

phone: 1-800-944-6190
fax: 1-503-280-8832

Table of Contents

Acknowledgements

I am indebted to Jørgen Hæstrup for his unstinting encouragement. While realizing that my writing is but a pallid footnote to his monumental *oeuvres* on European resistance movements, I gratefully acknowledge his support. My old friends from the occupation period, such as were still alive when the manuscript came into being, foremost among them Aage, Erik, Alfred, Valdemar, Viggo and Kurt, helpfully read several drafts, corroborating details and adding many more. Two of my colleagues at The Evergreen State College, professors Pete Sinclair and Mark Papworth, critiqued the manuscript from their vantage points as academic teachers. Bernice Livingston Youtz patiently proofread and offered valuable suggestions. As always, my wife Diane was my main source to sustain both inspiration and perspective.

Preface

The sun was setting over the Straits of Georgia, bathing Burrard Inlet in a golden glow. A glance through the window took in the spectacular scene: Lions Gate Bridge with Vancouver and Stanley Park to the left, the University of British Columbia on the opposite shore, the Inlet joining the Straits beyond University Point, and to the far right the mountains of Vancouver Island on the distant horizon. It gave me a pleasant feeling to have all this beauty spread out like on a Winslow Homer painting intended for my enjoyment, but it did not distract me from bellowing out the verses of *Vift Stolt paa Kodans Bølge*, as the baby resting against my chest continued his journey into dreamland. My young son, Joshua, and I had an understanding: I was to carry him and sing to him, he was to go to sleep without fuss. We always kept the bargain, and we both relished the evening ritual. Eight years earlier, a similar covenant had been equally successful in Barcelona with my older son, Thor. He had preferred the old Danish national anthem *Kong Kristian*, as loud as possible, to the discreet puzzlement of the building's Spanish tenants. Unable to focus on my face any longer, Joshua's stare became unsteady, and his eyelids slowly drew shut. The Danish song finished, I switched to *Joshua Fits the Battle of Jericho*, at the end of which he was totally asleep. I plunked him in his crib and stood for a few moments at the window, savoring the view, the fragrance of the nursery, and my good luck in general. In the distance, Thor's voice mingled with those of the neighbor children, and I wondered vaguely whether I might live to know my sons' offspring, if they have any. I had known three of my grandparents, though none of my great-grandparents, but Joshua was born three days after my 50th birthday, so my chances of grandparenthood are shaky and of great-grandparenthood, very slim. What a pity, I thought, that we have so little communication across generations. How marvellous it would have been to have had direct contact from an ancestor, male or female, telling about his or her daily life, problems, hopes, aspirations, failures and accomplishments.[1] What an absolute treasure it would have been to receive a message written by someone whose life thread had been spun out in a different age, a message intended for me, reaching across the chasm of time. It suddenly struck me that I ought to write such a letter. It seemed a good idea and quite a natural thing to do. Here I was, a product of the 20th century, having accomplished nothing earthshaking, yet taking part in and observing the contemporary scene. I should be able to convey to my descendants a feel for my century's life that no history book will allow them to glimpse. Looking at the sleeping baby, I felt certain that his grandchildren's appreciation of a note from me would far outweigh the slight effort of writing. I decided then and there to write a letter to my descendants. Soon.

* * *

Joshua took a sip of milk and said, "Time sure flies when you get older ... this year it seemed only about six months between my birthdays." Jean and I nodded serious agreement to this piece of 7-year-old wisdom, and our eyes met across the table. "When are you going to start your writing about these things?" she asked. "Soon," I assured her, "very soon."

* * *

Jean opened her eyes with difficulty and fixed her unsteady stare on me. A bottle suspended above the hospital bed was slowly releasing a painkilling medication into a vein in her thin left arm, threatening to extinguish the consciousness she fought to preserve. "Thor read poetry to me," she whispered, "it was so lovely ... He has such strength and sensitivity ... far beyond his years ..." Her voice got fainter, "When you write to our descendants, say hello from me ..." A hint of a smile flickered on her face as I nodded, unable to speak.

* * *

Joshua came booming into the quiet dining room of the chalet, slowing down just enough to greet our Swiss innkeeper, Monsieur Rochat, politely in fluent French. "Listen Dad, LISTEN," he kept his voice down to an urgent whisper, "just LISTEN to these statistics of the United Nation's 34-year forecast of population growth ... LISTEN, do you realize that West Germany's is the only population that will actually be smaller by 2020?" His youthful excitement enveloped our table like an ionized cloud as he grappled with the impending problems of world overpopulation. He left as soon as the meal was finished, and Diane looked at me over her coffee cup. "You ought to mention this when you start writing. When *will* you start?" "Very soon, now." She kept looking at me. "All right, then, tomorrow." Slowly, she took a pen from her purse and handed it to me. "How about tonight ... right now?"

* * *

Introduction

Blest is the man who has visited this world in its fateful moments ...

F. I. Tyutchev

One of the attractive aspects of being alive and observing the human condition arises from the swiftness of profound change in that condition and in the world around us. Or so I used to think. Actually, when visiting Denmark with my young sons, I became aware of the extent to which that country has changed, and the nature of the changes filled me with dismay. The pastoral Denmark I wistfully think of from time to time, epitomized by the town of Ribe where I was born, is gone with the wind as completely as Margaret Mitchell's antebellum South, replaced by a society of commerce and light industry, high-rise buildings and manicured tourist attractions. Realizing that my sons can never see the Denmark that was, I set out to describe it in some detail, affording them a backward glance through the looking glass.

Along the way I learned something about myself and my roots that had lain unnoticed in those unexplored recesses of memory that we all possess but rarely have reason or inclination to examine. Born in the borderland in the shadow of Germany, I had grown up with a vigilant awareness of the colossus to the south. Its presence caused neither fear nor hostility among us border people, just wariness, spawned by a past wherein the petty tyrants of medieval Europe and later an expansive Reich under Bismarck had to be kept at arm's length.

It was not until I got into the wrenching problems of German occupation during World War Two that it dawned on me that I was mining a vein of some contemporary relevance. What makes otherwise unremarkable young people fall out of step with their society and march to a different drummer? In a world increasingly torn by violence, very largely perpetrated by young persons not of a criminal bent, the question carries some weight. Moreover, resistance by civilians in response to suppression in that war was the apparent progenitor of certain postwar phenomena, including the plastique bombs used by innumerable terrorists, and aircraft hijackings. In their different ways they all declare objection to imposed conditions.

Researching the literature on resistance movements in general and the Danish one in particular, I found that historical accounts in some respects differed from my own experience at the time, both in substance and in emphasis. Historians often limn the resistance not only as far larger, but also as better organized than it was. They tend to leave the reader with the impression that events quite naturally – almost inevitably – went the way they did, when in fact chance

9

happenings, randomness and outright chaos tended to prevail. Moreover, I found little that dealt with the relationship and interactions between the internal, hidden and clumsy efforts of civilians, and the outside, organized and visible war, as it was perceived by the resistance participants.

No doubt, there are many and good reasons for this, one being that not everyone involved felt like divulging their activities and intimate thoughts to later investigators. Another reason could be that a historian's natural tendency to make order and sense out of the fragmented material may impose an overall tenor at odds with reality. However that may be, my aim became one of amending or perhaps supplementing history by describing our resistance efforts as they really were: haphazard and impulsive, triggered by the gamut of human emotions such as hope, anger, fear, courage, pride and vanity that might momentarily possess any one of us. That it was so, usually rendered our efforts uncoordinated and frequently ineffectual or wasted. On the positive side, it also made for an unpredictability that baffled German military authorities as well as the Gestapo.

In order to place in perspective the efforts of the resistance, I have juxtaposed its rise to the progress of the war that was spreading all around the globe, a struggle about which we knew at most the outline and which therefore only sporadically influenced our actions. At least in the first four of the five occupation years most acts of sabotage against the Germans formed a pattern of small, personal wars carried on by a few individuals with little or no mutual contact.

The unceasing work of Danish authorities to apportion equally the country's dwindling reserves and to hold down inflation made these small personal wars possible by removing the need to devote one's time overwhelmingly to hunting for the necessities of life. And yet, we had to carry on our normal work or educational pursuits while dabbling in the potentially deadly game of opposing the German Wehrmacht as spare-time warriors. It is also well to remember that the people most active were largely in an age group where interest in the opposite sex is at its peak. Such normal drives are not suppressed by extraordinary circumstances, rather the opposite.

The war narrative is far from a complete history of World War Two but is intended only to keep the reader abreast of the sequence of its main events. The focus is largely on Europe as the decisive theater. After America's entry into the war, the eventual outcome might seem to have been certain to any objective observer. But our view today is necessarily skewed by the advantage of hindsight; and in an ongoing war situation objectivity is a scarce commodity. In the occupied countries we understood to some extent that Hitler and the Japanese military rulers were fatuous in assessing American capability and determination. Nevertheless, the war in Europe in fact was a close affair, and at several points seemed to be going the wrong way.

Preceding the war narrative, Hitler's rise from penniless obscurity to head of state and his aggressive policies leading inexorably to war are mentioned, as they explain the cadence of events in the 1930s. As fate has willed it, they also coincide with my own story.

Letting fifty years pass before getting around to putting pen to paper may appear to diminish the result by losing or at least blurring much crucial detail, but that is not necessarily the case. The process of recall, of remembering things long past, is intriguing. I have found that by letting incidents rest for days (and nights) in one's subconscious, characters, names and places do come back to life. Human memory supposedly is never lost, it just becomes less readily accessible, and patience can often accomplish retrieval. I have confirmed the truth of that by cross-checking information and data with such old friends as are still alive. And there is one distinct advantage to very long hindsight. It sobers reflection and provides a perspective that obliterates apprehension about one's own rôle, of fear to have done less well than one would like to have been the case. Time replaces such concerns with a simple urge to describe what really happened.

I had the good luck to encounter some outstanding people in the course of the recorded events. Many of them did not survive the ordeal. Eternal life makes no sense, indeed it is a contradiction in terms. But as you read about some of them, they will live briefly in your mind, and that they deserve. History is replete with such unsung heroes.

Some things are discussed in detail simply because they have stayed in my memory better than others. These are incidents that particularly impressed me, or motivated me for better or worse. On the other hand, I have not attempted to depict the full horror of the Nazi concentration camps. I find that task impossible. And yet, we who experienced the camps have a moral obligation not to forget the innocent millions who died victims to one man's deranged fantasy of a master race. I believe Noberto Bobbio was correct when he wrote that the camps were "not one of the events, but *the* monstrous, perhaps unrepeatable event of human history."

Fortunately, far more accomplished writers have dealt with that subject. For vivid and detailed descriptions I recommend the books by Paul Thygesen, Niels Jørgensen and Herman Wouk.[2] Theirs are the best portrayals I know. To the extent that history does repeat itself, it must be in large measure due to the way in which horrors of the past tend to lose some of their dread. In many cases, passage of time confers an almost benign, romantic quality on human transgression. Written just after the end of the war, Thygesen's and Jørgensen's accounts of the camps retain their fresh immediacy.

Part I

Growing up in Denmark

—————

Nazism: Rising and Rampant

Chapter 1   July 1924

People will not look forward to posterity who never look backward to their ancestors.

Edmund Burke

I was born in Ribe in November of 1919, a classic Scorpio. Some people assure me that Scorpio is a good sign, and if good luck in life is a criterion, they must be right. My birthplace was a medieval stone house a short walk from the water-works, and at four I was able to make that journey on my own. In fact, my chief motivation for learning to walk must have been my need to get myself to the waterworks where my grandfather resided as master, for I considered this my real home, whereas the house where my mother and sister lived was a mere annex to which I had to return from time to time, tiresomely. I was very pleased to have been born in Ribe which I knew from my grandfather to be by far the best town in Denmark, situated near the North Sea coast on the peninsula of Jutland. Ribe is old, losing its origin in the mists of early Danish history. In the 12th century it held the king's residence, and it prospered and grew during the period when the Hanseatic League controlled commerce in the Baltic countries. My grandfather told me that in the late Middle Ages the town had 16 churches and was the seat of powerful bishops carrying out papal edicts on these northern fringes of Christendom. But now the town numbered only some five thousand people, and the two remaining churches towered with their immense bulk over the small houses clustered around them, like mother hens watching over newly-hatched brood. In the largest, the cathedral, my parents had been married, and my sister and I were later christened at its great bronze font. A fine Romanesque structure, it was built in the 1200s and still displayed some of the decorations dating back to pre-Reformation days, but from oil paintings on its white-washed walls in aisles and nave only Protestant bishops sternly looked down on the worshippers. The paintings showed the chronology of holy servants occupy-

Ribe as seen from the Nipsaa. Between the cathedral (center) and St. Cathrine church (right) the waterworks tower can be seen rising above the surrounding houses.

ing the bishopric in recent centuries, each bust draped in black and displaying a humorless visage. In most of the paintings the wife and children appeared as well, in modestly subordinate positions, of course, with infants who died in delivery or very young discreetly indicated by the addition of small angel wings. The heavy oak door providing main entrance to the narthex was huge and strengthened with iron fittings. Its present lock came from my grandfather's forge. Flanking the building stood bronze statues of particularly prominent Protestant bishops whose learnedness and diligence were being thus rewarded by posterity.

Around the cathedral the low brick and half timber houses huddled under red tile roofs, most of them only one or two hundred years old, but many of them dating back several centuries. The streets were paved with cobbles except for a few stretches where square pavers laid in a fan pattern provided a smoother surface for carriage or pedestrian. On the town's west side was the moat-encircled Castle Hill, in modern times only a greensward-covered area with an irregular surface hinting at subterranean ruins. But early in the millennium it was the site of a royal castle where among others Valdemar the Victorious had his residence from 1202 to 1241. He married the daughter of King Ottocar of Bohemia, Princess Dragomir, by sending his private emissary to wed her by proxy and fetch her by ship. A new queen was traditionally granted the privilege of receiving a "morning gift" on the dawn following her wedding night, and Queen Dagmar, as the Danes called her, asked as her gift the release of all peasants held for failure to pay tax. She instantly gained popular affection but unfortunately died young. A bronze statue on Castle Hill showed Dagmar in the prow of the ship carrying her to Denmark, anxious to glimpse the husband she had married *in absentia*.

16

The King's next choice for Queen was a Portuguese princess by the name of Berengaria. *She* chose expensive and ostentatious morning gifts necessitating heavier taxes on the peasantry, and it was said that for twenty generations common folk spat on her grave. As could be expected, Valdemar's choice cost him much in popularity, and six hundred years later local people still held him in low esteem for it. *Kings, take note!*

In the Middle Ages, the town's burghers had a deserved reputation for severity in punishing crimes of all kinds, rivaling Calvin in their delight at finding and visiting torture and death upon sinners. There was a local saying about an old woman in Varde, a town further north, who watched her son being hanged and muttered, "Thank the Lord, my son, that you didn't come before the Ribe court." In Ribe torture had normally attended capital punishment, an official response to the public's desire for entertainment. Few categories of miscreants got off with their lives but, surprisingly, medieval law allowed adulterers to do so. Standard punishment for such contumely to morality was to have the male offender being dragged by his penis naked through town.

Ribe was located four kilometers from the sea. The surrounding country was unrelieved by any hill or valley. Large, completely flat expanses of meadows stretch along the west coast of southern Jutland and continue down through Schleswig-Holstein and Ditmarschen all the way to Holland. Off the coast a fringe of islands, including Fanø, Manø and Rømø, had been split off from the mainland by storm floods in times past. Periodically the North Sea penetrated the coastal areas and ate away the land formerly tying the islands together and to the mainland, sometimes in swift, cataclysmic events. A great flood in 1372 washed away 30 parishes in one night and left memories of terror that persisted through generations of hardy coastal farmers; but eventually the danger was checked. Early in the 20th century a dike had been constructed along the coast to fend off the fury of the sea, and behind it the rains were now slowly leaching the salt from the soil and turning the marshy meadows into agricultural land. A small river, the Nipsaa, ran through town, winding its way to the sea and penetrating the dike through a double lock. Until the beginning of this century small vessels, Dutch *schouw* and other longshore craft, reached Ribe with trade goods and tied up at the stone quay on the west side of town. But in the 1920s such an arrival was rare. The town had sunk into a somnolent, peaceful state, bereft of vitality.

Although born in 1919, I really started life in the summer of 1924, for that was the time of my earliest memory: venturing across the narrow cobbled street from the waterworks to the home of my friend Aage Kjellerup, and this is what I remember doing one day shortly after midsummer of that year. The house of my destination was a two-story affair belonging to Aage's father, one of the town merchants. Reaching the other side of the street, I climbed the three steep stone steps, found the front door unlocked as usual, and stepped into the narrow hallway. The house contained an apartment on the second floor, while on my right the ground floor held the store where farmers and townspeople came to purchase their miscellaneous requirements. It was permeated by numerous pungent odors, none of them offensive, and they were noticeable in the hallway as well. The most dominant contributors to this olfactory mélange were two large open barrels holding marinated herring, whole fish averaging more than a foot in length which the clerks could grasp with wood tongs. Second was the coffee grinder, a large machine with two brass-plated wheels occupying three feet of counter space and with a quiet hum producing finely ground coffee from freshly roasted beans. Joining the distinctive herring-coffee duo were numerous aromas from less insistent, yet perceptible sources: dried fruit, hemp, tar marlin, kerosene, leather tack, varnish, honey and flour, the last from large burlap sacks open at the top to allow the clerks easy access with a scoop. To my left lay a storeroom where sacks and boxes were stacked.

The house had a portal access leading from the street to an interior yard closed on one side by a small stable where Mr. Kjellerup kept one draft horse for his delivery wagon. On the other side a seven-foot brick wall separated the property from a grade school next door, and we had devised a way to climb the wall to spy on the school children during recess. Above the portal was attic storage whence the hired man could lower sacks of flour and other goods into his delivery wagon or into any farm wagon backed into the portal. The hired man's name was Mathiesen. He was a somewhat fierce looking character whom Aage and I cautiously shunned while composing derisive couplets about him. In Danish the word fart rhymes with Mathiesen, thus providing us ample poetic raw material. When not employed on deliveries, he was kept busy chopping kindling wood in the yard. The six-inch sticks were carefully bundled and sold to housewives as starter for their *kakkelovne,* coke burning stoves that were the sole means of room heating in the cold season.

Aage's father, Mr. Kjellerup, reigned over this domain with cold inefficiency. He was a man of medium height with a small moustache and a permanently dour expression. Having taken over from the retiring owner a business that had prospered greatly during the years of World War One, his brusk personality and curt manner with customers had caused a steady decline in his trade and income. This aggravated his naturally pessimistic outlook, so that people tended to curtail contact with him whenever possible. His wife was of farmer stock, transplanted to the city as a young bride which, city folk never ceased to assure her, was her great and good luck. It had been her youthful beauty that had captured the attention of the city merchant, but that was rapidly fading, and her speech was becoming slurred by adenoids. Aage was the oldest child, followed closely by two girls of whom the youngest was still in diapers.

I scaled the long stairway to the second floor and knocked on the living room door. Told to enter, I took in the situation in a swift glance. The Kjellerup family was just finishing lunch, and Aage's mother was starting to clear the table. Aage was excused without comment, and we lost no time in heading back across the street. Despite some potential as a playground, we rarely used Aage's house

The top of the Ribe cathedral offered a commanding view of the town and its surroundings. The utterly flat landscape made it possible for the waterworks (lower right) to furnish water to the citizens by simple gravity feed.

because his father lacked empathy with the aspirations of small boys. By contrast, we knew that we were welcome at the waterworks, not just tolerated, and it had become our selected area of operations. To a four-year-old boy the waterworks was an immense affair, its square brick tower thrusting high above the one- and two-story houses of the town, dwarfed only by the two cathedrals. In the top of the tower was the water tank, feeding the water by gravity to the surrounding citizenry. In the basement were the two pumps and the engines, and a mechanical pointer connected through a long rod to a float in the tower's water tank high above showed the water level in the tank and warned when additional pumping effort was required to raise it. The engine room had yellow tiles on the floor, and the engines were painted grass green. When one or both were running, which was most of the time, the noise and vibration were pleasantly audible through the entire structure and seemed to infuse the building with a life of its own. The engine room smelled of warm oil, and everything was conspicuously clean. I was allowed to wipe the engine housings with white twist, a cotton waste from England's spinning mills, and under my grandfather's watchful eye I could lubricate certain bearings as well. Each engine was started by hand in the morning, as grandfather gripped the six-foot flywheel and threw his weight on the spokes. I was not heavy enough for that and waited impatiently for the day when I could turn the wheel. When an engine was not running and grandfather was not around, Aage and I would climb onto one spoke, and the great wheel would slowly, reluctantly, yield a fraction of a turn, but it took a modicum of speed for the engine to catch. Only grandfather could accomplish that. The engines drove the pumps in the adjoining pump room through twelve-inch-wide leather belts, and we knew the distinctive squeal of the belt when grandfather eased in the friction clutch to start pumping. If a fire occurred in town at night, an alarm bell activated from the fire chief's station would awaken grandfather who would hurriedly start both engines so as to have plenty of water available for the hosemen. After starting the engines, he would climb the stairway and the ladder to the top of the tower to see where the fire was, then return to the bedroom and report it to my grandmother.

From the back of the pump room a winding stairway led directly to the tower loft. It was unlit, so that one had to negotiate two full turns in darkness before emerging into the loft. From here a wooden ladder led to an upper loft above which the water tank could be seen, holding the town's supply of drinking water. The upper loft was strictly off limits to us, and at four we still obeyed the injunction.

On the exterior, two sides of the waterworks tower were graced by a tiny garden or yard in the European style. The part adjoining the neighboring property had a few square feet of lawn, and in a corner an elderberry bush screened an outdoor table and four chairs where my grandparents could take their Sunday afternoon coffee on the few days during summer when weather permitted. There was also an immense pear tree, certainly old enough to remember the laying of the first building stone. It produced annually a crop of small, scurvy pears, hard, strong-tasting and fiercely astringent, puckering your mouth at the first bite. The part of the yard facing the street was flanked on one side by the two-story gable end of a brick building along which a row of small, scraggly rhododendrons struggled to survive. The building's ground floor contained a barber shop where two oak barber chairs stood in a scented cloud of eau de Cologne. The barber's name was Milwertz, a small man of meticulously neat appearance and delicate, almost feminine features, and he lived upstairs with his wife and two daughters. On the opposite side, the yard was bordered by a plank fence and the building behind it belonged to the butcher, a heavy-set, choleric man whose name was Henry Petersen. The Petersen family had two sons and occupied the upper story of the small corner building, but the lower story was given over to the store which had a terrazzo floor sprinkled with sawdust and whitewashed walls where sides of beef and pork hung neatly on galvanized meat hooks and filled the room with the peculiar smell of cold, raw meat. In the middle of the waterworks yard was a small octagonal fountain with a sculpture in its center, a cherub riding a swan whose up-stretched beak sprayed water several feet into the air. The fountain served the practical use of holding grandfather's bait roaches (a local minnow species); trying to catch one in a small net, almost always unsuccessfully, kept Aage and me occupied for hours.

20

In the course of our early childhood we each fell into the fountain twice. It was only twenty inches deep, but the shock of the cold water and the ignominy of running home totally soaked stimulated us to caution. We were allowed in the engine room, even with the engines running, for there was a fence consisting of two parallel steel rods enclosing engines and pumps and designed to keep spectators at a safe distance. The rods were respectively two and four feet above the floor, so it was a simple matter to climb over, under or through them. However, grandfather had explained to us how a drive belt could easily catch and kill a man in seconds, and we intuitively sensed the danger. The engine room was no playground, but no matter; the waterworks provided plenty of other diversions.

* * *

From millions of men ... one man must step forward who with apodictic force will form granite principles from the wavering idea-world of the broad masses ...

Adolf Hitler

High above the river Lech in Upper Bavaria the old Landsberg Castle had been taken into use as a prison by the German government. This summer of 1924 it held an unusual prisoner, a 35-year-old man by the name of Adolf Hitler, a firebrand convicted of plotting and attempting to overthrow the government of the Weimar Republic. The attempt was bungled and was afterward referred to derisively as the Beer Hall Putsch. During his incarceration he spent his time working on a book describing his plans to resurrect the German nation from its present political and economic chaos. Inside Germany his name and that of his party were barely known, and then chiefly as butts of jokes. Outside Germany, the world as yet knew nothing of him.

This was soon to change.

Chapter 2   July 1926

Now 'tis little joy
To know that I'm farther off from heaven
Than when I was a boy.

Thomas Hood

I was sitting on the workbench in the waterworks basement workshop watching my grandfather working on a sewing machine that refused to stitch the way its owner wanted. This was my favorite vantage point, for I could observe how my grandfather used his tools as he applied them to the task at hand. I could also ask questions and invariably received sensible and courteous answers, for we held each other in enormous respect. In fact, there was great and true love between us, although I never recognized it as such. Neither of us was given to any display of affection, and I do not recall touching him aside from shaking his hand at arrival and departure when later on I began to spend my school vacations with my grandparents. But I would sit on the workbench and observe the old craftsman by the hour as he filed a key or restored a sewing machine to mechanical health, and it was soon obvious to me that such endeavors were noble art. Grandfather would go about a task with carefully controlled impatience, whether forging red-hot iron on his anvil, his hammer striking a note like a church bell, or adjusting the trigger on a shotgun, and eventually iron or machinery would yield to his will. Making machinery run, and run smoothly, was clearly satisfying to a man's soul. At times I might amuse myself by scraping iron filings from the workbench and creating showers of sparklets by letting them trickle into the flame of the gas light that was still used to illuminate the workshop, although electric lights had been installed in both engine room and living quarters; or I might fire up the forge, starting with an oily rag and some bits of wood, then piling on the nut coal, (nut-sized chunks of bituminous coal), working the bellows with a treadle pump until the fire glowed hot and I could bring the end of a small iron rod to orange heat and hammer it flat on the anvil. Once in a while grandfather would volunteer something relevant to his momentary endeavor, such as praising the file he was using as being a machinist's most important tool and with satisfaction relating how at the 1889 Paris World's Fair the Germans brought out an allegedly superior file only to have a British tool manufacturer cut it in two with one of *his* files. Grandfather always lauded the British, and not only because of the lingering legacy of England's dominant rôle in the Industrial Revolution. The German pressure in the border land dictated one's national preference.

In the course of many such sessions grandfather taught me much about how to make machinery behave, and in response to my questions he also told me about himself, in time establishing in my mind a tactile line to my ancestors. He was born in Agerskov, a small village south of Ribe and close to the German frontier. That was in 1860. Four years later Bismarck's troops defeated the Danish army, and the area became part of the Kaiser's Germany. It was Prussia's second try to conquer Schleswig-Holstein, the first attempt in 1848 having been repulsed by the Danes. Grandfather was a peaceful man, detesting everything military, yet he spoke with quiet pride as he told me how *his* father, Hans Christian Tarp, had fought as a dragoon in that 1848 war. The enemy cavalry consisted of uhlans, colorful Austrian lancers mounted on light, fast horses. The Danish dragoons were conscripted farm boys on heavy workhorses, the kind pulling the brewery wagons in today's beer advertisements. The husky farmers armed with sabres plowed like dreadnoughts through the German horse, earning for themselves the nickname of butchers. On the family wall hung a small picture of my great-grandfather, made by some etching process in those pre-photography days. It showed a strongly built, tall man sitting with his uniform coat unbuttoned to reveal a scarf, his hands resting firmly on a large, slightly curved saber, the face distinctly handsome with high cheekbones, dark hair and a prominent mustache. Between the wars he became one of the mounted police King Frederik VII used to keep order in the border area, but when Denmark lost the next war and with it Schleswig-Holstein, he moved with his family to Ribe where he became the town's policeman. This appointment was one to which he was well suited because of his great physical strength. Although he died well before I was born, old people in town still spoke about him and told me how his reputation usually was enough to keep the burghers in line. When he occasionally had to quiet a few brawlers, he usually did so by picking them up by the scruff of the neck, one in each hand, and smacking them together like rag dolls.

In consequence of the Tarp family's desire to keep north of the border, my grandfather, Niels Hansen Tarp, arrived in Ribe at the age of four, and he grew up there. His mother had died in childbirth, so he was reared by a stepmother, and unhappily so. More than half a century later he still spoke with bitterness of his childhood and how his stepmother boxed his ears mercilessly. He blamed his poor hearing in old age on that early abuse. As a young boy he was apprenticed to one of the town's three blacksmiths who taught him the craft well. He related to me that when he was 14, he had used the 14-pound sledge hammer ten hours every day. At 18 he passed his journeyman test and left town to go to Copenhagen, where he entered *Maskinistskolen* to become a marine engineer. After graduation, he sailed first in longshore commerce and later as Third Engineer in the *D/S Thingvalla* of the Thingvalla Line. The vessel was powered by both steam and sail as was common in that transition era, so that a sensible skipper could save his coal when the wind was favorable. The *Thingvalla* carried emigrants, mostly farmers who as second or third sons saw little chance of inheriting or acquiring land of their own. Hence those with the most vigor, energy and initiative set out to seek their fortune in the new world.

In 1887 the good citizens of Ribe built a waterworks to replace the town well, and a qualified man was sought to take charge of the pumps and the two one-cylinder coal gas engines being installed to drive them. Grandfather applied for and got the job, as he had quit the marine world after twenty-four crossings to New York – a fortuitous move as on the next trip the *D/S Thingvalla* collided in the North Atlantic with another ship of the same line, the *D/S Geiser*, with heavy losses of passengers and crew. The waterworks position carried a remuneration of forty kroner per month, plus living quarters in the lower part of the tower and in an attached building – more than enough for a man to get married and start a family. Of the actual wedding I have no concrete information. Unfortunately, it never occurred to me to ask about it. I know that two fine crystal glasses, etched with the couple's initials were among the presents, for I still have them. They must have been been ceremonial, or rather symbolic, for my grandparents drank wine extremely rarely, and never out of *those* glasses.

By the time I entered the picture almost forty years later, he was known to everyone in town for his industry and integrity. I understood from the earliest time that the waterworks was his kingdom and undisputed domain, and by natural extension it became mine as well. As my awareness of the world increased, this domain revealed itself to have more components than those supplying water to the townsfolk. In the basement, contiguous to the engine room, was also grandfather's workshop, for besides being master of the waterworks, he had a thriving business of repairing all manner of mechanical contrivances. Most important were bicycles, for they represented virtually the sole means of transport for people in town, and even more so for the farmers and peasants beyond the city limits. For longer trips, there was of course the railroad, and farmers with goods could use their horse-drawn carriages, but most traffic was by bicycle: swift, easy to use and within economic reach. By the time of my presence in the 1920s, there were half a dozen cars in town. The wealthy butcher next to the waterworks had a small Ford pickup truck, the gasworks manager owned an old Dodge Brothers sedan, and the veterinarian and the county doctor had automobiles as well, but these motor vehicles were seldom seen. The bicycle ruled. Accordingly, grandfather repaired bicycles by the score. Farmers brought them in miserable condition and invariably received a severe dressing-down. Grandfather would expound on the mechanical virtues of this technological marvel, emphasizing how uncouth and irresponsible it was to treat it with anything but reverence, scowling at the farmer if he ventured a feeble excuse about muddy roads or driving rains. As soon as the farmer left, grandfather would hang the bicycle on a special bracket in the engine room and start with a thorough cleaning, using twist and kerosene. Then came the repair, usually a punctured tire or a damaged wheel, and then general adjustment of brakes, chain and spokes. He would explain to me the intricacies of the rear wheel hub which allowed the wheel to run free when the pedals were stationary, activating braking when the rider pushed counter on the pedals. Most of the bicycles were German Adler or Danish Hamlet, and both of these were fitted with German Torpedo hubs, superior by far, said grandfather. Occasionally a cycle would appear with old-fashioned handlebar brakes. Grandfather and I looked down our noses at those as awkward, difficult to keep in adjustment, and unsightly.

Second in importance were sewing machines. Almost every housewife owned one, most of them being German Adler or American Singer, and sooner or later they seemed to appear on grandfather's workbench for repair or adjustment. If the machine was dirty or ill kept, its owner rarely escaped some pointed admonition when she returned to collect it in perfect running condition. The machines were all hand cranked, although a treadle model could appear, but no electrics. Grandfather also made keys by hand filing, repaired locks and occasionally made one from scratch, repaired shotguns, pumps, meat grinders, hinges – just about anything mechanical. He was a superb craftsman. Besides the lock on the cathedral door, much of the hardware in town as well as many of the small, decorative fences around graves in the cemetery came from his workshop. He also produced miscellaneous candlesticks, one model in the shape of a "C" to be sold on King Christian's birthday, numerous simple little sconces, and some hammered copper ashtrays with wrought iron feet. In the era before electricity reached the farms he had been called upon in the harvest season by the agricultural cooperative to run their locomobile, a self-propelled steam engine, which was taken from farm to farm to power threshing machines. In his spare time he made a perfectly working, miniature steam engine for the Latin school's physics room. He also made a seat to be bolted to the frame of his bicycle so that I at an early age could ride with him out of town to see the hill[3] in which a terrible troll many years ago kept a poor peasant woman prisoner until her son, Hans, helped her escape. I was too young to ponder the fact that Hans must have been the troll's offspring, as the woman had him after one year of captivity and cohabitation with that creature, but the story's authenticity was beyond question, for it had been related to grandfather by *his* father.

Above the workshop grandfather had a small office. It contained his desk, made of cherry wood and carrying a blotter and a brass paperweight in the form of a die. In the right-hand drawer, which he kept locked, was a money box with a compartment full of silver coins of ten and twenty-five øre. When he was at his desk, which was rarely, I would ask him to unlock and show me the treasure. Thus gratified, I would tell him, "Grandfather, you are enormously rich" and he would answer, "Not really. But you see, I am satisfied if I can earn just one øre more than I need." I believed this to be the epitome of modesty and thought it accorded well with his evident opulence. His desk chair was made of oak overlaid with a thin ply of cherry, the seat upholstered with crimson plush. I still have it, but the seat is now covered with an embroidery my mother made when the plush wore out. On the office wall hung a lithograph showing Napoleon on the British man-of-war carrying him into exile and imprisonment on St. Helena. He stood on deck at the mast gazing darkly toward the horizon, a small group of his officers clustered nearby, anxiously observing their idolized emperor. Below the picture stood grandfather's chaise longue where he took his afternoon nap every day from two to three o'clock. A small round table completed the furniture. It carried a large polished calabash pipe and a tobacco box of hammered pewter. The pipe was a gift from abroad, considered exotic and eliciting admiration from local visitors, but he had smoked it rarely, preferring his briar for daily use. When his tobacco supply ran low, he would purchase a yellow packet of *Cremo* and a green-and-white, heavily waxed carton of *Dark Mixture* which I was allowed to blend in the pewter box. The *Cremo* was fine-cut and of moderate fragrance, but the *Dark Mixture* was coarse and pungently aromatic, so that my hands for hours afterwards bore scented witness to the tobacco ritual.

In his workshop grandfather wore denim work pants and a denim work jacket, but for going out into the street on any errand he invariably wore his blue-black serge suit: jacket, pants and vest, with a hard-bill cap of the same dark cloth. With either outfit he wore a blue-and-white striped shirt with a detachable celluloid collar fastened in the back with a patent button, and a pin-on tie. It was the more or less standard outfit for men of his class, worn throughout Jutland and northern Germany in the late 19th and early 20th century.

He worked hard and well and derived complete satisfaction from doing so, but he observed Sundays as days of rest in the biblical sense. This was not so much because he wanted to relax, and certainly not for religious reasons; it was simply the thing to do. Custom. Proper behavior for self-respecting people. On Sunday morning he shaved as usual with his Gillette safety razor after sharpening the blade on a leather strop. A blue Gillette blade was good for several months when sharpened daily. He dressed only slightly differently from the rest of the week, using what had been his uniform hat when he sailed as a marine engineer four decades earlier. If an outing was scheduled in the summer, he also put on his uniform jacket which was of white drill with the Thingvalla insignia in the brass buttons. That also called for polishing his gold pocket watch, an Elgin he had acquired on one of his many trips to New York. "I bought it from a little girl on the pier," he told me. It was really gold plated, but we always referred to it as the gold watch. The chain, also gold plated, needed dunking in a saucer of ammonia in order to sparkle as only gold can do, and the ritual was always performed on the wood counter in the kitchen before our departure. Attached to the chain was a small fob in the shape of a ship's wheel, also gold, with a mother-of-pearl center.

It was perfectly obvious to me that grandfather was the most important man in town, the central figure without whom the town could not function at all. Only later did I come reluctantly to realize that there was an academically trained bureaucracy: the Latin school rector, the mayor, the town treasurer, and the bank director who constituted a different class, coolly polite but maintaining their separation from those without academic training, however indispensable. The merchants were a different class still, uneasily trying to safeguard what they perceived as their unique interests. They were at times joined by the town's two goldsmiths and two watchmakers who because of their craft training as well as their retail sales were in a position to wear two hats. Whereas grandfather enjoyed the friendship of many and the respect of everyone, he in turn thought his local world to be the best place on earth and its inhabitants the finest. It was simply not possible for him to imagine living anywhere but in Ribe. He loved the town, loved the part of the Jutland west coast where it was situated. He was not particularly loquacious, but over the years he told me bits of information and recalled incidents about the town and its people and about the surrounding countryside, and his love of the area communicated itself to me. Long before I was born, around the turn of the century, grandfather, together with a former sea captain, had owned a small pleasure craft powered by a steam engine after the fashion of that period. I often lamented to grandfather that he no longer had the steamboat. On the wall in his office hung an old photograph showing a Sunday excursion of ladies with parasols and gentlemen in their Sunday best under the boat's canopy, setting out on a cruise, grandfather erect and attentive by the engine, looking to have things well in hand. But by the time I was around, his hobby was fishing. He reckoned the sportsfishing season to last from the first haying in July until the autumn rains muddied the waters in late September. During that two and one-half months, come rain or shine, he would be off whenever the work load permitted. He had arranged with a man in town, a turner by the name of Christensen, to look after the machines in his absence. The turner was a heavy-set man with a huge Kaiser Wilhelm moustache. He treated grandfather with a respect bordering on awe and relished the opportunity to assume the prestigious waterworks responsibilities. So, when the wind was southwest and the sky overcast, Christensen would early in the morning be put in temporary charge of the machinery, and grandfather would be off on his bicycle to spend the day tramping along the local streams, stalking trout and pike and bass. He made his own rods of bamboo, suitable both for fly casting and for heavier bait. On his back he carried a wicker basket wherein the catch was deposited, swathed in fresh grass. He wore street clothes and on his feet, knee-length rubber boots. An old felt hat completed the outfit, together with a short raincoat when weather demanded. The fish to be caught were those who could trace their ancestral lines locally right back to the ice age. There were only three or four other sportsfishermen in town and thus little danger of depleting the stock.

As the bait roaches had permanent quarters in the waterworks fountain, nightcrawlers resided in a wad of wet moss in a clay flowerpot kept in the cool-ness of grandmother's wash house. Grandfather taught me how to stalk them in the garden at night, when they creep from their burrows to gather dead leaves. They always leave a small piece of their tail end in the burrow and will retract at lightning speed if warned by a heavy footstep or a warm breath. They are blind, however, and can therefore be stalked with a flashlight. One catches them by swiftly pinning the worm's tail end to the ground just where it issues from the burrow. The critter will retract instantly but cannot disappear into the dark safe-ty of the earth, because its retreat is blocked. One then pulls, gently or the worm will break, and for about twenty seconds there is a standoff between hunt-er and prey; then the worm tires and lets go. When this happened, we would drop it into the moss-filled flowerpot.

The door to the stairway opened and Aage entered, producing a licorice tape from his pocket. That was our favorite candy, and in our age group it was claimed to be made from horseblood. I jumped down from the workbench and we walked out into the garden, chewing on the licorice and debating how to spend the afternoon. Entertainment of children was confined to birthdays and Christmas celebrations plus *Fastelavn*, Shrove Monday, when young children wearing masks would go in early morning search of people still in bed, "whip-ping" them awake with home-made whisks while reciting an ancient chant,[4] en-titling them to be rewarded with a sugar-coated bun. But on the whole, we were expected to entertain ourselves, which suited Aage and me just fine. It was the summer of 1926, and being nearly seven we felt old and competent enough to explore the areas of the waterworks that had so far escaped our scrutiny: the upper reaches beyond the loft. With an air of innocence we strolled back through the workshop, continued through the engine room and pump room, and climbed the winding stairway, feeling our way step by step to the loft. We had checked out the loft many times, for this was where grandfather kept his stock of spare parts for bicycles on a long shelf. On rainy days we had spent many hours admiring and fingering these treasures. There were red cat's eyes reflectors for the rear fender, celluloid grips for the handlebars, bells for signal-ing, carbide lanterns that could cast clear light ahead but with small colored glass windows to the sides, green to the right and red to the left, dog pistols made of tin and to be loaded with corks that had a small powder charge in the center, pumps to inflate the tires, baggage carriers, chain guards, and countless other essentials. The dog pistols were a particular attraction. They were meant to scare off farmers' dogs that might charge the unwary cyclist, but we could easily visualize numerous other uses. To our dismay the pistols had mysteriously disappeared from the shelf, together with the ammunition. In reply to our in-quiries, grandfather had laconically answered, "Sold out." As we emerged from the winding stairway we routinely checked the shelf to see whether any new items had been added, then eyed the long wooden ladder leading to the upper loft. I started slowly climbing, grasping firmly each rung, with Aage close behind. The ladder just reached the upper loft, and when we stepped onto it and looked back down, we fell momentarily silent, for it was twelve feet between the floors and the distance looked far more intimidating from above than from below. The upper loft was empty except for three clotheslines which grandmother used to dry her laundry in the winter. Another twelve feet above could be seen the great water tank that held the town's supply of tapwater. It rested on three stout I beams imbedded in the tower's masonry walls, and another wooden ladder led to a small open platform in one of the four odd-shaped spaces between the cylindrical tank and the square tower. The platform was the transfer point from the last wooden ladder to a steel ladder riveted to the outside of the tank. I started toward the next ladder, saying, "Come," but lowered my voice to a whisper, partly so that no chance visitor to the main loft below could hear me, and partly in deference to the awesomeness the venture was taking on. On the transfer platform I waited for Aage, and the two of us climbed side by side the tank's steel ladder which was just wide enough for our bodies. At the top we grasped the edge of the open tank and looked down into it. It was about two-thirds full, and the water looked dark and ominous. We felt on our faces the coolness radiating from it and stood for some moments looking around uncertainly while hanging on with sweaty palms. In each of the tower's four walls were two window-shaped openings at the level of the tank. They were protected against bird intrusion by wood slats through which one could look down into the street far below but not out toward the horizon. "Look," Aage said in a low voice, "there is my house." And through the slats of the wall to our left the Kjellerup house was indeed visible in bird's eye perspective. We spat in the water to confirm our presence and watched the two sets of rings enlarging and crossing their patterns on the surface.

Then we slowly and cautiously made our way down.

* * *

If you wish the sympathy of broad masses then you must tell them the crudest and most stupid things ...

Adolf Hitler

To the south, Adolf Hitler had been released from custody and had published his book under the title *Mein Kampf,* My Struggle, a volume of turgid prose that few people could finish. Those who did discovered in its pages a manifesto detailing a complete political program based on a theory of racism with Aryans as the chosen people, a philosophy of the will to attain power, and even a precise notion of *entartete Kunst*, degenrate art. The author was under court restraint not to do any public speaking for two years and had thrown his energy into building up his political party, the National Socialist German Workers Party. The party had attracted a disproportionate number of social misfits and shady characters, pimps, murderers, alcoholics, and blackmailers, and in the party hierarchy a number of homosexuals. Some of the more respectable members repeatedly urged Hitler to get rid of the unsavory elements, but he rebuffed their suggestions several times, stating: "I do not consider it to be the task of a political leader to attempt to improve upon, or even to fuse together, the human material lying ready to his hand."[5] As long as supporters were useful to him, he would tolerate them.

In nearby Poland a highly skilled team of military code-breakers had since World War One monitored German military signals, i.e. coded information and orders flowing among military commands. This had enabled the Polish government to know that the German Weimar government systematically circumvented the restrictions on rearming imposed under the Versailles Treaty.

Then, suddenly in February of 1926, the Germans started using a mechanically produced cipher that defeated the best Polish cryptanalysts.[6] For the Polish intelligence experts involved in reading the German mind, this was tantamount to going blind.

Chapter 3   October 1928

*The love of man to woman is a thing common and of
course, and at first partaken more of instinct and
passion than of choice; but true friendship between
man and man is infinite and immortal.*

Plato

On the narrow platform at the Bramminge station I was waiting impatiently for
the arrival of the train to Ribe. It was six p.m. and I had been underway on
trains and ferries since leaving my mother at Copenhagen Central just after
eight in the morning. All this would not have been necessary, I thought irrita-
bly, if my family had just stayed in Ribe, where I had been perfectly happy. Instead, my father had two years ago obtained a position with a fruit importing
firm in Copenhagen, a fine career opportunity, but my world had thereby expanded in a most unwelcome manner. After the move I felt uprooted, displaced, a partial person compelled to stay where I neither fit nor wanted to be.
Our apartment was situated in the northwestern outskirts of the city in a rather
attractive neighborhood, but I despised every square foot of it. To make matters
worse, I had been compelled to start my education at Grøndalsvængets Skole, a
public school ten minutes' walk from home. It was a large, U-shaped brick
building of which one wing was for boys, the other for girls. We were kept strictly segregated as was customary at the time, the boys being taught by male, the
girls by female teachers. The arrangement seemed natural to me, as indeed it
was in the world of the 1920s. However, I hated every minute of school from the
first day. I was a Jutland boy, and my language revealed my roots. My classmates
spoke with a different accent and were wont to chide me for mine. I disliked
them all from the very beginning and resolved to keep to myself.

My resolve was strengthened and my exile made easier to bear by the knowledge that I had Aage, one true friend, in faraway Ribe. Our friendship was an

enduring bond, an unspoken commitment that neither time nor distance could diminish. It was an immense support, a secret weapon that gave me strength and patience to ignore the ignorant taunts of classmates. We wrote to each other, although the correspondence was intermittent, a letter perhaps every three weeks, and without great content, just a few sentences relating minor events, but the missive itself was a hand reaching across unseen miles.

Well into second grade my mother had taken me to school every morning, and I would predictably break into tears when the school building was in sight. She had been at her wit's end trying to dream up things to divert my attention from my miseries and had suggested cub scouts as a good project. Dubious, I had consented and spent an evening in a stone-cold cellar with two instructors who endeavored to teach a troop of five the rudiments of cub scouting. When mother collected me after two hours, my teeth were chattering and she rushed me to a *konditori* for resuscitation by means of hot chocolate. No more scouting. Mother then had suggested a woodworking course in town, and I spent a few months producing a bench for our bathroom, a serving tray, and some other useful items. School had remained a problem, however.

I was living through my first two school years in a state of mild confusion, usually unsure about where to go, what to do next, whom to address, and constantly wondering what the next hour would bring but without sufficient motivation to try to find out. My teachers were well trained in their subject matter but far too preoccupied with discipline to be noticeably friendly. We had two hours of *gymnastik* per week, physical exercise consisting mainly of calisthenics. The teacher was a retired army officer by the name of Parner who had once been on a big game hunting trip in Africa. When we rested for a few seconds between exercises, he would tell us about his prowess as a hunter, and in a quick aside caution us never to touch a negro. "They smell," he informed us in a low, confidential tone, twisting his nose meaningfully. Having never encountered a negro, we dutifully committed this item of incidental intelligence to memory. Corporal punishment was meted out for major, and some minor, infractions by means of a *spanskrør*, actually a thin bamboo cane. One or two whacks across the buttocks was standard punishment, and I had received it a couple of times. The pain was not severe, but the humiliation of being caned in front of the class was. We were rigidly graded and took our seats in the classroom according to our academic standing. Number one was in the front row on the teacher's extreme right, and low man on the totem pole was in the last row on the extreme left. Despite my non-functioning in the system, I managed to stay in the front row, usually well on the right. I am not sure how, for I never studied and my attendance record was horrendous. At the least sniffle or trace of illness, I would talk my mother into letting me stay home in bed, and I had succeeded gratefully in contracting most known childhood ailments from diphtheria (a light case) down through measles. In the 1920s medicinal treatment was still in its infancy, and our family physician, Fischer Nielsen, usually confined his ministrations to a small dose of acetylsalicylic acid, the early version of aspirin. The white powder was dissolved

The old Danish highway inn, landevejskroen, could be counted on to break up the tedium of wagon or bicycle travel. In the flat west coast landscape the inn was often situated at a bend in the road to make it visible from far off in both directions.

in a tiny tumbler of raspberry soda which made it my favorite medicine, certainly superior to raw cod liver oil or iron, the other two weapons in Dr. Nielsen's medical armory. Iron was prescribed whenever I appeared anemic, such diagnosis pronounced after my ear lobe had been pricked with a dull instrument and a drop of blood extracted therefrom had been matched to a color scale in the doctor's office.

Actually, it took all my stubborn prejudice to ignore or deny that life in Copenhagen was pleasant enough. To be sure, the city was a metropolis compared with Ribe, but in 1928 it was still quiet and placid. Traffic relied more on streetcars and bicycles than on motor cars. Parks and open spaces conferred an uncluttered impression very different from today's overbuilt and cramped state. Apartment houses were four stories or less, and each enclosed a yard devoted to clotheslines and bicycle sheds where *gaardsangere*, itinerant singers, would perform to solicit small donations from kitchen windows. Here also came from time to time *skærsliberen*, the knife-sharpener, with his handcart and grinding wheel to whom housewives could take their cutlery to have keen edges restored. Whenever the herring was running and catches were good, the herring vendor, *sildemanden*, appeared with his pushcart to peddle the silvery fish. Both *skærsliber* and *sildemand* announced their presence with age-old chants[7] that reverberated from the yard's pavement and brick walls. To entertain my sister and me, moth-

33

er played the piano, usually on Wednesday evening, and we would sing the songs we knew.[8] On Friday evenings father read aloud, usually some of Jeppe Aakjær's peasant stories from the Jutland peninsula.

While I was in first grade, my world had expanded in yet a different dimension: my grandfather gave me a bicycle. It arrived by freight from Ribe and was officially handed over on my seventh birthday. It was used, but grandfather had given it a new coat of beautiful black enamel, and he had reconditioned it so that it was far better than new. No Dane of the 1920s could really operate without a bicycle, and I started to teach myself the skill which is much like teaching oneself walking. I would lean it against a garden fence, climb onto the seat and push off. Two or three yards later we would crash together, my bicycle and I, and the attempt would be repeated. After countless crashes and bruises, the yardage covered slowly grew and eventually I soared like a bird given wing. The bicycle was intended to console me and reconcile me to Copenhagen, which it failed to do. But it was a major step in my gaining the world, something I had immediately realized. Black asphalt could take me any place, at least on the island of Zealand, and invoking ferries made the rest of the world mine as well. But even with these promising prospects, my resentment of Copenhagen remained as strong as ever. My grandfather sent me an old map of southern Jutland, and I spent countless hours studying it, memorizing place names, roads, and streams. It was clear to me that island dwellers, people from Zealand, Funen, and all the other Danish islands, were secondary citizens at best. The real Danes were the Jutes, stalwart, trustworthy, salt of the earth.

Fortunately, my Copenhagen exile was periodically relieved by vacations. There was the school vacation in summer, almost six glorious weeks, from late June into early August, and Christmas vacation provided ten days of joy. Both of these were occasions for family visits to Ribe. October brought the one-week potato vacation, a venerated relic of the past when farmers needed their children to help with harvesting of the potato crop. I would dearly like to spend the October vacation in Ribe, but it was not a time for family visits, so I was temporarily stymied. The October interlude was enticing, however, because it was still possible to fish despite the streams being swollen by autumn rains, and fishing had become my preoccupation and all-consuming hobby. It had started when grandfather taught me at the age of four to catch sticklebacks, using a five-foot bamboo stick and little hooks without barbs, made out of pins acquired from grandmother's sewing box. The sticklebacks, females dull brown but males blazing in red and purple, were given residence with the roaches in the waterworks fountain, where they thrived and multiplied until evicted in the late fall, when grandfather drained it for the winter. While I was still too small to accompany grandfather on real fishing trips, he and I would peruse his tackle box which stood on a bookshelf in his office. It contained a number of tobacco tins with lures and flies, hooks, leaders and swivels; we would review each item separately, noting its qualities and recalling particular fish caught on this or that lure. The same lures and hooks were used year after year, as grandfather rarely

34

lost any, so each item built up a history and career of its own. When I was seven, grandfather made me my first rod. It was bamboo, ten feet long and carefully selected as the best specimen from the hardware store's stock. First, it was cut into two sections and the knobby joints filed smooth without impairing structural strength. The cut ends were then fitted with brass tubing to allow the two sections to be reassembled when needed. Next, eyelets for the line were attached with China twine whippings which in turn were painted with black bicycle enamel. Finally, Grandfather mounted copper rings, carefully hammered to a perfect fit to hold the reel. The crowning touch was a coat of shellac to protect the wood against moisture.

On my first *real* fishing trip which had been last summer, my grandmother went also and insisted on walking with me along the stream, as she was deathly afraid I would fall in and drown, a fate that had befallen one of her many brothers in teenage. My embarrassment at her presence was alleviated when I caught a one-pound pike and turned out to be the only one to catch anything that day. This was the first of many fishing trips. When the weather was right – southwesterly breeze and some overcast – grandfather and I would strap our rods to our bicycles and set out for some stream, ranging as far as twenty kilometers from town. Geography dictated that the excursions go toward the east, the west wind on our backs hurrying us along in the morning hours. In the evening we paid the penalty, returning against a headwind that blew unobstructed across the flat landscape. Grandfather pointed out to me how one never needed to be in doubt about directions, for the trees along fence lines and roads all stooped toward the east, mute testimony to the ceaseless press of the west wind.

We would make periodic stops and lie on the roadside embankment, noting how the slightest depression yielded lee, listening to the wind whisper through the grass while we gathered strength for a few more kilometers. Along the roads stood stone markers indicating the distance in kilometers from Ribe cathedral. I soon knew the precise location of each one within many kilometers of town, as well as the few old milestones left from the pre-metric times, before the French Revolution gave Europe its modern and standardized measurements. The milestones were the more decorative, each embellished with the initials of the Danish king who ordered their placement. The roadside flora abounded in wildflowers such as *judaspenge*, Judas money, a weed of the dockum family with small, disc-shaped seeds resembling coins, and a plant with a spear-like, purple flower going by the local name of Priest Penis. Grandfather would show me how to produce an aromatic treat by rubbing wild thyme between my fingers, or we would test the springy resilience of the dry reindeer moss near the edge of a plantation. The plantations were groves of conifers dotting the countryside since the Danes had decided after the loss of one-third of their land in the war of 1864 to reclaim the heath that had spread in Jutland after the destruction of Viking Age forests. Companion planting of dwarf pine and Norway spruce had proven hardy enough to withstand the west wind and also to penetrate the ahl, an iron oxide-bearing sandstone fused into hardpan strong enough to blunt

35

plowshares. Occasionally a trip would end in rain, but we never set out when it was raining. If dawn broke wet on a planned fishing day I would continually scan the sky for a break and at intervals inquire, "Grandfather, do you think the rain will stop?" He always glanced at the sky and replied, "Yes, it always did before!" It did not escape me that he invariably turned out to be right, and I was well impressed with his infallibility as a weather prophet.

Our fishing areas lay along two streams, the Nipsaa and the Kongeaa. An *aa* is larger than a brook but smaller than a river. We lack an equivalent term in English and are compelled to label as river anything from the Mississippi down to a very modest water course. According to the Danes, their country has no rivers but does have a few streams meriting classification as *aa*. Grandfather had intimate knowledge of the two streams near Ribe and could relate valuable information about water levels, sluices and the farmers who owned the adjacent land. A sizeable stretch of the Kongeaa constituted the border between Denmark and Germany from the war of 1864 until 1920, when the Allies of World War One forced a defeated Germany to return part of southern Jutland to Danish sovereignty. The Allies were prepared to offer Denmark all of Schleswig-Holstein, which indeed was old Danish soil, but the Danes decided, probably wisely, to accept only areas in which the people by plebiscite expressed a wish to return. Accordingly, three zones were established of which the northernmost voted for return, while the other two opted to remain German. Along the Kongeaa grandfather pointed out the places where border guards used to patrol, German on the south side and Danish on the north bank. And he told me how by the summer of 1918 the German guards would sell their iron cross medals for a pound of cheese or a farm sausage, as the Allies, unable to gain a military victory, slowly were starving the Kaiser's Reich into submission.

On our fishing excursions we might stable our bicycles at some farm near the stream and walk from there. Such was the case in the village of Kalvslund near a tributary to the Nipsaa, where we chose the village blacksmith as a suitable *point d'appui*. Grandfather knew him, of course, and they often indulged in a brief chat while I impatiently watched the smith's two journeymen at work, usually shoeing farm horses or repairing wagons. The smith also did a bit of farming, as was common with village artisans, and he kept half a dozen pigs. They were trained never to defecate in the sty but only in a small enclosure in the outside yard to save him the work of cleaning. He was a powerful man, a prototype of smithery, and when he growled at one of the pigs for misbehaving in some manner, they all came to instant attention.

Most of the time, though, we left our bikes at one of the inns that dotted the countryside a few hours carriage journey apart, our favorites being Villebøl, Foldingbro, Kalvslund and Skallebæk. They stood like stout reminders of a prebicycle era of horse-drawn travel, their whitewashed walls gleaming in the black, half timber framework. Each inn was typically positioned at a curve in the road with the huge stable door thoughtfully open, so that weary travelers could proceed straight into its benevolent embrace. In the flat landscape it was visible from far off, allowing plenty of time to think up strong arguments for stopping. When entering, the visitor was enveloped by the smell of hay and horses. There is a distinct difference between the pungent, cloying smell of cows and the tea-like smell of the sturdy draft horse. We put our bicycles in the barn, and our arrival occasioned a brief chat with the innkeeper whom grandfather knew, as he seemed to know just about everybody throughout the county. When we returned to the inn by late afternoon, tired out after walking miles along the stream, leaping across ditches and negotiating barbed wire fences, grandfather would order a small libation to reinforce us for the trip home: a pilsener beer for him and a raspberry soda for me, sometimes accompanied by two or three *klejner*, local cookies baked by the matron. The inn had a common room for the farmhands and laborers as well as a smaller, more exclusive one for important city people like us. The rooms were very clean and neat but permeated with the odors of horse stable mingling with those of beer and stale tobacco smoke. When we entered, conversation momentarily ceased until sidelong glances by the locals had established our identity, reinforced by a whispered comment by someone that this was Tarp from the Ribe waterworks. Invariably, questions would be asked, politely and tentatively but revealing great curiosity about our catch and the fishing process. The farmers never fished and considered it an outright mystery that we were actually able to coax fish from their stream.

On the walls, the king and queen's pictures were prominently displayed together with some memento from *Genforeningen*, the return of northern Schleswig to Denmark in 1920. The favorite was a picture of the young King Christian X on his white horse striding across the now defunct frontier amid cheering throngs. The fact that these were border lands was always in the back of people's consciousness.[9] Because grandfather had been born in 1860 south of the 1864-1920 frontier, he was entitled to vote in Zone 1, the one that chose to return to Denmark. He told me how the voting had duly taken place amid much peaceful but jubilant celebration in 1920. Walking along the stream bed in the meadow solitude I reflected soberly on the good sense of many southern Jutes to move to Ribe before the 1864 war could make Germans of them. But for the foresight of my own great-grandfather, I could have been born a *Kraut!*

This fall of 1928, near my ninth birthday, I had finally extracted parental consent for my traveling to Ribe alone. My mother had been worried about letting me undertake so long a journey on my own, but by saving up for the ticket, 16 kroner and 80 øre, I had made my claim strong, if not unassailable, and had given it an aura of virtue, if not righteousness. In the end, relentless insistence had carried the day, and that was how I now found myself nearing the end of the journey which had involved three separate train rides interspersed by ferries across the belt seas.

A slight rain was beginning to fall in the gathering dusk as I stared down the track in hope of seeing the train. I was pleased to think of my bike waiting for me in Ribe. It had been shipped from Copenhagen a week before, for there would be far too much to do in the coming week to be operating on foot. I thought with relish how much ground the bikes had allowed Aage and me to cover the previous summer. My getting a bicycle two years earlier had enabled Aage to put heavy pressure on his parents to let him achieve equal status, and soon we both had wheels and could roam the town's cobbled streets swiftly and silently. Last summer we had undertaken our first trip away from home, a camping excursion to Fanø, a large island off the Jutland west coast that could be reached after a 20-minute crossing on a small, ancient ferry.

Our camping gear, acquired over a couple of years by being given prominent exposure on wish lists for birthdays and Christmases, consisted of a tent, sleeping bags, and a small spirit stove. The tent was made of canvas, presumed to be more or less rainproof for a couple of hours, and was of a simple A-design without sidewalls or ground cover, five by six feet in size and four feet high. Together with its two poles and 12 large galvanized spikes for anchorage, it was the heaviest item and added substantial weight when strapped to a bicycle's handlebars or baggage carrier. The sleeping bags were made of heavy woollen cloth and covered on the underside with oil cloth. Despite the manufacturer's assurances, they were not warm enough to ward off the cool northern summer nights, but we augmented their capacity by sleeping, or trying to, with most of our clothes on. The stove burned denatured alcohol which had to be carried in a glass bottle that needed many refillings in coop farm stores in the course of a trip, for the heating process was not particularly efficient, and potatoes, the Danish staple for main meals, required at least twenty minutes of boiling, equivalent, we discovered, to more than one bottle of alcohol. We carried some canned goods, extracted by persuasion from Aage's father's store, particularly frankfurters, of which he reluctantly had contributed two cans, each holding six of the little sausages. They could be heated in the can rather than in the aluminum cooking pot my grandmother had lent us for the trip.

We camped in the sand dunes with a view to the magnificent North Sea beach, a mile wide at low tide, and hard as concrete. The concrete-like quality of these North Sea beaches comes about because the sand is of extremely fine grain size. The fineness has historically caused great problems as it also made the dunes mobile during storms. To save adjoining farm land from being obliterated by westerly gales which could accrete several feet of sand overnight, the Danes finally at the end of the 19th century arrested the footloose hills by planting marram grass, a sand-loving, tenacious weed with extensive roots. Just how mighty a foe the wind-borne sand constituted is evident near the Skaw, Jutland's northernmost point. Here a village church was so completely buried during a sand storm in the 19th century that only the top of the church tower sticks up above the dunes.

Aage and I had experienced our own introduction to the moving sand as a storm blew in from the west during our first camping night and slowly but relentlessly piled sand against the tent wall. As we lay sleepless inside we could see the sand level mount outside, bulging the canvas inward. Every fifteen minutes or so we had to push out on the wall to keep the tent from collapsing. As dawn broke with moderating wind, we agreed that of such adventures truly memorable camping trips are made.

A small point of light appeared in the tenebrous darkness far down the track. It slowly grew and finally revealed itself to be the lantern of a small, wheezing steam engine pulling two old coaches. Amid a cloud of steam, the train came to a noisy halt, and a few people descended. Together with four other travelers I got into the 3rd class coach, and half an hour later we rolled into the Ribe station where my grandparents and Aage were waiting. I got off, my heart beating in wild anticipation but my face set in an expression of pleased unconcern. I felt on home ground.

***

We recognize that it is not enough to overthrow the old State, but that the new State must first have been built up and be practically ready at hand.

Adolf Hitler

In the 1928 elections the National Socialists had won a mere dozen of the 491 seats in the Reichstag and had managed to attract only 108,000 members. Undaunted by the modest numbers, Hitler was building his party to correspond in its structure to both Germany's government and German society, to establish a state within a state. It had departments of labor, agriculture, interior, justice, etc. It also had some of hitherto unknown identities: engineering, culture and race. When the National Socialists gained power, as Hitler confidently planned, the state-within-a-state would smoothly come into its own, become the state itself.

One Friday afternoon in 1928 a box addressed to the German Embassy in Warsaw was discreetly removed from the Railway Parcels Customs Office and after careful examination returned before the following Monday morning. The box contained a German *Enigma Chiffriermaschiene*, the machine with which a message could be encrypted in code or deciphered into normal text. In a follow-up to this event, a small group of students was chosen from those already studying mathematics at Krakow University. The chosen students were invited to take a special course in cryptology.

Chapter 4 July 1930

In the yard of the Postcoach Inn in Nygade the teamster had harnessed two enormous Jutland horses and was hitching them to the coach. The beasts stood stolidly, like mountains of muscle enclosing the wagon pole, while the man, a taciturn farmer, worked slowly, methodically, checking the traces for soundness and making sure they were seating securely on the whiffletree, running his fingers under the bellyband to feel its tightness, judging whether it would chafe if submerged in seawater during the journey ahead. He had made the trip scores, probably hundreds, of times but he had grown up on the island of Manø and had learned never to take the sea for granted. Today's tide dictated a 7 p.m. departure, in just a quarter of an hour, and the passengers had already taken their places on the plank seats of the postcoach, an ordinary farm wagon whose iron-rimmed wooden wheels were slightly oversized to give almost three feet of ground clearance. The front seat was the teamster's, and his oilskin coat lay waiting for him, for rain was expected later in the evening. The next seat had been claimed by Aage and me, and on the remaining plank sat two farm wives who had been in town to shop. The rest of the wagon was given over to miscellaneous goods, including our camping gear and supplies.

Around the wagon clustered our parents, and also my grandparents, discussing the venture they had been talked into allowing. Grandmother was quietly pleading for reconsideration in view of the deteriorating weather. Our fathers exchanged opinions in subdued tones, unsure about the risks attendant to a venture outside the realm of their direct experience but loath to reverse a decision already made. Our mothers found it impossible to visualize the details of the undertaking, and their confidence in a Royal Danish Postal Service coach,

40

The author visiting in Ribe at age 11. Fishing was of all-consuming interest, relentlessly pursued during summer and fall vacations.

however modest, contended with natural fears of the unknown to which their offspring were about to be exposed. Their conversation became an exchange of worries about their sons' ability to deal with contingent difficulties. We ourselves were boiling with anxiety but maintained outwardly impassive expressions, too wise to participate or be drawn into any discussion of the merits or safety of a venture already embarked upon. We smugly disdained giving any reassurance, or even reply to questions or to grandmother's entreaties, secure in the knowledge that we were committed.

This was to be our first excursion by transport other than our bikes. Emboldened by a few successful camping trips, including the one to Fanø, we had focused our sights on Manø, a small island three miles off the coast. It was situated in a wide intertidal area allowing a person to walk to it from the mainland when the tide was out. When the tide was in, however, it stood in the sea and was accessible only by boat. At low tide the causeway was visible, a thin bed of gravel deposited in a long, fragile ribbon to prevent wagons from sinking too deeply into the silt. Along the way stood a line of upturned "brooms," stakes with a fistful of twigs bundled and tied to the top end. Rammed into the silt, the stakes marked at intervals the edge of the causeway for the traveler's guidance, in case a returning tide had begun to cover the gravel before he could safely reach firm ground. It was clear to Aage and me that Manø constituted a suitable goal for our exploratory urges. Other than the handful of farmers inhabiting the place,

41

few people had visited the island, and this gave it a tempting aura of remoteness and mystique. The gravel causeway was not suitable for bicycles, and we recoiled in any event from exposing our precious bikes to the salty environment of the tidal flats, but we discovered that mail was taken to the island's few inhabitants twice weekly by a horse-drawn carriage. This sturdy conveyance became our chosen means of transport. Getting parental consent was a delicate matter, as we considered ourselves too old actually to ask for permission, so the plan was bruited offhandedly in the form, "We need some food for a three-day trip to Manø besides bread, butter, cheese and salami. What can you give us to take along?" The ploy had neatly deflected initial discussion of the trip per se, as our mothers suggested various comestibles, but grandmother quickly regained perspective on the situation and asserted that the trip was too risky. Relentless insistence interspersed with feigned injury to our dependability and competence eventually carried the day.

At length the teamster finished his preparations, mounted the front seat and donned his coat, spat heartily, and in seconds had the wagon rumbling across the cobbled yard and onto the street without a glance at the city folk left behind. We did not actually wave but raised a hand in a casual salute, hinting at preoccupation with matters more pressing than concern for bystanders. The stone pavement made the ride a teeth-rattling experience as the horses broke into a slow trot, and the deafening noise reverberated in the narrow street, but within minutes the highway macadam provided blessed relief. Shortly the wagon turned onto the gravel road toward the coast. A westerly wind was gaining strength as we passed through the three small villages we knew from our bicycle trips, and after an hour the dike was visible ahead. The horses slowed to a walk where the road climbed the embankment, and suddenly the tidal flats lay spread before us, as far as the eye could reach in the fading light. Emerging from the lee of the dike we met the full force of the wind, and the farmer looked ahead uneasily, gaging its strength and estimating its effect on the incoming tide. We felt the cold of the sea and the oncoming night and shivered in our light summer clothes. Grandmother had insisted on our taking raincoats along and had obtained parental backing, and we quietly slipped them on to break the wind. The team was kept at a trot as we entered the causeway but soon had to slow to a walk in the foot-deep water. Half an hour later we were half way to the island, and the water had risen to the wheel hubs. The normal schedule was to reach the island before the incoming tide, but strong onshore wind could upset the tide table. We passed slowly by the seemingly unending line of "brooms," and in the light summer night there had been no difficulty seeing as far as the next one ahead, but now rain started to fall, reducing visibility. We all sat in forward-bent positions, leaning into rain and wind, the teamster squinting under a shielding hand to get a bearing on the next broom. Aage and I sat close together trying to keep the rubberized fabric of our raincoats between ourselves and the plank seat on which rivulets of water sloshed sideways as the wagon wheels ground along on the gravel. Behind us the two women had covered their heads in their shawls, shutting out the world and leaving their fate to the coachman. After a while, the water was lapping the underside of the floorboards, and every few moments a small wave would break on the chests of the great beasts who patiently, tenaciously strained in their harness, dragging the wagon into the teeth of wind and driving rain.

As we hung on to the swaying seat, I thought about the summer's events to date, trying to blot out the discomfort of the wet and cold present and dwelling in my imagination on the recent months' events. At the end of March, Dr. Nielsen had prescribed that I start summer vacation three months early. I think it was his way of getting me and my many ailments off his hands, and I promptly took off for Ribe and the happiest spring of my school days. Arriving in Ribe, I found that grandfather had a wonderful surprise in store. He had purchased a boat in which we could undertake fishing expeditions up the Nipsaa. It had been on his mind for two years, but he had foolishly mentioned the plan to my grandmother who volubly and vehemently objected. She pointed out that the Nipsaa was deep and treacherous, every year taking the life of someone heedless of the danger; that the boys could not swim; that so-and-so had lost a child to drowning, and so forth. However, the previous summer we had both passed our swimming test, administered by one of Aage's teachers from the Latin School and performed in the very stream itself. This weighty argument had settled the matter, and grandfather had happily closed a deal he had long had simmering. The boat was a 16-foot wood-built *norsk pram*, a Norwegian fishing craft design which we without hesitation pronounced to be far better than any and all other boats we had encountered. It had received two coats of light blue paint – the perfect color, we decided.

Most important, it had a one-cylinder Evinrude outboard engine of 1912 vintage which grandfather had overhauled and painted so that it was better than new. Its sparkplug jutted forward from the cast-iron cylinder, menacing the elbow of the helmsman, and hand starting was accomplished by grasping a knob on the flywheel and giving it a strong jerk, clockwise, quickly letting go to avoid a broken thumb when the engine fired. Aage and I judged the two-cycle Evinrude to be vastly superior to any other engine we had seen or heard about. The tank held enough fuel for one and one-half hours' running, and an extra supply was carried in a five-liter tin can. We refilled the can at Ribe's only Esso station, for grandfather explained that Esso's red gasoline was the finest and most powerful product money could buy. We would watch the Esso man, a part-time truck driver, crank the red liquid up into the pump's five-liter glass reservoir – making sure it reached the full measure – and admonish him to let it run slowly through the hose into the can so as not to lose a single precious drop. Then we would add the oil, which was kept in a green bottle wrapped in a soft rag. The measure was an old tin cup from a thermos bottle that had met an untimely end in the distant past. Each item had its appointed place, the fuel can under the stern thwart, the oil in the bow. We carried oars, of course, for the rare oc-

The author's grandfather, Niels Hansen Tarp, in his boat on the Nipsaa near Ribe in 1931. The outboard motor was an Evinrude, model 1912.

casion when the Evinrude failed to justify our faith in its reliability. We were the only boys in town so endowed, at least if one disregarded the children of the wealthy attorney, Styrup, who owned an old mahogany-decked speedboat named *Melody*. It had a converted automobile engine that suffered from poor maintenance. On the rare occasions when it was taken up the Nipsaa, it would usually start with great fanfare and speed, passing us and surging out of sight up the stream. But we could always count on finding *Melody* later half beached in a meadow, its skipper sweating and cursing as he tried to restart the recalcitrant engine. As the trusty Evinrude carried us slowly past the marooned speedster, we assured each other that speed should always be considered secondary to endurance.

My reverie was suddenly interrupted as Aage's elbow dug into my ribs: "Look, there is a light!" Ahead a small light had appeared in the murk, and the shadow of land could be faintly perceived. The horses' brute strength had gotten our little party through, and close to midnight we were unloaded in pelting rain and pitch darkness on a bare, windswept spot amid a few clustered farms that were visible only as blacker masses in the wet darkness. Soaked to the skin and stiff from cold we swallowed our pride and asked the teamster for shelter in his hayloft. The man gave his consent with a grunt and a nod at the cow barn, adding a strong admonition not to light any matches. We reassured him as we carried our gear to the building and with the aid of a flashlight found the ladder to the loft. After hauling everything upstairs, we unrolled our sleeping bags and stripped off the wet clothes. The heat from the cows below rose and enveloped us in pungent smelling waves and after a while helped stop our shivering. Instead, we felt the full discomfort of a sleeping bag invaded by hayseeds, but before long nature took its course and sleep came.

The following day the uncommunicative teamster to our great delight let on that he had seriously doubted whether we would make it to shore that night in the worst spring flood he had known to occur. Accordingly, we decided that the Manø trip ranked among our most worthwhile adventures so far.

* * *

Instead of working to achieve power by armed coup, we shall have to hold our noses and enter the Reichstag against the Catholic and Marxist deputies.

Adolf Hitler

The Weimar Republic had managed to resurrect its economic system from the hyperinflation that had savaged the country after the World War ceased. But when the American stock market crashed in October of 1929, the effects were soon felt world wide. The basis for German financial survival, loans from abroad, largely from America, dwindled and the German economy slowed, throwing millions out of work. Great revolutionaries thrive on the misery of the masses: chaos, violence, unemployment and hopelessness. Events in Germany now produced all these conditions. Misery was at hand, and Hitler started with furious energy to make the most of it.

Chapter 5   July 1931

The distress of boyhood changing into man
The unfinished man and his pain ...
I am content to live it all again.

Yeats

In the narrow yard at the waterworks my father and Herr Lehman sat side by side on the green bench in earnest discussion. At the end of the yard Aage's bike dangled in a wall bracket near grandfather's outdoor workbench, and Aage and I were occupied lubricating the chain. It was not a very important project, but we pretended it to be so and that the task required our full attention, for Herr Lehman's two daughters stood at a respectful distance observing our endeavor with keen interest. Occasionally we threw a glance in the girls' direction, but neither side made any attempt at contact.

The Lehmans came from Leipzig every summer to visit relatives, for Mrs. Lehman harked from Ribe and had been a school friend of my mother's. In the evening, her husband and my father often sat on the bench in the waterworks yard and discussed the turbulent political situation in Germany. The Lehmans also brought their daughters, 13-year-old Astrid and 11-year-old Inge, whom we eyed with studied indifference and without actually attempting conversation, not because they spoke German and we didn't, but because they were girls. Boys and girls rarely mixed or played together, a custom that was subtly encouraged by the physical separation of the sexes in school. This had not prevented us by the age of ten suddenly to become interested in the girl phenomenon. In fact, we discussed the subject at great length, finding ourselves baffled by the concept of sex, a subject carefully avoided in the family. Nevertheless, the murky melange of chance observations and partly-understood incidental intelligence slowly gave way in our exhaustive man-to-man talks to a measure of coherence, so that now, by the end of grade school, we had pretty well surmised the general scheme of human reproduction, though details were obscure. Thus emboldened we had begun to subject the town's females of all ages to discreet but unrelenting scrutiny, routinely undressing them in our imagination and discussing their sexual attributes, at times arriving at somewhat bizarre conclusions. One rather heavy woman with a permanently bulging abdomen we decided had been pregnant, but her baby had died before being born. When encountering her, we would exchange furtive glances and nod knowingly: there was a dead baby in there, all right.

This summer, vacation in Ribe was as always idyllic, incomparably the high point of the year. The old houses and cobbled streets seemed perpetually unaffected by the passage of time. In the quiet morning hours housewives would scurry to the nearest baker to fetch bread or special breakfast rolls for the morning coffee, as if drawn by the fragrance wafting from the oven room behind the store. Some of the less affluent women who had no oven in their own kitchen would be there to pick up their own loaves, kneaded the night before and taken to the baker who for a small fee would bake them together with his own bread. The private loaves were usually large, yard-long specimens, for the less affluent families invariably were rich in mouths to feed. Catching the morning sun, a painter would be setting up his easel at some vantage point offering a street scene to his liking, and the town's street sweeper whose name was Juul could be seen with his broom and handcart, unobtrusively going about his routines. A few townspeople still kept cows, a valued privilege of ancient origin, and their small herds – at most half-a-dozen head – leisurely trod their accustomed way through the alleys to spend the day grazing the fens just outside town. Only the main thoroughfare bustled with activity as carriages vied with a few motor cars for its narrow passage, interrupted several times daily when an export truck, heavily loaded with fish from the harbor city of Esbjerg, passed through town on its way south to Germany, its iced cargo causing a window-rattling rumble. From bulky nests teetering on the ridges of red-tiled roofs storks would take to the air and majestically soar away to go fishing, while their young stayed behind, standing on red, reedy legs, peering over the rim of the nest at the world below. When the big birds returned at sunset to feed the young and roost for the night, they would enact a conjugal ritual in which they could be heard to *knebre*, to clatter their long, red bills in a manner to produce for half a minute or so a tone of slightly varying pitch. Going to bed just after ten in the evening, we could usually hear the near-total silence of the town broken by the strange, undulating sound from the nearest nest, finally trailing off on a rising pitch to an eerie, dying note.

The town's five thousand inhabitants seemed all to know each other, at least by sight, and despite its provinciality the local populace had some notion of the world beyond its horizons. The late 1800s saw the peak of the emigration exodus to America, and letters from sons and daughters who left for the new world brought whiffs of distant places to those who stayed behind. One example was an elderly spinster, Miss Krummelbein, to whom my grandmother turned when she needed a cook for party occasions. Her culinary talents were well recognized, and besides cooking she also imported mustard seed from Germany and produced her own immensely potent table mustard without which ham hocks and sausages could not be fully appreciated. While producing a gourmet dinner Miss Krummelbein (who behind her back was alluded to as "Boney" as she was quite skinny) would regale the lesser kitchen help with tales from her time in the United States, for she was one emigrant who after some years abroad had returned to the country of her origin with a small nest egg. While in the States she had seen the westward drive as the American frontier receded beyond the Mississippi and she liked to relate how she had been told that Chicago was a fine place to earn money, but if she wanted a husband she had to go farther west. Preferring money to matrimony, she had stayed in Chicago. Listening to her, one could tell that the Danish west coast dialect was very similar to English, bearing witness to the indelible Viking imprint on English vernacular. This circumstance greatly aided the early peasant immigrants from Jutland, and it even enabled me to understand Miss Krummelbein's rendering of occasional snatches of American comments she had retained from her faraway adventures.

Some time after midsummer, the annual fair created a high point of local excitement. Farmers brought livestock to be sold or traded with serious assurances, firm handshakes and, when the size of the deal justified, the downing of *kaffepunch*, a half-cup of black coffee topped off with aquavit, in the nearest restaurant. Besides its commercial function, the fair served as both social and festive occasion. In a meadow on the edge of town young farmhands competed at *ringridning*, a sport of horsemanship in which the rider gallops past a small ring suspended overhead between two poles and tries to spear it with a wooden lance. Contestants who had served with the dragoons had a noticeable edge on the rest, and when one of the great farm horses came thundering by and its rider succeeded in carrying off the ring, the crowd applauded enthusiastically. A local baker by the name of Koch made and sold ice cream which was locally thought to be the country's best, and farm wives hawked honey and cooked *æbleskiver*, apple dumplings, in their special cast-iron dumpling pans. Grandfather related to me that when *he* was a boy, an old dumpling-cooking farm woman used to hire him to gather large black slugs in the nearby forest, paying him two øre for each dozen. She used them to grease her dumpling pan, dropping a slug in each of the pan's semispherical cups. When the slug hit the hot pan, it would ooze clear slime that instantly coated the cup. The old women then would flick the charred slug remnant out into the fire and pour dough in the neatly greased cup. Her *æbleskiver* were recognized to be the fair's shiniest and most attractive.

Throughout the summer, Aage and I swam daily in the Nipsaa, often twice if the day was hot. Where the stream's westernmost arm ran through a meadow on the outskirts of town, two bathhouses had been constructed by the town fathers, one for boys and one for girls, with a suitable separation between them. They were simple sheds, sixteen by twenty-four feet, walled on three sides with boards and with the fourth side open on the water's edge. Bathing suits were never used by either sex, nor were they needed, for the sheds were almost three hundred feet apart and their open sides faced toward empty countryside beyond the stream. And, anyway, when one was swimming, the water conveniently covered one's nakedness. We often went for a swim after the evening meal, when the bathhouses were usually deserted. Swimmers were supposed to stay near the bathhouse, but excitement for that very reason lay in more distant excursion. The art was to draw no attention to oneself but to cruise along the reeds, gliding silently, furtively like a water rat, marveling at communicating in whispers which carry a long way across water when your lips are but a fraction of an inch above the smooth surface. In the gathering dusk the balmy air was pungent with the scent of meadow, the water felt lukewarm, and one could hear the reed warbler composing his mysterious melodies. By midsummer, the meadows along the stream yielded their first hay, and the aroma suffused the town night and day. This was also the tourist season, and a few dozen foreign travelers appeared, mostly Germans. One such family was the Lehmans.

Judging the bike chain to be adequately lubricated, we turned our backs on the girls in the yard and walked, slowly, through the arbor to the fountain in the waterworks' front yard, pretending not to notice the girls trailing along at a respectful distance. We inspected the fountain and counted its stock of minnows, raising our voices slightly for the girls' benefit. The process was suddenly interrupted by grandmother, calling from the kitchen window above our heads, "Niels, bring the girls in for strawberries and cream!" Aage said, with relief in his voice, "*You* have to tell them. In German." He was pleased to be without responsibility in this matter of communication, for it would be another two years before we were to start learning German in school. I thought quickly as we began walking toward the front door stairway. When we passed the girls, I said with a jerk of my head, "Come," correctly guessing that the word plus the gesture would be understood. The four of us proceded up the waterworks stairs and sat down together with the adults at the oak table in the dining room, where grandmother was serving the berries with sugar and cream while keeping up a running conversation with the guests. We ate silently, the girls venturing a few shy smiles while we deigned to look at them in a half-benevolent manner.

* * *

The Führer is the instrument of the Divine Will
that shapes history with fresh, creative passion.

Goebbels

A few miles south of the vacationing strawberry eaters at the waterworks, the legitimate government of the Weimar Republic was floundering; at its head, 84-year-old President Hindenburg was suffering old-age deterioration of his physical and mental capacities. Adolf Hitler had solidified the party and organized it for the rôle he intended it to play. Around him he had gathered six close associates, a group in which each member warily watched the others, jockeying for influence with the Führer, the designation Hitler insisted upon.

Gregor Strasser was a sought-after speaker and a gifted organizer. A genial Bavarian, he enjoyed great popularity both inside and outside the party circles, occupying the party's key office of political organization.

Ernst Röhm, a scarfaced war veteran, had brought to the movement many ex-service men, organizing them as *Sturmabteilungen*, or SA, stormtroopers who protected Nazi meetings and disrupted those of the opposition.

Hermann Göring had under a general amnesty returned from Sweden where he had fled after the abortive Beer Hall Putsch. Hitler found his connections useful and had appointed him to lead the small Nazi contingent in the Reichstag.

Joseph Goebbels, Nazi Gauleiter, or district leader, was a dwarfish, dark-haired man of restless energy whose fertile mind generated an unending torrent of ideas to further the Nazi cause.

Wilhelm Frick, a proto-typical civil servant, was the only drab member of the group, serving the party with unquestioning loyalty as he carried out his assigned tasks with teutonic efficiency.

Rudolf Hess, a World War One veteran and economics student uncritically devoted to Hitler, had become the Führer's most trusted follower and deputy.

Outside this small band of ruthless opportunists stood an odd, almost shadowy figure whom Hitler had given the task of building a black-shirted elite corps, the *Schutzstaffel,* or SS, for the Führer's personal use as a praetorian guard and counterweight to the SA. His name was Heinrich Himmler.

Chapter 6   July 1932

Fish say they have their stream and pond;
But is there anything beyond?

Rupert Brooke

From the bow Aage announced quietly, "This is a good place to tie up," and from the stern I nosed the boat toward the shore where Aage passed a clove hitch around a bunch of tall reeds. The spot was well chosen, for the fragile mooring was sufficient to hold against the sluggish current. The right bank was firm meadow where cows could be heard, grazing in the darkness. On the left the stream was bordered by a forest of reeds, half a mile wide, and the boat was situated almost hidden in the reeds with its port side exposed to the slow-moving stream. Aage lit a candle lantern – it was thought to attract the fish – and we settled down to our most sedentary fishing method. It was the end of July, and this late in the season the eel commenced its long migration, first toward the salt water of the North Sea, there to continue, drawn by some mysterious, genetically transmitted instinct toward the English Channel, and finally to cover the enormous distance across the North Atlantic to its spawning grounds in the Sargasso Sea. Tonight we would do our best to interrupt that journey at its inception by fishing in the middle part of the light Nordic summer night, using a special method locally known as *tatte*. With a blunt darning needle we had threaded a 3-yard strand of embroidery silk through a bunch of nightcrawlers, so that each worm had the silk through the whole length of its tubular body. Then the three yards of bait had been gathered into a loose bundle the size of a tennis ball, tied with two yards of line to the end of a broomstick, and the gear was ready. In the soft dusk of the summer night, the boat swayed gently on the edge of the current in 4-5 feet of water, the bait lowered over the side and nimbly jiggled just above the bottom. When the fisherman felt the tug of a passing eel biting into the bundle, he would lift it in one smooth motion up, over the gunwale and into the boat. With proper timing, the eel's hundreds of small backward-pointed teeth would catch in the silk just long enough to allow their owner to be lifted from the water into the boat, there to fall free and slide into the bilge.

This night's fishing turned out to be slow. We had heaved only a few specimens, sixteen or so inches long, from the small circle of dark water under the lantern's light and dropped them on the floor boards where they agreeably wriggled into the bilge. When catching eel, the wise fisherman avoids handling them. Nothing is slimier. And nothing is stronger than eel skin. We knew that our Stone Age ancestors inhabiting the Danish isles used eel skin to secure their stone axeheads to the handle, and we had both tried the daunting task of flaying an eel. It never ceases to wriggle and squirm, even without head and skin, on the frying pan, at least not until it is thoroughly cooked. Aage brought out coffee and sandwiches from our fishing basket, and we consumed the food in silence so as not to alert the fish we felt were passing below the keel. Large ones, too. Then we sank into silent inactivity, both contemplating the disagreeable circumstance of only a week remaining of summer vacation, and also thinking of the exploration we had accomplished. The moment a boat slips its moorings, severing its tie with the land, it becomes a miniature world onto itself. We felt keenly the responsibility this placed on us, for we knew that fate and destiny were ours to shape as we saw fit. Each trip had been a new adventure, as the town disappeared astern and we entered the domain of the reeds and sedges. The faint scent of *boat* would envelop us like an invisible aura, mingling with the potpourri of smells from the watercourse itself, of plants and mud and earthy meadows and bird and animal life, while we listened entranced to the reeds singing their incessant, monotonous tune, a low-pitch, dry rattle from thousands of stalks obediently swaying in deference to the press of the west wind.

The Nipsaa comprised vast marshy areas covered with forests of tall reeds through which the stream meandered, sometimes split into several channels. Here and there were patches of spongy meadow which yielded slightly to a person's step, giving a sensation of walking on a floating carpet. The farmers cut these patches with scythes, and after a few days of drying used small, flat-bottom scows to ferry the fresh hay to firmer ground. It was a world all its own, stretching upstream east of town for some five miles. Here and there a tern would be fishing, coots built floating nests, and now and then a lapwing would dash by overhead on erratic, unpredictable wing beats. Close to town a pair of migratory swans spent their summers, fiercely resenting our intrusions on their territory, often attacking the boat as we motored by. Paddling at maximum effort the big birds could just equal the Evinrude's top speed, and they often pursued the craft for hundreds of yards, several times attempting to board. Grandfather had pointed out that their powerful wings could break a man's arm, so we learned to fend them off with the blunt end of the boat hook. Such dangers notwithstanding, we had set about exploring this watery domain and soon knew the marshlands and reed forests intimately. Upstream of the marshy areas the channel wound through a landscape of sandy hills near the village of Varming, land only in recent generations reclaimed from the heather that covered much of the Danish peninsula after the depletion of the primeval oak forest. East of Varming our exploration ceased, as further progress by boat was blocked by a sluice which the farmers had built to divert some of the water during the dry season to irrigate the higher meadow land. Here the stream ran fresh and vigorous, and of all the areas we frequented on our fishing trips, grandfather loved this the best. So, therefore, did I. On warm days we all swam across the stream together, an undertaking involving some twenty yards of actual swimming, and after returning we would wait naked in the meadow solitude until sun and wind had dried us, then resume the fishing. Although well into his seventies, grandfather still easily swam the *aa* with us when the occasion arose.

Grandfather preferred fly-fishing for trout, grayling and an occasional salmon, but Aage and I chose to go after bass and pike, the latter our favorite prey. Nothing quite equals the thrill of feeling the lightning strike of a northern pike when a baitfish is skilfully maneuvered past a patch of floating eelgrass under which he is lurking. Then he is given slack line for ten minutes to swallow the bait and set the hidden hooks. When that time is up, the fight begins, the pike instantly seeking deeper water and cunningly trying to foul the line around reeds or other obstacles the stream might hold. Some of the strikers, the largest, we felt, would succeed in doing so, parting the line and leaving the fisherman disconsolate; but usually the fish would in the end succumb to our agility and endurance, tired out from fighting the steady pull of the flexing bamboo pole. Then he could be pulled close enough for the excited fisherman to land him with a net or gaff.

The end of Aage's pole suddenly dipped into the water and he let out a startled "Hey!", his grip tightening as something below tore at the bundled worms. This was definitely not the tentative nibbling of a passing eel, and he struggled to force the attacker to the surface. The head of a large pike momentarily appeared, its jaws pulled partly out of the water, still stubbornly clamped on the enticing worms, its body thrashing the dark water. The fish was as startled as the fisherman, but its grip immediately gave way as it let go the attraction without getting its teeth entangled. Aage dropped the frazzled worm bundle in the bottom of the boat with an outcry of disappointment. The episode had taken less than two seconds, and we looked at each other, barely comprehending what had happened. "No point in fishing any more," Aage said disgustedly, and I agreed. We threw out the rest of the bait, cast off the mooring line, and started the engine, hotly debating whether it could have been possible to land the pike, had we been prepared for the strike.

* * *

We tremble with desire for power, and
we are not afraid to admit it.

Adolf Hitler

On the same night as we were busy with our tatte on the Nipsaa, the Germans were tallying the results of an election in which the Nazis swept triumphantly ahead to become the largest party, winning 230 seats in the 608-member Reichstag. After the results were in, the President met with the Nazi leader and offered him a vice-chancellorship in a coalition government, but Hitler demanded the chancellorship and total power. The aging Hindenburg refused and instead gave the stubborn Austrian a stern lecture. The official communiqué stated that Hindenburg "regretted that Herr Hitler did not see himself able to support a national government appointed with the confidence of the President of the Reich, as he had agreed to do before the Reichstag elections." Breaking his promise, Hitler instead had demanded complete control of the state, and the communiqué went on to say, "The President gravely exhorted Herr Hitler to conduct the National Socialist Party's opposition in a chivalrous manner, remembering his responsibility to the fatherland and to the German people."

Infuriated, Hitler went to a mountain retreat in the Obersalzberg to brood on the results and plan his further moves.

Chapter 7   July 1933

*Disinterested intellectual curiosity is the
lifeblood of real civilization.*

George Trevelyan

Arriving on the highway from Hamburg, our car stopped at the Tinglev border crossing just south of Tønder. It was a Ford, model A, with a large trunk bolted onto the rear above the bumpers. The two doors bore a company logo, a banana invitingly half peeled and ready to bite into, on the background of a blue oval sticker with the word "Fyffes." A German customs official appeared, spruce in his grey-blue uniform, and politely waved the Skov family through, back into Denmark without any fuss. These days, the Germans were pleased to show off their country under the new National Socialist government, and all officials, including customs inspectors, were Nazis and under strict orders to convey the best possible impression to visitors. Besides, Germany needed foreign currency and tourists were welcomed with open arms, even to the extent of allowing them to buy special "tourist marks" at rates lower than the official exchange, one of the imaginative ideas of the Reichsbank President, Dr. Schacht.

By summer vacation this year, Ribe still appeared the dreamy, untouched oasis, but great activity was gathering momentum in the distance. South of the border Adolf Hitler had gained absolute power, German strength was swelling under the swastika banners, and order was returning to the country where tumult had increasingly reigned under the Weimar Republic. At the same time, peculiar phenomena occurred to vex the minds of Scandinavians: books by authors inimical to the new regime were burned in rituals likened to some latter-day auto-da-fé. The Nazis obviously did not accept political compromise, the way of life for democracies, always time-consuming and, some people would thoughtfully concede in private discussion, frequently frustrating. In July Herr Lehman came visiting from Leipzig as usual and on this occasion he showed my

55

father a photograph from his older daughter's confirmation party, a large picture of Hitler prominent among the presents.

Conversations with Herr Lehman made father curious to see the newborn Third Reich at first hand, and the result became our family automobile trip to the Harz Mountains. Although I had been inclined to stay in Ribe, the trip turned out to be a memorable experience. It etched in my mind a picture of a nation bent upon progress through hard work and discipline. In countryside, village and city, people were exerting themselves with Teutonic intensity toward ends they perceived only dimly, but which they confidently left to their Führer to sort out. At thirteen I had no understanding of and gave no thought to ultimate ends, but the here and now was quite within my grasp. I encountered enthusiastic youngsters my own age in the uniforms of *Hitlerjugend*, the Hitler Youth organization, clean-scrubbed kids extolling the merits of the new order. And there was evidence of the *Gleichschaltung* the Nazis had embarked upon, the orienting of the entire nation in one direction under Hitler's guidance. The idea had elicited mirth in Denmark when it had first been described in the press, and worthy citizens had chuckled at the thought of trying that in the North, but it was often admitted, particularly in the conservative press, that new solutions to old problems should not be rejected out of hand. In any event, it might well be instructive to watch.

Our family had stayed for a few days in Wernigerode, a small town in the Harz, picturesque, in some manner a German equivalent of Ribe and yet distinctly different because of the air of purposeful energy the citizens emitted. A young SA stormtrooper became instantly attracted to my sister, Angla. She was sixteen, pretty, and very unsure how to handle this attention. We were staying at a small *Gasthaus* finishing our evening meal in the garden when he marched in and introduced himself politely, clicked his heels, and requested permission to take Angla for a stroll in town. He was a clean-cut young man, his boots bright and shiny, the white, red and black of his swastika armband contrasting with his brown shirt. Father granted permission, and when he returned with Angla half an hour later, she told us how he had regaled her with compliments about her Aryan looks and Nordic background, much to her puzzlement and father's amusement. As we continued our journey the following day, we noticed that some hotels displayed signs *Juden unerwünscht*, Jews not wanted, and at the entrance to some villages signs showed the image of a stern stormtrooper shooing a small, bearded figure with a sack on his back, the inscription proclaiming *Jude, du bist erkannt*, Jew, you've been unmasked! At home, our circle of acquaintances did not include any Jews, although our apartment building had one Jewish family by the name of Pape. The eighteen-year-old Pape daughter was strikingly beautiful, but the family seemed otherwise unremarkable, just normal people. In my school, Grøndalsvænget, I knew of only one Jewish boy. His name was Jørgen Danmark, and he got involved in frequent, mostly successful, fistfights in the yard, possibly caused by some slanderous jibe. But Danish Jews were so few in number that most people had no personal contact with any. Consequently the German attitude and actions left many Danes more bewildered than repulsed, uneasily wondering whether the Jews actually might be guilty of conspiracies and evildoings such as the Nazis insisted.

At forty-one my father, Svend Skov, was in the middle of a promising career, a man of broad interests and keen intellectual curiosity. When he was only six, his own father had died from pneumonia, and he once told me how as a small boy he spent summer vacations with his uncle who was First Waiter at Steensgaard, a small castle on the island of Funen. The servants lived in a row of small houses flanking the stately driveway, beautiful half-timbered, thatched cottages, each the home of one of the staff essential to making the castle function in the manner intended by its designer and its occupants. The count and countess frequently gave weekend parties for the local nobility, and when Danish navy ships put in at Svendborg, a small port town some 15 miles distant, the officers eagerly responded to invitations from the castle and came in glittering regalia to dance with the ladies of the aristocracy. On these occasions my father was assigned the task of watching down the driveway for the arrival of each guest carriage. "Here comes the team of blacks from Egeskov!" he would call out, and out would rush the staff members' families to stand by the edge of the road, hats off and bowing to the baron and baroness from Egeskov as their splendid conveyance passed up the drive pulled by a perfectly matched team of four blacks.

This was at the close of the 19th century, and he had grown up seeing the automobile invented, and the airplane; the passing of a world war; and the merging of nobility with the ranks of common people in an ever more egalitarian society. In his younger days he had been a good athlete, excelling in rowing and rising to the Jutland division of the national soccer team. Shortly after getting married, he borrowed five hundred kroner from his father-in-law, my grandfather, and attended wireless school to become a radio operator. It was just after the World War One armistice, when radio communication was being adopted in ships, and the idea of being technologically avant-garde was, as always, of great appeal. After completing his training, he became "Sparks," as the operator's position was denominated at the time, on the freighter *S/S Normannia*. He immediately set about building from scratch the ship's radio transmitter, for that was considered part of his duties; only a few components were commercially available. The set he made had a range of about one hundred and fifty miles of morse code telegraphy, meeting normal expectancy then. On the transatlantic run the ship was out of range much of the time except for the occasional passing steamer, and he used his free time to write travelogues of the new and exotic lands visited at the ports of call. He was a good writer, and the leading Copenhagen daily *Politiken* bought his reports and published them with his own byline under the heading "From our Traveling Correspondent, Svend Skov," introducing the readers to the exciting worlds of the Caribbean and the Americas. After two years of constant travel, the *S/S Normannia* sprang a leak in a gale off the Florida Keys, and as procedure called for, he tapped out an S-O-S. The United States Coast Guard answered the call and took the entire crew off safely, father and the captain being the last to leave before the vessel went down. He spent two weeks in New York waiting for passage home and used the time to look at radio gear which was now being manufactured in quantity. He also took time to do some shopping and brought me back a tricycle from the United States, making me the only boy in Ribe so endowed.

When returning to settled life father worked for a couple of years as a clerk for the Alfa margarine factory in the town of Vejen, but in 1926 he obtained a position with A.W. Kirkebye, a large fruit importer in Copenhagen. This was when advertising and sales promotion were in their infancy in the U.S., and still novel and unexplored spheres of commercial activity in Europe. In Denmark the term *reklame* was coined to cover both concepts. With his knack for descriptive writing, father was a natural for such work, and he soon became *reklamechef*, manager of the company's newly created advertising department. He hired some very competent people, among them a young engineer, Mogens Lichtenberg. The small advertising team tackled the immediate task at hand, that of introducing bananas to the Danish market, a challenging problem when prospective buyers first need to be taught to remove the peel before eating the fruit. At the same time, scientists were making strides in understanding the relationship between nutrition and health, coining the word *vitamin* and describing these elusive substances. Father designed several advertising series built around the nutrition theme and lauded bananas as a modern way to health. The fruit was marketed under the English name of "Fyffes," and oval blue-and-white labels so identified each "hand." This was also the time when the possibility of using neon tubes was discovered, and father's efforts resulted in, among other things, the placement of an enormous neon banana on a downtown building, slowly rotating as a beacon for Copenhagen traffic. It was the largest such advertising sign in the city, and he followed it up with an advertising series that appeared in color in the Sunday edition of *Politiken*. The series comprised installments of a continuing story in which two children, Per and Lise, go on a trip to the lands where bananas are grown.

The bananas came from United Fruit Co.'s Jamaica plantations and were transported to Denmark in the company's specially-built cargo ships. After the bundles arrived in Copenhagen, they hung for some time in Kirkebye's ripening rooms where temperature and humidity simulated jungle conditions. The elaborate ripening treatment together with careful handling insured that the fruit reached the retail stores unbruised and at the peak of ripeness.

Father's career success was manifest in certain external benefits such as a company car, first a T-model Ford, later updated to the A-model in which our family undertook the German sojourn. Such opulence was rare, and I was the only boy in my class at school whose father drove a car.

During the early depression years painters and poets in desperate economic straits often tried to sell their output from door to door, and it seemed that a disproportionate number called at our apartment, having discovered that the resident combined appreciation for their art with some modest financial ability to purchase. A few small volumes of poetry found their way onto the family bookshelf, and a painting depicting two horses in a meadow came to decorate the living room wall after father bought those works from the artists themselves. Father kept up his interest in wireless communication by subscribing to an American magazine for amateur radio operators, one issue of which caught my attention as the cover showed in colorful detail a hunter in the wilds of upper Michigan launching a kite and lofting his radio antenna by using it as string for the kite.

In 1929 we had gotten our first radio, and father strung the antenna across the yard of our apartment building; broadcasts were feeble and occasional, yet brought in increasing measure music into our home. I became familiar not only with the works of Lehar and Tchaikovsky but also with an abundance of popular tunes flooding out of Germany to be sung and whistled all over Europe. Tunes such as *Das Gibt's nur Einmal* and *Bel Ami*, together with films such as *Drei an der Tankstelle* starring Willy Fritsch and Anny Ondra, and *Heute Nacht oder Nie* with the singer Jan Kiepura were instant hits in Denmark. The German influence during the Weimar years was overwhelming, cheerful, delightful.

Moreover, the Weimar spirit was infectious. Denmark's democracy had succeeded in elevating the economic conditions for working people, overcoming the traditional resistance by the conservative elements of the establishment to social improvements such as health insurance and unemployment benefits that removed much of the indignity of low income status. Solid citizens tended to shake their heads and assure each other that only fiscal ruin could be expected if people were paid good money when not working, but the measures were passed without violence and did not cause immediate financial collapse. Alleviation of econmic hardship combined with the relative prosperity gained by staying out of World War One to make Denmark of the nineteen thirties receptive and fertile toward the stimuli flowing in from abroad, including those from the turbulent republic south of the border.

The thirties thereby became a gay and lively period. New trends in architecture endowed apartment buildings with larger windows and with balconies. Abstract painting and jazz caused raised eyebrows in many quarters, enthusiastic approval in others. A huge output of popular music adopted the syncopated beat, and Danish film makers embraced the new technology of talking pictures, following the lead of *The Jazz Singer* and struggling mightily to adapt techniques and actors to the unfamiliar medium. After Hitler's accession to power, the inspiration from Germany had ceased, for National Socialism froze the new trends and started other quite different ones, but in Denmark they continued to blossom, fed by influences from the English-speaking world.

Our car quickly covered the last stretch of highway to Ribe. Arriving at the waterworks, I made a beeline across the street to Aage's house, and ten minutes later the two of us were on our way up the Nipsaa, savoring the chatter of the Evinrude while deep into planning our fishing trips in the days ahead. The visit to Germany merited only a passing remark.

* * *

What we saw in the course of our innocent sightseeing trip to the Harz was a gifted nation in the process of embracing absolute dictatorship. After several attempts and as many failures to form a workable government for the Weimar Republic, the eighty-six-year-old Hindenburg had finally in January appointed Adolf Hitler to the chancellorship.[10] Hitler immediately moved to eliminate or neutralize those whose consent had made him Chancellor. Three days into his new rôle he brought the higher echelons of the army to his side in a secret meeting, where he emphasized the urgent need for swift German rearmament on land and sea. Shortly afterward he met with a group of prominent industrialists in the Reichstag President's Palace where Göring now resided. The gist of his message was that in future the State would leave managers in firm control, keeping workers in their place and suppressing unions.

Having grasped the levers of power, the Nazis moved without delay to consolidate their gains and obliterate all opposition. Starting in grade school, Nazi indoctrination of the youth was made compulsory, and political *Gleichschaltung*, a coordination, began with the purpose of aligning all segments of the population, all elements in German national life, in the direction charted by the Führer. Germany henceforth was to be known as the Third Reich, its two historical predecessors being the Holy Roman Empire and the Reich under Bismarck. The process of Hitler's rise to power had coincided with the invention of the cheap, mass-produced radio of which he made effective use. His absolute control of all German radio stations enabled him to become a presence in every German living room.

The tragedy that befell the German nation was greater than generally realized, for the world tended to think of Germany in terms of the highhanded and intolerant Prussia or alternately the overweening Reich of Bismarck and the Kaiser that bullied its smaller neighbors and humbled France in 1870. But in the interlude between the country's defeat in World War One and the advent of

60

Nazism, the world briefly saw a different Germany under the Weimar Republic. William Shirer, who knew Germany of that period better than most, has described it:

> I was stationed in Paris and occasionally in London at that time (late 1920s) and fascinating though those capitals were to a young American happy to have escaped from the incredible smugness of the Calvin Coolidge era, they paled a little when one came to Berlin and Munich. A wonderful ferment was working in Germany. Life seemed more free, more modern, more exciting than in any place I had seen. Nowhere else did the arts or the intellectual life seem so lively. In contemporary writing, painting, architecture, in music and drama, there were new currents and fine talents ... The old oppressive Prussian spirit seemed dead and buried. And everywhere there was an accent on youth. Most Germans one met – politicians, writers, editors, artists, professors, students, businessmen, labor leaders – struck you as being democratic, liberal, even pacifist.[11]

This was the Germany now being ground out under the Nazi heel.

Chapter 8 June 1934

Boots, saddle, to horse, and away!

Robert Browning

The steamer backed water that sent eddies swirling between hull and pier. On the fo'c'sle, a deck hand hove a line that was caught by the harbor master, and the line in turn brought a steel rope that was made fast to an iron ring embedded in the pier's concrete. The same procedure was being carried out in the stern, and two steam winches slowly pulled the vessel to its alotted berth. Observing proceedings from the upper deck, I felt gratefully the complete cessation of motion as the moorings drew taut. The overnight trip from Copenhagen had met with inclement weather, and together with the rest of the two dozen passengers I had been miserably seasick all through the night, with a choice between the stuffy lounge, reeking of vomit, and the open deck where cold rain and spray after a few minutes had made my teeth chatter. Eventually I had found a space by an open half-door where intermittent gusts of warm air from the boiler pit below made my existence endurable. Twice during the night I had gone down into the cargo hold where my horse, Klaus, stood tied among boxes and bales of freight, no less unhappy than I at the turn of events. It was warmer in the hold than topside, but the motion and the fetid smells had quickly chased me back up the steel ladder to the cold sea air.

Two crewmen uncovered the hatches, folding the protective tarpaulins, while others readied the boomhoist and started to swing up cargo and deposit it on the pier. Within half an hour, Klaus was taken off. I had already carried his saddle ashore and now led the horse across the plank gangway and onto firm ground, tying him at a harbor water trough. The disheveled passengers were already gone, no doubt enjoying breakfast to replace what they had lost during the night. The only redeeming feature of seasickness is that it instantly vanishes when the offending motion stops. The harbor square was almost empty, the surrounding buildings glistening wet in the morning sun with the night's rain still dripping from their tile roofs and collecting in shallow puddles along the sidewalks and on the uneven pavement. A baker was doing brisk business, the store bell sounding a brittle note every time it was triggered by a customer's opening and closing the door, but the hour was still too early for other establishments fronting on the square. Klaus drank, rather tentatively, from the stone trough, while I saddled him and lashed to the back of the saddle his feed bag and a rolled-up multicolored blanket lined with hessian cloth. Then I swung myself into the saddle and started in a walk across the square, taking the street leading up over the hills circling the harbor and out onto the main road toward Ribe. Here I put Klaus into a slow trot, interspersed every fifteen minutes with a fast walk, a regime I knew the durable little Icelander could keep up for many hours. Around me lay spread the pastoral idyll of the Jutland countryside. Now and then I glimpsed a farmer tending a few cows, but there was no field work this early in the summer. Haying was at least three weeks off.

My aim was to reach Ribe, 43 miles distant, by nightfall. The road ran through Grejsdalen, a picturesque valley with scattered farms and small homesteads, the latter set up by the social-democratic government when it had taxed the old aristocratic estates out of existence. I knew this area from camping trips; in fact, I knew and recognized every curve and stretch of the road as only someone does who has pedaled it, uphill and downhill, on a bike loaded with camping gear. Reining Klaus to a walk and stroking the Icelander's flank, I contemplated the pros and cons of the different conveyance, while the gentle motion of the horse lulled me almost into the sleep I had missed during the night's exertions.

For my twelfth birthday I had wished for and received a course of instruction in horsemanship. My father decided to take the course with me, and during the winter months we went together to a riding school in town, the Frederiksberg Tattersall, where under the critical eye of the instructor, Søren Vind, we had both been introduced to the noble art of riding, English style. First, a few hours of trotting in circles with the instructor in the center keeping the horses on long leads, we novices without reins or stirrups hanging onto a soft saddle, getting the knack of jumping on and off a trotting horse, as well as turning ourselves so as to face alternately forwards and backwards. Then a few hours holding the reins and learning to balance while controlling the beast. Then a few hours with stirrups to perfect our posting. And finally graduating to an English hunting saddle and practicing certain subtleties such as changing from right to left canter, jumping hurdles, and so forth. I loved it, and the following year father bought me an Islandic horse. This small but stongly built mount has been in constant use in Iceland since Viking times, and the island's isolation has made it possible to keep the bloodlines free of admixture by other breeds. I named him Klaus, and he was stabled at a small riding school in Holte just north of Copenhagen. Thereafter I spent all my weekends and holidays on

At age 13 the author became the owner of an Icelandic horse, a small but powerful breed whose bloodlines have been kept intact in Iceland since Viking times.

horseback, exploring on my own the forests around Holte and elsewhere in northern Zealand. On Sunday mornings I would tag along with father and two business acquaintances who rented the school's horses to ride from Holte to Dyrehaven, the deer reservation where the royal family had a small hunting castle, Eremitagen, copied after the Russian Hermitage of Czarist days.

The riding stable was owned by Axel Koefoed, who kept four large hunting horses for rental, besides stabling Klaus. He had started his career as a journeyman carpenter, emigrated to the United States and enlisted in the cavalry, becoming one of Teddy Roosevelt's Rough Riders. Koefoed told me about the Cuban campaign and how the U.S. cavalry was unloaded from the ships by hoisting each horse in a sling and dumping it into the sea, each rider diving in after his own mount and holding onto its tail as it swam ashore. Mr. Koefoed was a tall, lean man with a fierce, red moustache. He always stood and walked ramrod straight, and as evidence of his military background he wore great cavalry spurs that jingled faintly when he walked. After his stint in the cavalry he became a Pullman sleeping car porter, frugally saved his money for twenty years and returned to Denmark with his wife, son and daughter to settle in Holte with the intent of making a living doing what he loved: managing horses. Unfortunately, his abilities were equestrian only. He had but scant business acumen, and in the course of a few years his life's savings slowly dwindled away. Being only twelve, I sensed but vaguely his struggle to keep the stable going against the relentless effects of the depression whose reverberations were felt even in the remote Danish society, like ocean swells spreading from a distant storm. I helped with cleaning the stalls, learning to separate manure from straw that was still usable as bedding when covered by a thin layer of fresh straw. And when called upon, I would with delight ride the rental horses to the blacksmith in Trørød for shoeing.

The blacksmith was old and grizzled and spat a great deal, for he chewed tobacco, a phenomenon with which I had been unacquainted until then. He pulled off the old shoes, which on Koefoed's horses often had been worn to pieces, removed the nails and cut the hooves down to the new growth. Then he selected a shoe of the proper size from a small stock he had forged himself and hung on the wall, heated it red hot in the forge and pressed it onto the hoof, melting thereon a flat, smooth surface amid a great cloud of blue smoke and the oppressive smell of burnt horn. Young horses were understandably jittery about having red hot iron pressed onto their pinkies, so the smith would growl at them to stand still and perhaps hit them in the belly with a backhand stroke of his hammer, but the older horses took it in stride. Attracted by the smoke, the smith's large dog in the meantime would eat the hoof trimmings. When the shoe was fitted to perfection by repeated trips to the anvil, it was doused in the water trough and nailed on. Finally, the hoof was filed smooth and given a painting with old crankcase oil to prevent dryness and also to make it look elegant.

It had not been easy to convince my parents that this summer it would be a good idea to take Klaus along to Ribe on summer vacation. It involved an overnight freighter trip from Copenhagen to Vejle on Jutland's east coast, the steamship company reluctantly agreeing to stow Klaus below decks with other cargo. But horse or no horse, Ribe was still the magnet that beckoned when summer came. In school I had established no close friendships; none of my classmates even knew that I had become a horse owner. In my general resentment of the Copenhagen environment I was determined to keep my life separate from theirs, a recognition, I thought, of the fact that my interests were different from theirs. I was satisfied with just one friend, Aage in Ribe.

To fill my Copenhagen days, I read voraciously. While in grade school, I had plowed through the medieval romantic stories by B. S. Ingeman, a writer whose fiction was set in the Danish historical scene of the 12th and 13th centuries, and from my grandfather I had received and eagerly read the animal stories of Svend Fleuron. I also bought one by one with my allowance all of the Tarzan books by Edgar R. Burroughs. They were already out of print, but I spied one in an antiquarian bookstore and eventually collected the whole set. Then Sir Walter Scott's *Ivanhoe* caught my fancy, and after that I went through most of the Arthurian legends in Danish translation. While in middle school, I discovered Jack London's works on my father's bookshelf, read them all, and found Kipling on the next shelf. The Danish translations were superbly good, just how good I could fully appreciate only years later after becoming competent in English. I also obtained a subscription to *Drengebladet*, a boys' magazine, and I devoured the Sunday funnies, notably Flash Gordon, Prince Valiant and Dagwood, unaware of their American origins. In 1934 Dagwood's children were born, both in the American and in the Danish comic pages.

The little Icelander proved his stamina while I contrived with miserly parsimony to preserve our joint energies as long as possible. At seven-thirty in the evening, the clatter of Klaus' hooves on the cobbles broke the evening quiet, as we arrived at the house of my grandparents.

This was the first time I could not visit them at the waterworks. The previous fall, water demand in Ribe had necessitated replacement of the waterworks' coal gas engines with electric pumps. The electric era was alien to grandfather, who at the age of seventy-three decided to retire. He had spent the last weeks before the changeover fussing even more than usual with his machinery, for those who understand such things know that a working engine has a soul of its own and that it can over the years bond with that of a man. Thanks to his forty-four years of loving care, the old machines were still in perfect running order. But life had passed them by, and on the appointed day a work crew had arrived at the waterworks, roughly pried them from their foundations and in the yard unceremoniously broken them into chunks of scrap with sledge hammers. Grandmother later told me that grandfather, unable to bear the sight of this destruction, had removed himself to the garden and wept in merciful privacy behind the elderberry bushes. By the time I arrived for the summer, they had moved to a small apartment in town, but their last days at the waterworks remained a wrenching memory.

* * *

*Shoot first and inquire afterwards, and if you
make mistakes, I will protect you.*

Göring, to the Prussian police.

On the day when I unloaded my horse in Vejle and set off across Jutland in the
pastoral Danish setting of peace and contentment, Adolf Hitler took action to
solve what had become a problem threatening not just his government but the
National Socialist movement itself. The SA under Röhm had grown to two-and-
a-half million, far larger than the national army, and Röhm wanted this force to
become the new army of Germany, under his command. The regular army, on
whose backing Hitler depended, naturally resented this threat and looked with
contempt at the cadres of SA streetbrawlers. Using lists prepared by Göring and
Himmler, special police troops and SS detachments rounded up not just Röhm
and his cohorts but many lesser opponents. Addressing the Reichstag afterwards, Hitler stated that seventy-seven had been summarily shot as "plotters"
against the State. Other estimates ran to more than a thousand. The Danish
press dutifully repeated the spurious Nazi claim that an incipient coup d'état
had been prevented.

After feverish efforts the Poles had succeeded in breaking the Enigma cipher
and were again able to monitor secret German despatches. One day, the Polish
military leadership was astonished to receive from its cipher team a decrypted
urgent signal that read:

> To all airfields: Röhm is to be brought here dead or
> alive.

The Poles fully understood the alleged plot for what it was: a purge by Hitler to
rid the Nazi movement of troublesome elements.

Chapter 9   June 1936

Bright youth passes swiftly as a thought.

Theognis

It was the last day of exams and also the last day of the school year at Efterslægtsselskabets Gymnasium. It was also the last day of public school for my class which was completing its *Realeksamen*, having taken the education path of people destined for business and industry rather than for university studies. Our education had entailed five years of primary school, four of secondary, and one of *realskole*. The class was being tested in oral German, the last subject on the schedule, and the proceedings stretched into late afternoon, for the exam committee took time to let each student reveal his proficiency, or lack thereof, in the course of quiet but insistent questioning. A knot of students gathered outside the door to the examination room uneasily awaited their alphabetic turns. Every fifteen minutes or so one of their number would emerge from within, the look on his face slightly dazed but overlaid with relief mingled with either pleasure or despair, depending on how he assessed the outcome of his ordeal. The little crowd would subject him to swift interrogation in hushed tones – "What did they ask you? What piece did you read?" – and try to guess what they might be shortly facing. Inside the room the committee was seated at a table in the center, one examiner and two monitors. At length it was my turn. I walked through the door and faced the committee.

Inherent in all human submission to being tested is a special thrill deriving partly from the element of risk in drawing questions or problems that may be beyond one's ability to solve, and partly from the element of self-discovery: how well can I really perform when under immediate, unrelenting compulsion? I thoroughly relished the feeling. With a good ear for music and tonal quality, I had early on detected the subtle differences in intonation that mark one person as a native speaker, another as a foreigner. Pronunciation should be no problem. I had committed to memory a sizeable list of the irregular verbs and conjugations that flourish in the Teutonic heritage, and my vocabulary was adequate to anything likely to be asked. Reading and translating a piece of unrehearsed text would be the acid test.

The examiner motioned me to the empty chair. "So, Niels, turn to page 122 and read the second paragraph." It was a poem by Heinrich Heine. I read the paragraph in German and translated it without mistakes. After four years of German, two hours every week, it presented a challenge but no real difficulty. The examiner closed the book with a nod. "Niels, wo bist du geboren?" "In Ribe, aber ich bin seit zehn Jahre in Kopenhagen wohnhaft." A short dialog followed in which one of the monitors threw in a few comments, more to demonstrate his own mastery of the language than to explore mine. Then it was over. I was dismissed and walked out into the hall where the crowd closed around me, quizzing me anxiously. After answering a few questions, I extricated myself, took my book bag and headed for the bicycle shed. Exam grades would be posted the next day and commencement was still a few days off, but I had no intention to waste one precious moment of my Ribe vacation by waiting for either. Now, school was over for good. My attendance record had remained execrable to the end, and on the way home I pondered why my school days had been so unpalatable, from first to last. It wasn't that it had been in any way difficult. Nor that the regimentation had been bothersome. And the teachers and the other students had been tolerable enough. Why, then? I wondered whether I was lacking in some qualities the world wanted. Or vice versa.

My mother was waiting for me, my clothes laid out on my bed, and dinner on the table. She had helped me buy a new bicycle, actually factory new, my first ever. It was a British *Hurry,* and the shop owner had acceded to my request that the rear wheel sprocket be replaced with one that had two teeth fewer than the standard. It made pedaling harder, but it also allowed a strong-legged cyclist – exerting himself without appearing to do so – to look unhurried and nonchalant when passing other bikers who were making less headway though pedaling furiously. An hour later I had the bike packed and ready, my clothes for the summer strapped to baggage carrier and handlebars. It was dusk when I departed, and I listened with delight to the song of new rubber tires against asphalt, while the city fell behind. As the summer night closed in around me, it became cold and I rolled down the sleeves of my cotton shirt. I was alone on the old road to Roskilde, ancient burial place of Danish kings and queens, but my cycle's swiftness kept me ahead of the shadows, its lantern stabbing a valiant shaft through the darkness while the dynamo's friction wheel against the front tire sang a steady tune, low pitched uphill, a tender whine downhill. As the highway's ribbon of asphalt passed under my bike's wheels, I thought about my present situation and what the future might hold.

My parents had divorced a year ago. This outcome of their marriage had been on the horizon for several years, and when it finally came, it was with relief

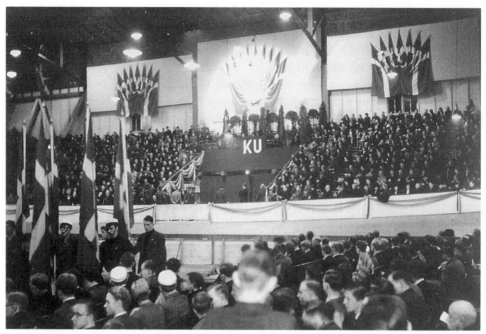

A public political meeting by KU, the Danish Conservative Youth Association, in Copenhagen, 1938. With an eye on the German threat, the conservative youth movement advocated a strong defense and gained some strength in the 1930s, but it could not match the numerical superiority of the social democrats.

rather than pain. Despite my youth and inability to imagine myself in a state of being married, I realized that my parents had never been suited for each other. Each was peculiarly unable to appreciate the other's many good qualities. Both were poor at managing money, and I remember their planning sessions when at the end of each month my father received his salary. They would then spend an evening setting up a budget for the coming month. The budget was never kept, and in spite my father's very good salary, they were always short. My sister and I had stayed with mother and had not seen our father since we had moved apart. Odd enough, I did not miss my father. We had not been really close, not the way I had been with my grandfather, and while I understood and admired my grandfather's skills in the workshop or when fishing, I was too young to appreciate my father's qualities in writing, or poetry, or in business creativity. Besides, nature programs us to be self-centered in teenage, enabling us to weather psychologic calamities that later in life would appear far more formidable. I knew of no other divorced family, but that did not bother me, and in my accustomed manner of preserving privacy I had never communicated the fact to any of my schoolmates. When I had arrived in Ribe the previous year, I had simply told Aage, "My parents have divorced." Aage said quietly, "Yeah, I know." We had not discussed it further.

70

My horse had been sold in the course of the divorce settlement. Partly as a result, my interests broadened in my last school year to include radio. In Denmark superheterodyne radio receivers were rapidly replacing older sets which consequently were sold secondhand at give-away prices. From outdoor stalls in Copenhagen's inner city thousands of radios, trade-ins from dealers' cluttered stock rooms were being hawked at prices as low as one or two kroner. Along with these conventional loudspeaker-equipped sets one could find yet older crystal sets which were unable to drive a loudspeaker but capable of producing reception audible in earphone headsets. There is something almost magical about snatching music or speech out of empty air simply with a small gadget in which an antenna's collected impulse is rectified by a delicate hair-thin wire touching a small crystal the size of a pea. No auxiliary electric power, no amplification, just magic! A magazine for amateur enthusiasts gave a one-page instruction with a diagram showing how to build a radio, and I had set about the task despite lack of tools and skills. I bought the components one at a time as funds permitted, first a four-by-six-inch piece of Bakelite for a face plate, then a bit of wiring, some condensers, etc. as the plans called for. My chosen set had just one vacuum tube, the last and most expensive item to buy, and could consequently only power a headset, not a loudspeaker, but at long last I actually got it working and could delight in listening to the Copenhagen/Kalundborg long-wave transmitter that covered all of the country. My listening preference was for popular dance music of which the State radio saw fit to broadcast only a single hour, starting at midnight. I managed to stay awake just to enjoy listening to the tunes of a small orchestra called Donde's Band[12] which was broadcast live from Lorry, a Copenhagen nightclub. The set was powered by one dry cell battery with a working life span of only three hours, and due to the late hour I often fell asleep with the earphones on, only to wake up with the radio silent, the battery dead, and no ready money for a replacement.

Nearing the end of my school days, I had come up against the need to make a career choice, the first major step in taking charge of my own life and leaving carefree childhood behind. The feeling was one of having the future move in close, staring at me expectantly. Like other teenagers, I had at best a dim idea about my own talents, or about the nature of the job market which in any event was rapidly changing, or about my own inclinations, preferences and goals, all of which were just beginning to form. In my case, however, I had no decision difficulties for the simple reason that my options were very few. The tight economic situation brought about by the divorce ruled out extensive studies, and I had instead taken aim – distant aim – at a career as a marine engineer, my grandfather's pursuit half a century earlier. Through the helpful efforts of my grandfather's first wife's brother, "uncle" Hans, I had obtained a commitment to begin an apprenticeship at Burmeister & Wain in Copenhagen in the fall. Uncle Hans owned Ribe Iron Foundry, a thriving enterprise and the town's largest industry by far. He and his wife were childless but had adopted a small Austrian girl, Ria, shortly after World War One. In the aftermath of that war, conditions in the countries of the Central Powers verged on starvation, and Denmark exerted humanitarian efforts to provide relief for children from these regions. Known as *Wienerbørn*, Vienna children, a large number of children from Austria were taken in by Danish families, usually on a temporary basis. In the Obbekjer case, Ria became permanently adopted into a loving home.

The apprenticeship prospect had for the moment fixed my career plans. Fortunately, the date when I was to start was ten weeks off.

It was 1 a.m. when my tires hummed across the stone pavement in Korsør. I drove through the silent town straight to the harbor and aboard the ferry which was loaded with only two freight trains and a few trucks. After buying a ticket I sought out the third-class lounge, stretched out on a bench and was asleep even before the ferry was heading across Storebælt. Two hours later I woke at the sound of a switch engine noisily hauling the freights off in Nyborg. Groggy, I staggered down to the main deck to get my bike and walked it onto the dock. In the northeast the sun was rising, reflecting brilliantly from the water of the Belt Sea. Dock and city were deserted except for the unloading activity. The squealing of train wheels and the clanging as they met switches and crossings floated through the still morning air, but to the sleeping town these were accustomed sounds, as the noise of children playing is to parents. I mounted the bike and started across the island of Funen, seventy-two kilometers. After Funen there would be the Lillebælt bridge, then eighteen kilometers to Kolding, and finally fifty-two kilometers to Ribe. I knew all of the distances by heart. By noon I had arrived in Ribe, having covered the 240 kilometers and the ferry crossing in fourteen hours.

Aage had lined up an apprenticeship to become a spare-parts man with Ribe's Ford distributor. However modest, almost every occupation in Denmark involved a four-year apprenticeship, or five if one started younger than sixteen. But before we were to start down our chosen career paths, ten glorious weeks of vacation stretched ahead, almost an infinitude of fishing and camping and softly warm summer nights, dancing at the forest pavilion, ogling girls at a distance, and drinking beer as our funds allowed. We had become interested in politics, both domestic and foreign, and decided to join the Conservative Party's youth organization, KU, a right-wing group that viewed Hitler as a much lesser threat than the Bolsheviks. KU had organized its own stormtroopers on the German model which we both wanted to join when we were old enough, at eighteen. To our annoyance, the social-democratic Danish government had outlawed uniforms in an attempt to discourage this sort of thing, but the stormtroopers had tested and found the allowable limit which included black boots, black pants and wide leather belts.

The previous October, during our last year of public school, Mussolini's armies had invaded Abyssinia. In 1896 an earlier Italian invasion had been repulsed by the Abyssinians at Adowa and, as Danish newspapers pointedly commented, it had been one of the very few European armies to suffer defeat at the hands of indigenous forces in the course of imperial conquest in Africa. But this time the Italians fought a campaign with odds to their liking, as they brought tanks and other modern weapons to bear against primitive tribesmen who had changed little since Lord Napier's expeditionary corps had defeated them half a century earlier. The war was front page news in Denmark but seemed to most people so remote as to be almost unreal. Equally remote, the fighting between Chinese forces and Japanese invaders aroused little interest and stirred no emotion, although it was reported in the Danish press. In July, violent events moved closer. Civil war broke out in Spain and we observed how European opinion divided, with socialists and communists favoring the Republican government in Madrid while Franco's side was supported by conservative elements all over Europe. A few Danish volunteers joined on each side, most helping the Republicans, but our middle-class orientation turned us against the Russian-supported government, so we rooted for Franco.

Like all good vacations, this one eventually drew to an end, and at the end of August I biked back to Copenhagen, prepared to enter a new and unfamiliar world, that of a workingman. Waiting for me at home was a 1922 edition of Holberg's Komedier which had arrived in the mail from my school, recognition for good performance in becoming a *cum laude* graduate. I scoffed at being reminded of school, but mother declared it was a fine thing to have, and put it in a prominent place on the bookshelf.

* * *

We have no territorial demands to make in Europe.

Adolf Hitler, to the Reichstag. March 1936

By the mid-1930s, the rest of Europe looked with varying emotions at the large nation in its center. Hitler had thrown off the limitations Versailles had clamped on Germany, by simply decreeing a law establishing universal military service and announcing establishment of an army of half a million men, to become known as the Wehrmacht, or Defense Force. He had expected France and Britain to protest but also to refrain from taking military action, and his political prognosis had proven true. He followed up with a "peace" speech to the Reichstag in which certain key statements,

> "... Germany needs peace and wants peace ... We solemnly recognize and guarantee France her frontiers ... Germany has concluded a non-aggression pact with Poland ... we shall adhere to it ... Germany neither intends nor desires to interfere in the affairs of Austria ...",

were what Europe desperately wanted to hear. Internally, German unemployment had been dramatically reduced by expansion of the armament industries, by pursuing development of synthetic substitutes for gasoline and rubber, and by establishing compulsory work service for young men to build superhighways of undreamed-of beauty and utility, plus significant strategic value in case of war. Germans were heeding the Führer's call to work hard and to strive for "guns before butter."

While Danish school children were preparing for their exams, Hitler had sent German troops marching into the Rhineland, ignoring the frantic warnings of his generals that the army was too weak to stave off military reprisals by France or England. In the event, the Führer's assessment of these adversaries was again correct; they merely watched passively, justifying their attitude with such casuistry as, "He is just moving into his own back yard." By this action Hitler abrogated an important provision of the Versailles treaty, one which had been a thorn in the German flesh, and the German public was jubilant. He followed the action with another conciliatory speech in the Reichstag, again assuring an anxious world with the statement, "We have no territorial demands to make in Europe."

The situation was quiet by midsummer, but in July Francisco Franco, the leader of a Spanish insurgency, made a secret appeal to Hitler for support. The Führer responded by dispatching selected matériel and technicians, and by sending a small air force, the Condor Legion. Its first accomplishment was the destruction by aerial bombardment of the Basque town of Guernica, with heavy losses among the defenseless population.

Chapter 10   September 1936

All aglow is the work.

Virgil

I trailed uneasily behind the office clerk who walked quickly through the maze of tool machines cluttering the hall. The noise and clatter was loud enough to drown out ordinary conversation, and when the clerk stopped at a fenced-in tool crib, he merely indicated by gesture for me to wait for the crib boss and disappeared. I stood near the door in the steel mesh wall enclosing the crib where tools were passed out through a chest-high opening to the requesting toolmaker who in return for each surrendered a small brass medallion with his identification number stamped on it. As several were waiting in line, the process lasted for some twenty minutes during which I waited, self-conscious in my clean overalls that still smelled of the clothing store, trying to keep out of the way while drill bits, cutting oil, milling cutters, micrometers and sundry other tools, most of them unfamiliar to me, changed hands. It was 7:10 in the morning on my first day in the world of the workingman, and the scene before me was Department 6, toolmaking, of Burmeister & Wain in Copenhagen.

Located in the central harbor area within shouting distance of *Børsen*, the stock exchange built by Christian IV in the early 1600s, B&W had by 1936 grown to be the world's largest diesel engine factory. The engines were marine diesels, huge affairs three and four stories high, whose destinations were the engine rooms of freighters plying the world oceans and in increasing numbers replacing coal-fired steamers. A few stationary engines were also produced, such as the standby power plant at the H.C. Ørsted power station, a behemoth whose 100-centimeter crankshaft was thought to be the world's largest. The motor division was its main business, but B&W also operated a shipyard building cargo ships, and less than a quarter century had passed since this yard had launched the world's first diesel-driven ship, the *M/S Selandia*, in 1912. Workmen still related with a chuckle how, when the *Selandia* visited England on her maiden voyage, old sailors along the Tyne waterfront had remarked that she must have run into a North Sea storm and lost her stack. Never before had a stackless vessel without sails entered a British harbor. Not resting on the laurels of past accomplishment, B&W was rumored to be pushing toward new horizons by attempting to build a diesel engine small enough to be used in a truck or bus. Most technical experts considered the project to be in the realm of pipe dreams, but the company's managers had seemed to lack the good sense to listen to their advice and accept the impossibility of miniaturizing a diesel to such an extent. Eventually, perseverance had been rewarded and a working truck diesel was at the stage of being tested.

I knew vaguely about these things, for B&W was a household word in Denmark, and I had been in touch with the metal-working field through grandfather whose early career as a marine engineer had been an exciting prelude to the quieter life at the waterworks. But at the moment, the noise and the torrent of new impressions combined to unbalance my mental equilibrium and threatened to make me appear a bumbling novice, something I was determined to avoid, however true it might be. I was a product of the middle class, and it was not unusual for middle-class children who could not afford academic studies to start their careers with a four-year apprenticeship in some trade. At the moment, more than half of B&W's incoming apprentices were of this group, the rest of blue-collar origin. The two categories were differentiated by the simple circumstance of age. The middle-class children had completed school at sixteen or later and then had to undergo four years of apprenticeship, whereas the working-class children almost without exception left school at fourteen and had to endure 5 years of apprenticeship. The stipulations were based on union rules or perhaps government regulation – the two were at times difficult to disentangle in a social democracy.

There was a temporary lull in the tool lending activity, and the crib boss turned his attention on me. "What's your name?"

"Niels Skov."

"How old are you?"

"Sixteen."

"Alright, you have been assigned to the tool crib for now. Take these chisels down to the smithy for tempering. It's on the ground floor over by the test hall." He pointed to a box on the floor, indicated with a wave of his hand the general direction, and turned his attention elsewhere. He belonged to the laborers' union, the lowest echelon of the blue-collar group, and he resented the middle-class kids, their polite speech, their different manners, their taking precious apprenticeship slots that by right should go to working-class youngsters. He glowered sourly after me when I willingly hefted the box and started in the direction indicated.

With the heavy box on my shoulder I picked my way through the maze of humming machinery, wishing my grandfather could see me now and thinking

Hedvig Sophie Tarp, born Riis, the author's maternal grandmother, at the birthplace of her brother, Jacob Riis, and herself in Ribe. The picture was taken on 3 May 1949, the 100th anniversary of Jacob's birth.

about how pleased the old man had been when I obtained the apprenticeship. Then I let my thoughts drift back to my time with my grandparents as a small boy, still too young to go fishing and largely in my grandmother's care when at the waterworks.

I knew my grandmother as cheerful, loving, infinitely patient, and possessing an inexhaustible repository of stories. Besides fairy tales she had also told me of her own parents who because they were long dead seemed immensely distant ancestors. My maternal great-grandmother, Caroline Bethine Lundholm, was born in 1823 and was married at sixteen to Niels Edvard Riis, a teacher and later headmaster at the Latin school in Ribe. In grandmother's living room hung a picture of her in middle age. It showed a kindly face with sunken cheeks from absence of teeth, one of the telltale signs of premature aging in a female body depleted by almost constant pregnancy. At the time the picture was made she had given birth to thirteen children, first twelve sons and finally in 1876 one daughter – my grandmother, Hedvig Sophie. Sadly, the labor of childbearing was largely in vain, for eleven of the twelve boys died as teenagers from tuberculosis, the scourge that loomed so deadly until the present century. My grandmother told me that treatment in her childhood consisted of drinking milk still warm from the cow at the early morning milking. As we know today, TB was spread largely through milk from infected cows, so the "treatment" must have been akin to fighting fire by dousing it with gasoline. The only surviving boy, Jacob, emigrated to the United States at the age of 21 and after much hardship made a name for himself as a writer and social reformer. Creatively using early photography to influence public opinion, he was instrumental in clearing some of New York's most miserable slums, working closely with Theodore Roosevelt who at the time was the city's police commissioner. The two men developed great mutual respect, inspiring Jacob to write a book, *Theodore Roosevelt, the Citizen*, while Roosevelt referred to Jacob as "America's most useful citizen." The Jacob Riis Park on Long Island was named in his honor.

Grandmother was educated somewhat better than the standard of the day for women of her class in a small town. Encouraged by her older brother's settling in America, she pursued on her own the study of English, and her father taught her some Latin as well, the subject of his teaching in the cathedral school. Although she found exiguous opportunity to practice the language, her English remained very serviceable throughout her life. She became my grandfather's second wife when she was twenty-six, his first wife having died in childbirth. Life with him was no bed of roses, as he was terrible-tempered. She once confided to me that she had on one occasion climbed all the way up to the top inside the water tower with my grandfather following her, and had told him that she would throw herself into the water tank – she could not swim – unless he mended his ways and curbed his temper. Whether this substantially helped their married life is doubtful, but the town did not suffer her drowning in its water supply, so it is fair to assume that grandfather took her threat to heart.

78

As a small boy I had of course no inkling of any such goings-on. Instead, I looked forward to the mid-afternoon hours when grandmother after serving the dinner at midday and being caught up on housework would retire to the bedroom to do her toilette. She would put on her dressing gown, sponge-wash herself from her porcelain washbowl for which she had brought a kettle of hot water from the kitchen to be mixed with the cold water from the porcelain pitcher. The wash water was afterward poured into an enamel slop jar and the pitcher replaced in the wash bowl. My grandparents never had a bathroom as such, with a tub or shower, or even a washbowl with running water. Their entire bathroom equipment consisted of a simple W.C., but that did not keep them from high standards of personal hygiene. After her sponge bath, grandmother would sit by her vanity mirror and brush her long white hair carefully before braiding and setting it. The entire ritual occupied an hour, and while very young I was allowed to be present. This involved ransacking the small drawers of her dresser which held her little cast iron nail file of a design very different from today's stamped steel models. There was also a small nail polisher, a silver frame covered with chamois on one side with which I would rub my nails in the hope of some miraculous improvement. Nail lacquer was unheard of. And there was a bone box with hairpins of which I was allowed on any given day to bend one into the shape of a swan. There were also hairnets as well as miscellaneous combs for setting her hair, and once in a rare while a small vial of perfume. Grandmother was very religious and I think she disdained perfume as a symbol of vanity. She alluded to it as patchouli. She wore no jewelry aside from a small locket carved in ivory and her wedding ring, a plain gold band she wore for sixty-one years. It was later to belong to my wife but no longer in usable condition, for over the many years it was worn paper thin and razor sharp.

The best thing about our toilette sessions was that she would tell me stories while she was doing her hair. She usually gave me a choice of a new story or one I had heard before. I was partial to *Little Red Riding Hood,* the real, unexpurgated tale in which the girl and her grandmother are both swallowed by the wolf, later to be saved when the hunter slits the wolf's belly open. Good stuff! She also told me about her parents and of events long ago which together with her white hair contributed to my firm conviction that she was very old. In fact, she was at the time only in her early fifties, but I would regularly lament to her that in all probability she would soon die of old age. The session ended when grandmother went downstairs at three o'clock to serve grandfather his afternoon coffee. I realized only later that grandmother had carefully chosen her toilette hour to coincide with his afternoon nap, allowing her a one-hour interlude of precious, uninterrupted privacy.

She was a superlative cook but usually confined herself to very plain meat-and-potatoes fare. She disdained seafood for her own consumption but patiently prepared the unending stream of fish brought home by my grandfather and in time by me as well. Her fishballs, made from pike filet, light as an elfin touch and served with caper sauce in *krustader,* small mille-feuille cups, qualified as unsurpassable in any gourmet repertoire. But she would rather have died on the spot than touch, let alone eat, any kind of shellfish, and she passed her prejudices on to my mother. Wine was consumed in the household only on grandfather's birthday and on Christmas Eve when the roast goose was entitled to be accompanied by a glass of red wine. Grandmother did also occasionally buy a bottle as a gift for someone in hospital. It was the favorite present for the ill, as conventional wisdom held red wine to be highly medicinally restorative. "Stimulates the blood," it was said.

Grandmother had strong religious inclinations which made her a Christian in the best sense of that word. She believed in helpfulness and generosity toward those in need, and in kindness and forgiveness toward everyone. She went to church regularly but alone. Grandfather took little interest in affairs of the soul, and she did not badger him about it. When I was six, she gave me a small pocket bible bound in suede and inscribed with a loving admonition to consult it for guidance and solace. Alas, with me her efforts bore little fruit. In her daily life she was tireless in helping the sick or unfortunate, and she was generally looked upon as a minor saint for it. She had only one child, my mother, who enjoyed her unconditional adoration and approval, all of which in turn was extended to my sister and me. I cannot recall grandmother speaking a single harsh word to me. Not ever. With her marriage to my grandfather she also acquired a stepson, the offspring of my grandfather and his first wife who had died when giving birth. He was referred to as Uncle Viggo, and over the years his story had become known to me, bit by bit. It turned out he was homosexual, and the intolerance of provincial society at the time had caused him to leave and emigrate to the United States as a young man, well before my time. It had been a great disappointment to my grandfather who insisted on lovingly maintaining "Viggo's room" in the water tower so that it would be ready "in case he comes back." Sadly, his absence was permanent. Viggo worked as a hospital nurse in Florida, where he lived with a male companion. Both became morphine addicts, subsisting in poverty, and eventually contact was lost when the rare letters ceased to come.

I stood in the smithy, awkwardly balancing the box of chisels and trying to decide where to turn, whom to address, what to do next. Two forges nearby had their blowers going and the coal piles in their centers were blazing white hot heat. At each a blacksmith was shaping some object on a large anvil, with an apprentice swinging a heavy sledge hammer in a steady rhythm, each blow precisely striking the blacksmith's tool. One of the smiths thrust the iron back in the forge for reheating and his apprentice momentarily rested his sledge and in a glance took in my predicament of uncertainty. He spat leisurely and said, "The foreman ... over there," indicating with his thumb a man in a noticeably clean work jacket some distance away. I nodded gratefully, approached the foreman and extracted information about the chisels' final destination. Having delivered the box, I started back to the tool crib with a glow of satisfaction: I had succeeded in my first actual task in the working world. Walking briskly, I already felt my surroundings less troublesome, the noise and activity almost familiar.

In the course of the day the crib boss, whose name I found out to be Larsen, gave me task after task from what seemed an inexhaustible supply. In the afternoon Larsen showed me how to fill out my time card and how to stamp it when the whistle blew at four-thirty. I washed up hurriedly at the cold water tap in the dingy washroom, unable to remove more than a fraction of the dark oily coating my hands had acquired during the day, and joined the crush of workers on bicycles streaming out of the gates and onto Christianshavn. Riding home through the city, I pondered the facts of my new existence, of four years of apprenticeship stretching ahead. Four years! Enough to constitute a small lifetime of its own. Could I handle it satisfactorily? Would I be a misfit, or would I fit in without in the end getting stuck as a machinist, a workman for the rest of my life? I dismissed the thought. Beyond B&W there were other worlds to conquer. I just wasn't sure where or how. Not yet, anyway.

Arriving home I related to my mother the day's events while applying a nail brush to remove the last evidence of the activities. I was being introduced to the simple fact that the metal working trades leave marks on their practitioners that daily demand stubborn effort to remove. The evening paper carried an editorial about the League of Nations' decision to lift sanctions against Italy over the war in Abyssinia. The writer's conclusion was that Mussolini had gotten away with facing down the international community, much as Adolf Hitler had gotten away with repudiating the Versailles Treaty and recovering the Saar.

* * *

Signor Mussolini had triumphed over the most ancient state in the world, Abyssinia, and also over its most modern institution, the League of Nations. I regard this as a lamentable event.

Winston Churchill

Italian fascism under Benito Mussolini had been the first right-wing dictatorship to take over a European country, in 1922. Compared with German Nazism it lacked a coherent ideology but was rich in folklore and imagery, military liturgy and uniformed maniples in their dramatic black shirts. Mussolini had proven himself a spellbinding orator, able to fire the imagination of Italy's masses.

The Danish commentator was correct in his assessment that Mussolini had faced down the League of Nations, but the true significance of Italy's foray into Africa to imitate French and British colonialism lay elsewhere. Until the Abyssinian adventure, Italy together with Britain and France had presented a united front against Germany in protecting Austria's independence. The Abyssinian war shattered this relationship as British and French objections drove Mussolini into Germany's embrace. Hitler and Mussolini agreed to pursue a common foreign policy, and their foreign ministers signed a secret protocol to that effect. Without revealing its contents, Mussolini afterward referred to this agreement as an "Axis" between Rome and Berlin. The European press picked up the metaphor, and Germany and Italy from then on were referred to as the Axis Powers.

Chapter 11   March 1937

Is sex necessary?

James Thurber

There were no empty spaces, so I finally parked my bicycle among dozens of others leaning against the ornamental fence of the H. C. Ørsted Park and crossed the street to the technical school on the opposite side. The building was from the 19th century, no older than others in the neighborhood but dilapidated from long years of housing trade school classes of teenagers in their prime, boiling with restless energy and impatient with mandatory school work. I joined the flow of bodies up the worn stairway and followed the diminishing stream that channeled into the third-floor corridor, finally entering a large classroom which was rapidly filling up. The room held four rows of wooden tables, four in each row, the black paint worn in spots and bearing the carved or scratched names of students from years past. At my back row table I was greeted by Poul Olsen and Bjørn Rødding, both apprentices from the boiler firm of F. L. Smith; the three of us had become friends in the course of our joint school attendance. Poul had dark hair and brown eyes, unDanish features that had earned him the nickname of Black Olsen. Bjørn had grey-blue eyes like my own despite the fact that his mother was Italian, a dark-eyed beauty his father had married after a hectic courtship while on a temporary assignment in Milan.

In many hours of tedious instruction, we had managed in quiet discussions to compare the work places where our apprenticeship contracts had committed us to spend four years of precious youth. As I became familiar with the place of my own apprenticeship, these exchanges of individual experience had given me a good perspective on my current situation. B&W's engine factory was rightly regarded as an outstanding learning ground for machinists. The plant comprised numerous departments or shops, set up by work specialty such as toolmaking, large lathe work, milling, forging, pipe fitting, foundry, assembly, testing, and so forth. We worked eight hours a day, six days a week. The work was physically strenuous, particularly the first year which was taken up largely by fetching heavy tools, air hoses, steel parts and supplies. This initial period served to acquaint the novices with the plant's physical layout and with the names of the hand tools and tool machines. The balance of the four years was devoted to all aspects of the art of transforming iron and metal into fine machinery. My own introduction by way of the tool crib had turned out to be a good way to start. Handing out and keeping track of drill bits and miscellaneous cutting tools for one of the tool machine departments had gotten me quickly through the first weeks of confusion when one had to commit numerous names and procedures to memory. My wage was ten øre per hour, and the pay envelopes in the first year of my working career contained 4.80 kroner for the forty-eight hour week. After three months I had been moved to a small, old milling machine where I spent the next three months milling large wrenches. The next transfer took me to the pipe department, where I was now working. The workplace hierarchy was rigidly structured by traditions evolved over generations. Each department or shop had a master, several foremen, and a workforce of anywhere from a couple of dozen to several hundred men, all organized into the numerous branches of the iron workers' union. Below the craftsmen stood the laborers who performed such unskilled tasks as transporting materials, cleaning and sweeping, and operating tool cribs. At the bottom of the hierarchy were the apprentices, ranging in age from fourteen to twenty-one. Being at the bottom, we addressed everyone else in the polite second-person titular, while we on our part were addressed in the familiar titular. In most departments each apprentice was initially assigned as helper to a journeyman whose tools he carried and whose errands he ran, while trying to divine the craft's obscure intricacies. The fact that there in some cases might be little difference, if any, in the ages of journeyman and apprentice was of no consequence. One was a man, the other a boy, by definition.

I exchanged quick greetings with Poul and Bjørn, and we uncovered our drafting boards on which an elaborate, half-finished projection drawing showed a matchbox in four different positions. The teacher entered, a small, bald engineer with a pointed black goatee which was responsible for his nickname of Mephistopheles. After a few instructions on how to proceed with the projection drawing, work got underway and he left the class temporarily to its own devices. A low hum of conversation settled over the group. Black Olsen was the son of a merchant marine captain, and Bjørn's father was an engineer, so both belonged like me to the middle class, and Danish society was still quite class conscious despite several decades of social-democratic government. Most of the others were working-class youths, and there was a constant verbal crossing of swords during class hours, as wit was exercised from either side of the social class barrier in practicing one-upmanship. Discipline kept conversation to a low key as everyone labored over the drafting boards, but quiet comments could be passed. Near the center of the group a tall mechanic apprentice produced a condom from his pocket and proudly held it up for everyone to admire.

"This," he announced in the accent of the inner city, "is what you need to fuck without worrying."

The room received the display and information in expectant silence. Then a foundry apprentice at the wall on our left contributed a comment that offered food for thought.

"My brother, he's 25, always says you should just fuck married women, that way there's no risk, see? No risk!"

The thought of chasing after married women was alien, startling, and also appalling. Not for any moral reason but because we would be at a disadvantage as the lesser experienced in such a match. We had all been instructed in the facts of life during our last year of public school, but the information had been rather summary, concentrating on the male anatomy, the nature of venereal disease, and the risk of causing a potential partner to become pregnant. Instruction to our all-male classes had given short shrift to the female aspects, so that female organs, menstrual cycles, etc. had remained in a shadowland of mystery. The overwhelming fact we had all absorbed, venereal disease being a minor risk, was that girls are tricky and complicated things who can get pregnant easily if you start handling them. Very easily! Hence, the conversation deserved, and had, our keen attention.

The mechanic was not about to allow himself and his condom to be upstaged by such theoretical gropings and persisted in trying to hold the attention of this audience.

"Nah, who wants to get into someone else's worn out broad. This rubber gives you complete freedom."

He went on to describe the merits of his prized possession, ending up making an impressive claim.

"I have used it twice and just wash it in soap and water in between."

Scowling sideways at Poul, Bjørn and myself, he added a sneering insult.

"But you guys down there in back probably don't even fuck yet, so you won't need any goodies like this."

The accusation was actually true, but fortunately unprovable. Our trio received it in silence, assuming looks of bored indifference as the best temporizing defense. Then Bjørn said over his shoulder to Poul and me, "Say, let me show you a little souvenir I just got from my family in Italy." He pulled a document out of his drawing tube and proceeded slowly to unroll it and pin it to the back wall with thumbtacks. It was a Fascist propaganda poster showing Mussolini's head in black silhouette with the single word *Duce* underneath. The artistry was excellent, capturing all the cocksure arrogance for which the Fascist leader by now was known to the world. The working-class youths, all socialists or communists, were aghast at the sight, and a cacophony of whistles and catcalls broke out as they realized what they were looking at. Several contemplated making a dive for the wall to tear the offending item to pieces, but Bjørn's square figure easily blocked the way. He was amiably conversing with Poul and me about the merits of Fascism and Mussolini's sexual prowess, while the noise died down. The crowd's attention had been diverted, the embarrassing accusation neatly sidestepped, but in the back row we sensed the need to keep the verbal initiative. When silence had been restored, Poul spoke up without taking his attention off his drafting board, "Say, Skov, next Sunday is Easter, and I do like to go for a swim on Easter Sunday." I let the remark sink into the minds of all the listeners while I with total concentration added two fine projection lines to my drawing. Then I lifted my pencil and turned to Poul, "Not a bad idea. I too appreciate the early spring swim season. Why don't we bike out to Furesøen Sunday afternoon and take our trunks and a towel?" We had deliberately made our language formal and stilted to annoy the inner-city listeners, and the startling suggestion had deftly changed the subject, the condom interlude forgotten. There was silence in the room for a minute while pencils were being diligently applied to vellum; then someone burst out: "For God's sake, who do you guys think you're kidding? It's still below freezing at night!" Poul slowly looked up from his work and raised an eyebrow in mock derision, throwing a contemptuous glance in the speaker's direction. "Well now, mustn't let a bit of cold govern one's plans. Mustn't be sissies. The early season is all to the good for the circulatory system, you know." As he finished, Mephistopheles came back into the room and started a long explanation of inverse projection principles. Having thus committed ourselves publicly, we felt obliged to go through with the proposal, and on Easter Sunday we took the shortest plunge of our lives in the frigid lake, its mossy bank still crunchy with frost. We felt the adventure well worth it, though, as we could offhandedly converse about it in class the following week.

We were all groping toward maturity in that intense process that varies from individual to individual, influenced by local environment, culture, class, family background, intrinsic personality and a myriad other factors, some dominant but many subtle, that human societies produce everywhere. Our work schedules, six weekdays of eight hours of demanding physical labor, followed on five of those days by two hours of evening technical school, left little time for social life. Occasionally, Sundays were spent on rest as the Bible suggests, but more often the inexhaustible energy of teenage impelled a project of biking or hiking in the Zealand countryside. Our needs were few. Good work clothes were essential, the best being one-piece coveralls of which I managed to keep two, allowing my mother time to wash one while the other was in use. Shop work gets a man dirty quickly, and mother insisted that one week was the limit between washings. I had just enough street clothes to get by: two pair of slacks, two shirts and a worn tweed jacket, plus one pair of leather shoes and one pair of work shoes, wooden clogs with leather uppers, good for the feet and comfortable on a cold floor in winter.

Our wants were few as well, largely because few are fostered in a well-ordered but frugal society. Still, two items appeared indispensable in order for a man to operate with a modicum of savoir-faire: a wristwatch and a fountain pen. I had recently acquired my first wristwatch, a Tissot with sweep second hand. Being somewhat ambidextrous but preferring my left for hammering, I wore the watch on my right wrist to avoid jarring it unnecessarily. It had a luminous dial that I observed with satisfaction in the darkness of my bedroom at night, and I had gotten used to winding it every night before going to sleep. A fountain pen was of equal significance. Typewriters were only for commercial establishments and public offices, so that the fountain pen held a solid and undisputed hegemony over the personal writing process.[13] Black Olsen and I had both purchased ours from a store doing a brisk trade in second-hand pens. The ones we chose after much shopping were 18-karat gold and had internal rubber bladders to be filled from a bottle of ink. Although we used the pens only to write a very occasional letter, we felt their possession to be a major step in our gaining stature and self-respect.

Beyond the watch and pen, I had a burning desire for a motorcycle. To me, owning a motorcycle was not just a passing fancy or a desire among others. It was a consuming obsession, overshadowing everything else and becoming an end in itself, dominating my consciousness and monopolizing my thoughts during all of my awake hours. I had not mentioned it to anyone, not even Black Olsen. Really important matters I could never discuss, only keep in my own mind and ponder, night and day, in desperate search for a solution. A new machine cost between two and three thousand kroner and was utterly beyond my means, and so was a used one, in principle. But one circumstance held out a slim hope. B&W operated three shifts, and whereas swing shift was inaccessible to apprentices due to night school obligations, graveyard shift was a possibility for volunteers, and it produced a weekly bonus of ten kroner, more than tripling the base wage. I had resolved to try my utmost to get onto the graveyard shift. And make some real money.

* * *

The whole education by a national state must aim primarily not at the stuffing with mere knowledge but at building bodies which are physically healthy to the core.

Adolf Hitler, in *Mein Kampf*

While we, three young Danes, tried to assess the adequacy of the evening school and of our technical training – which in fact was excellent – we were at the same time unaware how the quality of education in the Third Reich was experiencing a calamitous decline. An unemployed provincial schoolmaster who had been a Nazi party member and friend of Hitler's since the 1920s had been made Reichsminister of Science, Education and Popular Culture. In a very short time the school system from kindergarten through university became Nazified, textbooks and curricula changed to suit Nazi ideas. In the process, academic standards tumbled, as did enrollment in universities and engineering schools. Thus the National Socialist state proceeded toward a war-clouded future on the strength and momentum of a generation educated in the pre-Hitler years, when German institutions had been among Europe's finest.

We were equally unaware of the sinister implications of the racial policies being implemented in Germany. With an eye to the racist doctrines at the core of Nazi ideology, the Hitler government after gaining power had taken certain steps that would in its opinion strengthen and purify the Germanic national body. The steps included on one hand encouragement of early marriage and numerous children by the racially pure "Aryans," i.e. non-Jewish people. On the other hand, the government instituted compulsory sterilization for individuals believed afflicted by undesirable hereditary traits, and propagated the idea that the incurably ill should be killed, not cared for.

Although abhorrent to Scandinavians, these policies received little attention or exposure in the Danish press at the time.

Chapter 12   November 1937

The room was reasonably well lit, and I appreciated that, for this final scrutiny was important. I was kneeling on the concrete floor, minutely examining an old Rudge motorcycle. I was in the sales room of the Rudge dealership which occupied an old warehouse in the north end of town. The Rudge dealer had my particular interest, for I had just finished my driving instruction on one of their 500cc models, the *Special*, paying 35 kroner for the course. The dealer had recently acquired the BMW dealership as well and proudly displayed the new 500cc model with its revolutionary pinion drive and horizontally opposed cylinders, as well as the 250cc model which in my well-considered opinion was the sweetest machine human eyes could ever hope to behold. But they were all far beyond my economic means, and the best I could do was resolve to own one if and when I should ever become rich enough.

Fortunately, the dealer also had a number of used motorcycles for sale, eight to be exact, which together with four new ones stood in a row in the white-washed brick structure. The cheapest was a 250cc Rudge, the one I was examining, perhaps for the tenth time. It was a 1929 model and thus eight years old, and the price was 600 kroner. In the course of repeated visits, I had spent hours comparing, evaluating, estimating, and dreaming, running my approving eye for the hundreth time over the salient features of the little machine: brown paint, original and without scratches; a spring-mounted passenger seat; the manual gearshift on the right side of the tank; the cast iron cylinder of the Jap engine proudly displaying its overhead valves, actuated by push rods whose chrome plating had been worn through in places by many cleaning sessions over the years. It felt solid and dependable when I sat on it, promising me that we could do great things together. Its smell was wholesome, slightly distinct from the general odors of oil and rubber in the room.

I had already spent countless hours investigating other used machines at the dealerships around Copenhagen. The British models were the most common of imports seen in Denmark, with BSA, Ariel, Triumph, Rudge, Sunbeam and AJS all being well represented in the city. The Germans were selling NSU, DKW, BMW and Zündapp, while the Swedes marketed the Husqvarna. The American Harley-Davidson and Indian also were popular, and the different makes were readily recognizable by their color schemes which did not change from year to year. The green BSA, the olive Harley-Davidson, the flaming-red Indian – all of them kept their distinctive colors year after year. Only one Danish machine was produced, a blue four-cylinder Nimbus. The motorcycle dealers all proffered beautiful catalogs over which I had pored and salivated for other countless hours. Although per capita car ownership was high in Denmark as compared with other European countries, automobiles were still considered a luxury only a small minority could afford. This made the motorcycle a valued means of transportation and a status symbol as well.

By working graveyard shift for over half a year I had saved enough money, 150 kroner, to bring my dream within the pale of possible realization, and this Saturday afternoon in November was the day to take action. Last week I had turned eighteen and had immediately passed my driving test. Two days later I had picked up the license, a stiff three-by-five-inch folder in green cloth cover with my photo and the appropriate stamps. I was qualified. I was ready.

Getting up from the floor I walked to the small office where I was greeted by the salesman, a middle-aged man by the name of Reinhart. We knew each other well from my previous visits, and Reinhart began to fill out the contract that we had already discussed at length. I counted out the 150-kroner downpayment on the Rudge – one-fourth the total price – and handed the money to the book-keeper, an elderly woman. This was the first and, I thought, perhaps biggest deal of my life, and yet the woman seemed peculiarly unimpressed. We signed the papers and walked together out on the sales floor where I took possession of the Rudge, trying hard to look calm despite my pounding heart, giving, I hoped, the appearance that this was but a minor incident in my busy day. I pushed the motorcycle outside before starting the engine, put on my bicycle gloves of cheap imitation leather and waved goodbye to Reinhart as I slowly drove through the gate in the board fence and onto the dirt street in the late afternoon twilight. Testing the gearshift, I headed east and turned onto Strandvejen, the coast road leading north out of town toward Elsinore.

The driving instruction, confined to a small stretch of road in a quiet park, had been a firmly controlled and staid evening affair: one hundred yards down the dark and deserted roadway under the elm trees, accelerating to 40 kilometers per hour, then applying brakes gently and gearing down, signalling before a slow turnaround to the left, finally returning to start the tedious circuit over

90

again. Today, things were different and exhilarating. I reveled in speed and power, in messages from the wind in my face, in closeness to nature as city and suburb and countryside rushed past. The motorcycle experience was continuous action with constant need for vigilance, with unremitting demand for correct judgment, with subtle hints of danger. It was terrific! In fact, it was so superlatively wonderful that I thought it unlikely that life would offer anything to match it in the future. The machine under me felt alive and yet solid, a quantum leap from a bicycle. The road was devoid of traffic and flanked with villas behind garden fences. Eventually, streetlights petered out, and after a while I stopped, turned the engine off and sat in the cold and silent darkness, savoring the moment. From the nearby beach came the sound of waves and the smell of seaweed. I felt immensely privileged, certain that this motorcycle was about to open up for my exclusive access a world of adventure not available to my friends and acquaintances, and hitherto inaccessible to me. I could hardly wait! Cold rain brought an end to my reverie, and I started the engine and drove slowly back to the city.

* * *

We seem to be moving, drifting, steadily, against our will ... towards some hideous catastrophe.

Winston Churchill

On the same November afternoon as I was giving my chosen purchase one last going-over on the showroom floor, Adolf Hitler convened a highly secret meeting at the Reich Chancellery in Berlin. Summoned by the Führer were six individuals, the chiefs of the armed forces plus Foreign Minister Baron von Neurath and Colonel Hossbach, the Führer's military adjutant. The meeting had not been called for consultation or discussion. Hitler simply unveiled his irrevocable decision to go to war, and he did so to the small group of men who would be waging that war, directing Germany's armed forces. The Wehrmacht should lose no time in getting ready.

If Hitler's opponents outside Germany had read his book, *Mein Kampf,* the stark reality of his plans would have come as no surprise. Besides, already in 1927, Rudolf Hess, the Führer's deputy, had stated the long-range aim of National-Socialist policy to be the creation of a world in which the racially best people – as defined by Hitler – enjoyed supremacy, with lesser people kept subjugated and serving the master race. Hitler saw clearly that this state of affairs could be attained only through war, and his overall plan was to fight his enemies preferably one at a time, consolidating his gains quickly.

91

The conflict now looming would be fought for global domination along racial lines; would be of a nature quite different from World War One's struggle for relative standing within Europe; and would in extent vastly exceed that war. The true scope of Hitler's ambition was not to be grasped by the Western powers for some time yet. Their erroneous assumption of far more limited German aims therefore led to concessions that only whetted the aggressor's appetite.

Chapter 13   March 1938

The virtue lies in the struggle,
not in the prize.

Richard Milnes

B&W closed the plant for four days during Easter, giving the work force a brief period of glorious freedom. Resolved to waste no time in courting adventure, I had decided to travel to Ribe by motorcycle. To be sure, no one else I knew did such touring in the winter season, but so much the better. It would be adventure par excellence.

Ash Wednesday started as just another ordinary late winter's day. After a quick breakfast with my mother, I hurried down the back stairs from our fourth-floor apartment in Fredericiagade, a quiet street in the old part of the inner city. It was 6:35 exactly, leaving me just twenty-five minutes before I had to punch the time clock at B&W. Emerging from the protection of the stairwell into the early morning darkness, I glanced at the sky to check the weather. There was a light fog, and it was bitterly cold. In the narrow yard stood a low, wooden shed, partitioned into one-meter-wide sections, one assigned to each apartment for bicycle storage. I removed the padlock and opened ours, pulled out my treasured Rudge from its narrow confine, and clapped the padlock back on the door. I pushed it through the portal onto the empty street, primed the cylinder with a push on the carburetor plunger and engaged the kickstart once ... twice, and the engine caught. After turning on the headlight, I put it in gear and drove off, the engine noise muffled by the fog. There were no ice patches on the pavement this morning. Good. The winter of 1938 had so far been typical: temperatures hovering around freezing and with plenty of rain and sleet. Joining the thin stream of traffic through the heart of the city, I reached Knippelsbro, the harbor bridge to Amager, where B&W's plants were located. If a steamer captain should decide to leave just now, causing the bridge

The final parade in 1937 of Københavns Amts Skyttekorps, a volunteer rifle corps dedicated to serving in a supportive military rôle within the national defense in case of war. The Danish social democratic government ordered the corps disbanded as "not needed".

span to be raised, it could mean a delay of up to ten minutes, shaving my time margin to nothing. Fortunately, the bridge stayed put, and once across, I was almost there and nothing could delay me. Driving through the gate amid a cluster of bicycles carrying dayshift workers, I scanned the open shed provided for motorcycles and found an empty slot, parked the Rudge, and went to the washroom. It took only about a minute to change into my coverall, and another minute later I punched the clock with several minutes to spare. I was on a three-month stint in the department where huge bronze propellers were fitted to their shafts, or rather the aft-most section of the shaft which reached all the way from the engine to the ship's stern fitting. The propeller, usually from twelve to eighteen feet in diameter, was fitted onto the conical shaft end and secured by a key and a large nut. A crane coaxed the propeller onto the shaft, and if the fit between them was less than perfect – indicated by white dye on the conical shaft end marking the inside of the hole in the bronze hub – the hole was scraped, with a hand scraper, until repeated mounting of prop on shaft showed seating all along the conical surface good enough to satisfy the critical eye of the foreman.

The department master's name was Ebbesen, and I had a daily assignment of fetching his lunch pail from his home, a brisk fifteen-minute walk from the plant. Today Ebbesen was grumpy. The foreman had discovered a casting flaw in the propeller being fitted, and repairing it threatened to disrupt the entire work schedule. A normally phlegmatic individual, Ebbesen was cursing and stewing about how to dispose of the problem without unfavorable repercussions to his department, so I was glad to have his scheduled lunch pickup as a legitimate excuse to get out of the way. Leaving the propeller shop I took my usual circuitous route through the plant, turning the trip into an outing for my own pleasure. In the assembly building eight engines stood in various stages of completion. Two were being test run, their enormous bulks vibrating only faintly but emitting a subdued roar through the mufflers. I waved hello to a pipe fitter I knew, who was standing atop a half-finished frame, and continued my private morning walk, crossing the yard where a crane was gently lifting some large casting above a small cluster of men, and entered the forging hall. A steam hammer was shaping a white-hot steel ingot, each crashing blow cascading huge showers of sparks like successive eruptions of a volcano. I paused for a few moments to watch the ingot slowly attain the outlines of a crankshaft under the deft manipulation of two smiths, and wished for the hundreth time that I were able to paint some of these glimpses of my everyday working world. From the main gate I emerged into the street that ran alongside one of the canals girding the inner city. Fishing boats lay dormant along the streetside quay, their cargoes of cod and herring frozen on deck by nature herself during the previous night. Everything was powdered with a thin film of hoarfrost that the sun was trying feebly to remove. I compared the silent picture-postcard scene before me with the bustling activity just left behind and had difficulty deciding what was more alluring. Shakespeare was right; beauty is in the eye of the beholder, which I took to mean that it could be found anywhere. On days when I carried out this mission around nine in the morning, I sometimes encountered King Christian on his morning ride, winding his way through the city. Dressed in a military uniform, the King left Amalienborg Castle at the same precise hour every day to blend with his citizens in what had become a royal tradition not to be found in any other country. Mounted on his favorite horse, the monarch, now in his 60s, would ride alone along the boulevards and streets, without companions or security people. Here and there he might get caught up in early morning traffic, and at intersections he would patiently wait for a green light, towering above the crowd on bicycles and in motor vehicles. Pedestrians tipped their hats as he rode by, and some acknowledged his presence with a bow and a polite, "Good morning."

But on this day it was already getting close to lunch, and the king was long since back in Amalienborg. Taking two steps at a time, I ran up the stairs to Ebbesen's apartment, trying not to breathe too deeply of the stale cooking odors that always filled the stairway, snatched the lunch from his wife, and bolted for the outside to refill my lungs. Back in the shop, lunch restored some of Ebbesen's equilibrium, and I carried out my other duties while waiting impatiently for the workday to come to a close. At long last it was quitting time; I could stamp my time card, wash hands and face in the cold-water washroom, and rush for home. Mother had dinner on the table, but before we sat down to

Winter view of the canal near the Burmeister & Wain factory, the author's place of apprenticeship.

eat, I turned on the radio newscast. The announcer was in the middle of reporting that German troops had marched into Austria without meeting resistance and that an *Anschluss,* or joining, of the two countries was being effected in accordance with Hitler's wishes.

As soon as the meal was over, I made ready to leave. My few necessities lay ready on the bed, packed in a small bundle. I wrapped it in a piece of canvas to keep it dry, took it downstairs and strapped it to the passenger seat, then ran back upstairs to get dressed for departure. The temperature was hovering near freezing but was expected to drop during the night, so with luck I should be fighting cold rather than wetness. I put on long underwear, a woollen shirt and a pair of *Holmensbukser,* heavy black fishermen's pants whose wool stays equally warm whether wet or dry, plus a home-knit sweater. The crowning touch was a heavy black frieze coat, Danish military surplus acquired for ten kroner through my recent membership in a volunteer rifle corps, *Københavns Amts Skyttekorps.* The corps, together with two others,[14] had been disbanded by the social-democrat government the previous year on the pretext of being "not needed" as potential supplement to the army in case of war. It was widely believed that the true reason for dispensing with the volunteers was government fears of

96

a coup, an idea that struck most middle-class citizens as just plain ludicrous: a COUP? in DENMARK? Now, really! The coat was long enough to cover me down to my leather boots, which had been given a good coat of grease to make them water repellent. My gloves were of thin leather lined with cotton. They had large cuffs of a material made to look like leather, no doubt some paper product, and they extended over the wrists to close off the coat sleeves from entry by the wind. My head was protected by an old leather flying helmet of World War One vintage. Crash helmets could be bought, but they were not allowed for street use, only for professional racing. Governmental wisdom held that such helmets would be dangerous by enticing people to drive too fast. A woollen scarf and a pair of goggles completed the outfit. I was well aware that such clothes were skimpy protection against cold and utterly inadequate in rain, but they were the standard of the day, and I reasoned that one simply had to be philosophic about a bit of discomfort. Oilskins were not much better and in any event beyond my financial reach.

By seven in the evening I was off, heading for the ringroad that farther west would join the highway leading out of town. I had enough money to buy a return ticket on the Storebælt ferry, plus the 16-18 liters of gasoline the trip would consume. In my pack were tools to fix a flat tire and perhaps be of use in some unforeseeable emergency. What more could anyone want? Well, some weather luck would be nice. I was soon traveling west on Highway One, the road I knew so well from bicycle trips in summers past, and my excitement gradually gave way to urgent concentration on keeping from freezing. The road was desolate, but the familiar sound of the engine gave a comforting feeling of keeping the enveloping night at arm's length. The Rudge ran all right, but a moderate headwind kept my speed to less than 60 kilometers per hour. This was just as well, for the headlight beam reached only weakly into the darkness; full electric power was slightly beyond the dynamo's capacity. One after another I ticked off the small provincial towns: Roskilde ... Ringsted ... Sorø ... Slagelse ... their houses dark and tightly buttoned for the night, the motor noise echoing through the narrow streets as I barreled through. On the entire 107-kilometer stretch across Zealand the oncoming traffic totalled only three motor vehicles. When reaching Korsør, I found the ferry already loaded with two freight trains but only a handful of passengers.

After two hours in the freezing wind, my face felt afire in the warmth and sheltered comfort of the top deck restaurant, where I splurged by ordering coffee and a piece of *Smørkrans*. The ferry system was justly proud that its pastry was recognized as some of the country's best, but the reputation of its coffee was something else. It had suffered from being the butt of a series of jokes in the Sunday paper's popular comic strip in which a character by the name of Peter Plys had confided that the ferries had only one coffee bean which was passed around among them to be used and reused. One Sunday, Peter reported a serious accident: the coffee bean had fallen overboard and was lost in Storebælt! The following Sunday he announced in a reassuring bulletin that the ferry accident had turned out to be a blessing in disguise, for coffee could now be ladled directly out of the sea without any decline in quality. Although the joke was widely appreciated, public confidence in the quality of the ferry coffee had been noticeably shaken, for Danes like their coffee strong and take such matters seriously.

The landfall was made in Nyborg, and I debarked ahead of the trains, narrowly avoiding an accident in the near-darkness on the wet and oily ramp. Halfway across the island of Funen a light rain began to fall. In my bundled-up state it felt harmless at first, but shortly a fine trickle made its way down my neck and chest and started to soak my underwear on stomach and crotch. I stopped a few times and tried to prevent its entry at the collar, but a woollen scarf is of limited utility for this purpose. By the time I reached the Lillebælt bridge, the rain had turned to sleet and my goggles iced up and became useless. Fortunately, I had with me a pair of racing goggles, thin steel plates with narrow slits to see through. When I stopped to dig them out of my pack – a difficult project because my fingers were stiff with cold – I noticed that my frieze coat had become thoroughly soaked, both front and back. The thick wool cloth had absorbed such prodigious quantities of icy water that it felt to have gained fifty pounds. I got back on the machine with some difficulty and found the racing goggles to be working slightly better, but my field of vision was gradually reduced to less than fifty feet ahead, and my speed to little more than I could have made on my bicycle. It was by now well after midnight, and I found myself musing whether I would have swallowed pride and principle and sought shelter, had any been available along the highway, and had I had money for such indulgence. Forced instead to make a virtue of necessity, I gritted my chattering teeth and stopped every twenty minutes for a hundred-meter run down the road and back, fifty-pound coat and all, to get my blood circulating and force some life and warmth into my body parts. To take my mind off the misery of the present I thought about the Nazi troops now marching toward Vienna and wondered about the implications. Would there be a war in the immediate future? Or in my lifetime? Would Denmark be involved? Conservative press commentators insisted that Denmark's geographical position made the country highly vulnerable unless it demonstrated both means and intent to defend its neutrality, but the Danes showed no such intent, nor even any concern about their exposed position.

Time for another run to make my body functional again. I yanked the motorcycle backward onto its stand and started down the road, stamping my feet as I ran so the freezing slush splattered in circular patterns at each step. One hundred steps out, one hundred back, and my blood seemed to flow again. Then, back on the machine and on into the murk. With no gleam of light visible anyplace I ticked off the villages and inns, every one familiar from countless fishing trips, and I finally drove into Ribe, across the Nipsaa bridge to my grandparents' house. It was 3 a.m. when I hung my soaked clothes in the basement where they could harmlessly drip on the cement floor, and I sat down by the coke stove to let its grateful warmth reach me. Grandmother came out in her nightgown to greet me and inquired solicitously if I was "all right". Through lips stiff from cold I assured her that the trip had been fine. When she went back to bed I turned on the radio. The broadcast was now from Vienna where large crowds of Nazi sympathizers were welcoming the news of the *Anschluss. Sieg Heil! Sieg Heil! Sieg Heil!* In endless repetition the yells echoed into the night, the crowd fanatically spewing its adulation of Hitler and approval of his action, like a huge animal whose thumping heartbeat could be perceived on the airwaves.

* * *

Europe is confronted with a program of aggression, nicely calculated and timed, unfolding stage by stage ...

Winston Churchill

The Danish state radio's broadcast marked the culmination of a process of political moves coupled with military threats to bring Hitler the prize of Austria's subjugation. He correctly judged that neither Britain nor France would take up arms in defense of this remnant of the Hapsburg empire, and to assuage Mussolini he had slyly drawn the new German-Italian frontier at the Brenner Pass, thereby leaving Italy the slice of southern Tyrol it had gained by being on the victors' side at the formulation of the Versailles Treaty.

The military implications of Austria's Anschluss to Germany were enormous. In one stroke and without firing a shot, Hitler had placed his armies in positions that now flanked Czechoslovakia on three sides; he possessed Vienna, the gateway to Southeast Europe; and he had added seven million German-speaking subjects to the Reich.

Chapter 14 October 1938

What is strength without a double share of wisdom?

John Milton

It was 2:30 a.m. and a strong buzzer announced the end of the graveyard shift's coffee break. I got down from the steel table on which I had been sitting while eating my sandwich, and turned the lever that moved the lathe's drive belt onto the overhead main drive. With a squeal of leather against polished steel the spindle started turning. A few of the newer tool machines were powered by their own three-phase electric motors, but those were for the older toolmakers whose seniority entitled them to the best and most modern in the department's inventory. The younger men, and all of the apprentices, used older types of mills and lathes coupled to ceiling-mounted main drives. The piece on which I was working was an eight-inch piston for a small diesel, auxiliary power for some freighter's main engine, cutting grooves for the piston rings. I clicked in the feed and cast iron chips started spurting against a protective baffle as the vanadium cutter bit into the material. This was my last groove job. It required attention because each groove took less than five minutes, but after this I would start on a series of stagbolts. That would be an improvement in my work routine, for my tools could cut the tough bolt steel only slowly, each pass taking about forty minutes during which time I could read or take a walk and visit elsewhere. Strictly speaking, I was supposed to watch the machine, but the night foreman was too busy to concern himself so long as everything ran smoothly.

I drank the rest of the coffee and packed the small thermos in my shoulder sack. This lathe work was pleasant; it demanded skill rather than muscle. I had already done plenty of muscle work as I was shifted through a series of assignment periods, each lasting either three or six months. They had included pipe fitting, milling, forging, assembly, and black smithery, so far. I had particularly enjoyed working in the departments of pipe fitting and forging. To learn the secrets of good pipe fitting, I had been teamed up with a journeyman by the name of Mogensen, a man from Funen whose skill with steel pipe was inspirational. The work ranged from the piping leading from the fuel pump to the injection nozzles, heavy wall stuff with an outside diameter of about an inch, to cooling water pipes of diameters of eight inches or more. The pipe work was done directly on the engines in the process of their assembly, and I soon became familiar with these technical marvels of the diesel world. They were immense affairs, encircled by three or four galleries, usually two-cycle, double stroke, i.e. firing in both ends of the cylinders, which were typically some fifty centimeters in diameter.

In the forging department smaller items were produced by half a dozen smiths, grizzled veterans of the trade, who shaped the white-hot steel in its first step toward becoming a finished component. For heavy work the department had a large steam hammer that was used mainly to shape steel ingots into crankshafts when they emerged glowing hot from the furnace. For the small stuff, each smith had assigned to him one apprentice whose job was to swing a sledge hammer so that every blow hit with precision the tool the smith was using to produce the desired forging, and to do so with exactly the impact desired by the smith. It was a challenge because of the skill and timing it took to please the old guy, and at the same time it was superb physical exercise. But lathe work was tops. And the best part about being a machine operator, you could sing at the top of your lungs and nobody could hear you, not even the guy at the machine next to yours. During the long night hours I would sing to stay awake, anything that came into my head, popular tunes, Danish folk songs, American stuff currently on the dance floors of Europe from *Stardust* to Fred Astaire and Ginger Rogers' songs. I had a good memory for lyrics and could with equal ease reel off medieval folk songs or the songs from *Porgy and Bess*.

I had kept up my KU membership, had joined the junior stormtroopers and risen to the rank of platoon leader, and with enthusiasm was taking part in their activities. On the administrative side of politics, I had become a cell leader in the eastern part of the city's downtown area. KU had copied the cell system from the communists, and it worked quite well in keeping the membership on its political toes and contributing to worthy causes. The junior stormtroopers distributed conservative political printed material, undertook propaganda marches on the Nazi pattern, conducted para-military field exercises, held annual camps, and listened to the sages of the conservative party extolling the merits of nationalism and warning against the menace of Bolshevism. After the Nazis had drafted all German youth into organizations defined by age group, Germany spared no effort or expense to produce propaganda and instructional materials well designed to captivate young minds. In the KU we had managed to acquire several of the German manuals and were impressed by their quality, but despite our respect for some of the stated Nazi ideals, we did not consider joining the Danish Nazi party. We recognized it to be an unDanish product subservient to the Germans, just as the Danish Communist Party was willing to take its orders from Moscow. In an odd sort of way, our nationalism pulled us far toward the political right, yet kept us from joining the Nazis. We noted with interest that Charles Lindberg had received and accepted a high decoration from Hitler during a visit to Germany. Apparently even Americans were impressed with the Führer's actions. Lindberg had made his famous flight while my age group was in grade school, and we recalled the storm of excitement it had aroused.

Besides the political organizations there were other nationalistic groups exerting more quiet influence, and some of these had a distinct anti-German tint. The last war Denmark had fought was against Germany in 1864, and the defeat still rankled and was mourned on certain national holidays. Aage and I had joined an association called *18th April*, the date of the decisive battle at Dybbøl in southern Jutland in 1864, when breechloading Krupp cannon had demolished the Danish defense line of earthworks dating back to the Vikings. The association was highly respectable and comprised mostly older people, many of them families who had lost members in that debacle, and a few old men who actually had taken part.

Though disdaining the Nazis, KU was still so far to the right in the political spectrum that it was risky for a B&W worker to be known as a sympathizer, not to mention being a member, but natural contrariness made me enjoy the challenge of being out of political step. The workplace was a veritable hotbed of socialist and communist activists. The old smiths in the forging department were to a man socialists. They remembered the days when the Danish labor movement had confronted the country's conservative forces and the King had been on the verge of calling out troops to suppress the radicals. In the end the workers had prevailed without bloodshed and had ushered in the social democracy under which I had grown up and which had instituted social progress that I had learned to take for granted. Nevertheless, my political lights had in subtle ways been set by my middle-class upbringing. What was for the benefit of one class was deemed to be to the detriment of another in the simplistic world of class politics, and the visible, tangible class differences seemed to confirm this notion. Yet the crux of disagreement lay not in the social or economic realm. It pertained to the country's military preparedness. The middle-class parties insisted that the lesson from the past World War confirmed a strong defense as the best means to keep Denmark out of harm's way, but the workers would have none of that. They were suspicious of all things military and had for a generation waged a successful campaign not of vilification but of the far more effective means of ridicule.

Two journeymen came over from the center isle and stopped at my lathe. One of them was Julius Koefoed, son of the man who years before had owned the riding stable in Holte where Klaus had been kept. Julius was five years older than I and was saving up money to go back to the United States where he was born. He was convinced that Europe was heading for war and wanted to fight it, if necessary, on the American side. I did not know the other guy and Julius did

102

not bother with an introduction. He leaned on the edge of the steel table and came straight to the point. "Listen, I have a bet with Lars here that you can press one of those bolts." He pointed to a pallet of stagbolts parked near my lathe; they had been drop forged and were now awaiting finish turning. Taken aback, I looked at the bolts: three-inch diameter, a good meter long ... small enough to get a grip on, but heavy.

"Why me?"

"Never mind, just do me a favor and press one."

"Which hand?"

The two journeymen exchanged a meaningful glance and I realized in a flash that they had interpreted my question to mean that I could easily do it either way. Julius grinned, confirming my perception of the journeymen's interpretation.

"Doesn't matter."

In fact, I had been innocently wondering which hand might give me the better chance of success. As I was used to writing with my right hand but using a hammer with my left, I decided the left might be the better choice and walked over to the pallet. It was about a foot high, and I bent over to wipe the middle part of one bolt with a clean rag, clamped my left hand around it and moved it slightly. God, it was heavy! I realized that I would have to do it quickly, or I would run out of strength before I could get it up there. Turning my hand away from my body I took a deep breath, bent my knees enough to reach, gripped the bolt at the midpoint and hoisted it to shoulder height, crouched slightly and pressed it straight up, straightening my knees at the same time. Then I stepped out from under and dumped the bolt with a plangent thud on the wood-paved floor. Lars looked vastly disappointed but Julius exulted "I told you so!" As befit journeymen, the two departed with no further comment to me.

A few minutes before the day shift arrived, the shop steward strolled by and stopped at my lathe. He was a sandy-haired man of about fifty by the name of Nyrup who had taken a benevolent interest in what he considered my wayward political orientation. He had several times given me socialist pamphlets and on one occasion lent me a book about workers in the Greenland cryolite mines, all in the hope that this young apprentice might see the light, grasp the merit of social-democracy and turn away from right-wing causes. I had dutifully read the material and afterward pointed out, over Nyrup's strong objections, what seemed to me the fallacies in socialist thinking. It had all been friendly with both sides remaining unbending in our convictions.

"I hear you pressed one of the bolts," Nyrup said, chuckling at my obvious surprise, "didn't you know they both tried and couldn't do it? But more important, news just came that Hitler, that swine, got Czechoslovakia. The Brits and Frenchies let them down."

* * *

*The partition of Czechoslovakia under Anglo-French
pressure amounts to a complete surrender by the
Western Democracies to the Nazi threat of force.
Such a collapse will not bring peace ...*

Winston Churchill

Virtually everywhere along Europe's borders one can find pockets of minorities
cut off from the parental groups where their origins lie. Battles and treaties
quilting Europe since the Romans have failed to solve this problem. However
tortuously national frontiers are drawn, it has persisted.

In the South Jutland borderland where I grew up, a Danish-speaking minority lives south of the frontier and a corresponding pocket of German-speakers
exists north of the line. This was accepted as a fact of life to which the Danes
were largely indifferent, but the Germans have been notoriously fascinated by
ethnic introspection, searching and perusing their distant past in a manner that
has no modern-day corollary among European nations. It would strike Danes as
merely amusing if one tried to make them feel toward their Viking forebears a
kinship that could inspire them to great deeds or arouse them to fighting.
Danes simply don't take themselves that seriously, but Germans are different.
Ethnic roots, *Blut und Erde*, blood and soil, are charged concepts that touch sensitive nerves deep in the German psyche.[15] Hitler recognized the potential in
exploiting this German propensity, and Nazi ideas from the outset doted on it,
labeling the citizens inside the Reich's borders as *Reichsdeutsche* and those
stranded outside but of German stock as *Volksdeutsche.* Moreover, the Nazis took
their countrymen far beyond mere romantic attachment to ethnicity.[16] Besides
claiming the high ground as defenders of Germanness everywhere, Hitler introduced to his fellow Germans the notion of being a *Herrenvolk*, a Master Race,
who deserved as its natural right both space and preference over lesser peoples.
The message found a responsive audience.

The newly independent state of Czechoslovakia – created by the Versailles
Treaty – enclosed some 2.7 million people of German descent. In the summer
of 1938, wiping Czechoslovakia off the European map became Hitler's next
quest, and I had become old enough to follow with interest the political moves
of Germany, Britain, France and Czechoslovakia which were thoroughly reported in the Danish press. Nazi propaganda spewed all its venom at the hapless
Czechs, making the country a symbol of Versailles humiliation, an injury to the
German body, an affront to the German soul that must be eliminated, immediately and at any cost. The Czechs were made of sterner stuff than the Austrians
and not easily intimidated, but in four weeks of hectic negotiations Neville
Chamberlain, the British Prime Minister, and Daladier, the French Premier,
pressured the Czechs to accept Hitler's demands.

Part II

Wrath of Innocence

World War: From Warsaw to the Crimea

Chapter 15   September 1939

As long as there are sovereign nations possessing
great power, war is inevitable.

Albert Einstein

The new rubber swimming cap kept my hair out of my face; nearing the end of the seventh lap I decided that it was worth the two kroner I had paid for it. "Arms ONLY, just let your legs trail behind. NO leg work!" Mrs. Skule, the coach, walked along the edge of the pool and kept up a steady barrage of instructions to her half-dozen students, while we plowed through the routine exercises to perfect our crawl. I reached the end of the pool, put my feet on the blue ceramic tile as I turned and shot into the eighth lap. Mrs. Skule's figure was perfect, very sexy, nice curves, beautiful legs ... From my low vantage point I could see her legs well above the knees as her light smock flowed about her when she moved.

The pool was only a couple of years old, pride of the city administration. Located near Idrætsparken, site of field and track sports, the building was attractive with ample room for spectators, a worthy setting for international competitions. Proponents liked to point out how well justified it was by the upsurge in performance by Danish swimmers, particularly Ranghild Hveger and Inge Sørensen who had won several gold medals for the country. Too bad they weren't much to look at when one saw them at practice, which was frequently. Ragnhild was about nineteen and in a wet swimsuit she looked more like a salmon than a girl. Freckle-faced Inge was only fourteen, and I marveled at the way she always seemed to float in the water like a cork. It made me wonder what gave different people such different specific gravities. I was myself unable to float at all if I stopped swimming. My training had lasted the better part of a year and I was getting pretty good. Not that I expected ever to set any records, but the exercise gave me endurance. I had started last year, motivated by the incident in the shop, when I pressed a stagbolt to settle someone else's bet. It had been a revelation suddenly to become aware of my own physical strength, and only afterwards had I thought about the implications. Having started my apprenticeship as a normal adolescent, the heavy work had developed me in a most gratifying way. My muscles were hard, serviceable, but what could I do to improve myself further? I had joined a rowing club but realized after a couple of evenings sculling in the harbor that the members lacked discipline and drive; they were primarily interested in Saturday night parties and other social activities. Then I had thought of swimming: a useful skill, within my financial means, and offering uniform development of the human body. "Niels, keep your legs relaxed but STILL!" Mrs. Skule was hoarse, perhaps the effect of overusing her voice was aggravated by the scent of chlorine that always hung in the air. Beautiful legs, though. To keep her in my field of vision I breathed to the left on odd numbered laps, to the right on even numbered. I finished the last exercise, heaved myself in one smooth motion out of the water and onto the floor, nodded goodbye to Mrs. Skule and walked to the men's showers.

When I got on my bike outside, it was midmorning – I was still working the lucrative graveyard shift – and I enjoyed the ride home through the park. The beech trees had taken on fall colors. Here and there the wind was sweeping across the pavement small waves of reddish-brown leaves that my wheels cut through with a hissing sound. We were now living on the northeastern side of town, not far from the coast road along the Sound, where mother had found a cheaper apartment. I liked living with my mother; we got along well. Mother was born in my grandparents' home at the waterworks and had grown up in Ribe, probably a bit spoiled, I thought. She had left home at eighteen to attend a girls' school to learn cooking and simple home economics, and she also played the piano and took ballet. At twenty-two she had married my father, at which time she must have been pregnant with my sister. Perhaps she would have married him in any event, but pregnancy was a compelling reason, to say the least. Having a child out of wedlock was all but unthinkable for a girl from a good family in a small provincial town. After my father returned home from his travels as radio operator, they had started a dancing school and taught together for two years. For the rest of their eighteen years of marriage she had remained a housewife in the mold nearly universal in Danish society. Mother was cheerful, hardworking and efficient. She kept the family home spotless, saw to it that her children had everything she was able to provide, made few demands on us and never nagged. At the same time, her relationship with my paternal grandmother had been abominable. The two women's instant dislike of each other had proved to be enduring; they never changed their opinions or even relented in that regard, something that undoubtedly had contributed to breaking up the marriage. At my parents' divorce my father earned twelve thousand kroner per year, a very substantial salary, and the decree obligated him to pay his ex-wife one-third of this income. But two years later he had married a woman sixteen years his junior, resigned his position as advertising manager, and then moved from Copenhagen to the island of Thurø, where he bought a small orchard with an old thatched-roof farmhouse, fulfilling a dream about wholesome endeavor in idyllic surroundings. The dream unfortunately did not produce enough money to support his erstwhile family who found itself financially on its own in the late nineteen-thirties Danish society, where money was scarce and depression era unemployment lingered. I felt no resentment toward my father for our financial predicament. I knew he would have provided money, had he been able to, but I also knew that he was unlikely to succeed as an entrepreneur. His gifts lay elsewhere. Father had pursued a dream, and despite my youth, or perhaps because of it, I was tolerant of pursuing dreams. Mother was understandably resentful, but she was now applying her customary energy to the problems of being a provider. Although her career as a housewife had left her with little in the way of marketable skills, she tried her hand at various tasks. At the moment she was sewing leather gloves for a downtown store, work she could do at home, but even her speed and energy could not produce enough income by this means. Consequently, our financial situation was tight. My sister had become self-supporting as a nurse trainee, but I would be a liability for some time to come. And I disliked being a dependant, a family liability.

I parked my bike and ran up the stairs to our third-floor apartment and sat down to a late breakfast. The headline in the morning paper dealt with yet another German ultimatum, this time to Poland, and I turned on the radio to see if there was any further news. As we were finishing the meal the program was interrupted and the voice of the announcer brought a series of bulletins from the major news agencies, BBC, Reuters and Agence Havas. With minor changes in wording their messages were the same: early this morning German troops had crossed the Polish frontier at several points ... heavy fighting was in progress. Mother and I sat, momentarily transfixed, listening to the announcer's serenely calm voice reeling off a sketch of the opening phases in what must clearly be mayhem on a number of distant battlefields.

The night shift went on as usual. People talked only reluctantly about the drama beyond their border. Words seem pointless, even embarrassing, when one is totally unable to influence the flow of events. Instead they turned attention to daily routines, seeking solace in doing things familiar and respectably sensible and useful. On Sunday the radio brought the news of British and French ultimata to Germany, followed shortly by declarations that a state of war existed. Like the rest of the Danish population, mother and I dutifully listened to the state radio's announcements which turned to the effects on our country's domestic affairs. Practical matters were discussed and a number of decrees issued, such as rationing of miscellaneous imported goods and immediate curtailment on the use of private motor vehicles. In my case this firmly ruled out any use of my treasured Rudge, which overnight changed from being a source of sublime enjoyment to being an inert encumbrance and a financial burden. Two days later, I returned it to the dealer to avoid keeping up the monthly payments. Walking home, I realized with surprise that my regret was momentary, for my interest was now focused elsewhere, on the countries becoming embroiled in war, and whether Denmark would get involved as well. The clean-scrubbed, uniformed Nazi boys of my German trip six years ago came to mind. They would now be soldiers, my age, and in a mental picture I saw millions of them marching off to war, singing in exuberant expectation. I sensed that the deadly business would probably last a while.

* * *

Germany will never break the peace!

Adolf Hitler

In the spring of 1939 Hitler sent troops into the Memelland, a region of the small Baltic state of Lithuania that was essentially defenseless and at German mercy. The Reich now bordered Poland on three sides, and Nazi propaganda turned its sights on the border areas, painting these as intolerable wounds to German pride and well-being. However, it was noticeable even in Danish press reports that a change had taken place in British public opinion. Loath to contemplate another war, Britons had till then desperately wanted to believe in Hitler's illusory promises, but fatuity had its limits. Responding to public pressure, the Chamberlain government unilaterally offered Poland guarantees of support against aggression. The Poles eagerly accepted.

At this point, a Russian suggestion was floated in Berlin that Russia and Germany enter into a nonaggression pact. The pact was quickly concluded with a secret codicil that spelled out how to divide the spoils after a German attack on Poland had succeeded: the Russians would grab eastern Poland while Germany took the western part, thus wiping this ancient nation off the map of Europe. The codicil in effect turned the innocently labeled Pact of Non-Aggression into a deal to facilitate aggression by both signatories.

On 1 September, the Wehrmacht's armor smashed across the Polish frontier, three spearheads surging toward Warsaw. The British and French each sent Germany a formal ultimatum to cease hostilities and pull the troops back. Two days after the attack started, Neville Chamberlain in a subdued voice informed Britons over the radio that a state of war existed between their country and Germany. A few hours later the French followed suit.

The Poles lacked modern equipment and an effective defense strategy, and there was nothing that could be done by France or Britain to aid them. Poland's several neighbors stayed neutral with the exception of the Soviet Union who waited until German forces were fighting in the Warsaw suburbs. Then it fulfilled its secret agreement with Hitler, and the Red Army fell on the unsuspecting Poles.[17] It was all over in three weeks. Scattered units of the Polish navy and air force escaped to Britain and later fought with distinction on the Allied side.

Chapter 16 February 1940

There could be no honor in a sure success,
but much might be wrested from a sure defeat.

T. E. Lawrence

The snow crunched under the wheels of my bicycle as I rode through the gate. The street outside had been scraped reasonably clean and sand had been spread to render the remaining thin crust harmless. There was no slush, it was too cold for that, with the temperature at ten below the Celsius zero. I wore long underwear, and the scarf my mother had knitted kept cold air from getting under the zippered wool jacket. The gloves left something to be desired, though, and I kept flexing my fingers on the handlebars to keep them from getting stiff. When I reached the Finnish consulate, a sign on the fence outside informed that they would be open at eight-thirty, an hour from now. For a moment I pondered my options and decided to splurge on a cup of coffee in a nearby café while waiting for the Finns. The place was warm and cozy; apparently the owner managed his fuel ration well. I smiled at the waitress as I sat down and received an approving look in return. "Do you have a morning paper I could look at?" She disappeared and came back with *Politiken* and a small pot of hot coffee. With cream and sugar it tasted heavenly, as I slowly sipped it while scanning the front page.

The headline proclaimed another Russian regiment annihilated in a Finnish encirclement and described heavy fighting on the Karelian Isthmus. Despite reckless valor the stubborn Finns were giving ground, clearly being worn down by the hordes of Russians. A picture at the bottom of the page showed a small group of Danish volunteers leaving for Finland, doing, I thought, what a self-respecting person must. I went through the paper, methodically reading the numerous other items about the winter war. Collection centers in Copenhagen clamored for warm clothes for the Finns. From Sweden a small contingent of military pilots and several thousand other volunteers had left for Helsinki. A reporter described how the desperate need for artillery compelled the Finns to rely on light infantry arms. Another related how the Suomi machine pistol had become a favorite weapon. All praised the unflinching determination of these indomitable people.

It had all come about after Germany crushed Poland last September in a three-week campaign, creating the new military term *Blitzkrieg*. The British and French had declared themselves at war with Germany, a war that caught everyone except the Germans distinctly unprepared. The French huddled in their Maginot Line,[18] the enormous underground fortress complex built in the aftermath of World War One along their eastern border from Switzerland to Montmédy. The ghastly bloodletting in that first world war had seemingly broken the Gallic spirit, leaving the nation with no taste for war. The British, despite keen memories of their own terrible losses twenty-odd years earlier, gamely sent an expeditionary corps to the continent in a show of solidarity, but during the fall and winter of 1939-40 the main actors in the drama were sitting entrenched on the Western Front, warily eyeing each other. The war became known among English speaking people as the Phoney War. The French called it *la drôle de guerre*.

With the big powers' attention riveted on the Western Front, the Soviet dictator, Joseph Stalin, had demanded from Finland certain territories at Petsamo in the north and on the Karelian Isthmus. Negotiations eventually broke down, and Stalin at the end of November sent the Red Army in a sudden attack against Finland. Ignoring the hopeless 40-to-1 odds, the Finns fought instantly and tenaciously against their ancient foe from the east. Field Marshal C.G.E. von Mannerheim, seventy-two-years old and a national hero, came out of retirement to take command of the Finnish forces. Well known to all of us in Scandinavia, he had served Czar Nicolas II before World War One when Finland was a Russian province and had later fought the Bolsheviks to gain Finland its independence. Improvising new tactics with light arms, his troops annihilated one Russian regiment after another in the pitiless winter months and beat back the Russians on the Karelian Isthmus before they could reach the main Finnish field defenses in the Mannerheim Line. But lately the situation had changed and the Finns were yielding ground, clearly bleeding to death and needing help. Quickly.

I checked the time. The consulate was about to open, and I paid and left, noticing the friendly smile of the waitress who probably wondered why her guest was so preoccupied.

The consulate was already filled with activity as I was directed to a desk staffed by a young woman, where I came straight to the point.

"I want to volunteer to fight with the Finns."

As she looked up at me, thoughtfully, I felt I was being weighed, measured and evaluated, all in one brief moment.

"How old are you?"

"Twenty."

"We can't take anyone under twenty-one."

She was blonde, with grey eyes, and her voice carried just a trace of regret, taking the edge off the negative. She looked my own age, and that encouraged me to press further.

"What can I do, what would you suggest?"

She pondered my question for a moment.

"What do you do?"

I decided to stretch the truth by mentally completing my apprenticeship:

"I'm a machinist."

She looked more encouraging.

"We do have need for workers in certain categories to keep production going, releasing our men for the Front. You would qualify, and for that service you need only to be eighteen. I could sign you up for that."

"When can I leave?"

She smiled, for the first time.

"You will hear from us in about two weeks."

* * *

Only Finland – superb, nay, sublime – in the jaws of peril – Finland shows what free men can do.

Winston Churchill

The Finnish Winter War was a sideshow, to be sure, but one that briefly held the world spellbound. In January, Stalin placed General Timoshenko in command of the Finnish campaign. He called in massive reinforcements from all over the Soviet Union, brought up siege artillery and began a systematic destruction of the Mannerheim Line – unopposed, for the Finns had no long-range guns. In due time, the vastly superior numbers and arms told, and the Finns were slowly overwhelmed. In March they signed the Treaty of Moscow, ceding to the Russians the coveted areas of Petsamo on the White Sea and the Karelian Isthmus. The cost in human lives came high. Twenty-five thousand Finns and 200,000 Soviet soldiers perished on Finland's snow covered battlefields.

The Finns were from the outset doomed to lose, because in their case superior arms as well as numbers were with the opponent. As Napoleon once soberly commented, "God holds with the side that has the most bayonets."

114

Chapter 17   9 April 1940

If we seek merely ... peace, if we shrink from
the hard contests where men must win at the hazard
of their lives ... then bolder and stronger
people will pass us by and will win for themselves
the domination of the world.

Franklin Roosevelt

Nyrup looked at me from across the workbench. "You see, the Nazis let the Finns down too. No small country is sacred to those bastards."

I gave him a level, dirty look. "And your Soviets go them one better. Where are your Russians going to stand if Denmark is attacked?"

"Denmark will be all right."

Nyrup had sidestepped the question. He left, not wishing to pursue that line of conversation. What typical attitude, I thought bitterly while continuing my work. My application to the Finnish consulate had come to nought, for the war had ended before my departure. Furious about missing the opportunity to go to Finland, I had decided to apply for enlistment in the Danish army, although my apprenticeship was unfinished. I did not particularly agree with Montaigne's assessment of the intrinsic nobility of soldiering, but it seemed to me that Denmark might not stay neutral. Moreover, if my country became involved, lack of military training would likely doom me to passivity, and the rôle of onlooker was one I simply would not be able to endure.

One morning I had begged off from work, claiming to have to report for induction, and gone to *Tøjhuset*, a medieval building on the inner city canal adjoining the Christiansborg Castle that served as both induction center and military museum. Outside the entrance two large bronze cannon stood solemn guard. I read the inscription and saw they were 16th century navy guns, some of those that had made the Danish navy respected and feared on the northern

115

seas. Inside, the smell of ancient weaponry gave the visitor a feeling that the place was haunted by the spirits of long dead warriors. I filled out an application under the eye of an *Officiant,* the highest noncom rank, who watched me with something close to benevolence that there were still men willing to join without being drafted. Three weeks later, my application had been granted, and I was now under orders to report on 2 May at the barracks of the Jutland Dragoons, my great-grandfather's outfit. The dragoons were still mounted troops, albeit supplemented with some armored cars, a colorful military branch with glorious traditions.

It was almost quitting time, and I was cleaning up my workbench. Near the time clock a small cluster of dayshift arrivals had gathered, and I noticed an undercurrent of uneasiness emanating from the group, unusual at that time and place. I finished putting away my tools and went to stamp my time card. Two passing dayshift apprentices slowed momentarily,

"Niels, they say there are foreign soldiers in town."

"Have you seen them?"

"No, but they say there are some at Kgs. Nytorv."

I moved on, starting to hurry, skipped the washroom and got on my bike. I would be going across Kgs. Nytorv, so I should be able to see for myself. Traffic seemed normal, the day was cool and clear, a typical spring morning. I crossed Kgs. Nytorv, aiming for St. Kongensgade but traffic in that direction was being detoured to Bredgade by an armed soldier. His uniform was not the light grey homespun of Danish army issue but a darker, unfamiliar grey-green color. In Bredgade I passed the British Embassy. Outside the entrance stood another two grey-green soldiers. I slowed and rode by them looking as unconcerned as possible. They were about my age, nervously scanning the quiet street in both directions, and closeup I saw the German insignia on their helmets. Arriving home a few minutes later, I ran upstairs and joined my mother.

"They say the Germans are rolling into Jutland to protect Denmark from getting occupied by the British."

Her voice revealed more surprise than worry. By midmorning King Christian personally ordered the feeble Danish resistance to cease, implying that the country was under German occupation. On the radio, the King's voice sounded tired. No wonder. But what about Norway and Sweden? In all their thousand-year history no Scandinavian country had ever been under foreign domination, actually occupied by foreign troops. I thought of the Finns, how they had fought without a moment's hesitation. How different, the Danes. Accommodating, easygoing, soft.

I had to look again at the German soldiers and bicycled back downtown. Riding along, I kept scanning people's faces. My countrymen appeared to go about their business as usual. A bit concerned, worried perhaps, but obviously with no inclination to fight. Well, my countrymen be damned. I felt enraged, embarrassed, ashamed, but not really surprised.

116

Shifting my attention to the Germans, I scrutinized them in several slow passes on my bike. So this was what Hitler's troops looked like closeup: my own age, and clearly apprehensive about being on enemy, or at least foreign, territory. Silently, I measured myself against them and thought that I would be willing and able to take on any one of them. Or several, if necessary. Yes, it would surely have to be several. And I saw with complete certainty that I was going to fight, somewhere, somehow. There was hardly a decision process involved; it was simply so. One of the beauties of the intellect of youth is that decisions which later in life are pondered and soul-searched at length appear straight forward and simple. As if already accomplished fact, the thought consoled me.

The German attack came on a Tuesday. By nightfall on Wednesday it was possible to piece together what had taken place. In the early morning hours, the Germans had unleashed an armored thrust across the frontier to occupy Jutland. It met only feeble and scattered resistance from the Danish army which cost sixteen Danish lives. The flat, easily accessible land and a military establishment depleted during decades of disarmament made the German task an easy one. Yet more important, the Danes had absolutely no will to resist. They were the antithesis of the Finns, actually incapable of visualizing themselves fighting to kill. In consequence, the country lay supine before the Nazi onslaught.

On the same morning, a German freighter disguised as a coal transport had entered Copenhagen harbor and disgorged troops who quickly took the small military installations in the city. Against this sea-borne threat the Danish navy did no better than the army. It never fired a shot, glorious traditions notwithstanding. Also in the morning hours, Luftwaffe planes dropped leaflets exhorting the bemused Danes to cooperate, which they did with impassive inactivity.

The Danish press carried a German communiqué stating that the Wehrmacht had moved to protect Norway against a British invasion. The British radio reported fighting in Norway, where King Haakon and his family had fled Oslo and moved north with retreating Norwegian troops. I pondered the difference in behavior of the two kings. Norway's King Haakon was a brother to King Christian of Denmark. In the course of their long reigns the two monarchs' attitudes and dispositions evidently had come to mirror those of their subjects, Christian sharing his people's abhorrence of bloodshed to the point of becoming unable to contemplate resistance; Haakon striking the chord of stubborn intransigence characteristic of people in mountain regions.

The German purpose was not mysterious. Possession of Denmark and Norway gave command of the Skagerak, the waters connecting the North Sea with the Danish straits and the Baltic. It would also protect Germany's northern flank against attack.

During the following days as I rode my bike around Copenhagen and eyed the German troops and equipment, I was thoroughly purged of any sympathy with Hitler's aspirations. Whatever redeeming features the Nazi phenomenon south of the border had appeared to possess when observed from a distance, the close-up view suddenly presented a different and ugly aspect. Seeing foreign soldiers take charge in my country affected me deeply, as if touching some primeval, defensive instinct. Using force to solve international problems looks neither brilliant nor attractive if one is on the receiving end, but the experience helps a person gain perspective.

The German attack came on a Tuesday. The following Sunday I got up at three in the morning and bicycled to Elsinore, forty kilometers north of Copenhagen. The city is located at the narrowest stretch of the Sound, the strait between Denmark and Sweden, and is the site of Kronborg Castle, legendary setting of Shakespeare's Hamlet. It was built by Frederik II in 1574 to extract tolls from shipping passing into or out of the Baltic, and in centuries past the castle's nine-foot walls and 32-pounder guns easily commanded the strait and enforced the king's demands. Now a German sentinel stood on the ancient drawbridge, and modern German artillery pieces jutted from the picturesque stone embrasures, ready to control once more the Sound's traffic, and to repel if necessary any Swedish interference.

German soldiers were billeted everywhere in the city, as I found out when pedaling quietly through the empty streets to scout the situation in the very early morning hours. I stopped at a small hotel with an attached stable and a yard crammed full of horsedrawn artillery. There was no guard visible, and with nobody in sight I walked through the yard and made my way silently into the stable. A couple of dozen soldiers were snoring in the straw, their horses contentedly munching on good Danish fodder. Rifles and bayonets were hanging all around, and I was momentarily stunned at the vulnerability of this sleeping outfit. Realizing the impossibility of concealing a rifle on a bicycle, I finally grabbed two bayonets, hid them under my jacket and beat a quiet retreat. On the way back to Copenhagen, I threw them into a pond, feeling some slight satisfaction at having administered one tiny pinprick on the German war machine. Then I rode on slowly, with the cold air in my face, reviewing what I had learned and pondering the situation confronting me. It was quite beyond anything I had experienced or read about.

It seemed clear that by the nature of things, occupying troops were necessarily exposed and vulnerable when billeted in civilian homes, and for a short while that morning I had had opportunities to do damage, real damage, to the intruders – but how? Could I have killed some Germans? Perhaps, but I dismissed the possibility as too difficult to carry out silently and anyway something I had no stomach for. Not yet, anyway. Stealing weapons or equipment on a large scale? That seemed for other reasons even more difficult and impractical. A quantity of dynamite might have served both purposes, i.e. killing soldiers and destroying matériel, but I had never even seen dynamite, knew nothing about how to use it or where to obtain it. Then the thought suddenly struck me – fire! The stable had been loaded with inflammable material, straw, feed, ammunition, all enclosed within wooden stalls and beam ceilings. All I had needed was *one match* and the place could have become an inferno in seconds. The thought was both sobering and exciting as my bicycle glided silently through the crisp morning air.

* * *

Nowhere could the Danish soldier cope with the situation ... decisive leadership was missing ... the human material is good ...

General von Kaupish, Invasion Commander

As we correctly perceived at the time, the German action in one swift stroke gave Hitler's high command control of the Skagerak and protected the German northern flank against attack. Less well known was the importance of securing the sea lanes along the Norwegian coast. The lanes were vital for the transport of high-grade ore from northern Swedish mines.[19] Sweden was left alone. Its geographic location made it strategically of lesser importance; besides, it was already cooperating with Hitler's aims by supplying the ore to Germany's munitions factories and acceding to other German demands far beyond accepted norms for neutral status.[20] Little could be gained by occupying it.

The decision was made to strike against Denmark and Norway in April, code naming the operation *Weserübung*. Warnings from numerous sources, including highly placed German officers opposed to Hitler's plans, had alerted both Denmark and Norway to the imminence of attack, but both governments stubbornly refused to believe the danger. The invasion of Denmark was an unquestionable German success. Within hours after the King's order to surrender, German forces were in firm control everywhere.

In the simultaneous invasion of Norway, the Germans launched naval attacks on Narvik and Oslo and aerial drops of *Fallschirmjäger*, German paratroopers, at strategic points in southern Norway, but the Norwegians proved more obdurate than the Danes. In the initial attack the German battleship *Blücher* was sunk by coastal guns in the Oslo fjord, and the defenders' inaccessible, mountainous homeland lent itself ideally to holding tactics, so that the Germans needed two months to gain complete control. After staying with his soldiers to the bitter end, King Haakon escaped with his family to London and set up a government-in-exile.

Chapter 18   May 1940

Look with favor upon a bold beginning.

Virgil

The street was pitch black when I left home at nine. Immediately upon their arrival in April, the Germans had ordered a complete blackout of the country, and Copenhagen had overnight changed beyond recognition. When each spring day faded into evening, the city formerly referred to as "Paris of the North" now lay inert and invisible, as if stunned by events beyond comprehension. Newspapers gave helpful hints on how to live with the new requirements, how to make lightproof curtains, how much light a bicycle should show, how pedestrians could avoid accidents. Citizens took it all in stride, actually in good humor. Certainly no thought to obstructing German plans, I thought disgustedly. Not like Norway, where they were still fighting, according to British radio, or in France where Hitler had unleashed a mighty offensive. A relative had telephoned yesterday with an item of advice: when going out after dark, use sunglasses for the first few minutes, then your eyes adjust more rapidly to the dark. Thanks a lot.

On the positive side, darkness was just what I needed for my plans tonight. Feeling like a hunter looking for prey, I had spent a few weeks snooping around German motor parks, gun emplacements, offices, barracks and sundry other facilities in and around Copenhagen without finding any opportunity like the one I had missed in Elsinore. My draft notice had been cancelled, so there went my chance for some weapons training. The Danish army and navy had simply been discharged and sent home – and had obeyed without complaint! Adding in my view insult to injury, the government had urged the population to "quiet and restrained demeanor in the conditions now prevailing." Well, they could shove that piece of advice.

Tonight was the time to start in another track. Besides matches to set fires, I thought possession of a gun would be appropriate, just in case, and having noticed that officers and some noncoms carried pistols in leather holsters on their belts, I had chosen to begin my private fight against the Wehrmacht by supplying myself from this readily accessible armory. What better provenance?

I stopped in St. Kongensgade and parked my bicycle outside a small bar whose entrance had been supplemented with dark double curtain in deference to the blackout. I went through the improvised light trap, passing a German soldier going the opposite way, and squinted at the dimly lit room through a blue cloud of tobacco smoke. It was crowded with people, most of them soldiers and most of the rest, prostitutes, doing a brisk business. I smiled inwardly at the thought that the only Danes inflicting harm on the Wehrmacht were these ladies of the night, spreading venereal disease. Slowly, I made my way toward a coat tree carrying several uniform coats and belts, two of them with sidearms. Their owners at a nearby table had drained their glasses, apparently getting ready to leave. I pretended to be looking for someone, ignoring the waitresses. Nobody was paying attention to me. Good. At the table I was observing, a Feldwebel, the Wehrmacht's equivalent of a sergeant, got up and made his way to the coat-tree, took one of the two armed belts and strapped it on. He chatted for a moment with his drinking companions, then walked to the door with me trailing behind him. Outside, the man started walking toward the inner city. There was too much traffic to attempt anything here, so I unlocked my bike and followed him. Several blocks later he turned down a quiet street. This would have to be it. I rode past him, a couple of hundred feet into the darkness, parked the bike without locking it, and started walking back until my target came into sight at a distance of some thirty feet. My heart pumping an overload of adrenalin, I tried to walk with unconcern, just another pedestrian on some necessary errand in the dark. As we closed, I politely gave way on the sidewalk, veering toward the gutter on my right. The German was about to pass on my left, when my left fist shot forward with the power of a steam ram and into the man's solar plexus. The Feldwebel buckled in the middle with a hollow gasp, his head describing a downward arc, while my right fist traced a quarter circle, connecting with the man's jaw when it was passing midpoint on its way down. It was a roundhouse blow with all my weight behind it, striking less that a second after the first. The German slumped to the pavement with the muffled sound of a sack of potatoes toppling onto a concrete floor. I bent over the inert body to detach the belt with the pistol, fumbling because I had sprained my wrist in the encounter. I was breathing hard, but my mind was coolly evaluating performance and outcome. It was my first attack on another human being, and inexperience had made me use far more force than needed. My victim was out cold and I was wondering how much less force could have accomplished this satisfactory result, making a mental note that some experimentation would be in order. Fortunately, there were plenty of guinea pigs to experiment on. Finally, I had the belt unstrapped, but my right hand was shaking so that I couldn't get the holster off the belt. I stuffed the whole thing under my jacket, walked hurriedly to the bike and pedaled away. On one of the canal bridges I stopped and crossed the narrow sidewalk to the railing. Only a few dark figures were in sight as I slid the bundle out from under my jacket. Holding it on the outside of the railing, I unobtrusively got the gun holster free, dropping the belt into the water below while blessing the benevolent darkness.

Back in my room I examined my booty. It was a small .25-caliber pistol with only six cartridges in the clip and no spare. Not much to start a war with. Nevertheless, I enjoyed the feel of its cold, black steel when I drew it from the holster and was surprised at its weight. It was the first time I had held a real handgun. Denmark in the 1930s was probably the world's most peaceable society. A few shotguns were in the hands of duck hunters, but rifles were registered and owned only by a very few, members of clubs vying for precision target practice. Pistols simply did not exist in the hands of ordinary citizens. They can have only one purpose, to kill people, and were therefore considered something a citizen did not need.

* * *

The rejection of war that has developed in our population has made Denmark's situation one that renders impossible all thought of effective preparedness.

Thorvald Stauning, Danish Prime Minister

Immediately at the German occupation the Danish government avoided any appearance of approval of the *occupatio pacifica*, an internationally recognized concept without clear definition, and almost without precedent except for the German occupation of Luxembourg in World War One. It soon became obvious, however, that Germany's demands went beyond the military sphere and into those of politics, economy and ideology. In the Nazi view the occupation of Denmark was a natural link in the chain of events comprising the fates of Austria, Czechoslovakia and Poland. The Danish case in fact came close to that of Austria insofar as fighting had been all but avoided. The only lever now available to the Danish government was to refuse any and all further German demands. Weighing the foreseeable consequences of such refusal, the government looked at the conditions of citizens in other occupied countries and recoiled at the thought of causing anything similar to be imposed in Denmark.

This weighing of alternatives and the basis for decisions was not divulged to the citizens. Neither were the initial arguments between occupier and occupied which centered on three areas. First came the question whether workers and firms in Denmark should work for the Germans. There was little choice if the country wanted to receive coal and raw materials for its internal economy, and the Germans immediately demanded construction of airdromes for Luftwaffe use. Some large Danish engineering firms bowed to their government's pressure to oblige. Second came a demand to have Danish workers take contractual employment in Germany. This was also conceded. The third and very contentious point turned on maintaining law enforcement and jurisprudence. The Germans expected to take over in these areas as they had done in other occupied countries and pointed to the provisions of the Haag Convention. The Danes countered that their country was not at war with Germany and therefore the Convention did not apply. That argument held, and for the time being, Danish investigation and prosecution remained in Danish hands.

Chapter 19   October 1940

Mater artium necessitas.
[Necessity is the mother of invention.]

Anon.

Thank God it was fall, with long and dark nights. What I was up to definitely benefitted from the cover of darkness, and Scandinavian summers offered little of that; but summers are short and the fall season comes early. It was ten o'clock, and the street lay dark and quiet. The German staff car was parked at the curb in the middle of the block, its camouflage paint rendering it all but invisible until I was almost near enough to touch it. Leaning my bicycle against the wall of the apartment house, I walked around to the street side of the car and stood there for a moment, listening and looking in both directions for traffic of any kind. Last summer when Hitler had declared England beaten, Churchill had trumpeted an exhortation, "Set Europe ablaze!" to urge Europeans to resist the Germans by any and all means, including burning and other destruction of industrial resources supporting the German war machine. I liked that, the image itself and the defiance despite long odds. Tonight I intended to have my own small blaze, wishing Churchill could see my efforts. Then I lay down on the pavement and slid under the car.

Hitler's May offensive on the Western Front had scythed through the Allied lines and swept the British Expeditionary Force in a fighting retreat to the French Channel town of Dunkerque. A superhuman effort by the combined military services of Britain extricated the bulk of the troops, sans equipment. The French had surrendered after six weeks of fighting, giving the Third Reich the victory that had eluded the Kaiser's Germany in four years of bloody, all-out effort in World War One. Churchill's defiance had evidently triggered German preparations to invade England, for in the Wehrmacht's musical broadcasts eve-

124

The furrier shop in Griffenfeltsgade in Copenhagen, a useful contact point. At the entrance is Mr. Kaj Sander, Alfred's father, who owned the shop. Visible in the lower left of the display window is the white ermine collar that could be removed as warning in case of danger.

ry Sunday the song *Wir fahren gegen Engelland* had become the lead-off number, hinting at imminent invasion. Heavy aerial battles had raged throughout the summer in which both sides had claimed success. It had been possible to follow these developments through Danish press reports, heavily censored but augmented with radio news from Sweden and BBC in London. At the moment, Nazi intent was a matter for conjecture, but the heavy aerial bombardment of London, of late referred to as the Blitz, had not yet led to any invasion attempt.

At the end of August I had finished my four apprenticeship years and in the last month of the period had produced the mandatory journeyman test piece. The examination committee had decided on a drill bar. To produce this from raw bar stock entailed several machining operations as well as bench work, and the bar stock was first carefully marked with an identifying symbol, hammer-stamped into the raw material to ensure that another piece could not be substituted in case mistakes were made on the original. The first try was to be the only one, no second chance. I had passed the test, all was well, and I automatically became a member of the machinists' union, as B&W was a closed union shop. New journeymen were kept on the payroll for a month, then routinely laid off, but I had no difficulty in finding another job as a machinist. At that point in a young workingman's career, the new journeyman suddenly found himself making union wages, i.e. the same income as a family man of fifty but without any of

*Alfred Sander (1918-) who was instru-
mental in much underground resistance
work from 1940 until his escape to Sweden
in 1944. He is wearing the uniform of the
Danish Brigade that was formed and
equipped in Sweden.*

the many fixed obligations of the latter. For a while, the younger man's life typically resembled an economic bonanza, and the usual outcome was a short period of easy living, abruptly punctuated by marriage. That ending precluded further education and progress, and the labor pool was assured of another captive, lifelong member. A child of the middle class, I never for a moment thought of remaining in my blue-collar state longer than it took to save money for more education. After another month's work, I had enrolled full time at Copenhagen's Teknikum, a well-recognized engineering school that had granted me a partial scholarship.

The pursuit of education had not cooled my determination to pursue a private war against the Germans, and after the initial small step of acquiring a pistol, I had looked critically at my modest circle of acquaintances to try to assess who could be trusted as possible collaborators willing to attempt to injure the occupying power. Only two had come to my mind in Copenhagen. One was Erik Hansen, a military cadet in the army officers school. He was knowledgeable about weapons and other military items, and his mettle was such that he would be superlative under fire. The other was Alfred Sander, a furrier working in his father's shop in Blaagaardsgade, a street in the northern part of the city near the engineering school. I had known both of them in the conservative youth movement and knew that April 9th had caused both to experience instant catharses similar to my own in regard to Nazi ideas. The three of us had met in Erik's home and found ourselves in agreement, willing to inflict injury on the occupying troops but unable to propose effective ways and means. Together we visited some beer joints frequented by German soldiers and in one of

126

H. Erik Hansen (1917-   ) who worked with the author on numerous sabotage projects until his escape to Sweden in 1944. He went on to England and joined the British Special Forces.

them, Café Bernstorff, we acquired a second gun, this one a 9mm Lugar that another Feldwebel incautiously left on a coatrack behind his chair. However, when discussing how best to harm the Germans we still could not come up with anything very promising, and our work schedules were not compatible, so we had drifted apart for the time being. On my own I had been scouting the city to find a target to my liking and hoping for some inspiration on ways and means to hurt the Germans. Observing that their military vehicles not infrequently were parked here and there on public streets, the possibility of burning a car had struck me as attractive and probably easy, a satisfactory way of doing noticeable damage. After hours of searching through the city on bicycle, with matches and a thin screwdriver in my pocket and a plan of action in my head, I had found this Opel and immediately felt that opportunity was again smiling on me.

With my left hand I placed the sharp point of the screwdriver against the bottom of the fuel tank and struck the tool a silent blow with my right, piercing the tank just slightly and starting a drip-drip of gasoline onto the pavement. Sliding free of the car, I got up and checked again that the street was silent. Satisfied, I got the box of matches out, good *Tordenskjold* wood matches, struck one and threw it under the car where the gasoline drip had already made a small wet spot. The fuel caught with a bright yellow flame, larger than I had expected, and it momentarily illuminated the little street scene with me in the center. I grabbed my bike, jumped on and sped off. At the end of the street I stopped in the darkness and looked back. The fire had grown rapidly, and about one minute after I had struck the match, the gas tank exploded, illuminating the street and buildings on both sides. The street was still empty, and I started my bike leisurely, forcing myself not to hurry. This was my first planned and successful act of destroying German army matériel, and I relished it thoroughly. *Just wait, you*

127

goddamn Krauts. There are more matches where these came from. An hour later, I reviewed the result in the solitude of my bed. First and foremost, I was amazed how easy it had been. But I also realized how far out of step I was with the rest of the population in these private efforts to make war, and that meant I had to dodge not only the Germans but my civilian compatriots as well. Virtually none of my countrymen would look with favor on what I had done, including the police, but somehow it didn't bother me; it merely added to the element of excitement.

* * *

I have decided to prepare a landing operation
against England, and if necessary to carry it out ...

Adolf Hitler, Directive to the Luftwaffe

After the military success of operation *Weserübung*, Hitler had seized the initiative on the Western Front a month later. The swift rout of the British forces should in German eyes have made this adversary sue for peace, particularly when the French surrendered. The world at large agreed. How and why should Britain fight on, a doomed and futile struggle against hopeless odds? But Churchill rallied his countrymen by rejecting[21] any thought of surrender and instead inspired them to the struggle ahead with oratory that will live through the ages.

> We have differed and quarrelled in the past
>> but now one bond unites us all –
>>> to wage war until victory is won,
>>>> and never surrender ourselves to servitude and shame,
>>>>> whatever the cost and agony may be ...

> Let us therefore brace ourselves to our duties,
>> and so bear ourselves
>>> that if the British Empire and its Commonwealth
>>>> last for a thousand years,
> Men will still say:
>> "*This* was their finest hour."[22]

Frustrated in his expectations of a British surrender, Hitler decided to conquer and vanquish the stubborn foe by invading England. The high commands, both British and German, recognized that to succeed, the invaders must have control of the air above southern England before embarking, and in early July the contest began, later to be referred to by the Allies as the Battle of Britain. The contest reached a crescendo on 15 August, designated *Adlertag*, Eagle Day, by the Germans who attempted to destroy in one hammer blow the RAF fighters in the air. The attempt failed, and the imminent invasion threat faded.[23] Subsequent bombing of London, dubbed the Blitz, attempted to stampede the population to pressure the government to sue for peace. It also failed.

Chapter 20　　　　Christmas 1940

Friends share all things.

Pythagoras

Aage stood by the station building as the train pulled into the Ribe station, scanning the two small coaches filled with Christmas travelers. From the door of the second, I jumped to the platform, a haversack slung over my shoulder as total baggage. We shook hands with broad grins of pleasure and quickly detached ourselves from the crowd as we started walking down the snow-covered station road in the fading twilight.

"What Krauts are there in town?" We knew each other too well to indulge in small talk, and my question went straight to the subject that interested us both.

"Some are stationed at Missionshotellet which has been requisitioned; they seem to be infantry without much equipment. And there are some at Hotel Riberhus, again just more foot soldiers."

"Has anybody bothered them?"

"What do you mean?"

"I mean, has there been any demonstrable unfriendliness, anybody slashing their tires, or pissing in their food supplies?"

"Hell no. You know Ribe is a friendly town. Mrs. Falby, your grandparents' landlady, even invited two of them into her kitchen for coffee the other day when they made a huge purchase in her husband's grocery store."

"Paid for with our own money, of course, stolen from the National Bank in Copenhagen."

"No doubt, but what can we do?"

I had expected the question but hesitated, as we walked along silently in the snow. Then I replied, choosing my words carefully and speaking to myself as much as to my old friend, as I tried to articulate my thinking.

"As I see it, Denmark took a pitiful position when we knuckled under on the

Aage Kjellerup (1919-1994), the author's boyhood friend who started sabotage in Ribe and helped establish the Ribe group. He escaped to Sweden in 1944.

9th of April. Some of the other countries have been intimidated by the Germans too, but the Danes are at the bottom. And that goes for you and me whether we like it or not. Now, we can sit and wait for the English and French to get us out of this pickle, but we ought to do something about it ourselves as well. Look how the Norwegians did what they could. It wasn't enough to keep the Krauts out, but at least they did the best under the circumstances. Every German they killed was a small step toward beating Hitler."

"Are you saying we should try to kill some Germans?"

Again, we walked a piece before I could frame my answer.

"No. I think our careers would be too short if we tried, but we can get away with something else that will hurt them a little. I know."

Aage looked at me sideways. "How do you know?"

"Because I have been doing it. And it's not difficult."

Aage pursed his lips and let out a low whistle. "Tell me about it."

We had talked until late in the night, debating the merits and possibilities of doing harm of some kind to the German occupying forces, and we had concluded that destroying matériel was the best option. Our talk had touched on domestic politics, a topic that had interested us keenly as teenagers and KU members. The social democratic youth organization had then accused KU – not entirely unjustly – of sympathizing with the Nazis, but of late social democrats and conservatives had gotten together to "affirm their national loyalty," something we both thought should be demonstrated in more tangible ways. Our talk also turned on our mutual and urgent interest in world events which before had seemed distant, almost theoretical or academic, certainly not affecting us directly. The events of the past year had changed our attitudes in that respect by making us feel like participants, no longer just spectators, while at the same

131

time we both were unable to interpret what was happening in Europe, or to guess how it might affect our own country and ourselves.

I had related to Aage a story that had been much on my mind since I first heard it. A Copenhagen friend of mine, Oscar Førsting, had returned from a brief stint working in a factory in Hamburg, where one of his workmates had told him that his brother had been killed under the government's euthanasia program. Oscar's workmate broke down and spilled the story one evening after a few beers. His brother who had lost both legs in World War One had been unable to work and was therefore classified as a drag on the current war effort.

Aage's first reaction mirrored mine.

"There must be more to the story than that. Surely, they don't kill their own people just because they can't work!"

"That's what I thought, but I'm no longer so sure. The Germans are not like us, and the Nazis are ruthless."

Aage thought for a while, then returned to the here and now.

"I think your idea of doing what we can is good. Let's take a walk and look at the garages by Missionshotellet."

It was late in the night when we walked through the sleeping town, looking under a starry sky for targets of opportunity on which to test ourselves and vent our frustration. We both felt sure of being out of step with the bulk of our countrymen, perhaps almost all of them, but Aage had on this point been as unconcerned as I.

I had shown Aage the .25-caliber pistol, brought from Copenhagen, and had demonstrated its mechanical features with which I had familiarized myself. Holding it gave somehow substance, confirmation, to our plans and intents. This was a conquered weapon. It was designed for killing. It had been meant for killing Danes, if necessary, last April.

Now it was ours.

Aage had placed himself at the corner of the garage building, close to the fence separating the hotel garden from the street. He was clutching the pistol, safety off, to guard against the unforeseen. A snowberry bush leaning over the fence covered him from a soldier standing guard at the main hotel entrance forty yards away, but the midnight darkness was in any event too deep to discern anyone at a distance of more than a few feet. The garage building was a small brick structure holding four stalls facing the street, each closed with two hinged doors secured with a padlock. We had selected it as an easy target, hoping it would house some Wehrmacht vehicles.

At the number two garage I inserted a heavy screwdriver through the padlock and twisted, slowly. When the lock broke with a low click, I tucked the screwdriver in my belt and opened one door enough to slip through. Inside, I struck a match and the momentary glow revealed a BMW motorcycle with a sidecar. Against the far wall stood two bicycles with the oversize tires used by the Wehrmacht, and a 20-liter fuel can. I walked quickly toward the back as the match flickered out. In pitch darkness I proceeded, three more steps, my hands outstretched in instinctive prevention from running into something. I fumbled, found the fuel can and lifted it. It was light, empty. Putting it down quietly, I struck another match, looked around once more and walked back to the BMW. The match went out, but in the darkness I ran my hands over the motorcycle, here was the seat, here the tank. Under the tank I felt the fuel line; I drew the screwdriver from my belt and inserted it between the line and the tank. Striking one more match, I checked its position and leverage, blew out the match and slowly bore down on the screwdriver. The smell and feel of gasoline announced that a leak had been opened, and I stopped. A small trickle was best. Then I walked to the door in the dark, no more lighting matches. The outside darkness felt less intense, and the frosty air smelled good. I walked the few steps to Aage's position at the snowberry bush.

"All quiet?"

"Yes. What did you find?"

"A motorcycle. The fuel is dribbling out and ready to light, but you'd better do it, for my hands are soaked with gasoline. Here are the matches. We'll switch positions, and when it's lit, we run that way."

Aage handed me the gun, took the matchbox, walked to the garage door and opened it slightly.

"Phew, this is going to explode when I light it. Be ready to run."

He opened the door half way and stepped aside from the opening. Then he took two of the wooden matches, struck them on the side of the box and in a continuous motion let them fly into the door opening. The fuel lit with a soft WHOOSH and momentarily illuminated a slice of snow-covered street. Then he pulled the door almost shut, and the two of us sprinted down the dark and silent street, our footsteps making no sound in the snow. After fifty yards we turned into a side street and started walking normally.

* * *

The strong men, the masters, regain the pure conscience of a beast of prey; monsters filled with joy, they can return from a fearful succession of murder, arson, rape and torture with ... contentment in their souls ...

Nietzsche

The heart rending experience of Oscar Førsting's co-worker in Hamburg was our first direct indication of the German euthanasia[24] program, the extent of which came to light only after the war. The program of purifying the national body, started soon after the Nazi takeover with procedures of compulsory sterilization of undesirable individuals, had been expanded at the outbreak of hostilities. Euphemistically referred to as euthanasia, the program established a bureaucracy to select for killing and disposal certain categories of people with whom the new German superstate did not wish to be encumbered. With the assistance of the medical profession, the SS collected thousands of citizens from hospitals and other institutions, taking them to killing centers to be murdered and cremated. Routinely marked for murder were the physically or mentally handicapped, incurably ill, old and failing, babies born with serious defects, even World War One invalids. The program experimented with various methods of killing, from injections to starvation, and German efficiency quickly developed a corps of experts in all phases of bureaucratically organized mass murder.

On 10 January 1941, Goebbels noted in his diary that 80,000 of his countrymen had been eliminated so far, and that 60,000 more would have to go. By 1941 the New Order, as the Nazis liked to call it, was ready to spread its blessings beyond the Reich itself; a corps of experts in mass murder could look with confidence to solid employment into an indefinite future.[25]

Chapter 21   June 1941

*No occupation is as enjoyable as soldiering – an
occupation both noble in its practice ... and
noble in its purpose.*

Montaigne

At six o'clock the sergeant's voice rang through the hall of sleeping recruits:
"Up! Up! Get out of your fuck bags. Muster in twenty minutes." To the familiar
cry he then added a short comment. "Hitler attacked Russia this morning." I
was instantly awake, rolled out of bed and within sixty seconds was shaving at
the cold water tap in the yard.

This was not a real army barracks, merely a pavilion-restaurant in a beech forest
on the outskirts of Odense, Hans Christian Andersen's birthplace. After my
draft notice to the dragoons had been cancelled last year and all Danish military personnel discharged and sent home, things had gone so smoothly from
the German point of view that Hitler decided to use Denmark as an example of
occupied territory under magnanimous German rule. The Danes were therefore allowed to reestablish a small military force; I had immediately reapplied
and was again accepted. Since Aage's and my Christmas venture in the hotel
garages, there had been little time for sabotage. Aage was busy establishing himself in a new job, and I was immersed in engineering studies. My only subversive
endeavors came late in the winter when I had run into Svenn Seehusen, a
friend from our membership in the KU as teenagers. Together we had tried
with some success to activate a few old acquaintances from that period and start
them on a path toward effective resistance. An energetic and able individual,
Svenn was a natural organizer as well as suitably discreet about his activities.
   When the draft notice arrived in response to my application, it had ordered
me to report to a bicycle battalion in Odense in May. Actually, the outfit was not

The Danish Army's 5th Battalion, 2nd Company's 1st Platoon, May 1941. The author is fifth from left, second row.

a full battalion, just one company of 94 men, bicycle-equipped infantry. At first I had been disappointed. In a motorized society, soldiers on bicycles sound like a joke, but I had discovered that in several other countries the military kept bicycle units to fulfill certain rôles better than motorized troops. In Denmark where any location was reachable via small, hard-surface roads, the bicycle effectively conferred on the infantry soldier both speed of movement and ample load-carrying capacity. From our billets in the forest pavillon the two-wheeled columns could reach any point on Funen within a couple of hours.

The island of Funen presented a landscape of low, rolling hills dotted with tiny, prosperous farms. The local people spoke a melodic dialect that sounded enchanting on the lips of a young girl but invariably made people from elsewhere in the country laugh when coming from a grown man. Around the island, small exquisite castles lay tucked away, and the coastal fishing towns abounded with mementos from the sailing-ship era, when Danish full-riggers plied the seven seas. I mentally rejected Montaigne's uncritical view of soldiering, but in this setting basic training was enjoyable despite – or was it because of? – its built-in rigors. The training was thorough and comprised several different weapons, the main one being the infantry rifle, model 1889, which had served the army for fifty years. It was somewhat heavy, with manually operated bolt-action, but essentially a reliable firearm. Even the main German service rifle, *Karabiner 98k*, developed from the classic Mauser, was not significantly superior to the 1889er, though somewhat lighter. The battalion could deliver heavier fire power with the *rekylgevær*, light automatic rifles, and with heavier machine guns mounted on tripods. Both rifles and automatic weapons used 8mm ammunition which the Germans monitored carefully and doled out in small amounts from Danish army stocks. The ammunition was of American origin, received a quarter-century earlier in partial payment for Denmark's colonies in the West Indies, which the U.S. had purchased to enhance its security in World War One. The ammunition contained a lot of duds, and I wondered vaguely whether this was typical of American war matériel.

The sergeant's gratuitous report of the early morning radio broadcast was not expanded with further information, and after muster the company started for the firing ranges according to the weekly schedule. The ranges were located outside Odense in beautiful countryside sloping toward the fjord, where stray bullets would have minimal chance of doing harm. The lieutenant in charge dispatched the target teams to man the dugouts, and soon I was applying all my concentration to mastering the effective use of the automatic rifle. In previous weeks we had practiced at two hundred and four hundred meter distances in which the gun's weight was supported on two small legs attached to the barrel. Today's exercise turned on close combat in which the rifle was held hip-high by the shooter. The lieutenant pointed out how the muzzle tended to rise when the shooter let go a burst, and the recruits preceding me experienced the difficulty in varying degrees, while I tried hurriedly to devise the best way to counteract the problem. Obviously, the upward force of the left hand supporting the barrel should be reversed to a downward push while firing ... I tried to estimate the factors affecting the trajectories. Finally, it was my turn. I planted my feet well apart and clamped the weapon in a iron grip.

"All right, shoot when ready." I heard the lieutenant's voice in the background and ripped off a burst at the target twenty meters away.

"Stand down. Safety on." The lieutenant sounded bored.

The target team called out: "Number 412,[26] six shots, six hits."

A wave of excitement surged through me, though I carefully maintained an air of calm. This was what I had wanted to learn! Then I thought of the gigantic battle that must be taking place at this very moment, with Hitler's armor surging toward Moscow on the same roads Napoleon's grenadiers had followed one hundred and thirty years earlier. What were Soviet soldiers like? How would they do against Nazi troops, drilled with relentless Prussian precision and believing themselves to be a Master Race?

* * *

Poor as are the Russian peasants, workmen and soldiers,
he (Hitler) must steal from their daily bread; he must
devour their harvests; he must rob them of the oil which
drives their ploughs; and thus produce a famine without
example in human history ... It follows, therefore,
that we shall give whatever help we can to Russia and
the Russian people.

Winston Churchill

While German arms appeared successful wherever used, we took heart from the fact that Italian military operations were much less so. Mussolini's forces had been rebuffed on the Alpine front and in Greece. In North Africa, the Italians met with disastrous defeat at the hands of the British whom they vastly outnumbered, and in Ethiopia a British offensive enabled Emperor Haile Selassie to return to the throne he had lost in 1935.

The German high command had watched with dismay and contempt as their Italian allies had been repulsed from Greece and vanquished in North Africa. To save the Axis further embarrassment, Hitler dispatched in February two German divisions to Libya under the command of a hitherto unknown general by the name of Erwin Rommel. A month later the Führer implemented a planned attack on Greece, and in April his troops ran up the Swastika flag over the Acropolis. This enabled the Germans to complete preparations for *Barbarossa*, the attack on Russia, in June. Across a front stretching fifteen hundred miles from the Arctic Sea to the Black Sea, three German army groups smashed into the unsuspecting Soviets.[27] Hitler's plans for Russia amounted to annihilation through planned terror and starvation surpassing anything the Nazis had yet perpetrated. In his instructions to the service chiefs he emphasized this intent:

> This struggle ... will have to be conducted with
> unprecedented, unmerciful and unrelenting harshness ....
> German soldiers guilty of breaking international law ...
> will be excused.[28]

◀ *As was the case in Poland, Denmark in 1940 still retained mounted troops, the Jutland Dragoons, although a few of the cavalry horses had been replaced by light armored vehicles. These were not deployed for serious defense when the German attack came.*

Chapter 22   December 1941

Rejoice, Oh young man, in thy youth.

Ecclesiastes

When we emerged from the building, the cold struck my face with numbing force, making it momentarily difficult to breathe and stifling all conversation. In the voiceless rush of bodies toward the parade ground, sound was limited to the creaking of leather boots on snow, a curiously musical note, but the cadets were too preoccupied to pay attention. The ranks formed into straight lines, fingers on the rifle stocks avoiding the barrel where a trace of moisture in seconds could weld the three-fingered mitt onto the steel with an icy grip. The ranks were in position and came to attention in less than sixty seconds. Not bad. I almost chuckled when thinking what great stimulant to performance the cold had become. The platoon leaders could already be heard calling out the numbers. Another two minutes, and we were marching toward the training ground south of the barracks.

The Danish army's school for basic officer training, the *Kornetskole*, had in prior years had its home in the castle of Kronborg in Elsinore, where generations of tradition and centuries of history had combined to furnish an inspiring setting for shaping the young candidates. After the Germans took over the castle, the school had found a temporary substitute home in the barracks of the Royal Hussars just outside the city of Næstved in southern Zealand. In September we eight candidates from Odense had arrived by train in Næstved, walked the two miles to the barracks and reported for duty. Having been used to the improvised arrangement in the forest pavillon, we were suitably impressed by entering for the first time a real *kaserne*. Its two-story red brick buildings enclosed a spacious courtyard and were surrounded by exercise fields. The floors were of tiled concrete, and cadets slept ten to a room, each man assigned an individual steel bed. The buildings further accommodated shower rooms, a large

Kornetskolen, the Danish Army's school for warrant officers, endured briefly during the early years of the German occupation. Training was rigorous but suited more to World War One than World War Two reality. Here the trainees are digging trenches.

mess hall, infirmary and depots, altogether a vast improvement over the primitive quarters from which we came and enough to make us new arrivals feel that we had risen high above our previous status in the military world. In basic training in Odense I had applied myself to the utmost on target practice and succeeded at the end of the period in becoming regimental marksman with the automatic rifle. The marksmen, one in each weapons class, had been rewarded with prizes: a bronze ashtray which in my case held in its center a small sculpture of a young girl declining decorously in a mound of fruit. We also received for the left uniform sleeve a silver medal showing two crossed guns. As holders of this prized and envied decoration, we quickly acquired the reflex of casually posing with the left side toward people, so that they might enjoy the sight. For good measure we had also spent five kroner each to have the crossed gun symbol tattooed on the left forearm, forever to remind the world not to trifle with us. After six months a few of the recruits were allowed to apply for training toward officer's rank. I had jumped at the opportunity and considered myself very lucky, when I became one of those chosen.

In our new surroundings the class of '42 comprised some eighty men, and we were put through a training schedule that made time in Odense look like rest and recreation. The weather gods took fiendish pleasure in visiting extra severity on our ordeal, for the 1941-42 winter was unseasonably hard. The typical Danish winter season is dominated by rain and fog, and entire winters may go by without any snow at all, but this one was different. By Christmas the Belt Seas froze, parts of the Kattegat froze, and the Sound froze from coast to coast, so that a person with daring and some stamina could walk across the ice to Sweden. Our uniforms were frequently wet in the morning after their owners' exertions the previous night to wash away mud and restore a spit-and-polish appearance, and when we stood on the parade ground, the heavy, wet homespun cloth would freeze and actually crackle when we began to move. At the onset of the cold, the army instructors first considered it a stroke of luck to have the weather help in the process of toughening the cadets. But when the temperature dropped to twenty below zero Celsius, the rising numbers of severe frostbites became a nuisance. Exposed body parts such as ears will freeze quite rapidly, often without their owners being aware of any problem. In unlucky circumstances, an ear can break off, but if the calamity is discovered in time, circulation can be restored, somewhat painfully, by rubbing the frozen part vigorously with snow. After being thus thawed, the ear swells up overnight because the thawed tissue fills with lymph, so that for a day or two a man looks as if he has been endowed with a couple of water-logged apricots, and when he shakes his head the neighborhood is showered with effluent. I was lucky in avoiding serious frostbites. Only once did my left ear freeze along the edge before being treated to a snow rub.

To our unspoken relief, the training officer relented after a week of the deep-freeze with no end in sight, and all cadets were issued knitted tubular mufflers to wear around neck and wrists to stave off the worst intrusions of icy air. The

142

pitiless cold reigned even in our sleeping quarters and taught us to make our beds in a manner that gave a standard appearance of sheets and blankets but actually produced an arrangement in which blankets rather than sheets were next to the skin, for clammy bed sheets become quite unfriendly when the temperature really drops. Once a week we had showers, but the barracks' coal allowance did not suffice for water heating, so the showers were cold, and the water tended to freeze as it hit the stone floor in the shower room.

There was one heated common room in which it was possible to enjoy a half hour of evening conviviality around an ancient piano after cleaning and oiling weapons and polishing boots, belts and uniforms. Working hard, a cadet could finish these chores with almost an hour left before bed check. After a long day of sustained hardship, the recuperation wrought in the common room made everyone look forward to these precious minutes like a parched desert traveler sighting the next oasis. I used the time to write letters home and to try to divine from the tightly censored news what actually might be the state of the war.

Four of us had started a Sunday afternoon routine of walking the two miles to Næstved, a quiet provincial town. The precise destination of our foursome was a *konditori*, a cake baker, on the main street, where we would order coffee and help ourselves to the fine pastries on display. As we all did so simultaneously and consumed each pastry in one or two bites while inundating the waitress with charm and attention, we succeeded in preventing her from counting the delicacies consumed. After coffee we would pool our meager funds and make a show of elaborate counting. "How many did you have?" "Oh, I guess two ... no, maybe three!" The total always ended at about twelve pastries for which we counted out the required cash, leaving the depleted store and the befuddled but happily giggling girl with a flourish of courteous military salutes.

Three afternoons a week were reserved for classroom instruction, periods when we were permitted actually to *sit* like human beings and which we gratefully used to rest and nurse our constantly overstressed bodies. The instructor in combat tactics was a captain by the name of Olsen. He was held in great esteem, partly for his volatile temperament which had earned him the nickname Powder-Ole, partly because he on the infamous 9th of April when the Germans invaded had knocked out a German armored car, and had according to local legend done so in a manner we thought shiningly exemplary. Stationed near the frontier, he had positioned his four-man team with its 37mm cannon at a curve on the main road, and when the German column approached, he walked calmly to the middle of the pavement and held up his hand. Miraculously, the lead car stopped, its German commander no doubt confused by this unorthodox procedure. Powder-Ole turned to his men and barked out the order as if on a training ground: "Straight ahead enemy armored car. Fifty yards. Single shot. Fire!" The little cannon gave forth with a CRRUMP!! that knocked out the lead car, delaying the invaders for a few moments. Powder-Ole managed to survive the incident.

We had found out that his birthday fell on a day of classroom instruction, and we also knew that his favorite song was *Vift Stolt paa Kodans Bølge*. The routine called for standing at attention at his arrival from the corridor until he had walked to the blackboard and given the order to sit down. On the crucial day, however, the "sit down" order instead triggered the song. As twenty-five young voices bellowed out the hallowed lines, Powder-Ole stood at stiff attention with the class until at the end all sat down. Seemingly unruffled, he blew his nose and began his lecture without comment. But twenty-five pair of keen eyes registered that he also managed in the process to wipe a tear off his cheek.

The unavoidable jog at the end of the field training was almost over. Running was not my strong suit, and in the cold I hated it even more than usual. Sweat was streaming down my face while subzero air pumped in and out made my air passages hurt like hell. Rapid breathing also froze the hair in one's nostrils and at times caused bleeding when blowing one's nose. The group had started in tight formation a mile from the barracks but was now strung out, the good runners entering the parade ground, the stragglers several hundred feet behind smarting under the sergeant's scathing commentary. I was about half way down the line and did not seriously attempt any final sprint. I cursed my own foolishness in having volunteered for the automatic rifle when assignments were made. It now gave me a hopeless handicap. Besides, at the *Kornetskole* we had been introduced to the Soumi machine pistol, a weapon I liked even better and was making strides to master. The last stragglers fell into line and the class was dismissed. A few minutes later I sat in the polish room among a dozen other steaming bodies going through the cleaning process: first weapons, then boots, then clothes, then oneself.

"Hey, listen up!" Cadet Elo of the Royal Guard stood in the doorway holding a newspaper. "The Japanese have bombed an American base in Hawaii." The work continued in silence, nobody very interested. Hawaii was somewhere in the Pacific, half a world away, probably too remote to influence the events in Denmark.

Two days later the news came that Hitler had declared war on the United States. Again we could muster but meager interest, and there was practically no discussion of this event, although I recollected that America's late entry in World War One had been pivotal. Surely, adding America to Hitler's growing list of enemies must be significant. However, I had noticed that besides being deprived of reliable news, we in military service were all affected by a tendency toward lessened interest in the world at large, abandoning the broader view in favor of concentrating on the narrower tasks of here and now. Being in the lower ranks under military orders and discipline also appeared to affect the individual by mollifying initiative and judgment in deference to simple obedience and preoccupation with the present.

At the same time, there was little to cheer about in the war news. Over the summer and fall the Germans had gone from victory to victory in Russia and now stood at the gates of Moscow. There seemed to be no stemming the Nazi tide in that theater. In North Africa the situation seemed slightly better. The British had driven Rommel back to Cyrenaica, but Goebbels' press was crowing about victories in the Mediterranean.

* * *

These are not dark days: these are great days – the greatest days our country has ever lived ...

Winston Churchill

Initial German battle victories in Russia led Hitler to proclaim in October that "... the enemy in the East has been struck down and shall never rise again."[29] In fact, a German reconnaissance battalion had in early December pushed into Nimkhi, a suburb to Moscow, and had glimpsed the spires on the Kremlin, but that was their closest approach to the heart of Russia. As the Panzers drew near the Russian capital, the low, menacing silhouette of a formidable new opponent appeared in their gunsights, the Soviet T-34 tank. Designed with wider treads to suit Russian fighting condition, it was the only weapon in the allied armory that bested the best from Krupp's *Waffenschmiede.* On the sixth, the day before Pearl Harbor, Stalin ordered General Zhukov into a wrathful counterattack before Moscow that within hours had the invaders reeling. But the world at large,[30] particularly the occupied countries, received a skewed impression of these events, because Goebbels' newspapers and radio related only victories. On 7 December the Japanese catapulted the United States into the war by a surprise attack on Pearl Harbor, home base of the U.S. Pacific Fleet.[31] Hitler immediately ordered his navy to an all-out attack on American ships and in an address to the Reichstag declared that the Third Reich considered itself at war with America.

The date of the Pearl Harbor attack earned its own infamy in Europe as the Führer issued his *Nacht und Nebel Erlass,* the Night and Fog Decree. Its purpose was to winnow out people endangering German security and to do so with "effective intimidation" making the victims disappear without a trace, to inflict maximum anguish on their families and instill fear in the public.

Chapter 23 May 1942

Fire is the best of servants;
but what a master!

Thomas Carlyle

I had scouted the railroad yard with great care. At the east end of the switching area loomed the storage shed, a huge structure some six meters high and more than fifty meters long. A German military contingent was stationed in Næstved with the assignment of procuring fodder for the horsedrawn artillery the Germans still used, particularly on the Eastern Front. As collection point they used the shed, open on one side, that had been erected along the railroad tracks in the freight yard. Over the winter, the shelter had been filled and emptied several times, and at the moment it stood crammed full of miscellaneous fodder, mainly hay and potatoes, ready for transport south. I could visualize how welcome good Danish produce must be at its faraway destination. Well, this was one shipment that would be cooked before departure. A lone sentinel was guarding the place, and he was not due to be relieved for more than an hour. He walked his beat with mechanical precision, rifle slung over the shoulder, fifty steps toward the station building, fifty back to the corner of the shed.

It was almost dark, and the spring air carried a fragrance of moist soil and sprouting plants. In early May, two weeks ago, the snow had reluctantly released the land from its frozen bondage. This morning I had observed from the barrack's second floor windows how the dark fields were becoming faintly green as the soil – tilled for more than four thousand years – began to yield yet another crop. In June the school would similarly bring forth yet another graduating group of clear-eyed, eager Kornetter, budding officers ready to apply skills and energies in serving King and Country. Looming high in our priorities was the question of private uniforms. We were each entitled to one army-issue uniform of coarse khaki homespun cloth, fine for field use and daily work, but every cadet's heart was set on a tailored uniform of British woolen cloth which had to be privately purchased. Those who like me had saved up money had long since made a beeline for a certain old specialty shop in Copenhagen that still had a small stock of prewar imported cloth. My measurements had already been duly taken on a weekend furlough a month ago, and I had gone on to a bootmaker who after more measuring was now working on the brown leather riding boots that were needed to complete the outfit. The Army manual prescribed a jacket with high collar that precluded a tie, and jodhpur trousers tightly fitted from the knee down, the style used in most European armies. The epaulettes would carry a small three-pointed star that after six months would automatically become the five-pointed star of a second lieutenant. The cap would bear the coveted gold button with the kingdom's ancient coat of arms: three springing lions in blue enamel surrounded by nine red hearts. Fine prospects, I thought. Now, if the Germans would only let the present situation last until after graduation, leaving the Danish military to its own devices.

It was dark enough. Silently, I vaulted the low fence to the yard area and walked quietly toward the end of the shed farthest from the station building and the sentinel. At the corner of the shed's open side I halted and waited in the shadow. The guard, barely perceptible in the darkness, was facing in my direction while walking toward the shed's far end. Upon reaching it, he turned and began his walk toward the station building with his back toward the shed and me, unaware that a silent observer was standing in the shadows. The moment he turned, I stepped quickly into the shed, struck a match behind a hay bale and touched it to the bale without looking at the flame so as not to impair my night vision. Then I exited around the corner of the structure, putting the shed between me and the guard, and ran up an embankment separating the yard from a street without lights, continued running quietly in the darkness for about two hundred yards, then slowed to a natural walk and looked back. Less than two minutes had passed, but just then the fire burned through the tarpapered roof and the shed erupted like a volcano, illuminating the yard with an eerie, reddish glow that showed the guard running frantically toward the station building.

Twenty minutes later I saluted the cadet guard at the barracks gate, well before curfew time. The guard, Cadet Hansen of the field artillery, returned my salute. Without altering his rigid stance, and moving only his lips, he whispered "What's that glow on the sky near the railroad station?"

I turned my head and glanced in the indicated direction. "Hadn't noticed it. Must be some house on fire. Good night."

* * *

147

*Whenever you come across anything that may
be needed by the German people, you must be
after it like a bloodhound. It must be taken
out ... and brought to Germany.*

Hermann Göring, instructing subordinates

By February 1942 the Russian winter offensives were exhausted after bleeding more than a million casualties from the German ranks. Hitler's response to the Wehrmacht's flagging capability became a standing order: "No retreat. No Surrender."[32] He also convened the Reichstag to pass a law that gave him total, unrestrained life-and-death power over every German citizen, and by extension every human being in the immense area now under German control. An order by the Führer effectively was law as it was spoken. No man, king or kaiser or president, at any time in history, or even in tribal days, had been in a comparable position of power.

Hitler had explicitly ordered the Wehrmacht to act with merciless brutality, and German army commanders responded by placing masses of prisoners in "cages," which might be barbed wire enclosures or simply a field in which stakes marked the limits beyond which the POWs were not allowed to go, on pain of being shot without warning. My interrogation of German POWs after cessation of hostilities provided numerous details of this procedure. Hundreds of such cages held huge numbers of prisoners but existed only briefly, as the prisoners soon died of starvation and exposure, having been deprived of their fur caps and sheepskin coats. Frequently, epidemics ran riot through the cages. Then, flame-throwers were used to burn both the living and the dead. Hitler's insensitivity to torments inflicted on others was absolute,[33] and his attitude was adopted by his underlings.

The civilian population in German-occupied territory suffered comparably. In obedience to the Führer's wishes Himmler sent *Einsatzgruppen*, Extermination Squads, to follow closely on the Wehrmacht troops to round up Jews and "Jewish-looking" individuals and kill them summarily, by whatever means: shooting, hanging, burning. The *Einsatzgruppen* set to their task with a vengeance, but the numbers involved soon necessitated killing procedures on an industrial scale and in Germany obliging chemists and engineers set about devising methods and facilities scaled to satisfy Nazi ambitions.

Complementing the Aryan "cleansing" of the occupied lands, a thousand streams of loot were flowing back to the Nazi home lair. The fodder my fire consumed in Vordingborg would have been one tiny trickle out of many thousands. Together with foodstuffs went raw materials, industrial goods and components, military equipment, machinery, gold, art treasures ... It was a long list. Along with inanimate products came endless trainloads of human beings, randomly rounded up on streets in faraway cities to be crammed into cattle cars and transported, often for many days, without food or water and in freezing cold. The wretched survivors of the ordeal were herded into German factories and mines as slave labor.

Chapter 24   July 1942

Who waits until circumstances completely favor his
undertaking will never accomplish anything.

Martin Luther

The three small coaches and a baggage car rattled south toward Ribe, now only seven kilometers distant, pulled by an ancient little steam locomotive that spewed a large cloud of steam and coal dust when called upon to start the train moving from a dead stop. Nothing at all had changed. We were stopping at each of the tiny stations I knew so well, and in the silence when motion ceased, the conductor's voice was clearly audible as he walked along the train on the gravel platform and called out the station names I had memorized as a boy when coming this way full of happy expectations to vacation with my grandparents. My fellow passengers, a few farmers and other local people, eyed me with undisguised curiosity, for one did not see Danish army uniforms in these parts nowadays, but they asked no questions. The beautiful summer's day was fading into evening by the time the train wheezed to a stop in Gredstedbro, and when we rumbled across the bridge spanning the Kongeaa, I absentmindedly noted that the farmers had the haying well underway, so that fishing would have been possible. But my purpose was different this time.

The tasks that had been awaiting assignment to the class of '42 had been far from commensurate with the graduates' ambitions, although we had dutifully set about carrying out orders. Together with another Kornet by the name of Willumsen, I had been posted to a regimental headquarters located, without any regiment, in the small town of Vordingborg in the southern part of Zealand. In contrast to Ribe where I was now heading, no Germans were stationed in Vordingborg, and the two of us were spending a lazy summer exercising a few cavalry horses and performing some inconsequential chores at the headquar-

150

The author practicing for the Danish army officers' field sport competition, 1942. The Danish 9mm service pistol had the magazine forward of the grip, giving balance problems. The model was inferior to the German P-38 and Lugar models.

ters office. Villumsen was aiming for a military career and had graduated at the very top of our class, while I had come out a more modest number nine out of seventy-six. Prior to the commencement ceremony it had somehow become known that Villumsen had received piano training as a boy, a circumstance that caused his superiors curtly to order him to play "something" at our graduation party. He had chosen Franz Liszt's Rhapsody No. 2 as the only vaguely familiar piece to which he could find any sheet music. The performance on the poorly tuned grand piano of Næstved's best restaurant had been almost ludicrously poor but nevertheless elicited the solemn admiration of the rest of the class, certainly the most uncritical audience imaginable. Being career oriented, he was far too straight-laced to be a prospect for collaboration in any illegal activity, and there were in any event no German troops nor any other targets in Vordingborg to induce anti-German activity. So the summer months drifted by, as two young men performed their few simple duties in picture-book surroundings, while the continent of Europe was being consumed in conflagration all around.

On one thing Willumsen and I saw eye to eye: we were both fanatics about staying in physical trim. To this end we had devised a rigorous regime of swimming in the fjord and worked with equal diligence to improve our marksmanship with pistols. The Danish military pistol was an old-fashioned French model of 9mm caliber. The design dated from 1910, and it had the magazine located ahead of the trigger guard, a poorer arrangement than putting it in the handle as in the better-designed German Lugar or the P-38. The result was that the weapon's center of gravity shifted backward as successive rounds were fired and expelled from their forward location, very impractical and awkward. But we doggedly kept honing our skills, and by midsummer we had both qualified for entry in the army's terrain sport competition, a sort of military pentathlon involving a ten kilometer cross-country race, pistol shooting and hand grenade throwing. We had both finished the race in hot competition with young career officers, and I had won second prize overall, a small bronze cup.

Early in the summer I had on the street run into a former fellow apprentice, Helge, from our days at B&W. He was now earning generous journeyman wages in Copenhagen and was home in Vordingborg visiting his mother and nineteen-year-old sister, Augusta, to whom he introduced me. Until now, my life had been somewhat short on female companionship, and this had been only partly for lack of opportunity. Another reason was my firm convinction that I was not the type girls fall for. My favorite sources of intelligence on the subject of what beautiful women prefer had been provided by Hollywood movies. Films such as *Test Pilot* with Clark Gable and Myrna Lloy, or *Top Hat* with Fred Astaire and Ginger Rogers demonstrated beyond doubt that there was no substitute for a suave man-of-the-world image, and any mirror was ready to tell me that I was no Clark Gable or Fred Astaire. My big nose and coarse features left me few illusions. However, Gus was cute and attractive and I invited her to go dancing with me one Saturday night, counting on my handsome uniform to make up for my shortcomings. Miraculously, it worked like a charm! When I kissed her goodnight, she willingly melted into my arms, and afterward we spent most of the summer Sundays together. Our favorite haunt was Knudshoved, a long, narrow peninsula curving around a stretch of Zealand's south coast. Too remote for farming, it was an almost pristine area of wildflowers, stray sheep, thousands of shore birds, and soft haystacks.

Snooping around the somnolent headquarters offices, I had one day discovered where military travel tickets to the state railways were kept and promptly helped myself to a block of them. Technically, this was theft, but I reasoned that in my worthwhile efforts against the Germans, the Danish state should at least provide me with transportation. The tickets had enabled me to visit my mother in Copenhagen and also to embark on my present project, a visit to Ribe on a three-day weekend pass, something my meager military pay would not have allowed.

It had been bright and sunny when I boarded the train, as one could expect at the beginning of August. The backbone of the Danish state railroads consisted of a main east-west line whose eastern terminus was in Copenhagen which is situated on the Sound, opposite the Swedish city of Malmö. The line's western terminus was in the harbor city of Esbjerg on the North Sea coast, in peacetime the ferry port for transit to England. Another mainline ran from Copenhagen south to Gedser, export harbor for goods to Germany and the rest of the continent, and two north-south lines in Jutland completed the system. The westernmost of the two Jutland lines served the small towns along the North Sea, including Ribe, and continued down through Schleswig-Holstein to Hamburg. It was a single-track affair built in the heady days when steam was introduced in the late eighteen-hundreds, but it had essentially languished in low use, while the double tracks of the other Jutland line serving the larger and more prosperous east coast cities garnered the bulk of the traffic.

Coming from Vordingborg I had changed trains, first in Ringsted to the main east-west line, and again in Bramminge in Jutland in the late afternoon, this time from the Copenhagen diesel express to the diminutive train of the west coast line in which I was now rumbling along. Before each station, the conductor came to collect the tickets from the few passengers about to get out there, a procedure with which I was familiar. I had signed a fictitious name to my own travel pass after making it valid to Tønder, a station somewhat farther south. That way I could leave the train in Ribe without yet having surrendered the forged document.

Following the plan, I got off at the Ribe station, tore up the pass and dropped it in a refuse receptacle as I walked through the empty station building. That pass would never be traced. I left the building and started toward my grandparents' house. The sidewalks along the road were shaded by old elm trees from the afternoon sun and on each side a small park created separation between city and railroad, a picture of perfect peace and tranquility. I stopped on the bridge across the Nipsaa to gaze for a moment at the stream where Aage and I had spent countless hours fishing. Too bad Aage was away. He too had applied to serve in the army and was stationed someplace on Zealand. Suddenly, my heart started to pound in excitement. Right in front of me, on the other side of the water in the garden of Hotel Riberhus, a German gasoline dump had been prominently established. Two-hundred-liter drums were neatly stacked in rows, three high, on the well-kept lawn that bordered for some fifty yards on the stream. Just one soldier with a rifle patrolled the layout, pacing slowly back and forth. Here was a real target! Leaning leisurely on the guard rail, I could observe every detail hardly more than a good stone's throw away, and I realized how a shark must feel when closing in on a piece of bloody meat. While I was trying to memorize the precise layout, pretending to watch two swans feeding in the water below, a German platoon swung into view back at the railroad station and came marching toward me under the old elms, returning from some guard duty or other. I heard the *Feldwebel* in charge give an order, and with mechanical precision the column broke into song:

Auf der Heide blüht ein kleines Blühmelein,
Und das heisst
   Erika ...

I turned and watched them go by, enjoying every second of the singing. There were fewer than two dozen soldiers, but they harmonized the lyrics perfectly with both strength and enthusiasm. Why couldn't our soldiers sing like that, I wondered. The Danes had marching songs as well, but it simply was not customary for our soldiers to sing on the march. It was a traditional German feature the Nazis had wisely nurtured and given high priority during training, both in their youth organizations and in the military, sensing correctly that it touched something treasured in the national psyche, imbuing and firming an invaluable martial comradeship. The column passed and disappeared into the city, the voices fading but still echoing faintly off the brick walls of the old houses -

Wenn das Heidenkraut rotlilla blüht,
ist mein Gruss zu dir mein schönstes Lied ...

Six hours later I slipped stealthily through the barbed wire fence and crept across the lawn toward the gasoline drums. The velvet cloak of the northern summer night blurred things at a distance without offering any deep cover of darkness, and the night air was still and sweet, a faint gurgle audible from the stream. A soldier patrolled slowly in the aisles separating the rows of drums, his movements showing no discernible pattern, so I chose to worm my way toward an aisle somewhere in the middle, hoping to avoid his attention. Halfway down the chosen aisle I paused prostrate in the shadows between the rows, the thin civilian clothes I had changed into soaked from the dew-wet grass. The smell of gasoline was powerful in the warm air, causing me to see in my mind's eye the garden already ablaze with precious synthetic fuel burning out of control. My sabotage equipment consisted of a sharp-pointed screwdriver from my grandfather's shop, matches, and the small .25-caliber pistol I had liberated in Copenhagen long before. I readied the screwdriver to puncture the nearest drum, placing the sharp point against the end, near the edge. Just as I was about to deliver a quiet blow with the palm of my hand, the guard chose that very aisle for his random stroll. As he bore down on me slowly, I realized in a flash not only that I would be discovered at a distance of only a few feet, but also that discovery was inevitable in about twenty seconds. What infernally bad luck! How superlatively stupid to undertake projects like this the hard way. Why couldn't I have had a couple of tracer bullets and simply blown the whole dump sky high with one or two shots from the fairly safe distance of the bridge? The fragrance of the grass under my nose mingled with the smell of gasoline from the drums, fuel badly needed by the Wehrmacht and which I should have been clever enough to deny them ... But never mind all that, the moment of decision was bearing down on me in the form of a German guard with a rifle. He was almost upon me, and I decided to shoot him. Quietly I unlocked the safety catch on the small pistol. When he was about eight feet away I rose to my knees out of the shadows and squeezed the trigger. There was a CLICK, loud and clear in the night air ... the damn thing had failed to fire! The guard and I now reacted with comparable speed, both of us determined to save our lives. The German let out a hoarse cry, ran backwards a few yards, dropped to the ground, slinging the rifle from his shoulder into firing position with the reflexes of a veteran. I spun around, dashed past the corner of the barrel row and vaulted the barbed wire fence in a flying leap. As I landed on the other side, the first shot came, passing well over my head. At the second report, I was already safely lost in the shadows of the adjoining park.

The experience taught me never to depend on a firearm without first expending one of the precious cartridges to test it. Examination of the gun afterward revealed a broken firing pin. Sigurd Laursen, an old friend who had Ribe's only gunsmith shop and who many years before had been an apprentice in my grandfather's waterworks shop, replaced the firing pin, asking no questions.[34] I also learned another lesson about guns: when you really need a pistol, you don't need a small one.

The day after my abortive attempt on the fuel dump, the German outfit quartered in Hotel Riberhus and responsible for guarding the dump was a beehive of activity. More barbed wire was strung, additional guards were posted, and floodlights were being installed in the garden. In the afternoon, an old family friend dropped in for a visit at my grandparents' apartment. It was a criminal police official by the name of Østbirk. Close to retirement, he was a former neighbor whom I had known for many years and who from time to time had done a bit of private work in my grandfather's workshop, using grandfather's tools. Having timed his visit to coincide with my grandfather's afternoon nap, he chatted amiably with grandmother for a couple of minutes and accepted her offer of a cup of coffee. When she went to the kitchen to prepare it, leaving us alone in the living room, he pulled from his pocket the screwdriver I had left behind in the grass at my hurried departure from the hotel garden.

It was one of those rare coincidences that solve mysteries if they fall into the lap of an experienced detective. This particular screwdriver had been made by my grandfather from a fencing foil discarded a generation ago from the Latin school's sports program. It was unique, yet would have furnished no clue to anyone except Østbirk who had used it himself and knew it on sight. He was a veteran of the select criminal police force, known as a professional of the highest caliber, inscrutable, enigmatic, and tireless when in pursuit of a lawbreaker. As I found out then and there, he had also made up his mind where his national loyalties belonged. Squinting at me levelly across the table, he handed me the screwdriver and said evenly in his raspy voice, "I think you'd better put it back where it belongs before your grandfather misses it." He paused, then added, "Nobody else knows about this."

I took the screwdriver and said simply, "Thanks, I'll do that."

When Østbirk left after our coffee, I reviewed my actions in Ribe methodically to evaluate whether there might have been other slip-ups on my part. It was the first time someone had actually found out anything compromising about me without my volunteering the information, and it was unsettling. Østbirk would keep mum, but any fool could see that safety and freedom of action lay in not attracting attention or suspicion. If suspicion were ever aroused, it would be impossible to operate at all.

* * *

Strength lies not in defense but in attack.

Adolf Hitler

Immediately after the Pearl Harbor attack, the Japanese had let loose with a six-month victorious rampage that swept the Philippines, Guam, Wake, Hong Kong, Singapore, Malaya, Borneo, Sumatra, Celebes, Anboine, Java and Rangoon from Allied control. The Rising Sun empire builders were ecstatic, and the War Ministry in Tokyo defined the outlines of the intended Japanese holdings which made Hitler's immediate plans for territorial acquisition look positively modest by comparison. In addition to the already conquered areas, the new Japanese empire was to include Australia, New Zealand, Ceylon, parts of India, western Canada, Alaska, Washington State, Central America, Colombia, Equador, Cuba, Jamaica and Haiti, with several Southeast Asian kingdoms attached under Japanese control.[35]

In hindsight, the Japanese euphoria may border on the absurd, but a realistic Allied assessment at the time was one of clear and present danger to the world of the Pacific. Moreover, concentration of Japanese power in a thrust through the Indian Ocean combined with a successful drive by Rommel to the Suez Canal and beyond could link Germans with Japanese and project Axis power into areas critical to the Allied war effort. The threat never materialized due to the failure of the Germans and Japanese to orchestrate a coordinated strategy. It diminished when the Japanese advance was halted in May by the American navy in the Battle of the Coral Sea and faded away when the British shortly afterward regained the initiative in North Africa.

Chapter 25　　　September 1942

Be bloody, bold and resolute.

Shakespeare

We walked slowly across the stone bridge to Kastellet, trying to look deeply involved in some quiet discussion and hardly paying attention to anything around us. At the entrance gate we correctly saluted the German guard but immediately picked up our conversation as we continued our stroll onto the embankment enclosing the ancient fortification. Located near the harbor, Kastellet had before the occupation housed the Danish General Staff. It now served the German military administration and some troop contingents. The area was closed to civilians, but a couple of Danish officers discharging some sort of liaison functions had office space in one of the buildings which allowed us, two uniformed visitors, access during daylight hours on the pretext of visiting one of these offices. It was our second leisurely walk and a simple plan had sprouted during this reconnaissance. Designed in the 17th century, the fortress' old buildings enjoyed the protection of an earthen embankment outside of which a water-filled moat some fifty feet wide gave added security by Renaissance standards. On our initial walk we had located a shed filled with motorcycles that presented an inviting target and had also decided that our line of retreat should be crossing the moat rather than exiting past the guard and across the stone bridge.

"From that corner you can cover me while I set the fire," I said, nodding toward a building on our left, near the motorcycle shed.

Kurt looked in the indicated direction, taking in the area's detail without betraying undue interest.

"Even better, *you* can cover *me* from there while I set the fire."

I shrugged and dug a 5-øre coin out of my pocket, our accepted means of settling such disagreements.

157

Kurt Ridung (1921 –) with whom the author undertook several sabotage projects while they both served as warrant officers in the small Danish military force that was allowed to exist during the early part of the German occupation of Denmark.

"Heads or tails?"

"Heads."

A quick flick followed, and when the coin landed on the pavement, his face lit up.

"When *I* come out from lighting the fire, we run up to here and dive into the water below that elm, swim across, and by the time we have walked back, we will have stopped dripping."

Continuing our stroll, I thought once more that Kurt was an ideal partner for this sort of thing. Late in the summer, we had from different assignments been transferred to Copenhagen to serve with an under-strength company doing guard duty on some government buildings. We had been billeted into Gerners-gade Kaserne, an old barracks near the city's harbor area. The men of this small command were all near the end of their draft term and the good ones had long since been combed out for noncom or warrant officer training. What was left were the dregs of soldiery: lazy, recalcitrant, smart-alecky. After a week of having my orders carried out at an insultingly slow pace, I had singled out #27, the mouthiest and laziest and ordered him to carry some material up to storage in a remote attic of the old barracks. When we were alone and out of earshot in the loft, I told him pleasantly that I was unhappy with the way he carried out orders. He shrugged with an insubordinate sneer, and as I had planned, I hit him, just once. When he got back on his feet he shouted that he would have the Kornet cashiered, sent to the stockade, and so forth. I smiled amiably, told him to bring plenty of witnesses to the court martial, and dismissed him. It was a risky gamble. An officer striking a soldier, or vice-versa, was one of the most serious military offenses, and if proven would result in an immediate court martial. At reveille the following morning, #27 showed up with an enormous black eye and had become the butt of suppressed derision and half-whispered comment among the rest of the men. The company commander appeared not to notice anything unusual, and the attention of the noncoms seemed directed everywhere except at #27. Nothing further came of it, but I encountered from then on much less reluctance in having my orders obeyed smartly.

The incident had impressed Kurt Ridung who was a fellow graduate from the *Kornetskole*. He was of slight build but endeavored with some success to elicit respect from his underlings with a serious visage and an iron will. He never missed an opportunity to display arrogant contempt for such human shortcomings as weakness or fear, and he affected deft slowness of movement and speech that somehow conveyed to the world that his every move or utterance was of profound importance. The total effect belied his slight stature and projected the image of a handsome young officer naturally at ease when in command. In reality, a good sense of humor lurked under this carefully contrived exterior, and the two of us worked well together, enjoying each other's company and agreeing that a measure of arrogance should be part of a good officer's make-up.

In August, the BBC broadcast from London brought the news that a convoy had relieved Malta. We had studied the map and concluded that this British bastion in the Mediterranean must be vital to the North African campaign, being strategically placed in close proximity to Sicily. Puzzled that the island had not long ago fallen to the Axis powers, we speculated that it must be due to the Italians' by now notorious ineptitude at warfare. Mussolini's soldiers had been trounced in North Africa and even in Greece and we wondered about this peculiar trait in the Italian national character. Kurt claimed that in view of the glorious Roman accomplishments in antiquity, one should expect a quite different performance, but I argued that nations change over time, some profoundly so, and reminded him that the Vikings would surely have looked with contempt at the Danes of 1940.

In his attitude toward the Germans, Kurt had revealed himself to be a kindred spirit, and we discussed endlessly how we might influence the war in which we so far had been passive spectators. We found ourselves in agreement that, given competent manpower, modern warfare required a constant supply of matériel, and we doubted Germany's ability to keep up with America and Britain in productive capacity. This line of discussion always led us to conclude that the best we could do at the moment was to put as much German matériel as possible out of commission. Our orders specified two weekly trips to a firing range to keep up the men's proficiency with the rifle, and as the range was located on the island of Amager, this involved a march of some five miles through the city's downtown area, across the harbor bridges and into the open country beyond. Danish folklore holds Amager to be a favorite haunt of elves,[36] but in modern times the island had become better known as the location of Kastrup airport. No civilian air traffic was allowed, of course, and the Luftwaffe had taken the airport over, using it largely for training of pilots. As a result, an old *JU-52* carried out a daily routine of landing practice that took it across the firing range every fifteen minutes or so at a height of about 1200 feet. This soon proved too tempting a target. While Kurt kept the men busy improving their marksmanship, I took a shot at the plane from the cover of the bushes lining the range, timing it so that the sound would be drowned out in the general noise of rifle firing. To our disappointment, nothing happened, so we switched places, and Kurt managed to get two shots off when the plane passed overhead next time. Again, no effect could be observed. We changed back and forth and got several more shots off, but all to no apparent avail. This was most disappointing, for we had felt certain of hitting at that distance and had been confident of immediate and dramatic results, but we never bagged the plane.

We also tried to produce a bomb. Our training at the *Kornetskole* had been thorough and had comprised infantry arms up to and including the 20-millimeter cannon, but it had not taken in explosives, much to our regret. We did some experimenting and at one point scavenged several pounds of powder by siphoning half the charge off some cannon ammunition, but we were stymied by the practical problems of turning it into a usable bomb with a fuse that would give us at least a few seconds delay. All our trials accomplished was to singe us a couple of times and give us a healthy respect for the potency of gunpowder. Frustrated by our lack of success, we now had great hopes for the simple, direct approach to the motorcycle shed in the old fortress.

Kurt turned from a slit in the curtain and spoke in my direction as I lay stretched out on a couch in the far end of the darkened room.

"I think it's dark enough."

We were holed up in Lt. Larsen's small office in Kastellet and had spent four hours waiting for cover of darkness. We knew Larsen from the *Kornetskole* where he had instructed in small arms tactics, and he had been willing enough to lend us the office key with one laconic comment: "Don't tell me what you're up to, but good luck." It was encouraging, we agreed afterward, that a few officers were beginning to see resistance as the path to take. We had dressed in fatigues and canvas shoes, no shiny buttons and easy to swim in. Shortly after midnight, we walked silently down the street between the buildings, staying in the shadow. At the end of the street we had to cross an open space to the motor shed. It was possible to see a person in the darkness, but not to identify uniforms or other details. In case we were seen, it was best to behave naturally and hope to be taken for Germans, so we walked across the open space to the shed at a measured pace, side by side. Nobody challenged us, and the blackout curtains provided some insurance against unseen observers. At the corner of the shed I stopped while Kurt continued to the door and tried it. It had been open when we had reconnoitered earlier, but it was now closed and secured with a padlock. He ran his fingers over the lock and felt that it was inserted through two screw eyes. He drew his bayonet, stuck it between the screw eyes and twisted, slowly, slowly. The lock broke with a metallic click, clearly audible in the night stillness. We both snapped to peak attention, listening, staring into the dark, waiting for some reaction, feeling that anyone not inside the buildings must have been alerted. We remained silent, immovable for a couple of minutes, I with the safety catch off my pistol. Then Kurt pushed the door open. I could hear the faint noise of his fumbling search for a motorcycle, and moments later came the muffled metallic noise when his bayonet punctured the tank. Then, more fumbling, and again the noise of a tank being pierced. We had agreed to start the fire in two places. A few seconds later he stepped outside.

"Ready?" His whisper betrayed his excitement. The area was calm all around. I had heard nothing.

"Yes."

Kurt went back to the door, struck a match and threw it inside, pulling the door shut. We heard the instant WHOOSH as the fire caught, and the two of us dashed up the embankment. As we reached the top, a second WHOOSH from the shed blew the door out, announcing that the fuel in the second pool had ignited with explosive force. We ran down the embankment and plunged into the moat. The stagnant, lukewarm water had for years provided a fertile incubator for algae and sundry water organisms, and we emerged on the other side covered with slimy growth that we did not try or wish to identify. Across the moat noises and shouts could be heard from beyond the embankment, and we grinned happily at each other. Then we started to walk with unconcern in the pleasant darkness of the city, back to the barracks and straight into the shower room.

The following day the fortress was closed to Danish personnel.

* * *

The Battle of the Atlantic must, however, be won, not only in the factories and shipyards, but upon the blue water.

Winston Churchill, in the House of Commons

Although our puny efforts to diminish the Wehrmacht's fighting capability were but a drop in the proverbial ocean, Kurt and I were correct in perceiving matériel as one key prerequisite for successful conduct of the war. Despite her impressive industrial prowess, which had been boosted by the appointment in

161

January of Albert Speer as head of war production,[37] Germany commanded an ultimately smaller potential than the Allies whose productive capacity had been immensely increased by the addition of the United States. But the Allies' transportation problem was acute. It fell to Germany's submarines, the U-boats, to take central position in Hitler's efforts to sever the transatlantic supply lines, and the ensuing crucial contest became known as the Battle of the Atlantic. In the early stages it appeared to be going Germany's way.

Chapter 26   November 1942

There is no bore we dread being left alone with so much as our own minds.

J. R. Lowell

This was an easy piece to work on, the rim of a truck wheel in which the hub had been torn by a Russian 37mm cannon shell. I lined it up and clamped it in the chuck, engaged the lathe's carriage, and watched the cutter bite into the rim. Henriksen, the owner of the workshop, figured we could salvage the rim which was hard to replace, for the resilient steel alloy was in short supply, like almost everything else. The wheel had come off a Wehrmacht truck shipped from the Eastern Front all the way to this village of Toftlund in Southern Jutland to be reconditioned. I checked the stream of milky-white cutting oil to make sure that the feed was proper, and sat down next to the machine to eat my late-evening sandwich. My coat was hanging on a corner of the tool table, and from a pocket I fished a copy of *Berlingske Tidende*, a large Copenhagen daily. The war news was discouraging, as usual. Rommel apparently was riding high. In the East the Germans had introduced a new, more powerful Panzer. How long could the Russians withstand the onslaught? Turning to the war at sea, I estimated that if even half the German releases were true about the U-boats sinking American supplies en route to England, there must be more Allied war matériel on the bottom of the Atlantic than on all the battlefields. I pitched the paper into the trash and sipped my coffee ... coffee? Hell, I had all but forgotten what coffee tasted like. This stuff was black and commonly known as witches' piss. Yet people drank it with no complaint. The trouble with Danes was, they were good at making the best of things, and too damn willing to do so, almost considering it a virtue. I let my thoughts go back over the last few months, idly searching for something encouraging. Shortly after Kurt Ridung and I set the fire to the Wehrmacht motorcycles in Kastellet we had made a trip to Ribe, using the last of my military travel passes. There we had hatched a plan to impede German movements in case of an invasion on the Jutland coast. We determined that a machinegun in the cathedral tower could command the north-south highway more than a mile in either direction, and the tower itself was a natural fortress where a single determined defender could stand off an army. Being utterly unable to estimate the likelihood of an Allied invasion in the area, we had worked out the details,[38] confided our plan to nobody, but gave it our own code name: *Thermopylae.*

After my discharge in September from the Danish Army, I had been working now for two months, saving money toward getting back into the Teknikum to continue my engineering studies next summer semester, which would start in April. Choosing from the now numerous *Værnemagere,* firms working directly or indirectly for the Germans, I had first answered an advertisement seeking a lathe operator for a shop in Thisted, a small town in northern Jutland, and had easily landed the job. Good machinists were in short supply, and the little firm had a backlog of work despite round-the-clock activity, for damaged Wehrmacht matériel arriving in a steady stream by train from distant battlefronts found its way to such places. It was the shop's emphasis on automotive equipment that had attracted me, for every vehicle had a fuel tank, usually with sufficient gasoline or diesel oil to make it a tempting target to burn. But before I could do anything spectacular, a friend had told me about the firm of P. Schmidt in Toftlund, where hourly wages were higher. Besides, Toftlund was only an hour's bus ride from Ribe, enabling me to visit my grandparents and also keep contact with Aage. I had switched jobs, leaving my lathe in Thisted subtly maladjusted and with silica in the gear box that in the course of a few days would put it out of commission.

Schmidt's shop was larger and also far better equipped, having received over the past year sixteen tool machines from Germany, turret lathes and other state-of-the-art stuff. It was a pleasure to lay hands on such machinery. Henriksen apparently had no difficulty obtaining credits, and what used to be a small machine shop employing half-a-dozen workers had mushroomed into a sizeable enterprise. And it was by no means the only one doing a booming business repairing German equipment and producing parts and components for the Wehrmacht.

While I was still in Copenhagen after my discharge, Alfred Sander had called to set up a meeting. He had been very circumspect, and we used the telephone only to arrange where to meet, never hinting at anything illegal for fear of wire tapping. The meeting took place in a coffee bar, where Alfred and Erik Hansen revealed some sensational news. Erik had managed to get in contact with a British agent who had asked for help to receive a parachute drop from England. We had all been skeptical about its validity, for it sounded fantastic and far too good to be true, but we had of course agreed to help. A few days later we had received detailed instructions on how to proceed. First we had to go by train to the small

View of Ribe's main thoroughfare as seen from the cathedral tower. This was the only north-south route on the west coast of Jutland.

town of Borup, taking along our bicycles, and from there biked to a designated spot near the town of Jyderup. We had spent the small hours of the cool morning peering into a clear dawn sky, but no airplane came, and we had afterwards been told that the mission had been cancelled belatedly.

While waiting on the edge of the designated field, watching in vain for an airplane that failed to show, we had commisserated about our countrymen's lethargy and compliance with the demands of the occupying power. There was no denying that Danish society had settled rather easily and smoothly into the day-to-day routines of occupation. The country's infrastructure was intact and functioning. Absence of gasoline had eliminated private automobiles, but transportation by train or bus allowed anyone to travel anywhere. Buses and other essential vehicles had solved the fuel problem with gas generators, contraptions that burned wood to produce gas to fuel the engine. Neither as convenient nor as powerful as gasoline, the wood smoke still kept the vehicles running.

The tangible deprivations of war time, shortages or absence of all manner of consumer goods, had turned out to be not only of little consequence but actually to have some positive aspects. Most noticeable was the virtual elimination of money as an important factor in daily life, and to those who like me were in tight economic straits, that was decidedly a blessing in disguise. Wages and pric-

165

es were so firmly controlled that even a very modest income sufficed to provide the necessities; conversely even a substantial income could not provide significantly more than those same necessities. The first of these was food, which was available and rationed in adequate amounts. The adequacy of the rations was less a matter of generosity on the part of the Germans than recognition of the difficulty in starving a small and well-organized country whose main business derived from the food production of its agriculture.

The second necessity was best described as physical maintenance. With very few and low quality consumer goods to buy, people soon learned to extend almost indefinitely the service lives of the things they possessed of prewar quality. Clothes were mended and reconditioned, worn-through shirt collars reversed, good leather shoes repaired and given almost limitless life by care and gentle treatment. Urged by local authorities, communities organized exchanges of children's clothes outgrown by their owners, and published a stream of advice on how to stretch resources. Material that could be scavenged from less urgent purpose was used or traded, and sometimes unexpected sources were discovered. One example was British barrage balloons[39] which occasionally blew across the North Sea on the wings of westerly gales after having been torn from their moorings. They normally trailed twisted steel tails of broken anchoring cable across the countryside, snagging and ripping out powerlines, fences, small trees, and anything else in their path, easily doing more damage than a platoon of saboteurs. When brought to earth where no Germans were in sight, they were promptly slashed to pieces and spirited away to be turned into raincoats. Fur was in short supply, and some cat owners suffered disappearance of their pets who fell prey to a rash of illegal entrepreneurship. Cat skins, however obtained, were salable for a variety of end uses. In consequence of this market situation, most cats soon sported a close-shaven band around the midsection, their owners' attempt to render them worthless to the poachers.

Luxury goods were in brisk demand, but rather than lamenting their scarcity, people seemed to look at their provision as a challenge to ingenuity. Tobacco could be had in modest quantities from one's own tobacconist who tried to allocate his meager supplies with an eye to maintaining his customers' goodwill. English tobacco was obtainable only from the skimpy residuals of prewar stocks, but Europeans found out that it was perfectly possibly to grow tobacco on their continent, even in the temperate climate of the North. The local product had the same nicotine content as the now unavailable imports from Virginia or Cuba but fell short on fragrance and taste, in part because the proper additives for curing and processing were in short supply or missing. I was only an occasional smoker but had to admit to an increased desire for tobacco after it had become hard to get. It made me wonder whether I was unduly possessive or simply suggestible.

The absence of coffee and tea was by far the most annoying tribulation. No one ever managed to come up with a decent coffee substitute. The German ersatz was worthless, having only its color to remind the drinker of coffee. Tea

Ribe tower offered a commanding view of the surrounding countryside. The plan to obstruct German traffic in case of an Allied invasion on the North Sea coast called for occupying the tower and mounting automatic rifles in the upper peepholes.

substitutes from herbs, black currant leaves and fruit leaves found some acceptance. An old watchmaker of my acquaintance claimed that apple leaves, sold as tea, made passably good tobacco for long-stemmed pipes, though he had a low opinion of its tea-brewing value. I had tried the leaves on his recommendation but found them unpalatable either as tea or tobacco.

Alcoholic beverages were in short supply, but it was discovered that the strong beer traditionally brewed for Easter celebration could be further improved by letting it age for a few months, raising its already respectable alcohol content to

167

about eleven percent. As a nurse trainee my sister had access to the hospital's supply of pure medical alcohol. This allowed a small circle of us to experiment with concocting some homemade liquors, mostly at Christmas and birthdays. With some experience and luck in choosing materials for flavoring and coloring, we produced a drinkable whiskey and an almost believable *crème de menthe* liqueur.

Daily existence was affected also by electricity rationing which severely curtailed the amount of light people were able to use at home. When studying at the Teknikum, I liked to do my homework at night and on Saturday nights used to work straight through until birdsong announced the arrival of Sunday. I had found that both reading and drafting could be done without undue eye strain by using a mere twenty-five watt bulb. The secret was simply to move the lamp right down to within a foot of the object, book or drawing. The government had decreed that central heating be turned down, and hot water turned off in apartment houses, but the public bathhouse was fine for a weekly bath. Soap had been reduced in fat content from its normal eighty to forty percent. It was still usable at that percentage, but did not produce much lather.

Altogether, nobody could complain of severe hardship, and to top it off occupation life by no means lacked diversion or entertainment. Movies were not too great, for English and American films had been banned, and the news trailer, the German UFA newsbureau's Wochenschau, showed only Nazi victories, but stage plays and music were of high quality and in strong demand. In the summer, outdoor performances were popular, and while in basic training in Odense, I had attended in the old city park the operetta *Sommer i Tyrol.* As it happened, that particular evening was my first away from the barracks where I was due back at 10 p.m., and I had carefully pressed my uniform pants by placing them under my bedsheet and sleeping on them after moistening the creases. Making my way to my assigned seat down the rows of chairs on the park lawn, I looked around furtively lest an officer should be in the audience and expect to be saluted, and I was conscious of smelling of shoe polish and leather wax as if surrounded by an invisible cloud. The musical performance turned out to be an unforgettable event in the sweet summer night, and I memorized Sigismund's song, entitled in Danish *Man kan da ikke gøre for at man har Charme.*[40] In Copenhagen, musical reviews drew large audiences with such talented performers as Marguerite Viby singing *Kammerat med Solen,* and Gerda and Ulrik Neuman giving forth with *Den lille lysegrønne Sang* and many other popular tunes. From Sweden flowed the songs of Alice Babs Nilsson, a prodigy of sixteen reminiscent of Judy Garland with whom she was contemporary, and Norway's most popular singer warbled the sentimental *Maanestraalen.* There was certainly no shortage of artistic production. War's abundant tragedy tended to spur rather than inhibit the performing arts.

Of all the sources of entertainment, however, the radio reigned supreme. Every Danish home had one, and in the evening, particularly after sunset, all of the stations in occupied Europe were audible, although those of the British were blanked out by noise transmitters. The noise makers were only partially successful, inasmuch as BBC news from London usually could be heard on a good receiver carefully tuned to make the announcer audible above the din, but they did kill the enjoyment of English music broadcasts. On the other hand, every Sunday afternoon all of the radio stations in occupied Europe carried the *Wunschkonzerte der Wehrmacht*, a potpourri of orchestras and individual performers requested in letters from German soldiers at the front: "Members of a panzer division in France request *Lilli Marlene*, sung by Marlene Dietrich."[41] "And now we have *Drei Mädchen auf der Bank*, requested by *Fallschirmjäger* in Holland." The concerts were enormously popular with both soldiers and civilians. They always started with a Wehrmacht choir singing *Wir fahren gegen Engelland*, a rousing World War One tune threatening imminent invasion of England, a theme that was popular with the Germans early in the war while they were still filled with optimism about invading England, and toward that end were busily building flat-bottomed landing barges in the harbors along the Channel coast.

Monitoring the radio waves also afforded in an indirect manner some incidental intelligence about Allied air raid activity. By tuning in Brussels, Rotterdam or Amsterdam, stations in the path of Royal Air Force bomber formations en route to German targets, the listener at night needed merely to wait until the station suddenly went off the air, the telltale sign that a raid was underway. By switching to a station located farther east, such as Liege, Düsseldorf or Cologne, the listener could enjoy a broadcast from there until that station too went dead so as not to function as a guiding beacon for the oncoming squadrons. By switching progressively farther east, the listener could with the aid of a map ascertain both rough speed and direction to the target which might be deep in the Reich, perhaps Stuttgart, or even Munich or Regensburg.

On the whole, the citizenry was suffering remarkably little during the occupation so far. Public authorities were instrumental in maintaining this state of affairs, for they saw as their primary duty the protection of the public from hardship, rather than making any contribution to the war effort against the German occupiers. However I might personally disagree with their policy, in this they were broadly in alignment with the vast majority of the citizens: the Danes were still unwilling to fight. The occupation was bad enough to complain about but not bad enough to do something about. Danish restrained resentment of Nazi overlordship found outlet in what can only be described as gestures. For example, when the Germans began to withdraw from circulation Danish copper coins in order to use the metal in war production, and substituting cheap aluminum coins, citizens quickly hoarded the original product.[42]

Compared with their record elsewhere in Europe, the Germans still treated Denmark with velvet gloves. Overt interference with national life was kept to a minimum consonant with getting the Danish economy to serve their war effort. But one thing could not be concealed: the press was no longer free. To people who are used to complete freedom of the press there is something beyond simple annoyance in being muzzled with censorship. Having someone – anyone –

One of the Ribe cathedral tower peepholes, planned site for automatic rifle.

decide what a citizen should be allowed to know is, by someone with a tradition of a free press, almost immediately looked upon as an insult to one's intelligence, as indeed it is. And when the authority who decides what to censor is a foreign invader, it becomes intolerable not to be *permitted* to know what goes on in the world at large. It was inevitable therefore that illegal Danish newssheets had begun to appear from an embryonic underground press already in 1940, and by 1942 some 75 such publications had seen daylight, most of them very small, amateurish and occasional, but a bellwether, nevertheless. Still, going beyond mere writing – however illegal, inflammatory and insulting to the Germans – by contemplating a more concrete effort to resist was something else. If challenged on this point, people would insist that a small country such as Denmark could do nothing to affect the course of world affairs. The argument always filled me with exasperation, but in calmer moments I realized that it was a natural outgrowth of the national predilection for rejecting things military or violent, an attitude that remained dominant.

And yet. As we commisserated on our airplane watch, we had to admit that we were not entirely alone in being out of step with the country at large. A few incidents had occurred where people had committed acts harmful to the occupying power. They had been gleefully reported in the underground newssheets, while in the press they were officially stigmatized as being the work of misguided persons, something condemned in the strongest terms by the government. The words *sabotage* and *sabotør*, hitherto rarely used and barely known by the average person, were beginning to gain currency in the Danish vernacular. It was the wrath of innocence and so far not anything to make the Germans worry. It *was* but a straw in the wind.

The cutter broke through the rim and the hub plopped out. I stopped the lathe, removed the rim from the chuck and started the next job. This one was a front drive shaft for an SdKfz 251, an armored reconnaissance vehicle. The shaft had been torn, probably by a mine blast, and after some cutting and welding it was now ready for finishing. To spare the cutter, I started the first pass on low r.p.m. and slow feed, estimating it would take until the end of my shift, and sat down again. On my first Sunday off I had taken the bus to Ribe, where Aage and I spent the day together, catching up on each others' doings. A few changes had taken place in the town. In order to supplement the regular police forces, Denmark had early in the occupation created an auxiliary police contingent, *Civilbeskyttelsen*, or CB. The recently formed Ribe section comprised eighteen men, a force Aage had joined to supplement his income, and they were in the throes of getting organized. Looking at this group, I again toyed with the idea of trying to involve others in sabotage work, and I discussed with Aage the possibilities for more extensive sabotage actions. Torn between the convenience and security of working alone and the greater capability but heightened risk of being part of a group, it made us cautious to realize that, should we through carelessness become suspect, things would immediately be far different. In the end we chose to continue by ourselves, singly or together, for the time being. Besides, our efforts were not always successful. Attempting to burn a Bakelite factory in Ribe, we failed twice to do more than very light damage.

Despite such setbacks, I was becoming increasingly conscious that an ordinary citizen could get away quite literally with murder, so long as he attracted no suspicion. I had also begun to appreciate that my machinist background coupled with some engineering training in many ways were helpful. As a boy I had watched and quizzed my grandfather when he repaired door locks, and he had taught me how to make and use a skeleton key, something that now enabled me to gain access in the manner of a burglar to sabotage targets. When Aage and I pooled our knowledge, it was apparent that such simple skills together with growing experience would enable us to use more of the opportunities presenting themselves.

The midnight shift was arriving, and I started to clean up my machine and tool table. My shiftmate arrived and greeted me cheerfully. He was a middle-aged machinist who thought the war a bonanza, allowing him earnings he had never dreamed of. I replied curtly, handed him the work order on the drive shaft, put on my jacket and left. The cold night air was invigorating as I lingered outside for a few moments to let my eyes get used to the dark. Gazing at patches of stars through a torn overcast, I wondered about the sailors on that North Atlantic run, bringing the stores to sustain Britain. What would it be like to get torpedoed on a night like this? How long could one survive in the water? Ten minutes, at most.

Back at the inn where I had rented a room on a weekly rate the maid had prepared one last pot of coffee. While drinking, I scanned newspaper headlines. *U-boats sink five ships. Rommel forces British Retreat in Libya. Von Paulus' Army near Stalingrad.* I threw the newspaper on the bench in disgust and went to bed.

* * *

From now on all enemies on so-called commando missions in Europe or Africa challenged by German troops, even if they are in uniform, whether armed or unarmed, in battle or in flight, are to be slaughtered to the last man.

Führer Order, 18 October 1942

Actually, the Nazi tide had crested at the beginning of fall in 1942, but the fact was not apparent to us in occupied Europe. In the North Atlantic German U-boats were sinking Allied shipping at a rate the combined output of shipyards in Britain, Canada and the U.S. could not replace. On land the swastika flew over German troops from Norway's North Cape on the Arctic Sea to the desert wastes of North Africa, and from the Atlantic Ocean to the Volga River on the threshold of Central Asia. Hitler spoke grandly of the Russians being finally beaten, and of his armies pushing all the way to the Persian Gulf, even to the Indian Ocean to link up with the Japanese.

The reality was less favorable for the German side. Sensing this, Hitler in frustration sought to improve his military fortune by directing his armies to use ever harsher methods.[43] In November a new player appeared on the North African scene to seal the fate of the *Afrika Korps*. Out of the Atlantic mist and through Gibraltar steamed a combined Anglo-American force under Eisenhower. Code named operation *Torch*, it made landings in Morocco and Algeria, where fighting broke out in several places with French forces loyal to the collaborationist Vichy regime, and French naval units were sunk by the American fleet off Casablanca. Even so, Eisenhower quickly obtained the French colonial administration's cooperation.

Chapter 27   New Years 1943

The night that hides things from us.

Dante Alighieri, *Inferno*

At Christmas I visited with Aage in Ribe and found that the town's CB headquarters had been set up in the basement under a small bank located on the town square, a beautiful medieval half-timbered structure. I had known the building all my life but had been unaware of what the earth underneath it held. Passing through a cobbled yard behind the bank and down a stone stairway, we entered the cellar itself which had a number of columns built of munkstone, a large red brick used in the Middle Ages. Narrow at the base, the upper part of the columns formed low, graceful Gothic arches supporting the building above. A stove had been installed, plus two telephones, and an ordinary radio played popular tunes – altogether a picture of placid contentment as young men grasped at a taste of self-importance in the manner of children playing war. One of the telephones was a direct line to the water tower where two of the personnel were on duty as an observation and listening post to warn headquarters of direct evidence that an air raid was underway, evidence that could be gleaned by peering out of the small windows in the tower's slanted roof. Most of the men held regular jobs, and the extra income was less of an attraction than the excitement of manning the headquarters and carrying out the CB duties. Our arrival in the cellar failed to interrupt an animated discussion about the upcoming New Year's eve duty roster. Aage had been assigned this unwelcome duty together with another man, the latter badly wanting to switch with someone else in order to go partying with his girlfriend. He was offering twenty kroner to anyone willing to take his place, but there were no takers in the group, so I offered to substitute and was immediately accepted. To be sure, I was not a member of the CB, but my military background was known and regarded with respect, so it occurred to no one that the substitution could be in any way improper.

And so it came about that on New Year's eve 1942 Aage and I found ourselves climbing the ladders to the water tank as we had done many years earlier as small boys seeking a thrill. It was the first time I had been on these premises since then, but everything seemed hauntingly familiar: the creak of the wooden ladder, the smell of the loft, the cold iron of the tank's rivets ... the passage of time had altered very little. The top of the tank had been covered over to provide a floor, and four board walls enclosed a small cubicle whose ceiling was the tower's slate roof which had two slanted skylights, one on the south side and one to the north. A portable electric heater, a couch, two chairs, and a small table carrying a telephone and a hotplate completed furnishings and equipment. By half-past-four in the afternoon dusk became darkness. We made a pot of coffee, perused the last paper of the year and listened to popular music from Copenhagen on the radio.

At ten o'clock we heard the evening newscast. During the fall, events on the Russian Front had dominated the headlines, particularly the fighting in Stalingrad, where the German 6th Army under von Paulus was locked in battle with the Russians under Zhukov. This New Year's Eve a series of bulletins from Reuters again showed the Germans' anxiety about events there. To a thoughtful observer the reason was clear enough. Even the heavy censorship could conceal neither the extreme ferocity of the struggle nor the fact that the Russians slowly were gaining the upper hand.

To fulfill our assigned CB duty, we periodically opened one of the skylights to look and listen, but the night offered nothing but millions of stars in the frosty heavens. Close to midnight I poked my head out the south skylight and thought I heard a faint sound in the distance. I called Aage, and we both strained at listening as the sound increased to become a clearly audible noise similar to that of a slow-running motorcycle engine. Aage nodded thoughtfully.

"We have heard that from time to time. Nobody knows what it is – probably some kind of deviltry the Germans are concocting – unless the angels have taken to riding motorcycles."

The noise passed overhead and the heavenly motorcycle faded away somewhere in a northerly direction. Nothing had been visible, and without knowing the size or nature of the source, it was impossible to guess at its altitude, but it certainly did not sound like any airplane.

* * *

War is the business of Barbarians.

Napoleon

Breaking with traditional military conservatism, Hitler's orders called for German designers to pursue several new weapons systems. One such was the Fieseler Fi-103 flying bomb, later to become known as the V-1. Using a pulse jet for propulsion, the builders improvised a test range from a point in northern Germany to somewhere in southern Norway, following the Jutland west coast. What Aage and I heard on our watch that New Years' night was one of the Fi-103 prototypes working its way north on stubby wings at eight thousand feet.

On the Eastern Front, von Paulus' exhausted 6th Army fought its way into Stalingrad, only to become surrounded and bottled up. In the late summer, the Russians had shifted their aim from one of holding on in house-to-house fighting to the more ambitious plan of mounting a pincer movement to trap and annihilate the entire German 6th Army, code naming the operation *Uranus*. The Russian operation was carefully prepared. When the trap closed, Hitler refused to allow a tactical retreat, overruling his commanders who were unanimous in recommending a breakout from the city. Following orders, the German troops hung on, locked in savage street-to-street combat.

Chapter 28   March 1943

A wise man will make more opportunities
than he finds.

Bacon

For a few moments, I stood in the deep stillness of the auto repair shop to let my eyes adjust to the dark, going over the details of what I had planned to do in the next few minutes. My plan was simple enough, just a case of taking advantage of an opportunity that had presented itself.

In the course of the winter I had been in Ribe a few times, although Aage was no longer there; he had moved to Kolding, where he had found a job with the city's Ford dealer. We had as always discussed the war news which from our point of view had been improving. Stalingrad had turned out to be a battle like nothing in the war so far. It was over by the middle of January, and for once German defeat could be sensed not just in the trickles of news from London but even in the official German press reports.

When in Ribe, I usually visited the hospital where my sister was a nurse trainee. The walk from my grandparents' home to the hospital took me past Ribe Autoværksted, the Ford dealership and service shop where years before Aage had been an apprentice. Lately, the place had been crammed with Wehrmacht vehicles in various stages of repair, as the shop owner had eagerly sought all the German work he could garner. On my way back from a hospital visit late last night, I had surveyed the place carefully from the outside and found that the main entrance door held six small windows in its upper half and that the glass was missing in one of these. The opening was about six by six inches, just enough for me to reach through and unlock the door from the inside. After entering, I had in almost total darkness spent an hour familiarizing myself with the layout, for it was immediately obvious that the place was an ideal sabotage target.

176

The morning after fire devastated a Ford workshop and a furniture factory working for the German occupation forces in Ribe. German soldiers can be seen taking inventory of the military vehicles destroyed in the fire. The picture was taken by the criminal police technical division, despatched from Kolding to record and investigate. The author, who set the fire, received the file after the war as a memento from Østbirk, senior criminal investigator in Ribe.

The workshop occupied the lower floor of an old factory building, in times past a chicory processing plant, while the upper floor housed a furniture manufacturer who was known also to work largely for the Germans. Picking my way among the military vehicles cluttering the shop on the gound floor, I had discovered an adjoining well-stocked parts room. Inflammable material, mostly oil and rubber, was plentiful everywhere. Looking over the outside premises I had found a large pile of sawdust and wood shavings at the back of the building where also a quantity of planks were standing on end, leaned against the building and ready to be hauled inside by the furniture manufacturer through an upper floor window. After memorizing as many details as possible, I had departed as quietly as I had come, locking the door behind me.

Recalling what the nightly visit had revealed, I had spent the day laying a precise plan for setting the lower floor on fire, anticipating that the second floor inevitably would burn as well. In the evening I had gone again to enjoy a few hours with my sister and her nurse friends, but close to midnight I took my leave from the hospital annex and walked back through dark and empty streets.

At the auto shop I again used the entrance point of the missing window pane to let myself in, closed the door silently behind me and now stood here, ready for action.

With my eyes adjusted to the dark, I started methodically to carry out my plan. First, I piled a dozen tires into a weapons carrier that was blocking the main exit and proceeded to drench them with kerosene. Two barrels of lubricating oil were located near the center of the shop, surrounded by vehicles, and I started a slow outflow of oil from their taps onto the floor. Beyond the far end of the shop was the parts supply room into which I pushed a motorcycle and punctured its tank. The outflowing oil from the barrels was creating a widening pool, slowly covering the floor where the miscellaneous vehicles were being repaired, and it was now time for me to pour a trail of gasoline to connect motorcycle with oil barrels and weapons carrier. The trail ended below the small, glassless window in the main door which I closed behind me as I went outside.

Close to the building stood a British-made lorry, part of the German spoils from Dunkerque. I punctured its tank to start a slow drip. Then I ran around the building, digging matches from my pocket, and lit the curled wood shavings under the planks standing against the wall of the upstairs furniture factory. The flames flickered briefly and then caught rapidly in the tinder-dry material. Matches in hand I raced to the entrance door to the shop and threw a lighted match through the glassless window onto the gasoline trail inside. With the gasping sound of a giant boxer being hit in the stomach, the room belched into instant flame, and I bent under the lorry outside to light the small pool that had appeared under its tank. Then I sprinted into the surrounding darkness, slowed down after a short distance, looked and listened for any sign of life around me, walked to my grandparents' home and went to bed.

A few minutes later the sound of the fire department's truck echoed in the quiet street below as it raced through, horns blaring. I got out of bed, dressed slowly and walked slowly back to the scene, where a crowd had already assembled, both civilians and German soldiers. The entire building was an inferno of flame, both upstairs and downstairs, and the British lorry outside was already nearly consumed. The firemen concentrated their efforts instead on the municipal gasworks which was situated across the street, playing their hoses on its large coal gas storage tank to prevent it from exploding in the intense heat radiating from the fire. Shortly, fire trucks from Haderslev arrived to help. Running to hook up their hoses, the newcomers yelled that they had been able to see the smoke billowing skywards, illuminated from below by the fire, already when leaving the outskirts of their own town forty-five kilometers away, on the other side of the Jutland peninsula.

Mingling with the spectators, I heard only lament that many people would now be out of work. Old Mr. Lindberg, the gasworks superintendent who for many years had been one of my grandfather's fishing buddies and whom I had known all my life, turned with a knowing look on his face to a small group of bystanders and said quietly, "Well ... one thing I can tell you. This fire was set by English agents. Danes don't do this sort of thing."

To my regret, he was almost right. Danish civilians still gave little thought to detracting in any concrete manner from the Nazi war effort. After a few more minutes to satisfy myself that nothing was being saved from the flames, I went back home and to bed for the second time.

* * *

> *For the time of mischance comes to all.*
> *And a man cannot even know his time.*
> *As fishes are enmeshed in a fatal net,*
> *and as birds are trapped in a snare,*
> *so men are caught at the time of*
> *calamity ...*

Ecclesiastes, 9.12

At the end of January 1943, von Paulus surrendered the pitiful remnants of the German 6th Army, and some ninety thousand men trudged to the oblivion of prisoner-of-war camps in Siberia. Only five thousand of them would see their homeland again.

The fighting at Stalingrad had received too much publicity to hush up the defeat, but many other developments eluded public knowledge. One of these was the gruesome quirk in Hitler's tactical direction of the German war effort that he demanded the Jews be made to suffer especially when reverses occurred at the Front. Immediately after the surrender at Stalingrad, he issued orders that the Warsaw Ghetto be destroyed. SS General Jürgen Stroop was given three days to capture the Ghetto, but it took four months and 3,000 troops with tanks, armored cars, flamethrowers and artillery to subdue the Jews who unexpectedly fought back.[44]

Chapter 29   August 1943

*A man is more himself if he is one of a
number; so let us take that road together
and, as we go, gather what company we
can find.*

Hillaire Belloc

The drawing was almost finished. It was the tangible outcome of a series of calculations of stresses in the steel web of a bridge with a fifty-meter span, a homework problem in statics at the Teknikum institute where I was again enrolled.
With enough money saved from my machinist jobs, I had returned to engineering studies at the start of summer semester and had moved back in with my
mother. Sharing her apartment made economic sense, but the move in any
event seemed natural. Children of all ages think of home as being where their
parents live, until such time as they get married and establish real housekeep-
ing themselves. The Teknikum studies were demanding of time and effort, for
the institute's stringent performance requirements were meant to flunk out a
hefty forty percent of the student body before the senior year, and I intended to
be safely ahead in the remaining sixty-percent group. The study schedule
monopolized both my weekdays and weekends, but it had still proven possible
to find time for some extracurricular activity. I had thought again about joining
my efforts with those of some like-minded collaborators, perhaps one of the
small groups who performed the useful service of getting real news disseminat-
ed, but every time, I had opted to continue alone and with more direct action.

One day I had a phone call from Erik Hansen who had again made contact
with a British agent, this time through Svenn Seehusen, an old acquaintance
from our years in the conservative youth organization. The agent, recently arrived by parachute drop, used the cover name "Stumpen," and he had put us in
touch with Georg Quistgaard and his wife, Ellen, who were making prepara-

Aage Schoch, editor-in-chief of Nationaltidende until removed at German insistence in 1942. He was extensively active in the Resistance and became a member of the Danish Freedom Council.

tions to receive an air drop that was to be attempted from England. We had met with the Quistgaards for an initial briefing in their tiny apartment in Aabenraa, a short sidestreet in the old part of Copenhagen. Georg was a tall, gangly man in his late twenties whose appearance and behavior offered few clues to his background and education. Ellen was an attractive woman of about thirty who moved with unobtrusive confidence in organizing the couple's activities. As we discussed a few details, each of us trying to glean as complete a picture as possible without giving away much personal information, I watched Ellen with fascination. She was the first woman I had met among resistance contacts, and the way she acted elicited my unqualified admiration. At the end of our meeting, she had sketched the plan of operations without adding a single gratuitous detail, giving us only what we needed to know in order to do our part.

The group that was to receive the material – referred to by the English term "stuff" – had been thoughtfully composed by Georg and Ellen. Besides Erik, Alfred and myself, it comprised Svend-Aage Harpsø, a friend of Erik and Alfred's who was on his first serious action, Brian Clausen, Stig Jensen, Krarup-Hansen, Aage Schoch, Jens Sønderup, and the Quistgaards. For obvious reasons, it was necessary for us to know each other on sight, and Ellen had wisely arranged for our introductory get-together to take place in the lobby of the Palladium, a large downtown movie theater near the city hall square. Crowded public places were judged safest for such gatherings, and in the well-lit theater lobby we had introduced ourselves, all using cover names except one man, Aage Schoch. "Hell," he said with a smile, "you probably all know me anyway, so just call me Aage." He was right, we knew him. As editor of a large Copenhagen newspaper, he was known to too many people to make it worth the bother to try to hide his identity under a sobriquet. At the meeting we also learned where the drop was to take place, so that we could prepare transportation.

The prearranged location – our first on the island of Zealand – was a forest clearing in the countryside near Ringsted, a town sixty kilometers from Copenhagen. The actual spot was Gyldenløves Høj which we referred to simply as *Højen*, the hill. It was Zealand's highest point, but in the low Danish countryside this distinction was reached at less than five hundred feet of elevation, and it appeared as only a slight rise in the almost flat landscape. We would travel to the site by various means, Erik, Alfred and I having organized for ourselves the loan of a small milk truck, one of the few vehicles that could be legally on the road.

Final information about which night the drop would come was to be given by a simple code arrangement. The London announcer of the 7:15 p.m. news broadcast to Denmark would finish routinely by saying "Vi kommer igen med vor næste udsendelse kl. 21:15." ("We will be back at 9:15 p.m."). If he added the words, "Glem nu ikke at lytte," ("Don't forget to tune in") it would signal our group to spring into action.[45]

I scrutinized my drawing one last time. The railroad bridge over the Nipsaa in Ribe was of a similar type, and while sizing each component in the design for tension or compression, I had carefully noted the two critical points where explosive charges could most economically bring the structure down. Looking at my watch, I absentmindedly noted that it was close to the time of the BBC's news and was aware that Alfred as usual would be monitoring. He was ideal for this sort of thing, absolutely reliable and thorough. During lunch hour I often

182

visited him and his father in their basement furrier shop in Griffenfeldtsgade, a short stroll from Teknikum. His father was a small man with greying red hair and heavy bifocals. He was aware what we were up to, although in how much detail, I did not know. We never discussed any of our activities, but once when we were alone, he had shown me a small ermine fur piece in his display window.

"If one day that piece is not in the window," he said, "don't come in. It will mean they are after Alfred and may be watching this shop."

So, I had gotten into the habit of strolling past his window, glancing in to make sure the ermine was there, then turning around and descending the four steps to the shop. Alfred had been his father's apprentice and had learned the craft well. In the strong but not unpleasant odor from piles of furs fresh from tanning, predominantly mink, fox and seal, the father-son team produced the fashionable garments, stoles and coats coveted by most ladies. The visits were a good way to keep close personal contact, an agreeable routine of exchanging news and rumors, discussing the latest government decrees and the heavily censored releases from the war fronts.

I put the pencil down as my mother came into the room. "I am going to bed now," she announced, handing me a cup of coffee. She was used to my working at odd hours. Living with her in the three-room apartment on Frederiksborgvej was sheer luxury after my stint in the army and the subsequent half-year of living in rented rooms while working in various jobs around the country. On a day-to-day basis, mother and I always got along well. Her outlook was fundamentally optimistic, although she was keenly sensitive toward adversity. She was easily downcast when reality failed to meet her expectations or when financial disaster struck, which was often, but her discouragement was temporary, and of short duration at that. A generous endowment of dynamic energy and vitality combined with her inherently positive outlook were simply too dominant to permit gloom to linger. Her apartment was located well away from downtown but still in the city. Mother loved Copenhagen, and the apartment was ideal in her eyes. It had two rooms of about 170 square feet each, a small kitchen, a smaller entry, and a tiny bathroom with sitz bath, "telephone" shower and terrazzo floor. The kitchen had a wood counter with an enameled cast-iron sink and the indispensable *brødmaskine*, a hand-operated bread cutter without which a housewife could not function, for Danish rye bread cannot be properly cut by hand. Against the opposite wall a sheet metal table carried two gas burners for cooking, while a lower shelf held a gas oven. A door opened onto a three-by-five-foot balcony on the shady side of the building, which mother used most of the year to keep food and milk cool. The two main rooms had a door between them, allowing each of us our own domain with a modicum of privacy. Mine held a divan, a small table and a chair, and a drafting table by the window to take full advantage of available daylight. An old upright piano completed the furnishings. At the age of six my parents had briefly attempted to make me take piano lessons, but I had been dead set against it and unfortunately had won the argument. Older and wiser I had thought better of it though, and had recently started taking lessons after buying the old upright, actually a defunct player piano whose burnt-out mechanism I had removed, using the vacated space in the instrument's bowels to store some pistols and ammunition. Mother's room was on the street side and had a balcony about twice the size of the one off the kitchen. The room contained the furniture she had received for her wedding: a cupboard for dishes, a table, and a bench and four chairs for whose seats she had made slim pads embroidered with wildflowers. In style, the furniture was peasant-modern, painted dark green, and had simple, decorative carvings painted a rust red and showing my parents' initials intertwined on the cupboard's upper door. Belonging to the set, two narrow dishracks above the table displayed some blue-and-white china dishes that had belonged to my grandmother. In the far distant past a seafaring ancestor had brought them from China at a time when this lowest-grade tableware could compete in price with ordinary sand for ballast. Her room also hosted a divan and a chest. In the evening, mother would make up our divans as beds, having stored the bedclothes in the chest during the day. My walls accommodated some book shelves, but hers were decorated with a number of neatly framed prints of peasants in colorful national costumes, interspersed with ten small sconces, products of my grandfather's forge. They carried candles which she happily lit when she felt justified by a major holiday or a dinner party. It happened but rarely, for live candles were expensive as well as slightly impractical, because they always raised the room temperature so as to necessitate opening the balcony door, even in winter. The floors were six-inch wide pine boards, heavily embalmed because Mother at the slightest indication of wear would give them a good coat of marine spar varnish, investing the apartment for a day or so with the smell of a boatyard during spring outfitting. I think she looked upon the varnishing as akin to ritualistic rebirth from which she herself derived restorative therapy. The apartment had central heat by hot water radiators, and even during the war the building stayed reasonably comfortable. Hot water, however, was turned off when the war started and remained off for the five occupation years. I used the public bath, but Mother sponge-washed herself in the manner of *her* mother.

She would get up at six-thirty and call me fifteen minutes later, so I could be in engineering school at eight. As soon as I was out of bed, she put the bed clothes into the chest, elevating the bed to daytime divan status. She would then open her balcony door and retrieve a few items of laundry that had spent the night out there drying on two lines – waist-high, to be out of sight both from the room and from the street below – and water the nasturtiums in the flower boxes mounted on the iron railing. Low morning noises from the building mingled pleasantly with those from the street below, and every ten minutes the street car added a melodious note as the conductor applied his brakes at the nearby stop. Leaving the door open to air out, she would then move through the apartment like a swift but quiet cyclone, putting it in immaculate order. The process took less than ten minutes, and by the time I emerged from the bathroom after washing and shaving, our abode was fresh and inviting, the table in her room set with breakfast: for me, barley porridge cooked in milk; for her, coffee and toast with jam. We ate quickly and in silence, scanning the morning newspaper that had arrived through the front door mailslot about seven o'clock. After putting the dishes away, she would leave and walk to the old stockbroker, Mr. Pedersen, who lived in the same apartment building, six doors from us. On the way she would make a quick dash to the baker and procure for his breakfast three pieces of *morgenbrød*, the incomparable rolls, horns and buns that are indispensable companions to Danish morning coffee. Eliminating coffee and substituting ersatz or herb tea loomed by 1943 as the most outrageous calamity of wartime exigency, and it endowed the rôle of *morgenbrød* with even greater importance on the breakfast table. Early morning visits to a Danish baker become a memory to savor a lifetime. An empyrean fragrance swathes the bakery's immediate environs, reaching its breathtaking climax in the store and drowning the customer in the aroma of moist air waves gently wafting in from the adjoining oven room. When sailing in the Danish archipelago, it is never difficult to find the baker in an island village in the early morning hours. His is the highest smokestack, and if it is dark, one simply follows one's nose. It never fails.

Mr. Pedersen's apartment was identical to ours but more elegantly furnished. The floor was covered with two large Persian rugs, Bokharas. They were slippery to the touch when stroked with the pile, their crimson splendor implicitly protesting the incursion of feet in street shoes, yet welcoming them with luxurious softness. A faint but distinctive scent of African mahogany permeated the suite, soon to be traced by the perceptive visitor to its three main sources: a large and elaborate secretary bookcase together with an oval dining table in the study, and a commode in the bedroom, all beautiful early-eighteenth century pieces. Upon arrival, mother would mete out her cyclonic cleaning, simultaneously preparing Mr. Pedersen's breakfast, then to have a quiet cup of tea while they both listened to the state radio's twenty-minute broadcast of the morning service in Vor Frue Kirke, the city cathedral. Mr. Pedersen had been somewhat of a bon vivant in his younger days, but in his seventies he had turned quite religious and lost no opportunity to put in a good word on God's behalf. Mother was sufficiently indifferent to be tolerant of such endeavor, and she took her tea with a composure of pious reflection suitable to the situation, in reality enjoying this brief moment of relaxation, probably the only one in her day. At the last strophe of the organ, Mr. Pedersen would turn off the radio and Mother would depart to do the day's food shopping.

A few small stores were located on the apartment building's street level, an *ismejeri* (ice dairy) for dairy products and eggs, as well as a *viktualiehandler*, who provided the various delicatessen items Danes lump together under the term *paalæg* (literally: on-lay), things that go into the making of open-face sandwiches. Of the cornucopian choice available despite wartime shortages, mother usually bought some liver paté, herring salad and cheese. The paté was so common and so popular that the government had felt compelled to protect its citizens' palates by specifying minimum content of certain ingredients to insure quality, immediately giving rise to the mass market label *folkeleverpostej* (folk liver paté). Though liberally consumed, the product was held in low esteem, perhaps because masses of consumers dislike being referred to as masses. Young people stuck to the grey-brown paté's classic nickname *udtraadt neger* (squished negro). The herring salad maintained its prewar quality, for the herring supply was less affected than pork liver by war and peace. The salad was bright red, earning thereby its nickname *knust elevatormand* (crushed elevator man). The penchant for colloquial labeling and allegoric reference may strike non-Danes as excessively earthy but gives intimacy and flavor to the language and is inescapable. One of the delicate *wienerbrød* pastries is a case in point. It has a center of yellow vanilla cream with a small red spot of raspberry jam. Its translated nickname: the baker's sore eye. The war's effect on the cheeses was a lowering of their fat content, reviving the traditional popularity of *gammelost* (old cheese), a very sharp, whey-weeping, strong-smelling variety credited with inspiring the old joke about the blind man walking by a cheese store in Adelgade (a prostitute street), politely mumbling, "Good morning, girls."

The butcher and the baker had their stores down the street, a three-minute walk at mother's pace, where she would buy a small quantity of meat, usually veal or pork, and bread, of which Danes ate two kinds, the heavy, dark-brown rye which was used for sandwiches, and the light, white French bread suitable for breakfast and afternoon tea. The latter was shaped into loaves somewhat chubbier than the genuine French baguette for which it was named; it was also lighter of body, causing it to be deemed unusable after a few hours and necessitating that it be purchased daily, whereas the heavy rye could last for weeks. Returning home, mother would start meal preparation. As a rule, the day's hot meal was served at midday. It consisted of two dishes, the second being the main course, normally meat or fish, while the first served the purpose of taking the sharpest edge off one's appetite, doing so with soup or porridge. The soup might be meat broth but could also be a fruit-based sweet soup with prunes, sago and cinnamon. In summer, *tykmælk* was popular, individual dishes of milk cultured overnight after being seeded each with a spoonful of buttermilk and one of cream. Eaten with a sprinkling of grated rye bread and brown sugar it was a traditional dish predating yoghurt by centuries in Scandinavia. Another summer favorite was *rødgrød*, the tongue-twisting junket made from rhubarb, red currants, raspberries or, best of all, black currants and served with cream, the thought of which is enough to moisten the eye and gladden the heart of any Dane. The meal ready, mother would put mine in the haybox and take Mr. Pedersen's to him at noon. The haybox was a wood box lined with hay in which a pot could remain warm for many hours, or finish cooking overnight when it was put there boiling hot. It was a peasant relic of the past that war time rationing of gas and electricity had restored to honorable, if temporary, prominence.

Back in her own apartment, mother would spend the afternoon working on her dog hair spinning project. The spinning wheel occupied a corner of her room, and beside it a large basket held the carefully carded dog hair. She would run her fingers through it to feel the quality of this particular batch, then take up the spinning where she had left off the previous day. Listening to the radio while working, she would fill two spools with single strands twisted left, then combine the strands onto a third spool with a right twist to deprive the resulting yarn of any tendency to kink. It took notable skill to produce a satisfactory end product, but mother always succeeded. The afternoon gone, she would serve Mr. Pedersen his evening meal in his apartment. Customarily, Danes ate *smørrebrød* in the evening, open-face sandwiches, each person making his or her own, and if a beverage was served, it would be beer. Beer goes with food, coffee does not, except in the morning, as everyone knew. By eight she would be home again and spin some more, stopping only briefly to make us tea so we could discuss the day's events, but by eleven she made up our beds, closed the door between our rooms, and we would retire whenever our respective schedules allowed. The daily routine varied in the summer season, when she and Mr. Pedersen in the late afternoon took the streetcar to Tivoli to attend a concert and have dinner in one of the restaurants. And near Christmas she would make *nisser*, small Christmas elves, out of bright-colored yarn and market them through stores selling Christmas decorations. But always, always she was busy; she thrived on the activity, and the activity kept her cheerful. Her daily life contained much laughter and very few tears.

The phone rang and broke my coffee-sipping contemplation. It was Alfred, and his voice was tense despite his attempt to sound casual. "We can expect some fur deliveries quite soon; let us hope they will be good for our business." I knew what he meant. The drop was on for tonight! Without undue noise I put on my dark blue windjacket, retrieved my gun from the player piano, and left the apartment.

* * *

The keystone of the Fascist arch has crumbled and ... the entire Fascist edifice will fall to the ground in ruins, if it has not already so fallen.

Winston Churchill, in the House of Commons

In May Rommel's army, the *Afrika Korps*, met its end in Tunisia, as German and Italian troops surrendered with large quantities of weapons and supplies to the

Anglo-American forces. Having reached their objective in North Africa, the Allies in August launched their first challenge to Axis power in Europe proper. Under General Alexander's overall command, Patton landed with the American Seventh Army and Montgomery with the British Eighth in Sicily. This development caused the Fascist Grand Council to vote to restore constitutional monarchy and a democratic parliament. King Victor Emmanuel placed Mussolini under arrest, handed government to General Badoglio and dissolved the Fascist Party. Peace feelers sprouted toward the West, but the Italians proved no more adept at peacemaking than warmaking.

In the Führer headquarters attention was temporarily diverted from these changes in the Italian scene by developments on the Eastern Front. In the aftermath of their Stalingrad disaster, the Germans had built up their forces for an all-out effort in a salient near the city of Kursk. This pivotal confrontation, the largest armored battle in history, was joined in early July. It ended three weeks later when the Germans had lost one-half of their tank strength.

When Hitler returned his attention to the Italian scene where Badoglio was concluding a secret armistice with the Allies, he furiously ordered a daring airborne raid by a handful of SS troops to snatch Mussolini from his confinement at a mountain hotel high in the Abruzzi Apennines[46] and take him to safety behind German lines in Northern Italy. Here Mussolini proclaimed an Italian Social Republic under his leadership.

Chapter 30 August 1943

*Neither the lords nor the shōgun can be
depended upon to save the country, and
so our only hope lies in grass-roots
heroes.*

Yoshida Shoin

It was eleven in the evening, quiet, balmy and very dark, in Danish latitudes a typical August night with shooting stars, *kornmodsglans*, tracing thin, luminous trails on the horizon. The clearing in the beech forest – probably created as part of some forestry project – was less than two hundred yards long and half as wide. It was covered with grass and knee-high underbrush and was flanked along the perimeter by beech trees, their tall, slender trunks dimly visible as dark pencil lines connecting forest floor with leafy overhead canopy. Our milk truck was parked on a nearby forest road together with two local vehicles. We had four ordinary flashlights with which we were supposed to attract the attention of the pilot, and after arranging the four flashlight bearers in a line indicating the wind direction across the clearing, the rest of us were posted in pairs, spaced out under the trees along the edge of the clearing, and swallowed up by the night. Everything had been carried out quickly and according to plan. Now we could only wait in the almost total silence of the forest setting, the susurrant breeze barely rustling the leaves.

I was sitting together with Aage Schoch, and as he had cheerfully admitted his identity at the preparatory get-together, I asked him after a period of silence what form the German demand had taken, when he was removed as editor of *Nationaltidende*. He chuckled in the darkness, as he outlined how the German control and censorship of the newspapers functioned. Then he quizzed me in turn about my background: how long I had been involved, my education and work, what kind of resistance I thought most effective, or most easy. His questions were incisive, yet carefully skirted certain areas, and I silently admired the ease and fluency with which he extracted my profile without compromising my identity. As a reporter, he had obviously been a real pro.

"Did you train yourself to use a gun?" He posed the question with a note of genuine curiosity, as ordinary people had no touch with firearms.

"At the outset, yes, but later the Danish Army obliged to extend and improve on my training. That seemed only proper and fair, as I use those skills in a national cause."

"Although the government would disagree," he broke in, and we both laughed. Then he continued, "How can we get more people involved in this sort of thing?"

"You tell me. I've been wondering about that for three years."

"Why do you suppose it is so difficult to make people act, when they clearly dislike the Germans?" He sounded tired and just a bit exasperated.

"Have you considered that it could be just plain cowardice?"

"If your opinion of our countrymen is so low, why are you risking your neck for them?" I could sense him smiling in the dark.

"I settled that question long ago. What I do, I'm really doing for my own gratification."

We sat for a minute or two, listening to the wind and the faint sounds of the forest in the summer night. Then he said, "In a final analysis, perhaps we all are."

We lapsed into silence, and as the minutes ticked by, tension became almost palpable along the perimeter of the clearing. I felt my adrenalin rising and my heart beating faster. My excitement was heightened by the fact that flying had been a dream of mine for years, and I had been secretly cherishing a hope of getting myself to England and seeing some of the war through the gunsight of a Spitfire. One of my friends from the conservative youth organization had done just that. Home on a visit in the winter of 1939-40 before Denmark was occupied, he had held us spellbound with tales about his training in Sussex and about getting his wings. It would be easy enough for me to go to Sweden and, once there, I would stand a good chance of getting myself to England. But always there had been considerations of engineering studies or sabotage work that took momentary precedence. The closest I had come to a Spitfire until now was on the rare occasions when one had flashed by in the distance on some reconnaissance mission or other. I wondered whether my English would be good enough for me to go through flight training. In school I had had five years of English, three hours a week, four years of German, and one of French. Foreign language instruction was intensive and effective in Danish public schools, and I had always gotten top marks, so I felt pretty confident that I would be able to handle it. And now I was sitting here, expecting to be almost within reach of the Royal Air Force any minute!

Ellen materialized silently from the darkness behind me. "Do you have a gun?" She used the English word "gun." I did, but shook my head in denial, curious to see how she would react. "But you do know how to use one." It was a statement more than a question, but I nodded. "Take this for tonight." She handed me a handgun and disappeared. It was a .32-caliber Smith & Wesson revolver, a model I had never seen, fairly light, almost delicate. *This is really a lady's gun. It suits you, Ellen.* Examining it, I found that it would take both rimless cartridges and the older rim type, a practical feature when ammunition is hard to come by. My respect for her went up another notch.

It was shortly after 1 a.m. when a distant drone broke my reverie, and the flashlights were flicked on. The aircraft, a Lancaster bomber as far as we could judge, appeared suddenly above the trees toward the northwest, its low altitude making the black silhouette seem inordinately large, and moments later a cluster of parachutes came floating down like ink splotches against the night sky. We combed through the clearing and found where they had landed. Each carried a cylindrical body about the size of a large torpedo which was easily disassembled into sections, each one a barrel-shaped container fitted with a carrying strap and of a weight one man could handle. Georg had one group start gathering the containers, while four of us set about getting rid of the parachutes. The original plan, sinking them in a nearby lake, had to be abandoned for lack of rocks or other heavy material to overcome the natural buoyancy of the inexpertly bundled chutes, and we decided to bury them instead. To get them out of sight, we needed rather large holes, and we were soon digging feverishly. The forest floor was a mass of roots, difficult to penetrate in the dark with insufficient tools, but at length we were able to jam the bundles into the holes and cover them. Then we loaded most of the containers into the two local vehicles for transport to a temporary depot in the area, while two went into our milk truck to go to Copenhagen.

When we were ready to depart, Ellen appeared with the address of our destination in the city. I had forgotten about her Smith & Wesson, but as I was boarding the truck, she said evenly, "My gun, please." There was a faint smile on her face as she added, "You did not mean to keep it, did you?"

The question carried an implication that made my blood rise, so that my reply had a distinct note of resentment. "I have a collection of eleven German handguns, none of them obtained from ladies of my acquaintance."

As I turned to step into the truck, she said quietly, "I'm sorry. I shouldn't have said it the way I did."

Traveling back toward Copenhagen we relaxed after the excitement and physical exertion. I kept thinking about the disheveled state of the burial site but was otherwise supremely content at having taken part in a well-executed mission, and my companions seemed equally pleased. We were heading straight east, looking at the faint light in the predawn sky, and it came suddenly to me what Homer meant when he spoke of dawn searching the eastern sky with fingers of rose. The Quistgaards had with considerate aforethought purchased several packs of sandwiches, and our truck had been allotted one of these. It turned out to be luxurious stuff, including some crab salad which I tasted for the first time. The downtown Copenhagen scene was never complete without some *smørrebrødsvogn* in sight, a sandwich pushcart, even during the occupation years. These small carts sold sandwiches, the open-face, elaborate variety on thin half-slices of heavy, dark rye. Danes considered them one of civilization's necessities, and they were sold already packed and ready to go, the supply being replaced and renewed three times daily to assure the customer of getting a fresh product. The price indicated the content: four sandwiches for one krone would have spreads of liverpaste, salami and cheese. At a higher price, Italian salad and grilled cod roe might appear, and at the top price perhaps shrimp in mayonnaise or crab salad. My mother prepared my daily lunch sandwiches, so I had only once tried the purchased kind, and then only the cheapest. As the milk truck rattled back toward the city, we shared and consumed the unaccustomed luxury with gusto and decided that the crab salad provided a fitting finis to a well-spent night.

We got back on the city streets at the time when milk trucks properly should be out and about, and in the cellar of our destination we unpacked some of the containers and stared with awe and glee at the goods spread out before us. There were Sten submachine guns, which we saw for the first time; Albion revolvers and ammunition; plastique and 808 explosives; detonators with "pencils" for delayed action; and a multitude of other devices dreamed up by British ingenuity, such as a compression detonator cap to be placed on a railroad track to set off an explosive charge when a train wheel ran over it. We laughed with sheer joy at our sudden wealth.

I was intrigued by the Sten gun which was a far cry from the Suomi machine pistol I had trained on at the *Kornetskole*. The Suomi had a handsome wood stock and all its parts were carefully machined, so that the weapon exuded high-grade craftsmanship. The Sten looked like something put together from scrap with minimal tools in an amateur's workshop. It was evident, however, that the barrel was precisely machined, and I soon found out that its shooting qualities left little to be desired.

The plastique explosive resembled a child's modeling clay. A charge of it could be pressed onto the item to be blown apart, such as a door lock, or a vehicle engine, or a railroad rail. It was virtually odorless and could not be set off by incineration or rough handling, only by a detonator, a small metal tube a couple of inches long with a diameter of a pencil, open in one end. The detonator itself could be triggered by fire through insertion of a fuse in its open end or by sliding it into a "pencil." The pencil was a simple but clever device to enable us to delay detonation of a bomb by as little as twenty minutes or as much as twenty-four hours. It was color-coded and could be activated by squeezing the soft metal exterior, thereby breaking a vial of acid in the pencil's interior. The acid would then eat through a wire constraining a spring-loaded firing pin. The released firing pin would set off the detonator charge which in turn would detonate the main charge. The 808 explosive came in the shape of sticks the size of small sausages with the consistency of nearly solid gelatin and a distinctive odor reminiscent of marzipan. Besides all these paraphernalia our British benefactors had thoughtfully included a few packs of cigarettes! We left the cellar at breakfast time, impressed and delighted beyond description.

Two days later, worry drove me back to the hill. Had the parachutes been sufficiently hidden by our hurried efforts in darkness? This time I made the trip by bicycle in the early afternoon to be able to check the site in the revealing light of the sun. After approaching the area with due caution, I found that two of the bundles in fact did need better cover and set about repacking and compressing them to less bulk. Seeing a chute for the first time in daylight, I was struck by the delicate beauty of the silk which was camouflage dyed in rich colors of olive, gold and rust. Fabrics like this had long since been drained from merchants' shelves in the austere wartime economy, and it seemed to me the most exquisite material I had ever beheld. Suddenly deciding to keep a spectacular memento, I cut out a couple of the larger sections and rolled them into a small bundle. Then I dug the holes deeper and finished burying the chutes, camouflaged the site, and returned to Copenhagen.

The next day I took the silk to my sister's seamstress and instructed her to make Angla a dress from it. The seamstress also admired the silk, but I warned her to keep the matter to herself and to show the material to no one.

* * *

If we do not eliminate the evil called sabotage against the German Wehrmacht, it will be questionable whether we will be permitted to retain our own justice system.

Vilhelm Buhl, Danish Prime Minister

The drop of stuff that so delighted us that early morning in the Copenhagen cellar was the first to arrive on the island of Zealand. The developments that had led up to this point reflected the interactions between the situation in Denmark and the Allied conduct of the war, notably their support of resistance forces.

To an objective observer, Denmark was a gentle, civilized nation moving slowly – agonizingly slowly – toward an attitude vastly unfamiliar. Without any real precedent in European history, the German "peace occupation" of the country

193

Werner Best (1903-1989), German plenipotentiary in Denmark 1942-1945. At the surrender, he was arrested and in 1948 sentenced to death for ordering terror actions. The Danish supreme Court commuted the sentence to 12 years in prison. He was released and expelled in 1951. (Not to be confused with Dr. Werner Best, minister in Hesse 1970-73.)

had initially been just that: a peaceful occupation, satisfactory from the German point of view. The swift defeat of France and the British escape at Dunkerque had made deep impressions on the Danish public and was seen by many as validation of the Danish government's refusal to fight the inevitable, but the subsequent German failure in the aerial Battle of Britain gave rise to cautious optimism that Britain might hold out and in time defeat Nazism. In these circumstances the four million Danes sought solace and emotional sustenance by delving into their national past, by demonstrating support for the king, and by joining in communal activities from song meetings to hiking and field exercises.

At the beginning of the occupation, King Christian had appointed as Foreign Minister Erik Scavenius, a man of considerable experience who was bent on cooperation which he considered imperative due to Denmark's geographic and economic position in the shadow of Germany. The government accordingly embarked on a policy of economic cooperation, expecting in return to keep political independence. For a while it appeared to succeed, but ever-escalating German demands continually jeopardized the relationship.

In January of 1941 the Germans demanded twelve torpedo boats from the small Danish fleet. Negotiations reduced the number to eight, and these were handed over.[47] After the German attack on the Soviet Union, the Danish government was pressured into outlawing all Communist activity. The Russian campaign also encouraged the small and politically insignificant Danish Nazi party to solicit recruits for *Frikorps Danmark*, a volunteer battalion that was dispatched to the Eastern Front as a unit of the Waffen SS.

Although the Germans contrived to obscure the extent of the economic drain on the country, the foregoing and other events provoked Danish public opinion to increasing resentment toward the occupiers. Sporadic efforts at sabotage by a very small number of individuals who took matters into their own hands, were in the early occupation period ineffectual and vehemently condemned by the government, the police, and the general public. But no population group accustomed to the ways of freedom and democracy can long endure totalitarian overlordship without irritation, resentment, and eventual resistance. The policy of concession to German demands clearly brought only further demands. Replacement of the relatively well-behaved initial occupation troops with battle-hardened soldiers from the Eastern Front led to incidents of violence, while a steady decline in living standards galled wage earners. As time went by, acts of sabotage no longer seemed unreasonable, and after the slow start, resistance grew to become by the spring of 1943 a thorn in the flesh of the occupying power.

Workers in enterprises critical to the Germans rediscovered striking as a means of expressing dissatisfaction with the status quo. Introduction of German sabotage guards in some shipyards caused a series of strikes which spread to other groups in several cities, while concurrently the monthly cases of sabotage increased from 16 in January to 220 in August,[48] effectively undermining the policy of cooperation.

The Germans reacted nervously by ordering curfews in some cities. Ignoring the orders, people responded by street demonstrations and numberless street brawls with German soldiers. Danish authorities tried frantically to calm the situation but to no avail, exposing a widening gap between government and people. Caught in an ambiguous dilemma the police began to side with the street demonstrators. Under orders from Berlin the German administrator in Denmark, Dr. Werner Best, in August issued an ultimatum: the Danish Government must prohibit assembly and strikes; enforce curfews and German-monitored censorship; establish special courts and the death penalty for sabotage.[49]

The Government refused.

On 29 August came the irreparable breakdown of the Danish policy of half-hearted cooperation at the point of a gun. The date also marked the end of legally constituted government in the country. During the night German troops attacked and disarmed the small Danish military contingents they had allowed to exist. In a series of brief skirmishes 23 Danish soldiers were killed. A few Navy ships escaped to Sweden; the rest were scuttled by their crews. The following day the German military commander, General von Hanneken, formally assumed power. Referring to the Haag Convention of 1907, he declared a state of emergency, and declared King and Government to be superceded and replaced as functioning entities. On second thought, he decreed that the Danish Government must direct all civil servants to continue their work, and that it must then resign. The Cabinet patiently pointed out that the Haag Convention did not apply because no state of war had been declared or existed; that it was not

Hermann von Hanneken (1890-1981), German infantry general commanding the German forces in Denmark from 1942 to 1945. On 29 August 1943 he forced a German takeover of all governmental power. After the war, the Copenhagen city court sentenced him to an eight-year prison term, but on appeal he was acquitted and expelled.

inclined to order the civil service to continue, being anyway powerless to do so as it had been forcibly replaced; and that there was no constitutional provision allowing it to resign under these circumstances. After further deliberation the Cabinet requested from the King permission to resign. The King chose not to reply. Thus, legal government was in limbo, and continuance of actual day-to-day administration fell to the civil service department heads. Incredulous at the idea of law prevailing in the face of raw power General von Hanneken was for the moment stymied.

In the larger scheme of things, the Danish situation had come about under the influence of numerous factors, perhaps the foremost being the continued fighting of the Allies and the apparent reversal of German conquest, but the profound differences between German mentality and Danish in any event were too great to permit easy coexistence. With resentment blossoming into resistance, the British SOE (Special Operations Executive)[50] after a fitful start began in 1943 a serious program to put teeth into the fledgling Danish sabotage by aerial drops of weapons and explosives. The idea made sense, for the cost of getting weapons and explosives into the hands of local saboteurs and have them destroy a given target was obviously much less than that of going after the same target with conventional means, i.e. bombs carried by aircraft. The night missions to the drop zones were flown by the Royal Air Force,[51] sometimes by pilots of the Free Polish Airforce, a branch of RAF created from pilots escaped to the Allied side after Poland's defeat. Flying a bomber across the North Sea, traversing Jutland and the Danish islands at low altitude to find a tiny forest clearing without any beacons for guidance or crosscheck was an outstanding navigational feat, and the high rate of success testifies to the skill of the pilots.

While empowering saboteurs to diminish in sundry ways the enemy's war-making potential, the Royal Air Force itself went after the German industrial base with a vengeance. By the summer of '43, the British Bomber Command had come a long way since the days when a few of its planes, in a feeble retaliation for the London Blitz, had sent Soviet and Nazi negotiators into Berlin shelters.[52] Bomber Command under Air Marshal Harris had perfected its weaponry and its techniques of death and destruction to a degree never before contemplated in the history of warfare. On the night of 24-25 July, Bomber Command commenced operation *Gomorrah*, a series of five raids in which precisely timed waves of hundreds of specialized bombers successively dropped markers, incendiaries, parachute mines, and blockbusters. The resulting fires developed to an unprecedented magnitude, generating temperatures over 1,800 degrees Fahrenheit, causing spontaneous combustion of street pavement, consuming oxygen to suffocate people in their shelters, and creating winds up to 150 mph that carried debris and sparks to spread the fire yet further, until it was a monster conflagration like nothing ever seen by man.

Chapter 31 September 1943

*A desire to resist oppression is inculcated
in the nature of man.*

Tacitus

It was near ten in the evening, pitch dark and with that autumn coolness one expects in Denmark by the middle of September. For our purposes, a perfect night, and we felt this was going to be good, an order of magnitude better than anything we had done before. With nothing better than matches to work with, our only means of destruction had been fire, and not everything will burn. But now, in possession of the coveted explosives all good saboteurs dream about, we had elevated our sights. As our first target for a *real* bomb, we had selected the Ruko factory.[53] Located in the northern part of Copenhagen, the company had been a peacetime manufacturer of door and window hardware, locksets, hinges and such. It was now producing miscellaneous small items for the German military, and it was protected by *sabotagevagter*, Danish armed guards, who had recently appeared on the scene to protect installations the authorities deemed vulnerable. To avoid dealing with them, we had devised what we thought to be an elegant artifice rather than a heavy-handed frontal assault. Discreet reconnaissance had established that the factory's heating plant was shut down for the summer, and also that it was located in the same building as the power plant. We had decided therefore to lower our bomb down the chimney stack and into the heating unit, aiming to blow the entire powerhouse to bits.

Besides Erik, Alfred and myself our little group included Svend-Aage Harpsø who had hatched a novel idea to deliver the bomb. The powerhouse was situated next to a somewhat taller apartment building, and Svend-Aage insisted that we could swing the bomb like a pendulum from that building's roof and neatly drop it into the chimney. To give it a try, we made our way to the roof of the apartment building, carrying the bomb which was about the size of a basketball.

Svend-Aage brought a long line to which he carefully tied the bomb and lowered it toward the powerhouse chimney three stories below to start the pendulum motion. His scheme had sounded good in theory, but in practice it turned out to be impossible to make the pendulum swing at the necessary angle to the wall. Svend-Aage sweated and cursed through several futile attempts while the rest of us, choking with laughter, chided him mercilessly. At length we decided instead to get onto the powerhouse roof itself, which was accessible over a fourteen-foot wall from the city street.

Back at ground level Alfred and Svend-Aage went in search of a ladder and returned a while later with one of sufficient length, which they placed against the wall. It reached almost to the top, fourteen feet above the sidewalk. The four of us climbed quickly, swung ourselves over the wall and onto the flat roof of the factory building, and hauled the ladder up to prevent a passing pedestrian from seeing it and getting nosy.

Leaving Alfred with the ladder to be ready for an abrupt retreat, if called for, the rest of us proceeded to jump onto the adjacent powerhouse roof and reached the chimney stack which rose eight feet above the roof surface. With some effort I boosted Erik to the top of the stack, and Svend-Aage handed him the bomb which was wrapped in burlap, still with the line attached. Erik planted a twenty-minute delay detonator through the burlap into the explosive and slowly lowered the bomb down the stack. When it reached bottom, we made our way back to Alfred, lowered the ladder to the street again, and climbed back down. Alfred and Svend-Aage returned the ladder to the yard where they had taken it, while Erik and I went to the nearest public telephone booth and called the plant with a warning for everyone to get out.

As the nightshift workers left the factory through the main gate on the opposite side of the block from where we had made our approach, the four of us sat down in a beer joint several blocks away counting down the remaining couple of minutes. On time a powerful WHOOMP shook the building. The barmaid and the few patrons rushed to the door to look and listen in the darkness, while we discreetly toasted the removal of one tiny supply source of the Wehrmacht, marvelling at the ease of doing sabotage with the help of modern technology.

* * *

The sure way to miss success
is to miss the opportunity.

Chasles

The BBC in London kept us somewhat informed about Allied military activity in which the Soviets on the ground and the British in the air were throwing their weight against German hegemony in Europe. By contrast, events on more distant battlefields received almost no attention, nor could we estimate their importance. Across the vastness of the Pacific, America's growing military strength had checked the seemingly irresistible Japanese advance and had gone on the offensive. The first objective became the island of Guadalcanal in the southern Solomons. After a six-month battle the Japanese in February 1943 succeeded in pulling out 10,000 of the more than 40,000 troops they had committed. By then the tide of war had changed in North Africa and on the Eastern Front. The Japanese had lost the strategic opportunity of driving through the Indian Ocean and linking up with their German allies when Rommel stood at the gates of Egypt. The significance of Guadalcanal and its meaning for events in Europe should be seen in this perspective, as the war had become truly global.[54]

Chapter 32   September 1943

One man in a thousand, says Solomon,
Will stick to you like a brother.

Kipling

It was obvious even to my uncritical eye that the office was in a choice location. The third floor windows faced Gammelstrand, a street along the inner city canal, and on the other side Christiansborg Castle towered beyond a broad expanse of stone pavement, old trees and some monuments. Two secretaries scurried about, and newspapers were spread in greater or lesser disorder everywhere, not surprising, for this was the headquarters building of *Nationaltidende*, Copenhagen's second largest daily.

Through several intermediaries – nobody ever knew the ephemeral lines of grapevine in such matters – I had been asked to help organize the printing of *Hjemmefronten*, The Home Front, an underground newssheet that had mushroomed to impressive print runs. I was just beginning to realize that this explosive growth was due in large measure to the professional touch of the man slouched in a chair across the desk from me. His name was Niels Jørgensen, a *Nationaltidende* reporter and, as I was also just learning, the driving force behind *Hjemmefronten* and of the small organization of the same name which was producing and distributing it.[55] He was a tall, quiet-spoken man with steely grey eyes, an air of detached objectivity, and a slight tendency to overweight. I liked him, something I considered paramount in this activity. Niels Jørgensen explained in a few sentences that this was where *Hjemmefronten* was written but that it was produced elsewhere "in various places, and we try to make print runs of at least 15,000." He told me just enough to put me sufficiently in the picture, but offered no extraneous information, no small talk. I liked that too. In a corner of the room stood a man, slightly older than I, whom Niels had introduced simply as "Thies." He was tall and lean with grey-green eyes and dark hair, a combination most women would have found handsome, and was slouched against the wall with a bored expression on his face.

During the summer, steadily increasing sabotage had indicated that Hitler's policy of placating the Danes was failing, and the Germans had decided to replace conciliation with brute force. Once an occupying power takes this step, the course cannot easily be reversed later, because resentment and stubborn resistance build up exponentially with acts of suppression. My own reaction was probably typical, when in August the first execution took place. Reading the terse newspaper announcement, I had been momentarily stunned at the thought. The guy they shot was my age! And he hadn't done anything I hadn't done. *Why, the bastards!!* I had resolved then and there to avenge him. But before I could do anything to follow up the Ruko affair, our first bombing, the Germans had struck again. On 29 August the Wehrmacht had attacked without warning the small contingents of Danish military personnel still in service. The units were easily overrun and disarmed, though not without bloodshed. The papers did not announce losses, but from the Langelinie promenade several scuttled naval ships were in plain view, their stacks above water in mute defiance to the German attempt to seize them. The German actions had solidified the resistance, and groups began to organize on a wider scale. Until now, I had carried out my private war alone, with the exceptions of the parachute drop and occasional ad hoc ventures with three or four trusted friends. Instinct as well as common sense reinforced by experience told me that, so long as I was by myself, only a fluke accident could give me away. Besides, I liked working alone. On the other hand, underground news service, receipt of drops, weapons instruction, actions against larger targets, and much else required cooperation and organization. If properly organized, groups could obviously be far more effective than the sum of their members. All this became clear to me in the aftermath of 29 August, and when the request came to lend assistance to the *Hjemmefronten* group, that realization had propelled me to the office where I was now. Niels Jørgensen looked at me and motioned toward Thies.

"It would be a lot of help if you two could find a place to print this issue I am just finishing writing."

Thies and I looked at each other. As our eyes met for a brief moment, each of us tried to size up the other, estimating to what extent he would be willing to depend on this perfect stranger. Then we turned to Niels Jørgensen and simultaneously nodded consent, with assumed indifference.

At midnight two days later, Thies and I approached a printing shop by the name of *Westend* in a small pickup truck. Located in a half-basement near the central railroad station, it was a firm Thies knew from personal contact as he had done repair work on its printing presses, and it was protected by a couple of sabotage guards. I used a simple, direct approach, knocked on the door, and when a guard opened, stuck a gun in his ribs and told him and his buddy to hand over their guns *now*, which they meekly did. Then we herded the guards together with the half-score night shift employees into a back room where I could keep an eye on them, while Thies expertly typeset and printed 32,000 copies of the newssheet from the draft Niels Jørgensen had written. At 3 a.m. we loaded the edition on the pickup, gave each of the people in the back room a copy, warning them not to give our descriptions to the police, and disappeared into the city.

Thus began between Thies and me a close cooperation that developed into a lifelong friendship, for Thies turned out to be that one man in a thousand who, in Solomon's words, would stick to me like a brother. His name was actually Carlo Marqvard Thomsen, but early in his resistance work he had relieved a Danish Nazi by the name of Poul Thiessen of his German *Ausweiss*, a sort of general ID, after knocking him out in a bar fight. Using the ID for a while, Thies got used to the name and kept its shortened version as his cover name. Thies proved to be the ideal partner on sabotage and other such missions. A printing press mechanic by trade, he was an exceptionally fine craftsman and had intimate knowledge of just about every printing press in Copenhagen. He was also a good shot, a skilled driver, and absolutely unflappable under stress. He possessed an unlimited supply of bad jokes, terrible puns, and expressions and sayings so strange that I have heard them from no other human being. We were a good match, for I was a responsive and uncritical audience, even to the extent of endangering the two of us by often being unable to suppress laughter in some tight spot if Thies dead-panned a comment about the face of a German or the capability of some guard we were about to pounce on. Like myself, he had started his own war early in 1940, twice sabotaging the printing press of *Fædrelandet*, organ of the Danish Nazi Party.

Our activity ranged from printing of *Hjemmefronten* newssheets to sabotage, with considerable time and effort devoted to moving caches of weapons and explosives from one hiding place to another, usually one short jump ahead of the Germans.[56] We rarely needed resort to shooting, although on some occasions it became unavoidable, for the tempo and tenor of resistance were gaining momentum, as sabotage became more effective as well as more dangerous. The first such instance occurred one very early morning on Sdr. Fasanvej, a street in the northwestern outskirts of the city. We were driving in Thies' old car, a convertible Adler *Junior* with a fake operating permit, and found ourselves being pursued by a Wehrmacht car. The streets were deserted and allowed an unimpeded race which soon proved itself unequal, for though Thies kept his car in good mechanical shape and well tuned, the Germans drove an Opel *Kapitän*, a faster vehicle by far. We had with us in the car a Suomi machine pistol, a favorite weapon of mine from the days at the *Kornetskole*. As we rounded a corner Thies slowed down just enough to make the Adler into a stable platform, and I gave the pursuer a burst that riddled the engine and front tires. The *Kapitän* slewed out of control, leveled a cast iron streetcar stop and came to a halt half onto the sidewalk. "You slowed them down all right," Thies commented, deadpan, as he glanced in the rearview mirror at the steaming wreck receding out of sight.

On the lighter side we supplemented when time permitted the printed news with some unscheduled movie theater work to taunt the Nazis and appeal to the Danish sense of humor. Armed with a phonograph record of war news obtained from BBC broadcasts, and a slide showing a derisive cartoon of Hitler with a fly on his nose, we would enter a theater's projection room just before the performance, when advertising slides were being shown on the screen. The surprised audience suddenly saw our Hitler cartoon appear on the screen and was treated to a few minutes of uncensored news from the various battlefronts.

* * *

Knowledge is more than equivalent to force.

Samuel Johnson

The priceless gift of Polish cryptological Enigma hardware and data enabled the British in the spring of 1940 to set up a new intelligence system in Bletchley Park, north of London. It comprised a growing group of top-notch people, developing its own sources of information and an organization for processing and disseminating it. The system became known as Ultra and proved of incalculable value to the Allied military leadership, remaining a well-guarded secret never penetrated or suspected by the Germans. The relationship among the Allies opposing Hitler presents an intriguing aspect of World War Two, only one facet of which was the pooling of intelligence. Whereas the Russians never overcame their innate distrust of the democracies, a close cooperation based on mutual respect and good faith was born between the Anglo-American Allies even before America became a belligerent. In August of 1941,[57] Churchill and Roosevelt met on a battleship in Placentia Bay off Newfoundland, their first wartime meeting. In a joint declaration the two leaders pledged their countries to promote self-government for all peoples, freedom of travel, economic cooperation, and disarming of aggressor nations.[58]

After Pearl Harbor, when America in a famous phrase of Churchill's began "girding its loins" for the struggle ahead, top British and American leaders met in Washington for what became known as the Arcadia Conference, both to coordinate current Allied plans and to agree on longer-range strategy. The Russians were not willing to meet in joint planning and had made demands for recognition of their pre-June 1941 territorial gains. The British and Americans were not eager in that manner to reward the Soviets for what in their eyes was simple aggression. They chose to defer discussion on the subject and instead to respond to the insistent pleas from Moscow for material supplies.[59] Allied leaders followed up with a series of further meetings in the course of 1943, selecting Casablanca in January, Quebec in August, and Teheran in November. Stalin attended the Teheran meeting, but Russian suspicion of the democracies made Soviet cooperation rare and at best half-hearted, whereas the Anglo-American Alliance endured.

The wholehearted cooperation between the Western Allies to secure victory could not be matched or even approached by their adversaries. Under a Tripartite Pact established in 1940, Germany, Italy and Japan had set up a military commission for joint planning which had proven good for a few publicity pictures but not much more. Two fundamental reasons for the inability of Germany and Japan to plan and act in concert stood out in all their relations. One was Japanese failure to comprehend the primary German fascination with race and the extent to which it skewed German perception of the world. The other was their profound differences in control of the military and in conduct of the war. In Germany, control was in the hands of one single civilian, Hitler, who was accountable to no one. In Japan, control of the military rested within the military itself, with the politicians being effectively powerless while the army and navy cliques vied for primacy. Add to this the two countries' isolation from each other in geography as well as in culture, and their failure to act in harmony should not be surprising.[60]

Although BBC's news from London gave occasional mention of the Allied meetings, we in the resistance were far more interested in the concrete military operations, the movements of front lines. The Allied cooperation's profound influence on the conduct of the war, its salutary results on the battlefields, and the enemy's lack thereof, eluded us totally.

Chapter 33   October 1943

The best part of a good man's life
His little, nameless unremembered acts
Of kindness and of love.

William Wordsworth

Thies looked at me over the edge of his glass.

"The easiest, of course, would be to gather them here and ship them out from Lynettehavnen."

He was talking about the Jews. Two nights earlier the Germans had sprung an action to arrest all of Denmark's Jews and ship them away to ... nobody was quite sure just where. The action had evidently not been very successful, for it had netted relatively few, although we could not estimate how many. What we did know was that Jews at the moment were hidden away in homes and other places, desperately searching for ways to get out of Gestapo's reach. The obvious next step was to get them out of the country by moving them to convenient points on the coast, lining up transportation, and sending them to safety in Sweden.[61]

Thies' remark made some sense. Lynettehavnen was a secluded section of the vast Copenhagen harbor complex, and I was aware of at least one fisherman operating out of there who was willing to take "special passengers" when the need arose. The place could be quickly reached from the city's thousand hiding places, far better than transporting people up the coast toward Elsinore and exposing them in less populated surroundings. But I was also aware that the Germans were at top alert, probably trying to make up for their recent lack of success.

"Sure," I agreed, "and how would certain fishing skippers in Lynettehavnen feel about having numbers of people trooping out there, wandering around, looking lost and asking for passage to Sweden?" We both laughed at the thought.

We were having a beer in a bistro near *Nationaltidende,* discussing what might be done to foul the German efforts in this sudden people hunt. From our window seats we could see a nearby stop for the canal boats where at intervals passengers got on and off. The inner city of Copenhagen is surrounded by canals which in the Middle Ages served as part of the town's defense. They connect to the harbor and were now serving as watery avenues for a few motor boats supplementing the public transportation system. Using the canals much as streetcars used the streets, and charging the same fare, the canal boats in a small way helped offset the transportation shortfall caused by absence of private motor vehicle traffic. As Thies was watching two people board one of the boats, he pensively gave vent to another idea.

"You know, if we could grab one of the canal boats, that would be the perfect transport to take a batch of them to Lynettehavnen, directly to the fishing boat."

Now, that had some merit, so I added, "And we could put out the word and collect them right over there in front of *Nationaltidende!*"

Thies' laughter was flat, no modulation in pitch or volume, and even when he laughed, his face never lost its expression of enigmatic boredom.

"I wonder who would have the balls to do something like that, right under Gestapo's noses?"

I thought, perhaps for the hundredth time, that the reason we worked so well together was that we thought along similar lines and always recognized a good scheme. Finishing our beer, we worked out the details of the plan.

Tantalizingly visible in clear weather, the Swedish solution of last resort stood ever beckoning on the horizon. Between Sweden and the Danish island of Zealand the strait called The Sound forms a liquid ribbon in the north-south direction. The two countries were not always divided along this line. In Viking times, a thousand years ago, Danish kings included all of southern Sweden in their domain, but later monarchs with more ambition than ability could not keep the realm together, and since 1660 the Swedes have themselves ruled the area they possess today. It is their good fortune that their country – in pronounced contrast to Denmark – is blessed with the kind of borders that make for pleasant neighborly relations. Toward the east and south the Baltic beaches, toward the west the Sound and Kattegat, draw natural maritime borders to their kingdom. In the northwest their long frontier with Norway follows mountain ridges that discourage borderland friction. The remaining piece enclosing the country is the border with Finland. That stretch is in the Lapland region north of the arctic circle, an area coveted only by the nomadic Laps. In the greater scheme of international relations Sweden can therefore enjoy freedom from the kind of territorial squabbles that have plagued the rest of Europe since time immemorial.

At its southern end the Sound spreads fifteen miles of blue water between Copenhagen and the Swedish city of Malmö, but in the north it narrows to

Small commercial fishing craft such as these became instrumental in providing escape to Sweden for Jews as well as others sought by the Gestapo. Operating from tiny harbors on the many miles of Danish coastline, fishermen who were intimately familiar with their home waters proved adept in eluding German patrols.

barely two miles where it separates Elsinore from the Swedish city of Hälsingborg. At the German incursion, traffic of goods and people was immediately blocked between occupied Denmark and free and neutral Sweden. The greatest efforts to enforce the closure focused on the Sound, especially the sea lanes serving Copenhagen harbor. A total ban on shipping in and out of the capital had been deemed impractical, but traffic had been severely reduced. In short order a need arose to use Sweden as a refuge for people who had incurred the wrath of the German occupiers. With resistance becoming more common, a number of underground groups had evolved with the specialty of facilitating illegal transport of the growing number of persons in imminent danger of arrest and unable to endure the strain of a cat-and-mouse game with the Gestapo. Thies and I kept out of direct involvement with this unique branch of illegal activity, as our interests reached elsewhere, but we had contacts to a number of skippers and boat owners willing to help.

I stood at the iron railing bordering the canal and watched a family of four arrive and apprehensively sit down some fifty feet away on the bench for waiting passengers. The man was clutching a pair of gloves in his left hand, our recognition sign. The woman was talking to their two children, barely of school age, who each carried a school bag. Clever, I thought, for we had given strict instructions not to carry suitcases, a sure giveaway to a German observer. The school bags were natural, however, and probably held a few necessities. The family looked for all the world to be ordinary citizens, which indeed they were, waiting for a canal boat as part of the normal daily street scene.

When we had set about putting our evacuation plan into action, we found that we were far from the only ones addressing this task, though no competition appeared for our particular method. We had obtained through *Hjemmefronten* a boat sufficiently like the regular canal boats,[62] and for two days now we had shepherded Jews in groups of a dozen or fewer. A retired harbor pilot had proven willing to serve as skipper, the perfect person for the job. This was to be our last run. Intuition told us that two days should be the limit, and we both felt that we had developed some judgment as to how far to stretch our luck. The previous day, a German deserter had through mysterious channels been recommended for escape, and he had left with one of the groups. When screening him in a preliminary chat, we had noticed that he was about Thies' size, so we had relieved him of his uniform which we thought might come in handy some day. The man had been only too willing to put on some of Thies' old clothes.

I was contemplating how easy and smooth this project had turned out to be. In the distance Thies was approaching with three more people, and a minute later they were all waiting uneasily on the bench. Our boat hove into sight around a bend in the canal, and while we watched it approach, Thies came over to me and lit a cigarette. "Last batch," he mumbled. I nodded. As the boat put in to the landing below us, I looked at the people on the bench, then turned and spat in the water. That was our stipulated signal to indicate that this was the boat they should take. They all got up, trooped down the stone steps to the landing and aboard, the children chattering excitedly about the harbor tour they had been told they were taking. A moment later, they were all gone.

* * *

I must ask you to rid yourselves of all feelings of pity. We must annihilate the Jews.

Hans Frank, Statthalter in Poland

From the very beginning of Nazism, Hitler blamed an imaginary international Jewish conspiracy for just about every ill afflicting the Vaterland. Anti-Semitism was nothing new, of course.[63] A flame of tribal animosity that Christianity often has opted to fan rather than extinguish, it has historically persevered to various degrees in most countries of Christendom, but under the Nazis it became particularly indurated. In 1941 Hitler took the ultimate step by ordering the *Endlösung*, the Final Solution: extermination of Jews everywhere, actual genocide.[64] The timing coincided with a reduction in the euthanasia program. The reduction may have been caused by some public unrest and a denunciation of the murders by Clemens August Count von Galen, Bishop of Munster, in a church sermon in August 1941 that President Roosevelt referred to as "a splendid and brave thing."[65] But it may also have derived from the simple fact that established goals had been reached. Between 100,000 and 200,000 old, infirm and disabled Germans, including many war veterans, had been put to death by their fellow citizens. From this process, Germany now turned its trained core of experts in bureaucratically organized mass murder to the far greater task of annihilating the Jews of Europe.

Deportation of Jews to killing centers in Eastern Europe started in October of 1941. In the first year after the attack on the Soviet Union, one and a quarter million Jews, men, women and children, were put to death, and the pace of the program was accelerating. The mass murder program was not known at the time in Denmark (or elsewhere), but it was known that the Jews were being taken to concentration camps for no other reason than their ancestry, and that sufficed for the Danes to oppose the German plans.

After the August breakdown of Danish cooperation, the authorities in Berlin no longer felt any restraint from consideration of local sentiment and decided it was high time to eliminate Denmark's Jews. When the action was sprung during the night of 1-2 October, it netted only two hundred out of the country's seven thousand Jews. The rest had gone underground, hidden by friends and neighbors. The reason for the initial failure was that some highly placed German officials with more conscience than Nazi loyalty had leaked to Danish acquaintances that an action against the Jews was imminent. In response to the ensuing whispered information about the upcoming people hunt, a loose network came into being almost overnight to hide the Jews. The rescue effort involved many small resistance groups but was implemented on a large scale by ordinary citizens, people who would never have thought of undertaking sabotage but who rallied to this humanitarian cause without hesitation.

Despite their low numbers in Denmark as compared with many other European countries, the Jews' culture of diligence and learning had placed them in prominent positions in several fields. The best known individual was probably Niels Bohr, the atomic physicist, who was spirited out of the country and reached the United States to take part in the Manhattan Project. But locally people noticed immediately the loss of musicians, entertainers and actors such as Gerda and Ulrik Neuman, and Børge Rosenbaum.[66]

Although Thies and I had fun doing our small part, we actually paid little attention to the evacuation at the time; it was just a momentary distraction from what we mistakenly thought of as more urgent endeavors. Only years later did we learn that other countries, among them the United States, had shown a very different attitude in the Jews' hour of need. We were also surprised to find out that the Nazis had met with substantial success in a similar action in Norway, where many people actually assisted the Germans. Although thousands of decent Norwegians helped their Jewish compatriots, a dismaying number, people who would otherwise not have helped the Germans, continued a long tradition of anti-Semitism by taking part in registering, identifying, and handing over Jews to the German authorities.[67] This blot on the Norwegians' war record is regrettable, for they otherwise acted well, and we in the Danish resistance could have taken many a lesson from them, had there been any real contact between us at the time.

In retrospect, the quiet, unanimous Danish response in this particular affair is a bright spot in the occupation ordeal. The Danes undeniably lacked martial qualities, but they were not short on human decency and compassion.

Chapter 34 November 1943

*Boldness is ever blind, for it sees not
dangers and inconveniences; whence it
is bad in council though good in
execution.*

Bacon

It was almost ten in the evening as our group converged from various directions on the portal of an apartment house in Bredgade. Erik and I arrived together, each of us carrying besides our guns a small fire starter that we intended to field test tonight. Georg Quistgaard had parcelled out some of the material we had received in the parachute drop from England, and our share contained among other items a quantity of the fire starters. They were objects the size of a Havana cigar but larger around the middle, and they had a dab of sulphur at one end, so they could be lit like a match by rubbing on a matchbox striking surface. We had chosen as a suitable target a German marine administrative center located on the third floor of an elegant apartment house in the old Bredgade section of the inner city. The reason for this particular choice was a piece of incidental intelligence Alfred had picked up from a fishing skipper plying the Baltic fishing grounds. The man had reported that the Germans were conducting submarine exercises of some sort in the eastern Baltic. We knew from BBC that the Battle of the Atlantic was still being fought tooth and nail, and we therefore thought it a good idea to aim this small effort at the Kriegsmarine. Besides, the recent German action that had precipitated scuttling the Danish navy still rankled. Alfred was tied down listening for radio messages, but Erik and I had lined up a small team for the job, eight in all, counting ourselves. As we entered the portal, the other six appeared within seconds, and we ascended the stairway quietly to the third-floor landing. Erik and I stood side-by-side with our noses almost touching the door, the team getting tightly into position behind us.

It flashed through my mind that variants of this situation surely were being played out untold times and in untold places in the occupied countries around the perimeter of Germany: random groups of determined civilians making war on what was perhaps the best military machine since the Romans. Could we hope to make a difference? Was our effort merely symbolic, maybe even counterproductive in the larger scheme of history? Were we learning anything to be used in future human conflicts, or would governments and military establishments continue mindlessly to prepare for the previous war, too preoccupied to prevent the next one? Surely, if even one percent of Denmark's modest military expenditures had been devoted to preparation for this sort of thing, we could have been a thousand times more effective.

The quiet shuffle behind me had ceased; everyone was in place and ready. I pushed the doorbell button. We could faintly hear the sound of the bell, then footsteps from the apartment and into the entry hall. When the door opened I glimpsed a German marine guard, his face turning in a flicker from sleepy unconcern to acute surprise, then to horror, as the team behind us in accordance with our instructions fairly lifted Erik and me, like a human wave flushing us over the doorstep, bowling over the startled marine and pouring into the office beyond. I stopped in the main room from which four doors led to other parts of the apartment, one man rushing through each door to cover the entire layout instantly, leaving no time for any occupant to think twice.

There were only two Germans in the main room, one of whom like the guard turned pale and speechless with fright, thinking his hour of doom had struck, but the other man was unimpressed and put up a defiant scuffle. Fortunately, he was unarmed and was quickly subdued. A dozen or more file cabinets lined the walls of the main room, and those of us left there rushed to grab file drawers and started dumping their contents on a large work table in the center.

Erik had rushed to the kitchen where he encountered another marine, this one at the stove frying steaks. In his consternation at being suddenly interrupted by an armed intruder, the man jumped into a defensive *en garde* posture, holding his spatula like a fencing foil. Erik burst out laughing at the sight but waved his Lugar menacingly, and his opponent sheepishly put the spatula down. We herded the little group into the apartment's bathroom and piled more of the center's documents onto the table in the main room. Demonstratively insouciant, Erik lit a cigar with which he in turn ignited his firestarter, planting it in the middle of the paper pile which immediately caught flame. I scratched mine on a matchbox, noting that it lit readily, and threw it into a file cabinet that was still half full.

We exited back down the stairway, but on the way we heard the familiar sound of a police car arriving with its horn wailing. Alarmed by the commotion below, an old lady in the apartment above the Marine office had called the Danish police. As we reached the portal at street level, the police was deploying on the sidewalk in front of the building. The other end of the portal led to a small garden, through which we made a quick getaway, and after jumping several fences we dispersed into the city.

An hour later, Erik and I discussed the action with Alfred and could report that the firestarters worked just fine.

* * *

We have broken the back of the U-boat war.

Winston Churchill, November 1943

The Danish fisherman's information was more than idle scuttlebut. The Kriegsmarine, the German navy, at this point did use the Baltic Sea for training of submarine crews. In May, Dönitz had been forced to withdraw his U-boats from the North Atlantic, predictably causing the supply stream from America to England to take on flood proportions. In September the U-boats were ordered back to the Atlantic battleground to try to stem the tide. They managed to sink sixty-seven merchant ships but only at the forbidding cost of sixty-four subs, and the buildup for a cross-Channel invasion of the European mainland continued, accumulating immense Allied stores of weapons, food, transport equipment and fuel. An Allied joke at the time told that only the upward pull of the barrage balloons hovering over cities and military installations kept the island from sinking below the sea under the ever growing load.

Chapter 35   December 1943

*Every one of us must purposefully and tirelessly
obstruct German interference and exploitation in our
country ... by sabotaging every task forced upon
us by the Germans in areas of administration and
economic life ... Those of courage and ability must
attack points of vital importance to the occupiers,
such as war production, communication and
transportation.*

Danish Freedom Council proclamation
29 October 1943

It was close to seven in the evening when I entered the Vartov Building, and winter darkness had long since descended on the city, making Thies barely visible as he trailed thirty steps behind me. A man at the entrance motioned me to follow him, and we walked together down a long corridor. Carrying my large briefcase in my left hand, I stuck my right in the pocket of my trench coat and closed it around the Colt, a .32-caliber automatic that had become my favorite gun for everyday use. As always, its cool steel felt reassuring as I kept half a step behind and to the right of my guide, and the knowledge that Thies was hovering in the shadows outside the entrance gave me added peace of mind. There was after all something to be said for not working alone. Our walk ended as my guide opened the door to a large room where a group of men was seated. My guide veered toward a chair and sat down, while I placed myself at a table standing against one wall, put my briefcase on it and turned to face the audience watching me in silence. Feigning unconcern, I swept the group slowly with my eyes, counting forty-two, all men and almost all about my age, with two or three somewhat older. This, I thought, was definitely more efficient than dealing with three or four saboteur recruits at a time, but I could not assess whether it carried more or less risk per capita instructed. I opened my briefcase, extracted a stick of 808 and a dab of plastique, and picked up my career as a teacher.

As resistance in the fall of 1943 had become a reality known to every citizen, it was inevitable that someone would attempt to claim and exercise leadership, and indeed a small group did constitute itself as a *Frihedsraad*, a Freedom Council.[68] Consisting of a few well-known and respected individuals with contacts to some of the sabotage groups, the Council proceeded to issue a ringing call to resistance.[69] I was aware that Aage Schoch was one of the founders, and knowing about his presence in the group pleased me, for he had gained my respect and confidence at our brief encounter while waiting for the parachute drop at *Højen*. I still retained my aversion to organizing the resistance in any overall sense, for I believed a congeries of small, autonomous groups to be both effective and far more difficult for the Gestapo to destroy. Niels Jørgensen and I had discussed the subject several times and were in essential agreement, but he had pointed out – correctly, no doubt – that most people tend toward organization rather than solitude, so the process was destined sooner or later to take place, and he thought we should take part in order to help make the organizing ultimately as safe and sensible as possible. Even the provision of news by miscellaneous underground newssheets had taken on a measure of order with the creation in February of a *Bladudvalg*, a newspaper committee, of which Niels was a member.

We were both convinced, however, that common sense was sorely needed in these efforts, for at one point a scheme had been advanced by one group in an attempt at organizing. It involved the collection and filing of *Soldaterbøger*, military identification records, of all former soldiers joining active resistance. The system would have offered the Gestapo a potential opportunity to unravel and eliminate such organized groups in one fell swoop, something Niels had immediately realized, so that he vigorously opposed the proposal.[70]

My own reluctance to organize the resistance that was finally sprouting had been prompted by my preference for operating alone or with just a very few contacts, and it had been reinforced by disappointment with the military establishment. In my opinion, career officers should have been the logical core of resistance – what else are they all about? – but on the whole, the officer corps proved unequal to any such task. I had encountered one colonel, Vagn Bennike, who under the alias Gustav Olsen was organizing receipt of parachute drops in Jutland, but active resistance by and large was manned by civilians. It remained an enigma to me whether this was due to military men's inability to act independently on their own judgment and without orders from above, or whether it simply arose from a mindset incapable of waging war as guerrillas rather than in textbook formations. Perhaps the pacifist attitude of the population at large had to some degree infected the military as well, dousing fighting spirit. In any event, with few exceptions such as Colonel Bennike or Erik Hansen, the Danish military establishment had shown itself to be largely a waste of

216

the money taxpayers had expended. At the same time, I observed with amazement how the unprecedented situation in which Danish society found itself exerted psychological pressures on many people to choose in the course of daily living whether to resist in some way or mentally submit. The occupation in a sense functioned as a gigantic screening process of sifting wheat from chaff, and I soon realized that I was poorly able to predict how any given individual would react. People of whom I expected courage and firmness all too often would fade away when the reality of everyday existence called for taking a stand, while others from whom I would have expected nothing much proved to be steadfast, even veritable heroes. The gods dole out their allotments of courage in unequal shares.

Despite the fact of modest but firming resistance, and despite resistance having gained a measure of respectability, sabotage was not something many ordinary people dreamed of doing, and it was potentially a capital offence for those caught by the Germans. Even so, by late fall Thies' and my contacts had become extensive, and my days had turned into a flurry of activity, as I devoted all the time that could be spared from engineering school to various resistance projects, some with Erik, Alfred and Svend-Aage,[71] some with Aage Kjellerup and Kalle Frederiksen in Ribe, some on my own or with miscellaneous other individuals, but most with Thies. I had also begun to meet requests for instruction sessions for would-be saboteurs. The first such affair had been organized by Svend-Aage at Nordisk Kollegium and had involved almost two dozen people. The requests mysteriously seemed to come out of nowhere, always by word of mouth from people with whom I had had some touch, however fleeting. Such projects carried an obvious risk. Thies and I discussed the pros and cons, realizing that the more people who saw or talked to one of us, the stronger the likelihood that we would become known to the Germans. But we also reckoned that the war could not last forever and what we did should help shorten it. We were in any event loath to turn any requests down, for they were proof positive that our countrymen had come around to getting involved.

In the end we decided to work together on a few instruction sessions. I would do the instructing, while Thies would "ride shotgun" on the projects to cover me against unforeseen trouble. The meetings were impromptu, never in the same place twice, never with the same people twice, and only with people I didn't know and who knew me only as "Aage." Except for the first session and the one tonight, we had kept the groups small, usually six or fewer people. Like most civilian populations, Danes were poorly prepared to do sabotage. Few had served in the military, and of those who had, even fewer had touched a handgun. By comparison, Thies and I both had military training, supplemented by a bit of mechanical know-how and a fair amount of actual sabotage experience, gained on a trial-and-error basis. Besides, as the old saying goes, in the land of the blind, the one-eyed man is king.

After my first session I had made up a kit consisting of a small sample of 808, a dab of plastique, some detonators and "pencils," and a piece of explosive chord. I also included one each of all the different handguns I could lay my hands on. The selection included a 9mm Parabellum (Lugar), a 9mm Long Parabellum, a 9mm Walther P-38, a 12.7mm Belgian Browning, a 7.65mm Dreyse, a 7.65mm Walther, a 7.65mm Deutsche Werke, a 6.35mm Deutsche Werke, a 9mm Danish army pistol, a .38-caliber Albion revolver, a .32-caliber Smith & Wesson, and my Colt automatic. It was a hefty load, straining the leather of my roomy school briefcase, and I had to be careful when putting it down while riding on a streetcar, for it tended to emit a tell-tale metallic klunk.

Both Thies and I were by nature inclined toward keeping a low profile, minimizing the chance of attracting attention. Except when home or at the Teknikum institute, I used the name Aage Jørgensen to make tracing and discovery just a little harder. Jørgensen is a common Danish name, Aage is my middle name. Easy to remember. In July, the Germans had made inquiries about Thies at his parents' home where he was then living. Fortunately, he was away at the time, but it had prompted him to move to a vacant Jewish apartment in Hovgaardsgade. We had a few such hideouts available after the Jews had been evacuated and their homes stood empty. I opted for the convenience of staying with my mother in her apartment on Frederiksborgvej, but I got into the habit of being daily prepared to face a Gestapo agent on my arrival home from school. My mother was happily unaware that when she opened the door to our apartment to let me in every afternoon, the Colt in my pocket was aimed at her heart, safety off. She knew nothing about my being a *sabotør* besides a diligent engineering student. That sort of knowledge could only make a parent worry to no good purpose.

I finished my talk and demonstrations and took a few questions. The group had been paying close attention, and I was cheered by the prospect of forty-two new entrants to the thin ranks of saboteurs. I told them to give me three minutes to get lost before they started filtering out, picked up my straining briefcase, and left. Back on the street, I walked to a nearby stop of the Line 16 streetcar. When it arrived a few minutes later, I got into the open front compartment where the driver stood. Thies materialized and got on right behind me, and when the car started up again, we could talk safely in the near-darkness, the noise of the wheels against the rails drowning out our voices.

* * *

Of all the evils that infest a state,
a tyrant is the greatest.

Euripides

The end of the fourth war year found Germany in an unenviable position. The Red Army was keeping the initiative and was nearing the frontiers of Poland and Romania; the Allies were advancing in Italy; and an invasion of Western Europe clearly loomed. This much was clear to us in the occupied countries. What was not clear to us but entirely shrouded in secrecy was the fact that Germany's deteriorating position motivated certain people within the Reich to try to get rid of the dictator. The plotters faced a daunting task, for Hitler was under constant heavy guard of elite SS contingents fiercely committed to his protection. Despite the omnipresent secret police and the merciless reprisals awaiting such dissidents and their families, a few Germans of exceptional courage persisted in hoping to remove him and make peace with the Allies before Germany was overrun or totally demolished by the aerial bombing. Several attempts were made, one of which in March of 1943 narrowly missed, when a bomb placed in Hitler's airplane failed to detonate.[72] Information about such incidents came to light only after the war.

Chapter 36   Christmas 1943

Violence and injury enclose in their net
all that do such things, and generally return
on him who began.

Lucretius

Grandmother had cleared the dinner table, and together with my mother she was washing the dishes in the kitchen. The two women's gentle voices could be heard through the half-open door, as they in unbroken conversation talked about the thousand things mothers and daughters everywhere discuss endlessly. Grandfather had lit his pipe and settled in the armchair with the newspaper, and I decided to take a walk to get some fresh air. As soon as my Teknikum vacation started, mother and I had taken the train to Ribe to spend Christmas there with my grandparents. My sister had finished her training and was now a nurse at the Ribe hospital. We could all be together for the holidays.

The night was cool with a million stars overhead, and the Milky Way painted a broad, shimmering splash across the heavens. Ribe lay dark and silent, but distant sounds announced that a train was pulling in to the railroad station. It sounded like a freight, and out of idle curiosity I began walking toward the station to see what it might be.

The station was deserted except for two employees working in the office behind blackout curtains. I walked through the building to the platform where the train was standing, and became instantly alert. It was a freight, all right, but a military one, about three dozen flatcars loaded with Wehrmacht vehicles in camouflage paint, and without any guards in sight. The locomotive wheezed plaintively, as if impatient at having the journey interrupted. Obviously, the driver was keeping up steam, ready to continue. I returned through the station building to the unlit street and started running for home. Mounting the stairs, I could hear the women had finished the dishes but were still talking in the kitchen. Quietly, I went to my room, got a firestarter and a Sten gun out of my suitcase, left without anyone hearing me, and started running through the dark, empty streets back toward my target. A few minutes later, I was waiting on the railroad embankment just north of the station yard. How I wished there had been time to get Aage Kjellerup or Kalle Frederiksen, for there was enough work here for all of us, but I was afraid there wouldn't be time to find them before the train left. My breathing slowed to normal as the minutes ticked by. In the distance the engine was still wheezing intermittently.

I had brought from Copenhagen a quantity of plastique, detonators and some fuse, together with the Sten submachinegun, all for the purpose of showing Aage and Kalle what such materials looked like and how to use them. The stuff had been packed in my suitcase and in the Copenhagen Central station checked directly to Ribe. The Germans had recently taken steps at the Storebælt ferry to guard against transporting such contraband, so that passengers now had to open the handbaggage for inspection, but the Krauts ignored – or had forgotten about – baggage not carried by the traveler but checked through to the destination.

The three of us had decided to blow up the high tension line carrying power from Haderslev north, probably to Esbjerg, and had selected a spot near Seem, a village four kilometers east of town, where the power line crossed the road to Haderslev. This would be our first attempt to blow up a power line, but we had looked it over in daylight and thought it an easy enough project. The line was carried on pairs of wooden poles, each pair cross-braced with steel cables to form a simple tower. In the dead of night we had bicycled to the chosen spot and put a plastique patch on one of a pair of poles, lit the fuse and blew out a one-foot section of the pole, expecting the tower to come crashing down. But to our surprise, the other pole had proved strong enough to hold the strain all by itself. Approaching gingerly, we placed a charge on the remaining pole, warily, lest it should suddenly break and dump on us the three copper wires suspended with their deadly charge high above. Then we retreated a safe distance while the plastique did its work and blew a one-foot section out of the second pole. But to our utter amazement we saw the tower still standing, the two poles balancing neatly, each on top of its own stump, held precariously in position by the overhead wires. With extreme caution we set a third charge and finally brought the line down in a spectacular shower of sparks, just the way we had visualized to start with.

The following night we had destroyed a Wehrmacht truck by putting a gob of plastique on its engine, while it was parked at a small workshop just south of town on the highway to Tønder. We had used a "pencil" to delay detonation, but the delay turned out longer than intended, probably because the acid ate through the firing pin wire too slowly in the freezing temperature. We had planned for the blow to come just after midnight, but it came instead in the forenoon when the two mechanics who owned the shop had already started working. Unhurt by the flying engine fragments, they were scared out of their wits. It should be a while before they would want to take Wehrmacht work again. I had been pleased to see Aage and Kalle impressed with the material, and tomorrow we would test the Sten in a plantation well out of town.

Kalle was employed at the moment as a laborer with a construction firm doing contract work for the Wehrmacht, and he related to Aage and me how his work gang had devised their own form of sabotage. They were building coastal artillery emplacements on Fanø, the island where many years before Aage and I had gone on our first camping trip. They were heavy-walled structures requiring many tons of concrete which Kalle and his workmates had managed to sabotage by a simple and hard-to-detect method. When the concrete was being mixed in a large rotating drum, one man would slip a small quantity of sugar into the mixer with the result that the concrete subsequently refused to harden properly. When the forms were stripped off, the contents simply collapsed. Kalle and his workmates had taken turns donating their sugar ration to the project.

A sudden release of steam announced that the locomotive was trying to get its load moving again. Chooo ... chooo ... chooo ... chooo ... The train was slowly pulling out and I could see the light on the engine drawing nearer. I moved back from the embankment to be out of the sparse beam from the hooded lantern, and when the locomotive had gone past, I jumped without difficulty onto one of the flatcars. The vehicles were strapped down; most of them were diesel powered, but I located a *Kübel*, a small scout vehicle which I knew had a gasoline engine, and punctured the gas tank. By the time I was ready to ignite the gasoline, the train was rumbling along at moderate speed, and as I was digging in my pocket for the firestarter, a bullet suddenly smashed through the *Kübel's* windshield. I ducked behind the vehicle and tried to figure out where the bullet came from, for the noise of the train had drowned out the report of the gun. A second bullet solved my problem, for this time I saw the muzzle flash. The shooting came from a small wood brakehouse on a flatcar three cars farther back. Some of the flatcars on European trains had such brakehouses, two-by-three foot structures, five feet high, mounted high at one end of the car, open on one side and having one-foot-square, glassless openings facing front and back to give a man overview to manipulate the mechanical wheel brakes during switching operations. Offering protection against inclement weather, it was the perfect vantage point for someone guarding the freight, and evidently a soldier was holed up in this one, obtaining some shelter from the icy wind.

As I lay on my side close to the *Kübel* my thoughts flashed to that summer night a year and a half earlier, when another German guard had chased me like a rabbit from the gasoline dump in the Riberhus hotel garden because my firepower was insufficient, and I felt grimly grateful for the Sten under my windjacket. I readied the gun, rolled over onto my stomach to bring the target into view and squeezed off a burst that stitched a lethal pattern across the full width of the brakehouse. For an instant I visualized what it might be like inside, when the wood wall in front of my unseen adversary suddenly erupted in a shower of splinters and bullets. *Sorry, Nazi soldier, but your rotten government should not have sent you to my country.* Then I put the thought out of my mind. He had tried to kill me, but it was my good luck to be better armed for the contest. Even in the hands of a marksman a rifle was a poor weapon on a rattling and lurching freight car, but the Sten was absolutely perfect for this situation.

Without waiting to investigate further, I lit the firestarter and threw it under the *Kübel* where gasoline was accumulating. As it caught, I jumped off the flat-car onto the grass embankment, scuffing my knee in the fall. The train proceeded into the winter night as if nothing had happened, the fire building slowly but surely, like a cheerful Christmas candle. Apparently the engineer was not looking back at his freight, or perhaps there was no instruction for dealing with this sort of occurrence. While the train receded into the distance, I limped the opposite way along the railroad track, back toward town.

Plodding along into the darkness of the empty road, I wondered about the heavily loaded freight disappearing behind me. Aage had commented on the amount of such military traffic, as he had also observed it in Kolding on Jutland's eastern north-south rail line, much of it apparently through-traffic to and from Norway. Why would the Germans bother with so many troops here in Jutland, not to mention Norway? It couldn't be for keeping the Norwegians in line, and it couldn't be for fear of a Russian invasion in the far north; the terrain there formidably favored a defender. Neither of us had been able to suggest a plausible explanation.

* * *

The attack will come; there's no doubt about that anymore ... If they attack in the West, that attack will decide the war. If the attack is repulsed the whole business is over.

Adolf Hitler

We were stymied about German motives for excessive garrisoning in Denmark and Norway simply because their reasons were not based on logic or sound strategy. Hitler and his military planners had been taken in by an elaborate long-term program of deception perpetrated by British strategic planners through the Ultra intelligence network. By subtly feeding faulty information to the German Abwehr by means of double agents, the idea of a possible invasion in Norway had been planted and nourished in the minds of the German planners.[73] The result was that in November 1943, when the German leaders kept a reasonable force of fifty divisions in France and the Low Countries, they kept a comparatively massive force of eighteen divisions in the far smaller areas of Norway and Denmark.

At the end of the year Stalin let his ambassador to Sweden air the suggestion of a Finnish exit from the war on certain terms rather than unconditionally. The terms involved a return to the 1940 border; exchange of Hangö for the Petsamo area; internment or expulsion of German troops; and reparations of $600 million, payable in goods over five years. Urged on by the United States, the Finns decided to investigate the matter.

Chapter 37 January 1944

In all things it is better to hope than to despair.

Göthe

A half-dozen passengers got into the open driver's compartment at the Griffen-feldtsgade stop, among them Alfred Sander and a blonde woman. When he had called me an hour before, there had been suppressed excitement in his voice. Or perhaps worry might be a more accurate term. The driver started the street-car and stomped repeatedly on the floor button with his *træskostøvler*, leather boots becoming at the bottom wooden clogs. The stomping produced a ca-cophony of clanging by the car's bell that cleaved the morning traffic ahead like Moses' injunction parting the Red Sea. Alfred leaned close.

"Do you know this lady?"

He was shouting, but only I could hear his voice in the infernal din of the front compartment. I glanced sideways at his companion and her blue eyes mo-mentarily met mine, but she did not smile or give any hint of greeting or recog-nition. As straw blonde instead of brunette, her appearance was substantially changed, but the face was etched in my mind so that I would have recognized her anywhere. It was Ellen Quistgaard, unmistakably, and no less attractive in this disguise. I nodded slightly in puzzlement, and Alfred continued.

"They took Georg. Ellen wants to talk with you."

I nodded again, and Alfred got off as the streetcar slowed to a stop, its brakes screeching. In another few minutes we would be at the city hall square, and I decided to take Ellen to a second floor restaurant with a view of the square. It would be as good a place as any to talk.

Having Georg in Gestapo's clutches was serious, and the trail could possibly lead to Erik and Alfred who had kept contact with him. And it came on top of losing Aage Kjellerup and Kalle Frederiksen. Truly, calamities did come in

*Ellen Quistgaard (1915-1990), a fearless and effective organizer and courier, escaped to Sweden af-
ter her husband, Georg Quistgaard, was caught and executed by the Gestapo in 1944. Ellen later
made her way to Washington where she worked for the Danish Ambassador, Henrik Kauffmann.
The picture shows her at her desk in the embassy.*

droves! A few days after New Years, Aage and Kalle had arrived from Ribe, having narrowly avoided arrest by getting out of town only a step ahead of the police. I had supplied them with a small cache of explosives which they had kept
hidden in Kalle's brother's garden shed. The hiding place was badly chosen, for
the brother, who knew nothing about the cache or about Kalle's resistance activities, had found the stuff and in a panic rushed to the police. Various clues
provided an easy trail to Aage and Kalle, who therefore had to get away. They
took the train to Copenhagen and within hours we had them on a fishing boat
to Sweden. Thank God the transport system was working so smoothly. Counting
in my mind the people I knew who had recently taken this escape route, I was
appalled at the number just from my small circle of acquaintances. Seehusen
had left a couple of months ago, and the hemorrhage of good people had increased since then.

Aage's and Kalle's departure had posed an immediate problem, however, for

Kalle Frederiksen (1917-1988), one of the early Ribe saboteurs trained by the author. Tough and fearless, he crossed on foot the frozen Sound from Sweden one night to visit his family.

we had together liberated a Wehrmacht motorcycle and some weapons which at Christmas had been very temporarily stashed in a small forest east of Ribe, near the village of Varming. It was an area Aage and I knew well from countless fishing excursions years before. While we were together in Copenhagen, I discussed with them their possible replacement, and they recommended six individuals from the Ribe auxiliary police force.[74] I had been acquainted with these men most of my life, but it had been only a nodding acquaintance, so we discussed their selection at length, and both Aage and Kalle vouched for their suitability. In the event, their judgment was fully justified. The six men were in every respect prime manpower: dependable, resourceful, and unimpressed in the face of danger. When after Aage and Kalle's departure I had made a quick trip to Ribe and suggested to the six that they form a resistance group, I pointed out not only the risk but also that should they get killed, their countrymen would in all probability feel no gratitude but think that their actions had been foolish and useless. The group had responded by asking me to get on with showing them how to shoot and use explosives. From monitoring the radio waves they had noticed increasing activity in the air war, with Allied planes raiding Germany in ever higher numbers, and they would like to play a small part if an invasion should finally come. We scheduled some training sessions for later on, but for the moment, the group dug a shelter in the forest and got the motorcycle under cover and camouflaged.

Ellen was fingering her coffee cup, the only outward sign of her concern and preoccupation, as she looked at me across the white tablecloth. The restaurant

227

Viggo Hansen (1916- 96), a founding member of the Ribe sabotage group.

was half full, and there was a hum of conversation that allowed us to talk in low voices without being heard.

"I was away in Jutland when they came to our apartment and took Georg. We had agreed on a signal to warn of just such an emergency, and it had been activated when I returned." She did not spell out what the signal was. Typical of her, I thought.

"Did they find any stuff?" I had to know in order to assess the seriousness of Georg's predicament.

"We had none in the apartment, but there was some shooting. A British agent was staying with us and he got away, but they got Georg." Then she came straight to the point. "Would you be willing to help me get him out?" Her blue eyes held mine and never wavered.

The situation she had described was about as bad as it could be. To shoot your way out of a Gestapo raid was fine only if you succeeded. Otherwise, a death sentence was almost certain. Georg would never get out alive unless rescued somehow.

"What do you have in mind?"

She laid out a plan with her customary precision and economy of words. She had found out that he was being held in Vestre Fængsel, the city's main prison which had been taken over by the Gestapo, and it was common knowledge that interrogations took place at Gestapo headquarters in Dagmarhus, a building on the city hall square. We could actually see the place at this moment from our window seats. Transport back and forth had to be by automobile, and it should be possible to waylay it on a busy street. The plan was simple enough. The sticky point would be to find out about the route and when he was being transported, and I had no idea how to do that. Neither did Ellen, but she was working on it. Having put me in the picture, she came back to her request.

"So, will you help me do it?"

"Have you talked with anyone else about this?"

"No."

I was both surprised and flattered that she was asking me. She certainly had numerous connections but hardly knew me. At our three previous meetings, we had spoken only a few words to each other.

"Yes, of course I will do what I can. If you can find out when and where."

"How many will you need to be for the job?"

I thought for a moment. One man to stop the car, one on each side, one for reserve. And they would have to be very good for this kind of action.

"Four should do it, and I can get them on short notice."

I was observing her closely, and she seemed relieved, as if the scheme were already accomplished fact. That made me uneasy, and I felt obliged to repeat the substantial caveat. "But we can do nothing unless we have accurate and reliable information about time and place."

She nodded, got up to leave, and I helped her put on her coat.

"I'll be in touch through Alfred," her voice was calm and even, neither resigned nor hopeful.

"All right," I said, "but for heaven's sake, be careful." It came out of me almost involuntarily and I felt foolish, realizing that it was the first time such an admonition had been uttered in our group. She was turning away as she pulled on her gloves, but my words made her hesitate, as if trying to fathom their meaning. Then she turned back toward me with a sudden smile that made my heart leap.

"I will be."

* * *

It was not till 1943 that we possessed sufficient and suitable aircraft for striking heavy and continuous blows.

Winston Churchill

Early in the war the Luftwaffe had without compunction used bombing of cities to further German conquest by terrorizing civilian populations, and had even tried in the Führer's own words to "erase the cities of England." In 1943 the tables were turned. The Allies commenced a combined bombing offensive that visited awesome vengeance on the cities of the Reich. However swiftly the Germans repaired the damage, the disruption of their economy was severe, and Luftwaffe units were recalled from distant locations to assist in the defense of the skies above the homeland. With these measures the Germans felt confident

Stone mason Valdemar Sørensen (1917-), a sturdy member of the Ribe group, suffered ill health effects from the concentration camps but gradually recovered after his return.

of winning the aerial contest, for they now had the advantage held earlier by the Royal Air Force in the Battle of Britain. Each bomber shot down meant a large crew killed or permanently lost to imprisonment; each fighter shot down meant one pilot killed or possibly surviving to fight again. Against these discouraging odds the Allied airmen grimly fought on through 1943, their efforts attenuating German strength on the Eastern Front where aerial and artillery resources were withdrawn and diverted to home defenses.

Chapter 38 February 1944

'Tis only noble to be good.
Kind hearts are more than coronets,
And simple faith than Norman blood.

Alfred, Lord Tennyson

We remained in the standing-room entrance compartment until the door closed with a thud and a pneumatic PSSSSHH that started the S-train moving. Through the door's glass window I had my eyes fixed on the buildings a quarter of a mile away, clearly visible across empty fields from the earthen dike carrying the elevated track.

"What are you looking at?" Ellen inquired.

"Take a look yourself at that group of buildings over there to the right, and keep looking."

Today was Sunday, and I had invited her for a hike in the countryside north of the city in the hope of taking her mind momentarily off Georg's problem. And also because I enjoyed being with her.

We had been together several times since our meeting in the restaurant a month earlier, and each time she had merely shaken her head before I could articulate a question. To make things even worse, our side had sustained further losses, when at the end of January Erik and Alfred had decided to go to Sweden. As we had feared, the trail that had led to Georg enabled the Gestapo also to track down Stumpen, although they did not get him alive. He managed to take the poison pill carried by all of the SOE agents parachuted into Denmark.

One day my lunch hour visit to Sander's furrier shop was preempted. My routine check of the show window revealed the ermine collar missing, and I continued my stroll down the street without stopping. In the evening, Alfred called me at home, and when the three of us got together I learned that Stig Jensen wanted "the four Kornetter" – his way of identifying Erik, Alfred, Svend-Aage and myself – to go to Sweden. Erik and Alfred were ready to go, Svend-Aage had agreed to leave shortly. Would I go with them now? After thinking it over, I declined. With the other three out of the country, I could think of no trail leading the Gestapo to me. They had left the following day, but their escape nearly ended in disaster. Through one of our contacts in the evacuation network they had been directed to a villa in Elsinore, where they would be picked up for departure across the Sound. However, as they walked from the railroad station, a man on a street corner one block short of this interim destination stopped them and after asking where they were going, told them that the villa had been taken over by the Gestapo and advised them to return to Copenhagen. After parting with him, they went instead to a nearby Coast Police station, as we knew this branch of the Danish police establishment to be involved in the evacuation network. The police obligingly took them to a point south of town where a Swedish motorboat collected them just after dark, and two hours later they were safely in Hälsingborg on the Swedish coast. A few days later I learned that plainclothes agents had made inquiries at both their homes.

Losing Erik and Alfred seriously diminished the small circle with whom I felt unconditionally at ease. We had made a point of annoying the Gestapo, just on principle. One evening we had planted explosives in some German cars parked outside Gestapo headquarters in Dagmarhus by using the passing streetcar as a screen between us and the guards at the entrance. The upshot was that the streetcar had been rerouted the following day. Erik had also taken a dislike to a German truck parked near his apartment at Landbohøjskolen, the agricultural college, so we put a bomb under the driver's seat and took that out of commission as well. The streetcar, this time Line 4, again served as convenient distraction. But such fun and games had now come to a halt.

Before we parted, Erik had handed me a brown paper bag. "Here is a goodbye present for you," he said, laughing. I looked in the bag and found it contained about a kilogram of a coarse, white powder which he identified as trinitrotoluene, more commonly known under its abbreviation, TNT.

"We scavenged it from a clutch of handgrenades," he added, "and I thought you might put it to use."

We were always short of explosives, and when I told Thies about the bag, he had suggested the workshop of a motorcycle dealer by the name of Rheinhart as a suitable target. Before the war Rheinhart had imported Triumph bikes from England, but his workshop was now repairing German vehicles on a scale large enough to justify protection by *Sabotagevagter*, Danish armed guards.

Rheinhart's shop was in Sejerøgade, a sidestreet to Lyngbyvejen, the main artery leading north from the city into the Zealand countryside. I had arranged with Ellen to meet me at Lyngbyvejen's S-station for a nine o'clock departure, and as it happened, the workshop could be seen from the train. The coincidence tempted me to time the bang to go off when she might see it. After all, what could be more cheering?

Our preliminary reconnaissance had shown the workshop to be situated behind a board fence with barbed wire strung along the top to discourage intruders. The fence had a large double gate with a button to ring a bell inside. Thies and I had met at the main gate at eight-thirty, and Thies brought with him what he referred to as "two recruits," Anton and Poul. Standing on Thies' shoulders I peeked over the top of the fence. The workshop was a dilapidated sheet metal structure, separated from the fence by some fifty feet of parking area which was largely empty at the moment. In the corner of the building was what appeared to be an office, and smoke was rising from a primitive stove-pipe chimney poking through the wall. That had to be where the guards were, and we expected no one else around on a Sunday morning. Thies switched positions with me to fix the same picture in his mind, and with a few words we instructed his "recruits" to be ready to pounce on the guard. Then I pushed the button. The sound of the bell could be heard, then the opening of a door, probably from the guard office. Then steps.

"Who's there?" The voice was annoyed rather than concerned.

"Here's a package for you, automotive parts I have brought by train from Odense."

The sound of a bolt being slid back told that the man was none too bright, and Thies made a disparaging grimace that made me cough with suppressed laughter. The door began to open, and the four of us gave it a sudden shove that bowled the guard over, Anton and Poul jumping on top of him, while Thies and I raced across the parking area and burst through the door to the guard room, guns ready. One man at a table in the center of the room dropped his newspaper and coffee cup. Another was sleeping on a cot along the opposite wall. Their guns were hanging on pegs near the door, ancient pistols for which it would be hard or impossible to scrounge ammunition. Seconds later, Anton and Poul herded their quarry into the room, and we put the three captives on the cot where they sat sheepishly at the point of one of their own guns in Anton's hand. Poul ran to get the brown paper bag off my bicycle's baggage carrier, while Thies and I made a quick survey of the premises. The shop had three German vehicles in various stages of repair. In the center stood a Ford, its V-8 engine partly dismantled. I put the bag on the engine, activated a pencil of 20-minute delay and stuck it in the TNT powder. Then we assembled our little group and marched it to the front gate, on the way telling the guards to warn any passers-by that the place was about to blow. Anton and Poul were sent off, happy as larks to have acquired the guards' three old pistols, and Thies and I got on our bicycles and took off in the opposite direction leaving the empty-handed guards behind. At the end of the street we parted. Five minutes later I met Ellen, silently proud of the speed and smoothness of the little action. Now, if only the trinitrotoluene would do its work.

The S-train was going into a curve that in a few seconds would take us out of sight of the buildings. It was 23 minutes since I activated the pencil.

"Sorry," I mumbled to Ellen, "maybe there's nothing to watch for after all."

Just as I finished the sentence, a column of dust and debris shot into the air above one of the buildings. The timing could not have been better, and I relaxed as we turned toward each other.

"You have obviously been busy this morning," she said, and barely audibly she added, "and you have more to show for your efforts than I do."

She was alluding to her attempts to find out about Georg, all of which had proven fruitless. Was he still being interrogated? How much had they found out? Had he been sentenced? Questions were multiplying, unanswered and unanswerable.

We got off in Holte and spent the morning hiking through forests where the frosty paths crackled underfoot. We lunched at the Fortunen restaurant and continued our hike through Dyrehaven, in former times the royal hunting preserve but now a public park, where I used to ride Klaus as a boy. Despite the sunny weather, we saw only a few hikers, and we were speculating whether it was the war that kept people cooped up at home. Along the way we discovered a common interest in poetry, and we both remembered J. P. Jacobsen's *Gurresange* as our favorites. Ellen sympathized with Tove, King Valdemar's mistress, whom his jealous queen had scalded to death in the bathhouse while he was away on affairs of state. I remembered and could quote the beautiful stanzas describing the King's grief when he stands at the shore of Gurre Lake, recalling the sound of Tove's step and turning when he imagines hearing them again, only to see dead leaves, stirred by the wind.

When we ran out of poetry, I tried with moderate success to cheer Ellen up by telling her snippets of sabotage events, selecting only the humorous details of which there were many. Without giving identifying details I told her about a recent visit to my Ribe group during which Viggo Hansen and I had biked south to Skærbæk with the intent of blowing a large transformer station located there, but found it too well lit and too well protected. On our way back we settled instead for a small transformer house on the road to Sdr. Farup, where we set a plastique charge with a delay detonator on the transformer itself and closed the door to the house neatly behind us. It blew the next morning, to the consternation of a German platoon who had until then been having a restful stay in the village, enjoying Danish farm hospitality. Another group member, Niels Christensen, was a mailman whose rural route included some farms where German soldiers were billeted. Niels and I had paid a visit to one of these farms in the village of Vester Vedsted where we collected three rifles and some ammunition and hid them temporarily in a large haystack nearby.

Secure weapons storage presented a problem, and after some discussion we had decided to put the firearms in the subterranean depot where the group had earlier stored the motorcycle. Viggo made a strong box for the material in his father's carpentry shop, and we packed the box carefully, wrapping in oily rags three rifles, several pistols and some ammunition. The box was about four feet long, sixteen inches wide and ten deep. It was sturdy enough and, loaded with the weapons, beastly heavy. Nevertheless, I set out with it on my bike, carefully balancing it on the handlebars, a task to tax even a seasoned biker. The distance to be covered was six miles, and on the way I had an experience that gave rise to much amusement afterwards. About halfway to the depot I ran into a Wehrmacht regiment on maneuvers. The force had been divided into two opposing groups for the occasion, with the soldiers of one group dug in about half a mile away in a pine plantation while the troops of the other group were lining both sides of the road in front of me, using the ditches as trenches. The ones in the trenches were getting ready to advance on their opponents' position in the plantation, the regiment's equipment train in the meantime standing temporarily abandoned on the road in the wintry sunlight. I had to dismount and pick my way carefully, pushing my bicycle with its heavy burden through the clutter of wagons, motor vehicles, shouting officers and staff cars, but to turn back would have led to suspicion. I tried but failed to think of a plausible explanation in case they decided to turn their attention from the war game at hand to the interloper in their midst. Fortunately, it did not become necessary; all went well. Nobody thought of inquiring about the heavy box balanced on my bike.

Ellen listened attentively to my chitchat, making occasional comments and asking a few questions. When describing the expression on the face of the guard as our two recruits pounced on him this morning, I actually had her laughing. These were things I had never discussed with anyone, not even Thies, for it could only pose risk to both teller and listener, but Ellen's case was different. Or so I told myself.

"If you should ever get caught," I said, "feel free to tell these stories to the Gestapo."

"Do you think I would?"

"I would want you to, for you could use it to draw their attention from other things. Besides, you don't know my name, so what harm could be done?" She thought about it for a while in silence, as we were nearing the end of our walk.

The tired winter sun almost touched the horizon, and shadows from the naked beech trees were lengthening, dark streaks across golden snow patches, when we had tea in a forest café in Klampenborg. The cups were fine Bing & Grøndal china and the tea was a black current brew that we both liked. When the waitress left us, Ellen sat for a while without speaking. Then she fixed her gaze on me and suddenly blurted out what was on her mind.

"Stig Jensen wants me to go to Sweden."

I had met Stig only twice, once in the Palladium lobby for the briefing, once again when we collected the first drop, and both times only under his cover name. Later I had by sheer coincidence, and without intending to, learned his real name. He was middle-aged and had some business in the Nyhavn quarter. He was actually the one who kept direct touch with the British agents to organize drops on Zealand, and I was aware that Flemming Juncker who had been in our original receiving group on *højen* did the same in Jutland. I had also deduced that Ellen's cool courage, competence and resourcefulness, coupled with her already deep involvement with the air drops, had placed her in a key position as courier between Stig and Flemming. Small wonder that Stig wanted to see her gone. She knew far too much, and now that they had Georg, she was exposed.

"I think that's an excellent idea."

"Would you go?"

"Certainly," I lied.

She looked at me, and I felt as though her blue eyes read my every thought. Then she spoke, her tone of voice, matter-of-fact.

"You are not telling the truth."

"I have many times thought of going to Sweden and on to England," I retorted lamely. "Truthfully, my greatest ambition is to join the Royal Air Force."

"That's different."

"But you too could go on to England, perhaps even work the other end of our supply line. Maybe you could send me an occasional note in one of the containers."

She smiled, very briefly.

"We had better get back to town. I want to call Georg's parents from the coin phone in the S-station and see if they have any news."

The walk to the station took only a few minutes in the gathering twilight. The path ran along the beach, and a light easterly breeze carried scents of seaweed mingled with those of fishing boats. In the far distance, lights twinkled on the Swedish coast. We walked silently, and I thought this had been the most perfect day, ever. And Ellen was the most attractive woman I had ever met.

At the station, she telephoned. The conversation lasted no more than a minute, then she emerged from the booth.

"They've sent him to Germany."

I thought for a moment. Executions were normally carried out in Denmark, probably with the intent of added deterrence. That it tended to have the opposite effect was something the Germans had not understood.

"I think that's good news. His chances of staying alive are better there."

She was relieved, and I realized that we had both been fearing, if not expecting, a swift death sentence and immediate execution.

"I also have to check in with Stig." She returned to the phone booth, digging in her purse for coins.

The conversation took a lot longer than the last one, and I sat down on a bench across the room where I could keep an eye on both the booth and the few passengers. Finally, she came back.   "They knew about Georg, and they insist that I leave tomorrow. Passage has already been arranged." I knew pretty well who "they" were, and they were right to insist, but her voice indicated that she was not in agreement.

I put my arm around her. "Ellen, you know you should leave. You have no excuse for staying any longer."

She did not answer, but as we walked out on the platform, she took my arm. "My place is no longer safe. May I stay with you tonight?"

She was aware that I often slept in an abandoned Jewish apartment in the Eastend. I waited a moment, to drain excitement from my voice.

"Of course."

* * *

I can only win the war by dealing out more
destruction to the enemy than he does to us.

Adolf Hitler

While we in the resistance movement administered our pinpricks to the German war machine, the air war proceeded with unremitting fury into the winter of 1944. Besides diverting resources to fighter aircraft production so that by this time half of Germany's industry worked for the Luftwaffe, the Germans had dispersed their manufacturing facilities and put as much as possible underground, often using abandoned mines for shelter. But the additional fighter strength was to no avail against recent American progress.[75]

In their efforts to strengthen air defense the Germans added more and more antiaircraft artillery, so that 1944 saw one-half of all their artillery deployed on the home front, pointing skyward, being served by 1.1 million personnel, and consuming ammunition at a voracious rate. At the beginning of the year Hitler ordered a bombing counteroffensive against England, although bombers were in short supply. The offensive, dubbed the Baby Blitz by the Allies, lasted from January to May; it had little effect but lost Germany 300 bombers.

Chapter 39   March 1944

Women sometimes forgive a man who forces the
opportunity, but never a man who misses one.

Talleyrand-Perigord

Perhaps it was just the bright morning sun, or perhaps the feeling of spring in the air. For whatever reason, the Copenhageners were crowding the sidewalks of Strøget, a fashionable shopping street at the city's core. It was gratifying to see people actually jostling to look at window displays that contrived to maintain an air of elegance despite wartime shortages. The crowd studiously ignored a sprinkling of German soldiers, gawking with disbelief at what to them appeared an affluence the Vaterland had not known for years.

The winter semester at Teknikum had ended three days ago, and I had passed the tests with better results than I had hoped for. Finishing my education was high on my personal agenda, but I had decided the war had even higher priority and therefore had not enrolled for the summer semester. Instead, I had moved out of my mother's apartment and gone underground, as Thies had done months before. Caution seemed to be in order. Finding a place to stay was no immediate problem, for I had access to a couple of Jewish apartments and had chosen one in Hovgaardsgade.[76] This morning I was on my way to see Thies and Niels Jørgensen at *Nationaltidende* to discuss another printing of the newssheet.

In front of me a woman stepped off the curb to cross the street, and as she did so, a paper bag she was carrying broke and spilled its contents of apples in all directions. She bent down, trying to reach as many as possible, and I jumped in pursuit of some of the ones farther away. We retrieved them all, each of us cradling eight or ten, looked at each other and burst out laughing at the awkwardness of having nothing to put them in.

"That was kind of you. Winter apples are hard to come by. Let me get something here at Illum's to carry them in." Her voice was melodious, slightly nasal, her smile revealed a dimple in her chin, her hair was medium brown, her eyes hazel with finely arched eyebrows, the bright morning sun revealed just a touch of makeup, and even my undiscerning eye could detect that it had been expertly applied. And she was perhaps three or four years older than I. In one glance I took it all in and decided she was a dead ringer for Ava Gardner, my favorite American movie actress.

"Yes, sure," I said, trying not to drop any apples, "go ahead and I'll follow you." Walking behind let me observe her more closely. Yes, Ava had nothing on her. Once inside Illum's, the most expensive of the city's fashion stores, she moved with confident grace and immediately had a clerk scurrying for a bag. It took but seconds to get the apples securely packed, and she thanked me again with a smile, while I desperately tried to think of some way to delay parting. "Well, I must be off, shopping." There was that dimple again, and I smiled back with all the charm I could muster but unable to think of anything more to say.

Continuing my walk down Strøget, I reviewed the incident in my mind and decided that the chance of running into her again was the same as the chance of finding another woman remotely as beautiful: Zero! So I turned around and walked back to Illum where I slowly and methodically combed through the establishment until spotting her on the third floor, absorbed in the process of trying on a pair of shoes. From a safe distance I saw her linger before a mirror, turning from one side to the other, apparently pleased and in the end deciding to take them, but ordering them to be delivered.

When she left, I did some lightning-quick shopping, picking out a pair of chic, painted sandals – not difficult, for everything at Illum's was chic – and told the clerk to get me the same size as the shoes he had just sold to my girlfriend. When he opened his order pad to check the size, I read her name, upside down: Gurli Lyngesen. I was not sure how to put this piece of intelligence to use, but a telephone directory would certainly yield additional information as a first step. I felt clever and smug as I continued on my way to meet Thies and Niels.

Thies and I had been busy through the winter. Most of our activity was spur-of-the-moment, opportunity stuff that came about in response to requests or tips reaching us through the numberless channels crisscrossing the underground, or through other members of the *Hjemmefronten* group. We both liked this modus operandi and thought ourselves well suited to it. We also felt the risk to be minimal as we usually needed only each other to depend on.

In February we had attended a meeting in Café Odin[77] with several members from other groups and most of the *Hjemmefronten* members. It had been called by Steen Hansen, a diligent underground organizer, and we discussed group composition, overall coordination, and whether a recently proposed "sabotage stop" should be rejected or carried out. Thies and I did not agree with stopping the sabotage and argued strongly against letting up on the pressure it exerted on the Germans. Two days later we had punctuated our arguments by blowing up Reinhardt's motorcycle shop. In another small action four of us from *Hjem-*

mefronten entered the Frederiksberg public swimming pool, an indoor affair which was frequented by several German military personnel. While they were frolicking in the pool, our group broke into their lockers and carried off their handguns. We speculated afterward with much hilarity about their explanations when they returned to their outfits disarmed.

At times I missed Ellen Quistgaard and wondered how she got along in Sweden. There was never any word from the ones who had made the trip. They had been removed from the lives of those left behind, almost with the finality of death. When leaving, she had plunged her Smith & Wesson in my coat pocket. "I know you don't accept guns from lady friends," she whispered, trying gamely to sound lighthearted, "but please pretend you took this from a German." The gun had since occupied a special shelf inside the old piano, but I rarely used it. Seeing it conjured up memories of our time together and made me daydream, to no avail. Ellen was gone. Unobtainable. Inaccessible. She was out of my life in every practical sense. Although not given to introspection, I had begun to realize that my views and philosophy of life had gradually changed from the long range to a narrow focus on the here and now. It was not a matter of conscious choice. It had simply been fostered by my present lifestyle.

When I reached Niels Jørgensen's office, Thies was there, and Niels had just finished another newssheet draft. As usual, Thies and I would be doing the printing, and Thies was gathering papers and getting ready to leave. The *Hjem-mefronten* newssheet was becoming a popular paper, hardly surprising with Niels' writing talent and publishing experience behind it. The increasing load kept our group busy gathering the news and distributing the printed product.

"I have picked a print shop called Mayland to do the honors this time."

Thies announced his choice as if we could have our pick of Copenhagen's printing industry. Actually, he selected our targets very carefully, using only places where he had worked and knew the presses and local layout.

"Are there any guards in this one?" I liked to be prepared for the kind of opposition to expect.

"Nah, the outfit is too small, but they do have three people working night shift, so the machines will be warm and ready to run."

"Listen," Niels was addressing me from behind his cluttered desk, "I have had a request from *Københavnsledelsen* to have a representative from our group work with them. I know your reluctance to organize, but I want you to think about representing us." *Københavnsledelsen* was a Copenhagen organ working to contact and coordinate groups for possible military action. I doubted that any military operations would ever come about, and any organizing effort meant severe potential risk to many people.

"All right, I'll think about it." I might as well sound positive.

At the door, Thies suppressed a smile and deadpanned, "Yes, that's well worth thinking about."

"OK, guys, see you later." Niels Jørgensen was already occupied with the papers on his desk, oblivious to the note of sarcasm in Thies' remark.

The telephone directory indicated that Gurli Lyngesen owned a beauty salon in the Frederiksberg section of town. No wonder she looked so immaculate. On the morning after Thies' and my printing assignment I went to a flower shop and ordered a bouquet sent to her at the salon address. I lingered over the choice of flowers, going through the store's sizeable inventory. Roses were too presumptuous. African violets, too modest. Carnations, too formal. I finally settled on six gerbera, two each of three different colors, and had the clerk add a few sprigs of gypsophila to the bouquet. They looked sufficiently exotic to match Gurli's sophisticated appearance. I did not enclose a card. *Let her wonder who sent them. Mystery peaks a woman's interest.*

In the afternoon I went to the address listed in the phone book. It turned out to be a mezzanine location in the Falkoneralle, a pleasant Frederiksberg street. An almost unobtrusive sign above the window identified the establishment as Salon Capri. I was greeted by a soothing fragrance, hints of perfume and women's toiletries, and a low buzz of hair dryers. The three chairs were occupied by middle-aged matrons to whom three employees in white smocks, women in their thirties, devoted their attention and skills. The place was tastefully decorated and the clientele, so far as one could detect in their bundled-up state, was definitely upper crust. Addressing the nearest employee, I asked to see Miss Lyngesen. I said "Miss" without hesitating, and judging from the woman's reaction my guess was correct. She disappeared into the back and returned with Gurli, who looked quizzical for a couple of seconds before she spoke. "Oh ... YOU ... "

"Yes, I would like to take a moment of your time, if I may." We were the objects of keen attention by everyone in the place, but she instantly regained total composure.

"Oh, yes, please come into my office." Inside, she closed the door and turned toward me, "What in the world are you doing here?" but her voice carried only slight reproach.

"I have just a small present for you." I handed her the parcel with the painted sandals.

"A present? You ... but ..." Then her natural curiosity took over, and she slowly unwrapped the contents. "Oh, they ... they are exquisite!" *Thank you, Illum, for knowing what appeals to the female fancy.* "But I can't accept them. I don't even know you."

"Why don't you accept them as a favor to me, in return for my helping you catch your apples."

Suddenly, a thought struck her. "Ah, YOU are the one who sent the flowers!" The gerbera bouquet was in a vase on her desk.

"You have no proof of that."

She smiled. "My girls were all curiosity and thought I was just trying to keep them in the dark, when I had no ready explanation."

"My name is Aage Jørgensen. Will you have dinner with me tonight?"

We had dinner at Esplanaden, a second-floor restaurant with a view toward the moat surrounding Kastellet which Kurt and I had swum across on a night outing almost two years before. Gurli was gregarious in a low-key manner, and it was easy enough to keep conversation going. She had had her salon for five years, a business that had been only positively affected by wartime hardship. The reason, she asserted, was that women made up for other deprivation by making themselves more beautiful, something I had never considered, but when looking at her I was prepared to believe anything she might tell me on the topic of beauty. She was not married but had some attachment – she left out a closer definition – to a man somewhat older than she. I experienced an instant surge of jealousy. She was the first woman entrepreneur I had met, and I was intrigued by her obvious business competence which showed clearly when she talked about her salon. I posed questions and she answered and explained, and as she talked, I watched the lively play of emotions on her expressive face.

She had a cousin in the United States with whom all contact had been lost at the beginning of the occupation. That made us speculate about the Americans' war with Japan, without being able to imagine what the current status might be in that conflict. The German news services showed little interest and never reported much from that part of the world.

It was close to midnight when we left the cozy atmosphere of the old restaurant and caught one of the last streetcars. Taxis were not to be had, of course, a mere memory of luxury belonging to a bygone era, but the streetcars served very well on Copenhagen's comparatively modest commuting distances. The car was nearly empty, and from the rear platform we could sense the street trailing away behind us, as we stood close together, swaying with the motion of the car. A few more blocks, and we would be leaving the inner city's narrow streets behind and enter the broader boulevard to Frederiksberg, a separate township but in reality a suburb.

Suddenly, a powerful detonation tore out part of a building slightly ahead of us on the left side of the street. The driver slammed on the brakes and the car came to a grinding stop that threw us against the forward wall, while descending debris showered the vehicle with the pattering sound of giant raindrops. As we stepped gingerly onto the littered street, my mind was racing. *Get out of here fast, but don't walk ahead past the site, for there may be unexploded stuff still lying about. Go back one block, then get to a parallel street and bypass the site before they cordon off the area.*

I grabbed Gurli and pulled her with me back in the direction we came from. Walking was slow at first, for we had to pick our way through the litter. We reached the sidestreet and could move faster. Gurli took off her high-heeled shoes and we started a slow jog. At the next corner we turned in the direction of Gurli's apartment, but we had only gone a few hundred feet when hooded lights appeared behind us. I pulled her into a doorway and watched one truck go by, disgorging soldiers at the nearest intersection and proceeding to the next. It was bound to be a futile effort to catch the saboteurs, but we could well end up in the net, and the last thing I wanted was to be picked up for someone else's sabotage.

Gurli leaned against me, panting from the run. "I must say, you know how to make an evening exciting. What do we do now?"

I was delighted that she reacted so calmly, no trace of panic. "We get out of here through back yards. How good are you at climbing fences?"

"It isn't what I usually do after dinner, but I'm afraid this outfit won't survive tonight's entertainment, anyway."

I made a mental calculation of the area that was being encircled. We would need to get over at least one more block, away from the streetcar route. Our doorway led to a corridor that ended in a small yard, bordered in the back by a bicycle shed. I reached up and lifted myself to the roof, then bent down and got Gurli's hand. With a swift heave, I had her on the roof. We walked across to the other side, I handed her down into the neighboring yard and jumped down beside her. This yard was large and empty, and the building to which it belonged had several doors to it. We tried them all and found them locked, but one was decrepit enough so that I succeeded in forcing it open. I held Gurli's hand as we fumbled our way along a passageway in utter darkness, turning twice and ending in a stairwell that had a door to the street. Like all street doors, it was locked from the streetside but could be opened from inside, and we opened it slightly and peeked out. Noises could be heard from the nearby streets, but ours looked clear, and we started walking.

It was well after midnight when we reached Gurli's apartment. She took one look in the mirror and burst into laughter. "Your dinner invitations certainly leave their marks. Even the city's clothes exchange would reject this dress." She looked at me and added, "How far away do you live, and how will you get home?"

"Oh, it will be about an hour's walk." I was lingering at the door, trying to prolong what had been in my opinion an absolutely perfect evening. "Unless you would let me stay."

She looked at me for a long moment, a smile playing at the corners of her mouth. "All right, you'd better stay. No telling what other troubles you might get into."

* * *

*Modern infantry weapons are too deadly, and
frontal assault is only for mediocre commanders.
Good commanders do not turn in heavy losses.*

Douglas MacArthur

Had we been better informed about progress in the far-away Pacific theater, we would have been greatly encouraged, for the Americans were steadily advancing westward in two thrusts. The southern thrust under MacArthur went in two branches, one through New Guinea toward Vogelkop, and one through the Solomons, both branches leapfrogging with modest losses. Admiral Nimitz' Central Pacific thrust went through the Gilbert Islands and the Marshalls. As U.S. cryptanalysts had cracked the secret codes the Japanese used for their diplomatic signals around the world as well as for battlefield intelligence, the American commanders enjoyed an immense advantage,[78] although it was initially wasted by lack of professionalism in handling cryptologic material.[79]

Actually, Japanese commanders in the field often did not bother to put their communications into code. After all, they knew how strange their language looked and sounded to foreign eyes and ears. What neither they nor the American public knew was that the military intelligence services had 6,000[80] first-generation Japanese-Americans, some drafted but many volunteers, who served in every major battle in the Pacific. They translated documents, questioned captives, eavesdropped on radio talk between pilots, even read diaries and poems taken from bodies of dead enemy soldiers. This service, an unsung saga of loyalty, was kept secret by the government both during the war and for decades afterwards. Major General Charles Willoughby, intelligence chief at MacArthur's headquarters, estimated that the service of the Nisei saved over one million lives and shortened the war by two years.

Chapter 40   Mid-May 1944

The camomile, the more it is trodden on,
the faster it grows.

Shakespeare

Svend Barber finished *Gem du dine Kys* on the old upright, and the tango stopped. His name was really Svend Andersen, but as a barber working in Milwertz' salon next to the waterworks, his identity had over the years merged with his occupation. He earned a bit extra from piano playing, mostly popular tunes rendered passably well at private parties. I led Gurli outside for a breath of fresh air and we walked slowly away from the building toward the dike that drew a straight line of darkness against the horizon. It was after ten o'clock, but the May evening refused to let night overwhelm the deep cobalt of the western sky. The 30-foot steel gates of the double lock – the farmers' guardian against storm floods – loomed as black squares in the almost black dike as we ascended the narrow strip of concrete stairway to the top of the dike. We were now on a dirt path that led us in a few steps onto the top of the lock gate itself which carried a two-foot wide wood trestle where we paused, ensconced on both sides by iron railings. The gate was half open, and from the darkness below came the faint gurgle of water leaving the embrace of the Jutland mainland to enter the North Sea in one of nature's countless cycles of our watery planet. We were standing on the *kammersluse*, the lock in the sea dike three miles west of Ribe where the Nipsaa issues into the North Sea.

Gurli leaned against me with my arm around her. "This has been all so perfect. The place is serene compared with Copenhagen. And your friends treat us like we were something special."

Feeling her this close always distracted me and started my heart pounding. "Yeah, uh ... they're a good bunch. I was born here, you know ..."

In three Ribe visits over the past two months I had given the group some minimal training. We had pawed through my selection of handguns, memorizing their features of loading and safety locks, but without firing any as our pistol ammunition was too precious. One of the German infantry rifles we had liberated on Niels Christensen's mail route had served for firing practice, for Niels subsequently had gotten a good quantity of ammunition as well, and a stretch of heath six miles east of town had offered a secluded place for our exercises. My Sten gun had elicited much admiration; we had thrown two hand grenades and fired a few rounds with a Wehrmacht signal pistol, red flares that descended under a tiny parachute. Finally, we had reviewed whatever explosives and related paraphernalia I could scrape together.

I had arranged my last trip to coincide with my grandparents' golden wedding anniversary on 3 May. This had entailed a formal dinner at Hotel Klubben for a sizeable gathering. Our family was small, but my grandparents had a large circle of friends, built up over a long lifetime in the town. My sister had become engaged to a member of the town's police force. His name was Ole Kuhlman, and he was involved in some radio traffic with England. I did not know what or how and didn't ask. Ole and I had rented formal attire for the dinner party, for both of us the first occasion to wear tailcoats. As the only, and therefore oldest, male of my grandparents' family I was obliged to make the main speech to the anniversary couple. After careful preparation and secret rehearsing before a mirror, I had carried it off well enough to produce tears from my grandmother and general applause from the rest of the assembly.

Timing my instruction and firing practice around the anniversary dinner had inspired the Ribe sabotage group to organize tonight's party to celebrate completion of our training plan. Gurli and I had arrived by train in the afternoon. I had excused myself for a couple of hours to sketch the location of a German artillery emplacement near Vester Vedsted, about two miles from Ribe. I had mentioned this heavy gun to Skern, an acquaintance in Copenhagen who channelled such intelligence through Sweden to England, and he had insisted that I plot precise coordinates to the place right away. If an invasion should come on the North Sea coast, the information could be of real value. I borrowed a bicycle and rode out to the village with paper and pencil, completing a precise sketch in less than half an hour. With the aid of a geodetic map the task was an easy one, for my training at the *Kornetskole* had included such simple mapping. The location was a farmyard where the gun had been dug in and camouflaged among some fruit trees. Sketch in hand, I returned to town, feeling our trip to Ribe doubly justified. Skern would be happy.

The evening's program comprised transport from Ribe by chartered motorboat on the Nipsaa to the dike, where the lock keeper ran a small restaurant, Slusehuset, whose specialty was fried eel. The restaurant was not operating this early in the season, but he had proved more than willing to open it for a special occasion, so we had it all to ourselves. Perfect. The dinner had been outstanding: sections of large eel served with boiled potatoes and parsley sauce.

Occasions such as anniversaries are in Denmark customarily celebrated with a good deal of formality. Here the Tarps' 50th wedding party poses to commemorate the gathering of family and close friends. The author can be seen in the standing back row, 6th from left, between cousin Ria Obbekjer and brother-in-law Ole Kuhlman.

Through her connections in Copenhagen Gurli had obtained eight bottles of miscellaneous table wine which had flowed and raised the spirits further. The members of the group, Viggo, Valdemar, Kjær, Niels, Johannes and Jens Carl had brought wives or girl friends who had been given sundry, partly diverging reasons for the party. But who cared about reasons? A party was always welcome. Chic and elegant, Gurli's appearance was distinctly different from that of the local women who at first had eyed her with tongue-tied awe. The same was true for the men, but the wine had quickly removed all traces of inhibition, and when the music started, Valdemar with an air of suavity had asked her to dance, setting an example the others hastened to follow.

After that first hectic night, Gurli and I had seen a great deal of each other. Every week I spent several nights at her apartment which was "clean," i.e. no clue or connection could lead the Gestapo there, for she had never been involved in any illegal activities. She was intelligent and perceptive and had despite lack of tangible evidence deduced my involvement in sabotage or some other resistance activity, but she asked no questions. She used to tease me about my abys-

Ole Kuhlman, a member of the Ribe police force, was involved in radio contact with England. He and the author both knew the other was engaged in underground activities but studiously avoided getting to know details, a common pattern of behavior to preclude accidental revelations.

mal ignorance in regard to women's beauty aids, and one night she gave me a quick rundown on dyeing of hair; then she offered to change my hair color, if I thought it a good idea. The suggestion left me momentarily speechless, for despite the lightheartedness of our conversation, it was clear that she suspected my extracurricular work. The idea was worth considering, particularly with a new ID card to go with the new image. However, my natural color was the washed-out medium brown that makes Danes all look somewhat alike, so I decided that a radical change would make me conspicuous and thus could well be counterproductive.

When she accepted my invitation to the Ribe trip, I had to tell her my real name, as I was known there in my true identity. She had looked thoughtful, then smiled.

"I like that name. What other surprises do you have for me?"

"Nothing, nothing at all. Not now, anyway."

She gave me a long, lingering kiss, pushed me away and held me at arm's length.

"Dammit, Niels, I want you to be more careful."

"Whatever makes you think I'm not?"

She looked away. "I just know. Well, let's hope the war will be over soon."

I had told Thies about Gurli, and we agreed that I should keep her name and address to myself. "Just let me know the approximate street location for planning purposes," he said thoughtfully, then added, "you can never have too many hiding places."

The party ended an hour after midnight, when Svend Barber stopped playing. "Union rules," he declared. Gurli and I sat on a bench in the bow of the tour-boat as we motored back to town in the near-darkness of the spring night, a blanket wrapped around our shoulders against the coolness. She was leaning against me with her eyes closed, the scent of her hair conveying her presence, conjuring up pleasant images. I was aware of having become very fond of her despite constantly reminding myself that this was no time for dalliance, let alone serious attachment. What lay ahead? More years of war? How long could the various belligerents continue to spend lives and resources? Was Germany getting beaten? Where exactly *was* the Eastern Front right now? As always, it was infuriating to have no overview of events, no basis on which to forecast.

The eastern sky was turning pink as we debarked and walked back to Hotel Munken, the small establishment where we were staying, very properly in two single rooms so as not to upset the provincial mores. The proprietress had allowed me a street door key when she heard that we would be in late, and we tiptoed upstairs without waking anyone. "We will take my room," Gurli announced softly.

We left on the morning train for Copenhagen and had lunch on the Storebælt ferry. When we boarded the train in Korsør for the last stretch to Copenhagen, I bought a newspaper. Scanning the standard German news releases, my eye caught another headline. Nine saboteurs had been sentenced at a German military court, four of them to execution. One of them was Georg Quistgaard. They had brought him back from Germany.

The simple words in black and white on the page in my hand stung me like a physical pain. I closed my eyes and recalled Georg's face, a face I should never see again. What would be the effect of notices such as this? Would those few of us who had taken up sabotage lose heart, be cowed by ruthlessness and overwhelming power? How many could we lose and still amount to anything? But as I watched the ditch and embankment along the rail line tearing by, covered with grass and wildflowers, an old saying about the camomile came to my mind. Perhaps the feeble Danish resistance was becoming like that lowly herb: the more it is trodden on, the more it grows.

* * *

*Rumania was already trying desperately hard
to surrender unconditionally ...*

Winston Churchill

Our frustration at lacking a clear picture of the war situation was shared by millions of Eastern Europeans fighting on the German side. Being a German ally was proving to be a costly and altogether unhappy experience for the countries

249

Hitler had enlisted in his Russian venture. In the fall of '42 the Italian, Hungarian and Romanian armies on the Eastern Front had been torn to shreds in the Russian encirclements preliminary to the German disaster at Stalingrad. Relations between Germany and the three satellite countries were further shaken when Hitler refused to allow retreat by German and Romanian forces cut off in the Crimea. In May the Russians were able to crush this pocket with its 120,000 defenders.

In the north the Red Army had been building forces to succor Leningrad which by April was truly freed. For a while the Germans retained a toehold on the Narva River. Although militarily insignificant it may have been what induced the Finns to reject in April the Russian peace proposal.

It was not a good decision.

Part III

Slated for Oblivion

———————

World War: From Normandy to Berlin

Chapter 41 26 May 1944

*We should never so entirely avoid danger as
to appear irresolute and cowardly; but, at
the same time, we should avoid unnecessarily
exposing ourselves to danger, than which
nothing can be more foolish.*

Cicero

I emerged from the printing shop into the sunshine and afternoon bustle of Blaagaardsgade, a street in the old north end of town. Something was bothering me, gnawing at my subconscious, but I was so damn tired and preoccupied that I couldn't drag it into the realm of clear conscious thinking. The last few days had been hectic. A week ago I had met Hanne. She was a petite brunette divorcée, five years my senior, very good looking and very sexy. Our brief relationship had quickly become rather intense. Actually, I had made it my business to meet her, for she was also a secretary at the criminal police laboratory where murder weapons were stored, or so I had been told.

On our first date I learned that she was involved with one of the groups organizing transport to Sweden, and she had with her a Swedish newspaper, obtained from one of the transport skippers and much prized for its uncensored war reports. Over coffee we spent an hour perusing its contents and discussing snippets of information about the viewpoints and actions of the neutral countries. It was pretty obvious that the neutral countries were getting a free and profitable ride through a war the Allies were fighting to create world conditions that ultimately would benefit the neutrals as much as the victors.

Hanne revealed that the crime lab where she worked contained several usable handguns in addition to an array of knives, axes, hammers and other implements used by those preferring cruder methods. The laboratory was situated in a quiet location on the edge of a park, Fælledparken, and on our second date

This picture, retrieved from Gestapo files, was taken by a street photographer in Copenhagen, showing the author with Hanne Schlederman the day before he was caught by the Gestapo. He stuck the photographer's ticket in his pocket where Gestapo later found it and obtained the snapshot.

we arranged that, when leaving in the evening, she would unhasp a certain ground-floor window to permit me easy entrance. The next night I had entered the lab via the unlocked window and combed through the miscellaneous weaponry but gleaned only three usable handguns and a few cartridges. The rest of the collection was ancient and of calibers to which it would have been impossible to find ammunition. Danish murderers were few to begin with and obviously lacked interest in modern equipment.

While rummaging around the place I became aware that the Colt I carried had worn a hole in my right rear trouser pocket, so I shifted it to my left rear pocket, making a mental note to do some mending at the first opportunity.

The following day I had learned that Thies had been caught. When I tried to call him, our prearranged code warned me that something was wrong, and I went to his parents' address for a further check. Their living room window faced the street and was filled with potted plants, among them a geranium in an old porcelain pot. We had impressed on his folks that if they had knowledge or even reason to suspect that Thies was caught, that pot should be removed. Casually, I strolled down the sidewalk past their window and cast a sidelong glance at the plants behind the panes. The porcelain pot with the geranium was missing. Later in the day I discovered that Holger Søderberg, another member of the *Hjemmefronten* group, had been shot and killed in his apartment by Gestapo agents.

I spent the next two days cautiously checking on other group members and established that Niels Jørgensen and four others had been arrested. As I was unable to contact anyone else, it looked possible that the entire group had been

254

caught, myself excepted. In my apartment – known only to me – I pondered what to do next. A new issue of *Hjemmefronten* was in the process of printing at a small print shop with a cooperative owner, and it should by now be ready for distribution. I had not been to the shop myself, but Thies had told me about it and I would have no trouble finding it. If in fact I were the only one left, it seemed incumbent on me to get the paper out. Besides its intrinsic value it would appear to be evidence that *Hjemmefronten* was still in business, thereby perhaps helping those now being interrogated. It suddenly became urgent to get the next issue into circulation.

I had reached that conclusion this afternoon, on 26 May, and had immediately phoned an acquaintance I could trust, Torben Halkjær, and asked him to find some means of transportation for a large quantity of newssheets and be prepared to move in the evening. Then I went to the print shop in Blaagaardsgade, where I found that the issue indeed was ready. The printer's name was R. Markussen. He was a small, rat-faced man with close-set eyes that seemed to dart glances in all directions simultaneously. He told me in a nervous half whisper that Thies had been there four days earlier and had mentioned that some of our group had been caught. The man's behavior should have alerted me, but nervous people were only too common, and as this guy knew of some of the arrests, his fear seemed natural enough. Besides, I was thinking about the date I had lined up with Hanne that night, wondering whether I could keep it. I told him I would return late in the evening with transportation, went downstairs, and was walking back down the street toward the nearest intersection.

Something bothered me about Markussen's story, and as I stepped off the curb at the intersection, it suddenly struck me what it was: Thies would not have told him about the others having been arrested! I almost stopped in my tracks but mechanically kept walking, my mind far from this street scene and racing to assess the significance of what I had just realized. When I was half way across, jostling my way in the afternoon crowd, a man coming toward me suddenly stepped into my path and stuck a Walther pistol in my face hissing "Hände hoch." The gun almost touched my nose and my left hand shot up in a reflex, moving it out of the way, while I twisted my right hand awkwardly toward my *left* back pocket to get my Colt out. At that very moment two gorillas fell upon me from behind, twisting my arms together in front and clicking handcuffs on my wrists.[81] An Opel *Kapitän* materialized with a rear door open, I was shoved into it with a man on each side and one on top of me, and we sped off as quickly as traffic allowed. The entire operation took fewer than forty-five seconds, and we were gone before people in the street realized that something was happening. I was in the hands of professionals.

The Gestapo car, with me in the back seat being smothered by agents, proceeded directly to Dagmarhus. In peacetime an elegant downtown office building across from the city hall, Dagmarhus had been requisitioned by German security police for headquarters. The driver maneuvered smartly through the crowded streets, but not so fast as to attract attention. On the way, the agents frisked me, but only cursorily, thereby missing my Colt because of its unusual location in my left back pocket, and I was feverishly wondering if it would be possible to get to it with my hands cuffed in front. Alas, on the way up in the elevator the agent in charge – he was the one who had initiated the arrest, and I later learned that his name was Marquart – told them to search me once again, and this time the Colt appeared.

"Why didn't you tell us you had this?" he demanded furiously in broken Danish.

"You never asked me," I said, and then had to laugh at the ridiculous logic. He struck me in the face, and in the confined space of the elevator I noticed that he was shaking. It made me realize that the bad guys' adrenalin was at least as high as mine, and I found that somehow comforting.

They hustled me to a fourth-floor office and into a chair, and Marquart lit a large cigar and sat down.

"Well, Aage Jørgensen, we finally got you." He spoke in German which was translated by a burly agent, and I realized that his Danish outburst in the elevator had been a slip. Very well, I understood German easily enough, so I could play the same game to gain time.

"No, you didn't," I said truthfully in Danish when his question had been translated, "My name is Niels Skov, so you have the wrong man."

The agent smiled and pointed to a thick file on his desk, "We will now put your real name on this and get started."

I tried to think fast. Although the possibility of getting caught had occurred to me – how could it not? – I had never actually thought through what might then happen, and I was sure the others hadn't either. Why the hell hadn't we done any contingency planning? The answer was essentially because we knew nothing about the actual scenario that would unroll after an arrest, something that had already become clear to me when Ellen and I tried to get some basic information about Georg. We were in the truest sense of the word amateur players in a game where our lives were the ante and where the rules heavily favored the house. I saw in a flash that my own attitude had been a mixture of arrogance and naiveté in assuming that my charmed career could go on forever. Did they have enough on me to shoot me? That question was soon answered, for as they dug into my file it became readily apparent that they had enough on me to shoot me several times over.

I understood pretty well the workings of the Nazi mind. It was radically different from the mind-set of free people and more like that of the communists with whom I had had fleeting contacts. To the Nazis, an opponent fell into one of only two categories: he was either a knave or a fool. In their view of the world it was simply not possible to be honorable and intelligent and still be against the Nazi cause. People of a democratic tradition can look upon opponents with a measure of respect, ascribe the differences between us to cultural diversity or the vagaries of human nature, and treat a vanquished enemy with decency; but such an attitude conflicts with a totalitarian outlook. The totalitarian mind lacks tolerance, which it equates with weakness, and it lacks the self-assurance to admit the possibility of its own imperfection. In fact, the mere suggestion of imperfection was tantamount to treasonous criticism. To the Nazi, anyone working against Hitler's will was at best misled and hence was expected immediately to repent and recant when caught and enlightened; or he was thoroughly evil, a manifestation of subhuman qualities such as one could expect to find in lesser races. In neither case did he rate humane treatment.

I tried to look contrite and read immediate approval in their faces. Then I analyzed for a moment our diverse goals. They wanted information: names and details that could lead them toward further arrests. I, on my part, wanted time. After all, every new day held the promise of something – anything – to change the situation. I might escape. Or the war might end. Or Hitler might drop dead. At least two of those three possibilities were bound to come to pass sooner or later. And I had four years of sabotage to talk about, most of it done on my own, most of the rest done with people who were either dead or in Sweden. I could talk for a long time without endangering anyone but myself. What simpler strategy? Besides, while listening to me, some of the Gestapo would be kept from doing mischief elsewhere.

Marquart had become impatient at my silence and suddenly tried a more coercive approach. I was sitting in an armchair, and on a signal from Marquart three of the agents closed in, grabbed me and pinned my left hand to the armrest, palm down. Marquart was puffing on his cigar, and he now walked leisurely across the room, stood a moment in front of my chair looking down on me, then reached over and slowly stubbed out his cigar on the back of my hand in the soft area between thumb and index finger.

The pain was briefly excruciating, surging through my body, and despite my extreme effort to prevent it, tears filled my eyes. There was an ugly black spot on my hand, and I smelled burning flesh, *my* flesh, dammit, and in a rush my anger far overcame the pain. These goddam Kraut bastards, marching into *my* country, lording it over *my* countrymen, flouting good Danish law and common justice, burning *my* goddam hand ... I nearly choked with fury and felt the blood draining from my face while I tried to regain my composure. Walking back to his desk, Marquart spoke in German with his back to me.

"Maybe now you would like to talk?"

I waited, pretending not to understand until it was translated, then hissed my reply at the interpreter.

"You'd better tell him he'll need a lot of cigars."

A man had entered the room through a door behind me, and he now walked into my view, waved the agents away from my chair and addressed me in a friendly voice. He was in his forties, and he introduced himself, the first one to do so, as *Kriminalrat* Fritz Schweitzer, in charge of this section of the *Sicherheitsdienst*. He seemed not to notice the smell of burned flesh but told me, quietly and earnestly, that I was in deep, deep trouble and that it bothered him to see a young man in this position. But he, the *Kriminalrat* himself, might – just

MIGHT – personally go before the military court and try to save my neck, if – but only IF – I would understand that my sabotage had been a terrible mistake, and IF I would take the only intelligent path, which was to redeem myself by cooperating with him to try to prevent others from getting into the same lamentable position. The appeal was almost pathetically insincere, but it gave me just the opening I needed to make cooperation appear genuine.

On the spur of an impulse, I asked him if Niels Jørgensen also was being held in his section. His face darkened,

"Ach ja, Niels Jørgensen, but that man lies, he LIES!"

It was comical to see his expression of righteous indignation which accompanied the words, but I tried to look shocked at the thought. All right, I said, in response to his sincere and reasonable promise I would tell them whatever I knew. Everyone in the room relaxed and cheered up; coffee was ordered, and I started to talk. In slow and elaborate detail.

That initial session lasted far into the night, everything being written down and typed, but we covered less than the first occupation year. When it was over, we got back in the Opel and they took me to Vestre Fængsel, the main Copenhagen penitentiary which the Germans had taken over. Two prison guards led me to a small cell, told me to undress and to lie down on a steel cot hinged to the wall, cuffed my hands together and chained them to the cot, and left me with the light on and a guard outside who checked on me randomly and frequently. I could hear him outside and *felt* his peeking through the lens in the door. I closed my eyes and reviewed my situation, and for the first time did I feel really CAUGHT. I was absolutely, totally unable to do anything except lie like a lump of meat and wait for somebody else to make the next move.

The coarse blankets were scratchy, the chains were cutting my wrists, and the charred spot on my left hand throbbed in protest against the cigar treatment. I now knew exactly what freedom was: it was what I had just stupidly lost.

Then I fell asleep.

The metallic noise of a key unlocking the cell door woke me with a start. What was the time? Early – before seven, I estimated, but there was no way to tell. A sullen guard entered with a thick slice of dry rye bread and a mug of pissy ersatz coffee. He fumbled with my handcuffs and chain and finally got me detached from the cot. I ate my simple breakfast and looked over my surroundings. The cell was bare, conspicuously clean, and smelled very faintly of concrete and steel. It was the most unfamiliar environment in which I had ever slept. The floor was smooth concrete, measuring about eight by thirteen feet. The walls were concrete as well, and so was the ten-foot-high ceiling which held a recessed light bulb protected by steel mesh. Mounted on one wall a small, open box about sixteen by sixteen inches served as an open cabinet which at the moment I did not need, for I had retained no possessions whatever. Below it a shelf some fourteen by thirty inches formed a simple table. In one corner was a small cast-iron sink with a brass water faucet above and an enameled chamber pot on the floor below. Hinged on the wall opposite the table was the steel frame cot with a cheap canvas mattress stuffed with seaweed. A heavy, low wood stool completed the furnishings. In one of the short walls sat the heavy steel door, and in the opposite wall was a small, high window. I could just reach the window ledge and chinned myself to look out between two stout steel bars that daunted any hope of escape via the window route. Outside was a small yard, seemingly unused, with a tiny flower bed in the center.

After about an hour, two of Marquart's agents arrived and took me back to the Dagmarhus headquarters for more interrogation, and it was late afternoon before I returned to prison. During the transport I had been handcuffed, but when we got back the guards brought a small chain and padlock which proved less uncomfortable than the handcuffs. When they left me, I set about inspecting the premises more thoroughly. My cell door carried the number 412 on the outside, and although at first glance the cell seemed utterly devoid of anything but its spare furnishings, this proved on close scrutiny to be not so. Minutely intensive searching by a prisoner with nothing but time on his hands will reveal things no guard can hope to find. After a couple of days I noticed that a few stitches were missing in one seam of the seaweed mattress, and inside the tiny hole was a two-inch stub of pencil. Between the box-shelf and the wall it was mounted on was a paper-thin crack that with some coaxing produced two razor blades. *Thank you, unknown previous occupant!* I set about attacking my beard with one of the blades, no razor or mirror, and found such shaving to be possible but so slow that one side of my face could grow a respectable beard while I worked on the other.

While I tried to memorize everything that was said during interrogations, so as not to contradict myself later, my brain had neatly divided itself into two branches. One, the minor one, dealt with routine tasks: eating, sleeping, exercising, seeking news, interrogation. The other branch, the important one, devoted full time to planning escape, and my mind remained so compartmentalized during my stay in prison. Always, always and everywhere, the idea of escape dominated my consciousness. To that end, I began to analyze my new environment and routines.

As for the prison itself, even my unskilled eye told me that it was built by people who knew about such things: lots of concrete, steel bars everywhere, no internal communication, no chance even of gaining some idea about overall layout. Not encouraging. That left the visits to Gestapo headquarters and the trips back and forth as possible opportunities for escape. Interrogations took place in a fourth-floor office and I pondered the chances of surviving, in running condition, a jump to the sidewalk from that height. Poor, I decided. Going to the toilet, I was accompanied by Randschau, the interpreter, and another agent, both young, about my age. Randschau was like me from southern Jutland, but his roots were in the small minority whose homes for generations had been north of the border while their loyalties had stayed south. He was blond and proud of his Aryan looks, used the cover name Johnsen, was my height but at least twenty kilos heavier. And it wasn't fat. He was a bear of a man who on the Russian Front had lost part of his sight in one eye but otherwise seemed in as good shape as I. The other agent was no slouch either, and they were both armed with automatic Walthers in shoulder holsters. Going back and forth between prison and Gestapo headquarters, we traveled in an Opel, one agent in front with the driver, I in back with an agent on each side. In downtown traffic we waited obediently at stop lights where I found myself a tantalizing four feet from carefree people on bicycles: craftsmen, office workers, students, house-wives, suntanned girls – all of them my countrymen, not one of whom wished me dead. On the other hand, as I soberly reflected, not one of whom could be expected to give me any effective help on an instant's notice. On the way we passed over the railroad line which near the main station is underground but only partially covered, so that one can from the street look down on the rails and see them disappear into tunnels. If I succeeded in bolting from the car and vaulting the four-foot stone fence, could I survive the twenty-foot drop to the rails, dodge the bullets and make a running escape through the tunnels? High-ly unlikely, I had to admit. In the evening I visualized every remotely imaginable scenario, both before and after going to sleep.

* * *

When a fellow says it hain't the money but the principle o' the thing, it's th' money.

Frank McKinney Hubbard

The impression we gained from close reading of the Swedish newspaper that spring day in 1944, just before I carelessly wandered into the Gestapo ambush, was basically correct. As the belligerents exerted themselves in life-and-death struggle, the behavior of the neutrals was of more than academic interest. Their aggregate trade with Germany added up to important quantities of both raw materials and finished products which the Reich could ill do without, particu-larly this late in the war. A glance at the record of the individual countries in-volved reveals that they acted – as most countries do – from motives of avarice, need and security, tempered by momentary assessments of the likely final out-come of the fighting.

Spain under the dictatorship of General Francisco Franco was clearly Axis oriented. Hitler and Mussolini had both assisted Franco during the civil war, their help being decisive on more than one occasion. When war came, the Spaniards came through with useful submarine support and provided tungsten and iron ore for the German steel industry.

Like Spain, Portugal was a producer of tungsten and supplied substantial amounts to Germany, but the Portuguese under Oliveiro Salazar were rather more friendly than the Spaniards to the Allied cause. The difference stemmed from their close relations with Britain and with Brazil. The latter relationship went back to colonial times, and Brazil had joined the Allies.[82]

Straddling the straits to the Black Sea and guarding the gate between Europe and the Middle East, the Turks watched anxiously as German forces positioned themselves in Greece and the Eastern Mediterranean, and they saw with equal concern the Soviets thrown back as the Germans encroached on the Black Sea areas. In return for chromium sales to both sides Turkey obtained modern armaments, built up her military strength, and managed to sit out most of the war, stalling off urgings from the Allies, particularly Britain.[83]

Of all the neutrals, the Swiss had the best of luck and ended up profiting handsomely. Over three and a half years Swiss industry worked hard and very profitably for Germany despite strong Allied pressure, producing arms and ammunition in ever-increasing quantities. The Allies finally put a stop to Germany's Swiss armory by threatening to blacklist Swiss industrial firms working for Germany. The sobering prospect of being excluded from major markets in a postwar world dominated by the United Nations got Swiss attention.

In World War Two Swedish public opinion leaned toward the Allies, but Swedish government and industry circles chose a policy of accommodating German demands, which were numerous. The output of high-phosphorous iron ore from the Gaellivare mines in northern Sweden and the high-quality ball bearings produced at the SKF plants were urgently needed by German armament manufacturers, and through most of the war, Sweden kept up a brisk pace of delivery.[84] German pressure for concessions was intense, but Sweden accommodated Hitler over and above the minimum to satisfy the demands, postwar apologia notwithstanding.[85] In August of 1943, an American air raid on the ball bearing center at Schweinfurt sustained terrible losses: 60 Flying Fortresses downed out of 220. Public opinion in the United States became enraged at the idea of Swedish supplies making up for German losses American fliers had given their lives to incur, and the American government aired the possibility of bombing the SKF plants. The Swedes at length agreed to cut the export by 60% – against economic compensation by the Allies.

The Swedish position was in part motivated by fear of Russia, the ancient enemy, and in part by influential circles friendly toward Germany. In any event, Sweden's record during the war did not square with her citizens' generally Western orientation, and the country's humanitarian exertions when the Reich was collapsing regained her only some of the international respect lost. Those Westerners who expected somehow more from Sweden than from the other neutrals were disappointed.

More worrisome than opportunistic profiteering was the narrowly parochial view the neutral nations' behavior reflected. That the world public was unable to see the Nazi designs for what they were, a deadly menace to Western civilization itself, is understandable. Even those being rounded up for extermination could not quite believe what was happening to them until the last moment. That responsible governments so utterly failed to grasp the extent of the threat and failed to do what they could to contribute to a German defeat is another matter and harder to accept. The Swedish and Danish governments saw as their duty the protection of their people from hardship and danger. This is certainly a defensible attitude in democracies, but if it becomes overriding, crowding out a sense of mutual responsibility among nations, it does not bode well for the maintenance of peace and order in a crowded world to which one would wish national governments to be attuned.

Chapter 42   June 1944

Stone walls a prisoner make, but not a slave.

Wordsworth

Randschau turned toward me, grinning from ear to ear.

"Now you'll see, Niels, they will be thrown back into the Channel to drown!"

"Who will?"

We had arrived minutes earlier for interrogation at Dagmarhus, where it had been immediately noticeable that the Gestapo headquarters was boiling with excitement. In Marquart's office four agents were talking and laughing excitedly. One of them was Randschau, the interpreter, who had just addressed me.

"Oh, you don't know, of course. Well, the *Engländer* and their American friends have landed on the French coast and are trying to breach our *Westwall* line, the fools! Now you'll see us deal with them! This may end the war soon."

So, the invasion was finally on! I asked Randschau for details; his answers indicated that none of the Gestapo crew really had any. I then tried to make my own assessment of the probability of an early but different end to the war. What was likely to happen? Would the German fortifications prove impenetrable? Or would Hitler try to fight a two-front war?

I hadn't the slightest idea.

My interrogation had been proceeding in the previous days, further swelling my already sizeable dossier. With a terrible memory for names, I had carried on me a small pocket calendar[86] in which I had noted the names of the Ribe group when Kalle and Aage suggested them prior to their departure for Sweden. Sensing that the notes might lead my captors to the group, which it did, I spent long nights reproaching myself for having acted so carelessly. Carrying the calendar was inexcusable on my part, and more than anything else showed our amateurish approach to the fatal risks of playing hide-and-seek with the Gestapo.

Altogether, I was learning – belatedly – some lessons that would have made us very difficult to catch, had we known them earlier. On the positive side, Gestapo never caught the scent of any of my other contacts, for in the interrogations there had been no difficulty in confining my disclosures to the people now in Sweden or the ones who were already dead. Georg got blamed for a great deal. Erik and Alfred came out as prime public enemies. Aage and Kalle also were given more than their due. Although I had never worked with Holger Søderberg, I spun a few stories about him as well, just to kill time. But my interrogators obtained no clue to lead them to Kurt Ridung, Aage Schoch, Stig Jensen, Ole Kuhlman, the remnants of the receiving group, Colonel Bennike who was busy in Jutland, Sigurd in his Ribe gun shop, Førsting who kept my small repository of papers and notes, Vilspang[87]who was busily building an armored car on an old truck body, Skjern who was quietly working on his espionage projects, or the many others. Nevertheless, the capture of the Ribe group made the Gestapo's haul painful.

People react differently to incarceration and prison life. After the initial shock of no longer having control of my own destiny, I adapted rather quickly. Prison routine assumes its own magic monotony, one day dragging the next one along in a mesmerizing succession without beginning or end. I worried a good deal that my healthy body would atrophy for lack of exercise and not be ready for a maximum escape effort at a moment's notice, so I diligently chinned myself and did pushups to stay reasonably fit. Chinning on the window ledge was much harder than on a bar, but after two weeks of practice, I could do it one-handed. In my cell I was still kept chained, but it had turned out to be of no great consequence, only a minor inconvenience. The chain was wound in a loop around my wrists and clumsily fastened with the padlock; only the first few nights did it link me to the bed, and I soon figured out how to hold my hands when the guard put it on, so that I could squeeze it off after he left. When the key rattled in the door in the morning, announcing the arrival of the guard with my breakfast, I often had to dive under the blanket to find and put on the chain just in time for him to enter and remove it. It puzzled me at first why they bothered to put the silly thing on someone in solitary confinement, particularly after I found out that I was the only one so adorned, which explained the guards' inexperience and ineptitude in using it effectively. Later I discovered that it was meant, not as a security measure, but to humiliate me. Seen in that light it pointed up the psychological chasm separating Gestapo from the people they were hoping to intimidate. Far from humiliating, other prisoners saw it as a mark of distinction.

The prison guards were a disparate lot, varying in age from early twenties to early forties, and largely uncommunicative. Only one of them, a man in his mid-thirties from Essen, volunteered a bit of small talk. He was a clean-cut chap with blond hair and blue eyes, always wearing tennis-type shoes of grey canvas to accommodate some foot injury suffered on the Eastern Front. He was a fervent Nazi, and his eyes lit up when he told me in hushed tones about the happy lifestyle Hitler had allowed his fellow Germans to enjoy, the emphasis on sports to build healthy bodies with the consequent marvellous records German athletes had racked up at the 1936 Olympics, the healthy *Arbeitsdienst*, the work service corps which had abolished the scourge of unemployment and built the glorious autobahns, and the Volkswagen automobile project on which so many frugal citizens had made downpayments to become car owners as soon as the war was over. Progress all around, thanks to the Führer. He also described his young sons going off to do their *Hitlerjugend* exercises on Sunday, their swastika pennants gaily streaming from their bicycles. He moved himself almost to tears describing the wholesome happiness the Führer had brought the fatherland by such means and how his sons would soon be old enough for army service, although victory would surely be won before that milestone was reached.

I reciprocated by telling him about my own exploits in KU before the war, trying simultaneously to gain some news about events outside. When I emphasized KU's similarity to the Nazi organizations, shading the truth somewhat, he expressed his surprise that I could have erred so badly as to oppose the Wehrmacht. Though unable to justify my actions to his satisfaction, I did glean some bits of news indicating that Danish resistance was making a nuisance of itself. Reflecting afterwards on our little exchange, I wondered where I might now have been myself, had my great-grandfather remained south of the Danish border so that I would have been born a German. I might well have swallowed the Nazi appeal as the Essener did and with *élan* have thrown my life away on some distant battlefield in the service of a foul cause. Was there any profit in being an activist? Probably not, but I decided that we are born with and stuck with certain predispositions.

Suddenly, Randschau stuck a photograph under my nose. The daily trips to Dagmarhus and the incessant questions were becoming a boring cat-and-mouse game, and I disliked the rôle of mouse. It was late afternoon, and the interrogation had been going on for six or seven hours. I had lost track of time.

"Niels, who is this woman?"

The picture showed me on the sidewalk of a downtown street together with Hanne, the secretary of the criminal police laboratory. I had never seen it before, but after a few seconds I remembered. The day before my arrest a street photographer had snapped it, one of those – at the time common in Copenhagen – who randomly took snapshots of passers-by, handing each a numbered ticket by which the photograph could be purchased by mail for a small sum. I had absentmindedly put the ticket in my pocket and forgotten the incident. But my interrogators had found it, obtained the picture, and wanted an explanation.

"She is a girl I met just the day before you picked me up, name of Inge. We had coffee together in Tivoli and had a date to meet later. Don't know her last name or address, but if you can find her I'd sure like to share my cell with her."

My reply elicited some guffaws and renewed examnination of the snapshot.

After a few more questions, they dropped the matter, but it was one more inci-
dence to prove that they missed very little, and that I needed always to be ready
with plausible explanations.

Marquart came in, still distracted by the news from France. He looked at the file.
"Enough for today. Take him back."

* * *

*People of Western Europe: A landing was made
this morning by troops of the Allied Expeditionary
Force ... I call upon all who love freedom to
stand with us now.*

Dwight Eisenhower,
broadcast on 6 June 1944

Often forgotten today, Allied military planners expected the Normandy invasion, code named *Overlord*, to be a close thing, and so it turned out. Despite the
scale of the undertaking – by far the largest combined operation in history – its
success was due in large part to a brilliant and elaborate Allied deception
scheme that led the Germans to believe that the Normandy landings were a
mere distraction, with the main attack yet to come in the Calais area. Numerous
Allied actions had been carefully orchestrated to support the deception, and
the Germans were completely taken in.

Eisenhower was in overall command with sole power of decision to call a go
or no-go, depending on weather. This turned out to be crucial, as a storm blew
in from the Atlantic, strong enough to prevent landing operations. However,
the meteorologists were able to predict a 36-hour "window" of abating winds, an
opportunity Eisenhower decided to grasp. Having lost their weather stations on
Greenland and in Canada, the Germans were unable to forecast this passing
feature in the weather front. Feeling certain that amphibious operations would
be impossible for at least two weeks, several German commanders were absent
from their units.

German reaction to the invasion was a mixture of indecision and incompe-
tence which assuredly contributed to the Allied success. When the troops
poured ashore, von Rundstedt and Rommel, the two commanders in charge,
could not on their own authority commit a Panzer reserve nominally under
their command. Hitler dithered, fed in reinforcements piecemeal, and kept on
believing the Allied deception. When the mistake became obvious, the five initial beachheads had been consolidated into one, and the Americans were
poised for a breakout in the west.

266

Chapter 43   June 1944

A key rattled, unlocking the door, and one of Marquart's agents walked into my cell. He was a small, slightly older man with red hair who had been present but quiet during the interrogation sessions. He sat down and made himself comfortable before starting to talk. Then he commented about the weather, unseasonally hot for our latitude, and finally got to the point. My case had been completed, he informed me. The case and I would now be *endgültig*, finally, disposed of. He phrased his statements so that it was unclear whether the military court, the *Kriegsgericht*, had already handed down a verdict without my presence, or whether it was about to do so, but the outcome was not in question.

"When?" I asked.

He did not know precisely, but I had *noch ein Paar Tage*, a few more days left.

What he was chatting about in a totally detached manner did not really come as a surprise. I had all along realized that in the end my case could be wound up only with a firing squad. Gravamen of the accusations were nine charges, all potentially carrying a death sentence: destruction of German war matériel, sabotage on Danish industrial plants, recruitment and instruction of saboteurs, printing and distribution of illegal newspapers, traffic with the enemy (parachute drops), evacuation of Jews, possession of firearms, espionage, and murder. Of these they had very ample evidence on eight, the murder charge remaining unproved.

It was close to the end of June, and about a week before I had run out of stories to tell. My instinct had told me to delete the cases – few, anyway – that had involved shooting and bloodshed, and I later found that Thies had done the same, but otherwise I had been generous with all manner of details. Some of the incidents could be quickly verified, others took longer, and I endeavored to think of as many as possible of the latter. Eventually, though, I was running out of material, and the Gestapo knew it. Interrogations ceased abruptly, and I was left in my cell to dream up escape scenarios, ever more farfetched.

No further news about the invasion had come my way, but I figured that if the Germans had been able to throw the attackers into the sea, they would surely have boasted about it. One day shortly after the invasion excitement I had found the headquarters in an uproar once again; this time there was even more exuberance.

"The Führer has now unleashed the ultimate weapon on Great Britain, our V-1, a fantastic *Vergeltungswaffe*.[88] The war will be ended any time now."

Again Randschau was assuring me, and himself, of imminent and final German success. It was not difficult to see how badly they wanted to believe Hitler able to pull a rabbit out of a hat, but again I was incapable of making any kind of reasonable guess about what influence the V-1 might have on the war's outcome or duration. The only thing certain and obvious was that people believe what they want to believe and tend to construe all available evidence to support their beliefs. Was I guilty of wishful thinking myself? I wondered.

After three weeks they had allowed me to shave and granted my request that they contact my mother for some clothes. The next day a set of underwear and a shirt had arrived. The shirt was new and had French cuffs with silver cuff links I had never seen before. And I had never owned any shirt with French cuffs. As I fingered the cuff links, it suddenly struck me that they were the shape of an abstract "H" – Hanne! So they hadn't gotten her, and neither had she apparently taken refuge in Sweden.

The day after the clothes arrived an unexpected occurrence had put me temporarily in touch with Thies. The daily prison routine was altered to let the prisoners file into the yard for half an hour of exercise. For reasons only Gestapo knew, if any existed, I was not allowed to take part in this daily outing, but hearing the midmorning opening of cell doors and exit of prisoners had told me some change was afoot. Then one morning, the familiar noise of cell doors being opened did not skip No. 412. My cell door swung open too, and a new guard looked in, checking a list in his hand.

"Du bleibst da sitzend!"

The order to remain seated was appropriately brusk and his index finger pointing to the cell stool left no doubt about the meaning. Turning away from my door, he raised his voice in a shout.

"Alle 'raus."

The order echoed off the unyielding concrete walls, and everyone else emerged to walk in single file, ten feet apart, down the middle of the corridor toward an exit at the end which led to the yard. I watched for the first time my prison mates one by one as they passed by. Suddenly, there was Thies, in view for less than two seconds only fifteen feet away! He looked at me sideways without changing his facial expression of detached boredom. My cell remained open until half an hour later they all returned to their respective cells, and Thies and I had a second glimpse of each other as he walked by.

The following day the procedure repeated itself, but as Thies walked by he unobtrusively pitched a tiny ball of paper through my door. I put my foot on it and stood stock still, half expecting a guard to come tearing and cursing, but nothing happened. Nobody had noticed! An interminable half hour later, a guard closed and locked my cell door. In the dead angle close to the door that could not be viewed from the peephole I gently unfolded the small ball. It was sheet of toilet paper, better suitable to write on than modern soft tissue, and it was covered on both sides in the smallest possible writing.

> Well, this stupid Kraut guard obviously made a mistake by exposing you to the cruel world thru an open door but hoping he will be as stupid tomorrow I'll send you this and if you have something to write with we'll set up regular mail service on top of the cistern above the toilet in the second stall so when you take a shit look there and leave me a note at the same time I don't know why they honor you with that chain on your wrists but by all means don't let it go to your head ...

The letter went on in Thies' characteristic style, one unstoppable sentence, bringing me up to date on the issue we thought most likely to affect us. The invasion had succeeded; at least the British and American forces were still in France.

On my next trip to the toilets – we were allowed one daily visit just before the evening meal, otherwise the enameled chamber pot had to serve – I obtained toilet paper for a reply, and we had established a correspondence, somewhat irregular, depending on the availability of the second stall.

The redheaded agent had stopped talking and was looking at me expectantly, obviously curious about my reaction to the prospect he had portrayed of my impending demise. I opted not to satisfy his curiosity on that point.

"What about Thies?"

He didn't know.

After he left, I reviewed once more everything that had transpired since my arrest. It struck me that I had made yet another bad mistake by not attempting a break, however desperate. Interrogations finished, I could now only wait passively in my cell to be finished off; there would be no further opportunities to escape during transport. Suddenly the chances I had rated so low seemed quite promising. Bolting through a fourth-floor window or jumping twenty feet to a railroad track while dodging bullets had some merit after all – at least compared with being taken out, reduced to an undignified and futile struggle when being tied to a stake, and shot. I spent hours trying to think of some insult to shout at them just as they were pulling the triggers. Oh, what use? Who'd ever know? A bunch of goons who wouldn't remember beyond their next glass of beer. Damn! I was only twenty-four, way too young to die. At night in the privacy of gentle darkness, I tried a philosophic approach. Sure, I'm only twenty-four, but measured against eternity, twenty-four and one-hundred and twenty-four are equally long. Besides, what really matters is not how long you live but what quality of life you have enjoyed. I had to admit that my life had been a completely happy one. I had been favored by luck and circumstance, no real regrets about anything ... Trouble is, I decided, a good life merely sharpens one's appetite for yet more good life. Then I pondered whether I was afraid to die. I was not worried about going to hell, which I considered nonsense. On the other hand, paradise was surely equally nonsensical, so there was nothing to look forward to. What then was death to be like? Oblivion, probably, and that was nothing to look forward to, but nothing to be afraid of either. Yet, I had to admit to a feeling of fear, the kind we harbor, probably instinctually, toward the unknown. When I get out of here, I thought, I will never again allow myself to be unhappy in the course of daily living. Not for one minute. Then I realized that I had resolved "when" not "if" I would get out.

My decision four years earlier to fight the Germans had been immediate and spontaneous, voluntarily made, my own initiative. I had wanted active involvement, and I got it. Would history now assign me a rôle of unknown martyr, taken from his prison cell to be summarily liquidated, mourned by a few family members, then forgotten? Introspective analysis did not come naturally to me, but the confinement's solitude inevitably led me to do some, as I pondered the prospect of my approaching end. Was there solace in prayer? Many people apparently derived fortitude as well as peace of mind by praying, and I could see how fervent focus on one's wishes might lend a measure of confidence in one's ability to influence the course of events in a favorable manner. But unless prayer rests on a basis of belief in an omniscient and omnipotent god, it loses credibility, or perhaps efficacy. And my exposure to the Lutheran dogma had failed to kindle any firmness of belief. The idea that man should arrogate to himself a central position in the universe seemed to me then – as it still does – a notion childishly naïve, not to say presumptuous and vain. As for other religions, I knew little or nothing about them. The thought struck me that the Danes' low affinity for religion might have been a clue to their unwillingness to risk happiness, much less life, in the war, but I dismissed the explanation. So far as I knew, the main participants did not to any greater degree lean on God for strength and endurance. I wished I had some better understanding of philosophical systems. My education, firmly oriented toward things practical, had been sadly deficient in that area, and I resolved also to remedy that shortcoming. When I got out.

* * *

*This form of attack is, no doubt, of a trying
character ... In all up to six a.m. to-day,
about 2,750 flying bombs have been discharged
from the launching-stations along the French coast.*

Winston Churchill
in the House of Commons, 6 July

Hitler's launching of the V-1 "flying bombs" against England temporarily lifted Germany's sagging spirit. A pilotless airplane powered by a pulse jet, the V-1 was an early forerunner of America's cruise missile, and the bombs caused heavy damage until British ingenuity devised counter measures.[89] The demonstrative celebration I witnessed at Gestapo's headquarters was indicative of hopes that enough time could be gained for the Reich to allow new and spectacular weapons to shift the fortunes of war in Hitler's favor, but this was not to be. The lack of success was not due to any shortage of imaginary concepts on the drawing boards of Germany's designers. In 1939 the Germans had flown the world's first pure jet, a Heinkel 178, and two other jets took to the air in 1943, but the Allied bombing offensive delayed production so that only 200 became operational before the Red Army overran the factory. Only at the end of the war did the Allies discover German efforts to build a "New York bomber" to operate over the United States from bases in Western Europe.

With a rocket-propelled missile, the V-2, German engineers had by spring, 1944, taken the lead in a field of immense potential. The Allies had some intelligence information about German progress, and a bombing attack on the Peenemunde research station in August of 1943 was made specifically to delay the V-2's completion.

The German navy looked in vain toward new developments in naval warfare with which to recapture the initiative. Extravagant plans for superbattleships with 18-inch guns to outclass anything afloat anywhere had been shelved in the fall of 1941 when the Russian campaign proved to be more than a three-month affair. A new submarine design raised hopes of cutting, once and for all, the supply stream from America without which the Allied war effort would be stymied, but the estimated development time ruled it out. Instead, a modified electroboat version was put into production in two sizes, but Allied bombing again disrupted the Germans' desperate race against time.

A trend toward gigantism that intermittently appealed to Hitler gave rise to experimentation with monster tanks such as a 1,000-ton behemoth, nicknamed "Mouse", but nothing of practical value came of this tinkering. The ultimate in artillery size became the V-3, code named HDP *(Hochdruckspumpe),* that embodied a 150-yard barrel through which a series of explosions would drive a projectile all the way to downtown London. It reached only the planning stage.[90]

The Germans developed three nerve gases, Sarin, Somar and Tabun.[91] They were tested on prisoners of war and concentration camp inmates, but Hitler decided against using them at the front, as he believed (wrongly) that the Allies also had nerve gases. The Germans also performed butchery on hapless prisoners in the name of medical research, but to no avail other than sadistic gratification. The Japanese worked extensively on biological agents and in the process killed thousands of prisoners in tests. Some of the products were used in China but never against their Western adversaries. In 1945 they blew up the experimentation facilities, killed the surviving prisoners, and tried to cover up all evidence.

Overall, the secret weapons programs consumed vast amounts of resources, yielded little in return, and never came close to being cost effective, let alone offering a realistic hope of making a decisive difference.

Development of an atom bomb, the one weapon that could in German hands have altered the course of the war and of history, foundered on a miscalculation by German scientists about how large a quantity or critical mass would be needed.[92] The Germans arrived at far too large a figure, and as Hitler expected a quick victory, a project costly in resources and stretching over several years had no appeal. In contrast to their German allies, the Japanese understood the atomic bomb potential and had a better grasp of the problems, but they lacked the resources to pursue a program of development.

Chapter 44   July 1944

My time should have run out already, and here I was doing embroidery with my hands chained, something not nearly as difficult as it sounds. It had taken me only a week to do the needlework – a forest scene with an elk – in cross-stitch, about two-thirds of a square foot, and it was nearing completion.

After my mother had been informed of my whereabouts and had sent the parcel with clothes, she had, unbeknown to me, pestered the Gestapo daily with requests for permission to bring me food. With the unrelenting persistence only parental love can fuel, she actually wore them down. They first gave her angry lectures about how bad I was ... "ein ganz böser Kerl, Frau Skov!" And when it had been translated to her, she patiently explained to them that there must be some mistake, for I had always been a very good boy, etc. In the end they probably concluded that she was slightly daft. To my immense surprise I had one day been fetched from my cell to a visiting room where she was waiting. Seeing her, I came for one brief moment close to feeling regret. She had lost weight, in fact she seemed to have diminished in size; and her auburn hair had turned noticeably grey. She had aged twenty years in little over a month. On my cot in the dark that night, I cried, the only time I remember doing so during that period, for it had dawned on me that parents are the real losers in war.

She brought a basket full of delicacies which I was permitted to eat on the spot in the visiting room but not take to my cell: *frikadeller* (small meatballs), cheese, fresh strawberries ... I wolfed it all down while we talked, two guards hovering over us with sour miens. She also brought a piece of needlework can-

273

vas and some yarn. She had been told by some that prisoners were being tortured around the clock and by others that we were bored. She preferred to believe the latter and consequently thought the needlework would be in order. There was also a pack of small cigars which the guards reluctantly let me take to my cell. Being only an occasional smoker, I nevertheless enjoyed the cigars a lot but found to my surprise that tobacco didn't taste like anything in the dark, although the glowing red point seemed like company.

The day after the redheaded agent's visit, my steel door had swung open and let two men into my cell. They were about my age, clean-cut in that inimitable way that marked them as young Germans of the Hitler period, wore civilian clothes, and spoke Danish only haltingly, so we used German. At this point it could serve no purpose to deny that I could speak the language.

"In the Danish army you were *Scharfschütze* with machine pistol, and you volunteered at one time to help the Finns against Russia ... If we could work out a chance for you to come with us to fight our common Bolshevik enemy, would you be interested?"

"Keep talking."

They explained that they were in charge of collecting *eine kleine Spezialtruppe*, a commando squad, to be parachuted behind the lines on the Eastern Front to harass the Russian Rear. My thoughts were already racing ahead ... Oh, to get my hands on a Schmeisser submachine gun and again be able to influence my own fate. Moreover, if there were *two* of us in that situation, the possibilities would skyrocket.

"Are you making this offer also to Thies?"

They claimed not to know his name and did not like the suggestion. So, I would be alone, but with luck I could still take out an entire squad and surrender to the Russians. If only I had spoken a few words of Russian! I had a quick vision of myself in German uniform, hands over my head, at gunpoint trying to communicate with a bunch of scruffy Russkies, in German.

"Hey guys, I know what you're thinking, but things are not really what they seem ..."

It was all I could do to keep from chuckling. I would assuredly end up dead, but so would I by waiting here; by taking my chances with these two characters, I could at least take a bunch of Nazis with me.

My visitors were now describing the fun and games of *Spezialtruppen,* but I was only half listening, simultaneously contemplating what such an adventure would look like to the rest of the world. Beyond a shadow of doubt, everyone would think me a turncoat and a coward. My mother was the only one who would uncritically accept whatever I did, but she would know what everyone else was thinking, and there were people who would remind her of it for the rest of her life. The decision was not hard after all.

"Thanks, fellas, but no thanks. I am very good with a machine pistol, even your heavy and clumsy Schmeisser, but my skills are not for hire."

Their faces changed, first to surprise, then contempt, and I knew precisely what they were thinking. *Those opposing the Führer really are criminals who cannot be reasoned with. The Gestapo showed poor judgment in suggesting this ... and what effrontery about the Schmeisser.* They left me abruptly to my solitude and my musings about what the morrow might bring: a firing squad or further uncertainty?

A few days later, on the morning of 1 July, the faucet over the small sink in the corner of my cell refused to yield a drop when it was turned on. No breakfast appeared, nor any other meal the rest of the day. In the afternoon, the prisoners were lined up in small groups outside the building under heavy guard and ordered to dig a latrine trench. I spotted Thies a short distance away, but it was impossible for us to talk. After using the trench for its intended purpose, we marched back in single file to our cells. The next three days passed without food and with only one small water ration, but with daily visits to the latrine trench. Then the water was turned back on, and the prison routine returned to normal. This had been my first encounter with being hungry, really hungry, and I observed with interest that my body seemed unaffected except for the nagging desire to eat.

I had never been a fussy eater and was without any dislikes except one, heavy pea soup, actually pease porridge, which in Denmark usually was cooked on a ham bone smothered in yellow split peas. In the evening of the day when the water was turned back on, I heard the food cart coming down the hall, rattling its way with agonizing slowness from cell to cell, and realized that our fasting ordeal must be at an end. We were finally about to get fed again. The cart kept up its snail's pace, as I worried feverishly whether it would run out of food before reaching cell #412, but at long last it stopped outside my door. Getting a grip on myself as the key turned noisily, I assumed a position of indifference, as if preoccupied with something or other of greater importance – they weren't going to see me standing with my tongue hanging out, drooling like a dog waiting for a handout. The door swung open and an ambrosial whiff of hot food wafted in on the breeze. The guard unlocked my chain and handed me a bowl of pease porridge and a chunk of dry black bread which I put on the shelf with studied indifference. As the door clanged shut, I sat down and took in the sight: it was without a doubt the finest and most desirable meal I had ever seen, and I relished every drop and every crumb. I've had a soft spot for pease porridge ever since.

The interruption in the prison routine with an interlude of minor hardship was puzzling at the time. In my solitary confinement, however, I was blithely ignorant about the reasons. Obviously, something important must have happened, but the only thing important enough to affect me in my current predicament was the invasion and the outcome of the war. Or so I thought. As week after dreary week went by, even the expectation of imminent death began to lose its dread and was replaced by the calmness of resignation. The Danish summer of '44 was dry, sunny and lovely. In the tiny flower bed visible from my cell window grew one single rose, and when I chinned myself to window height twenty times every morning, I glimpsed its progress from bud to blood-red, magnificent bloom.

My correspondence with Thies via toilet cistern had been a welcome but brief diversion. We never alluded to any of our sabotage cooperation, nor to any interrogation experience. Instead, we wrote about personal and family affairs, and Thies never tired of reviling and belaboring the Germans in terms of choice obscenity and to speculate about when our countrymen would see the light. If everyone started to resist in a serious way, the Krauts would in his opinion panic with unpredictable results. That led him in one of his letters onto a different track.

> ... and you know people panic over the smallest things like late last fall my cousin who has the cabin near the furesø swimming beach went to check that all was secure and he was down in the cellar that has a small window toward the beach it is up high in the cellar but just at ground level hardly noticeable if you look at it from the outside and while he is rummaging there in the half dark because there is no electricity a guy strolls up outside and my cousin peeks out to see if he's a burglar because he looks kind of suspicious as he looks all around him but then he drops his pants and squats down right in front of the basement window to make a call on nature and after much labor and groaning he delivers an enormous turd and my cousin sees a chance to do something unusual and grabs a shovel from the garden tools he has stored for the winter and opens the window real quiet-like and sticks the shovel out at the critical moment to catch the turd and silently retracts thru the window and the guy wipes himself with some dry leaves and gets up pulls up his pants and is ready to leave but before he does he turns around to admire the result of his efforts and there is nothing there so he looks left and right and all around and even up in the air as if a turd could fly and then he totally panics and runs away as if the devil himself is on his heels so you see if people panic over something like that you can imagine what real trouble would do to the Krauts ...

The story in Thies' inimitable style had made me laugh so hard that I wondered if the guards heard me. The scatological yarn was in every way vintage Thies and for some reason helped me keep the world and its inhabitants in perspective. But there had been no letters from him after the interlude of dry water taps and outside latrines. My own lay uncollected on top of the cistern in the second toilet stall.

To occupy my mind, I fell back on my half-completed engineering education and designed – in mental pictures only – a line of farm equipment appropriate for Danish agriculture, feeling certain that it would be a smash hit in the post-

276

war market. My inventory of songs also proved a source of diversion. Although my memory for names is deplorable, I remember numbers and poetry with ease. When working as a machinist and operating a lathe or milling machine, I had been in the habit of singing the night shift away, anything from historical folk music to popular tunes, the noise of the machines drowning out my voice. Singing stimulates the mind and keeps one's repertoire alive and fresh. In my solitude I now constructed a mental, alphabetized file of folk songs to which I knew all the lyrics, starting with the national anthem. There is probably not one Dane in a thousand who knows all the verses to the national anthem, but if I start singing it, the words dutifully come to mind, out of somewhere. It is an ability of questionable value; but then, we are stuck with the aptitudes nature has allotted us.

I finished the embroidery, having sewed my name, date and place in the corner. The elk looked impressive, I thought, standing proudly by a forest stream, bellowing a mating call, no doubt. I wondered if I would ever see an elk in the wild. Tomorrow I would try to smuggle my handiwork out to my mother by hiding it in a batch of dirty laundry.

* * *

He that is slow to anger is better than the mighty ...

Proverbs 16:32

After the upheavals of the summer of 1943, Denmark's "department head rule" had continued, with German authorities neither approving nor rejecting the arrangement. Occupation policy instead became subject to some of the internecine rivalry endemic among the different tentacles of the Nazi octopus. In the fall, SS-Gruppenführer Günther Pancke had been posted to Copenhagen as Polizeiführer, Police Chief, in Denmark and immediately joined in the ongoing fray between the military commander, General von Hanneken, a brutal and not-too-bright soldier, and the civilian administrator, Dr. Best, a prototypic German *Herr Doktor* with transparent hopes that his Nazi career would lead him to fame in the position of *Statthalter*. The natural outcome was a political and administrative zigzag in which the German civilian administration urged negotiation and persuasion toward the Danes, while the military took the hard line of advocating martial law. The SS just opted for terror actions, its customary method of operating.

After overrunning the Danish military installations on 29 August, the Germans had demobilized the small army and navy contingents. The Danish officer corps, having no taste for irregular or partisan warfare, set about organizing an "underground army" to be used in case of an Allied invasion in Denmark, an uncertain prospect conveniently in the future. The general public, however, responded by increased sabotage.

As 1944 began, the SS together with auxiliaries recruited from among the Danish population embarked on a program of random vandalism, dynamiting Tivoli, the Royal Porcelain Factory, the Royal Yacht Club pavilion, and sundry other historic and revered landmarks. Making use of informers, they also succeeded in catching or killing a number of saboteurs, but the resistance fought back by shooting informers who could be clearly identified and tracked down. The Germans in turn retaliated on Hitler's orders with "clearing murders": five random street killings for every informer liquidated. In these activities a group of Danish auxiliaries organized into a unit called Schalburgkorpset, the Schalburg Corps, became notorious as they operated under the aegis of the SS.[93]

By June, 1944 the situation had deteriorated so that the Germans after a large sabotage incident clamped a tight curfew on the entire Copenhagen area. In response, the blacksmiths at B&W downed their tools the following day at 2 p.m. and went home on the pretext of needing to tend their vegetable gardens before curfew time. But at the 8 p.m. curfew, hundreds of thousands of citizens crowded the streets in the balmy evening, making a point of defying German patrols. Surprisingly, the Germans backed down the following day and reduced the curfew to a few midnight hours, but under the influence of their zigzag policy a simultaneous statement announced the execution of eight saboteurs. That brought the public mood to a boil.

The result was an all-encompassing people's strike, shutting down factories, offices, stores, and all forms of transportation and communication. Only water and electric power supplies kept functioning. In the streets of Copenhagen people eagerly erected barricades to obstruct the German patrols, while exulting in a feeling of solidarity, citizen-to-citizen, facing the common danger. For once, the Germans put their internal disagreements aside and in impotent fury ordered operation *Monsun*, a plan prepared in order to punish the city. General von Hanneken placed the capital under martial law; set up road blocks to close down all traffic into and out of the city; called Wehrmacht units from all over the country to Copenhagen where they shut off water and electricity supplies; placed automatic weapons at street intersections; and with patrols and armored cars unleashed a street terror that in a matter of hours caused hundreds of civilian casualties.

Up to this point Danish authorities had stayed on the sidelines, but implementation of *Monsun* raised the specter of subjecting entire sections of the capital to destruction by bombardment or artillery fire, with potentially appalling losses among civilians. The Chief Mayor together with a few members of Parliament obtained German agreement to cancel curfew and blockade in return for their making an appeal to the citizenry to call off the strike. The appeal was made, but the country's Frihedsraad, the self-established Freedom Council which had begun to speak on behalf of the growing resistance movement to the remnants of constitutional authority, published a different appeal, urging citizens to keep up the strike until the Schalburg Corps was removed from the city. The citizens chose to heed the Council, and the strike continued.

In full psychologic retreat, the Germans moved the Schalburg Corps to Ringsted, a city well away from the capital. This finally caused the Freedom Council through the underground press to urge people back to work, calling off the strike.

During this confrontation in the summer of '44 which had followed that of the summer of '43, the ministerial department heads who had been left with the unenviable task of making the best of a hopelessly messy political situation had striven valiantly to prevent convicted resistance people from being sent to prison or concentration camps in Germany. Over strenuous Danish protest this had happened two years earlier to Communists arrested in the wake of the ban on Communism. These had first been interned in a Danish camp at Horserød in Northern Zealand against a German promise not to send them south. The promise was subsequently broken and most of the Communists deported, ending up in the concentration camp Stutthof. After much agonizing, the department heads had decided to build another facility in their attempt to keep resistance prisoners in Danish custody, reasoning that even a small delay of eventual deportation would justify the effort. The result became the Frøslev facility. It received its first complement of prisoners in August, 1944.

In the aftermath of the July clashes between unarmed Danish civilians and German military forces, the Germans eased up on executions for a while and transferred a number of prisoners held in custody, some under death sentence, from Vestre Fængsel in Copenhagen to the comparative comfort of the Frøslev camp. The timing was most fortuitous for us of the *Hjemmefronten* group.

Chapter 45

August 1944

You can never plan the future by the past.

Edmund Burke

Thies fished another cigarette out of the blue pack of North State he had received by mail from Cordia, his fiancée. He lit it with an expression of intense pleasure, blowing the smoke into the crystal-clear air of the early autumn afternoon. The blue North State was the stronger variety that he preferred over the yellow. Then he summarized our long discussion about the appropriateness of our plan to escape.

"Staying here we can't do anybody any good."

We were sitting on the sunny side of our barracks hut, leaning our backs against the wall and observing the leisurely life of the Frøslev camp, where our fellow prisoners were going about a variety of activities. A short distance to our left Birger Mouritzen was whittling on an oak paper knife with a mermaid handle, carefully shaping her breasts to a barely believable size. In the shade of the next hut a group was playing bridge.

It was over two weeks since I had arrived in Frøslev from Vestre Fængsel, and it had been some change. One morning in late August, four SS guards had walked into my cell. I half expected to be carted off for execution, but instead they had sullenly removed my chain and ordered me to line up outside together with some two dozen others. We were put into two military trucks and under heavy guard rumbled out of town, across Zealand and onto the ferry to Funen. The guards did not allow us off the trucks while on the ferry, and after landfall the trip continued across the island of Funen to Jutland where we turned south toward the border. We were beginning to think ourselves on the way to Germany, but the trip ended just north of that fateful line in the village of Frøslev, where we drove through a gate in a barbed wire fence and were finally told to

The author as a prisoner in the Frøslev concentration camp in Denmark in August, 1944. Before being sent to Germany, he was photographed by the SS, and the picture was later retrieved from Gestapo files.

get off. To my delight Thies appeared at the tailgate the moment I hit the ground and for a moment forgot his imperturbability.

"So, they finally brought the hard core down here!" He was shouting, pounding me on the back and dragging me away, urging the rest of the newcomers to follow.

"Did they get my Ribe group?" I had to know, for it had been on my mind for so long.

"Yes, I'm afraid so. I have told them that it couldn't be because the Krauts squeezed their names out of you."

We had been walking to a barracks where Danish personnel was busy setting the tables. Upon entering, we could hardly believe our eyes: milk, fresh bread, beef patties, steamed potatoes, gravy, jam ... we sat down, solemnly and momentarily silent, and started to eat dinner. Except for the food my mother had brought me at her one visit, this was my first real meal since my arrest the previous May.

Frøslev was a concentration camp established under an agreement between the German and Danish authorities in an attempt by the latter to prevent Danish citizens who had run afoul of the Gestapo from being sent to incarceration in Germany. The guards were German, but the camp was run by the Danish department of prison administration with Danish mess personnel. But why should the Germans have relented to the extent of sending what they considered serious criminals, even condemned prisoners, to this prime retreat? The answer had become clear after dinner, when Thies and I sat down by ourselves to compare notes. For openers, Thies relayed a lot of information and news about which I was utterly ignorant.

The break in the prison routine when we went without food and water at the beginning of July had been caused by a general strike in Copenhagen that spread to the rest of the country. An increase in executions, various German terror actions and a restrictive curfew had brought the showdown. To get the population back to work the Germans had backed down. The stubborn action by our countrymen had evidently saved the lives of those of us who had been singled out for execution. Niels Jørgensen had ascertained that six of us from the *Hjemmefronten* group were thus prevented from prematurely departing this world. Frøslev had been completed shortly after the general strike, and compared with the Vestre Fængsel prison it was a vacation retreat. The Danish personnel showered us with kindness and good food and bought the guards' connivance by giving them the same treatment.

Thies showed me a *Berlingske Tidende* newspaper report on an attempt on 20 July to assassinate Hitler. Unfortunately, it had been a failure. It had caused some changes in the Nazi hierarchy with Himmler being put in charge of the home army, and Guderian being put on the General Staff. The paper also reported that the Americans had landed on Guam. To assess the significance of that item, we tried but could not establish exactly where Guam was.

Next, we compared interrogation experiences. With Thies they had also tried a rough approach, hitting him with a typewriter on top of his head, but he had persisted in a story not unlike mine. Not knowing what the other might be telling, we had both minimized the extent of our activities together. Without prior discussion or plans for this turn of events both of us had also sensibly omitted mention of any incident in which shooting had taken place.

What was to be learned? How did they catch both of us so easily?

The answer was that we had both failed to get to our guns fast enough; if a handgun is to be of real value, the owner must be able to draw it and fire in not more than one second. We had both felt confident about our marksmanship but had neglected the time element in bringing the skill to bear.

We concluded that in any situation where one is being arrested, held up or otherwise detained by bad guys, the chance of regaining freedom is better the earlier the attempt is made. Time is on the side of the opponent who will endeavor to strip the prisoner of weapons, handcuff him, put him in a cell or other secure place, or otherwise put him at maximum disadvantage. Really quite elementary, we thought, but nevertheless well worth remembering, and we resolved to stay mentally prepared for quick action, should we ever be held up or otherwise threatened by an enemy or other opponent. Our experience made it easy for us to appreciate that the victim's momentary confusion and hesitation, natural concomitants of surprise, work strongly to the aggressor's advantage.

The next two weeks had been pleasant enough. The *Hjemmefronten* people and five of the six in my Ribe group had already spent several weeks in Frøslev

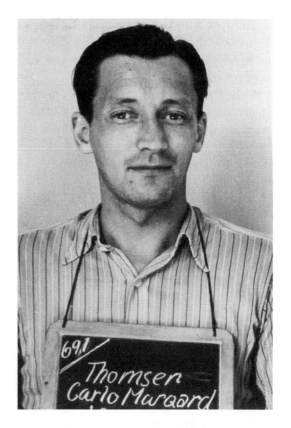

Carlo (Thies) Marqvard Thomsen (1914-1985) as a prisoner in the Frøslev concentration camp in Denmark in August, 1944. Before being sent to Germany, he was photographed by the SS, and the picture was later retrieved from Gestapo files.

when I arrived. They were the only ones I knew among the camp's population. We debriefed each other and pieced together a picture of what had taken place. The *Hjemmefronten* group had been betrayed by Markussen, the rat-faced printer. Thies had been arrested in the print shop where Gestapo agents had been waiting when he came to typeset the newssheet. The notes in my pocket calendar had given the Gestapo enough of a lead to find most of the Ribe group.

A gentlemen's agreement of sorts existed in Frøslev that no one would try to escape unless everyone else did so too, as otherwise the Germans were bound to clamp down, install an all-German administration and impose harsher conditions, perhaps even send all of us to a German concentration camp. We had heard about these camps where rebellious elements were kept in confinement, but practically nothing was known about them. Still, we were sure Danish custody was preferable.

Thies and I discussed at length this self-imposed restriction and concluded that it played into the hands of the Germans. Better for some to escape than for everyone to wait like lambs before slaughter. Besides, the Allies seemed to be making only slow progress in France, and for all we knew, the war could drag on for years while we stood by passively. The reasonable thing to do was to get back on the scene and put our recent experience to use. With what we now knew about how the *Sicherheitsdienst* functioned, we should be able to elude capture indefinitely. We would also know how to rescue a prisoner being transported from prison to interrogation.

While the two of us were contemplating the matter one afternoon, the sudden chatter of a machine pistol had broken the quiet of the camp. An SS guard in one of the towers had gunned down without warning one of our fellow prisoners. The ostensible reason for the shooting was that the prisoner, who was not known to Thies or me, had strayed too close to the barbed wire perimeter fence, but it appeared to be, and no doubt was, a simple case of intimidation. That particular wanton killing had made up our minds for us: We decided to make a break for freedom. The same afternoon we had laid a plan of sorts. Getting out would not be too difficult. There were no minefields or dogs or trip wires; and once out we could easily make our way back to Copenhagen and pick up where we had left off. Only doing it better.

One of the mess personnel came from the SS guardhouse, making some inquiry at the bridge table and was sent in our direction.

"Is one of you Niels Skov?"

I nodded.

"They want you in the office. Your brother and sister are here to visit you."

Thies and I exchanged glances. He was aware that I had a sister but no brother. I got up and walked to the office, setting my face in an expression of pleased anticipation while wondering what would come next. Visits were not allowed. When entering the visiting room, I found to my delight Hanne and Torben Halkjær. With false ID cards and a box of genuine Cuban cigars, they had bribed their way from the sentry at the public access road to the camp commander himself and obtained permission to see me. With the Gestapo looking for them all over the country, they had walked into the lion's den, an audacity to take your breath away.

We spent fifteen minutes together and were able to chat and exchange a fair amount of veiled information, while an SS guard in the corner watched us indifferently from under a cloud of blue smoke from one of the Cubans, his personal bonus. Hanne carried on a low continuous chitchat into which she wove brief items of important news. The Allies were making good progress; Paris had been liberated. After fifteen minutes, his cigar half smoked, the guard signaled that the visit was over. Hanne embraced me and with her lips at my ear gave me the message that was the purpose of their visit.

"Day after tomorrow at 2 a.m. we'll be outside the fence between second and third guard towers."

Torben shook my hand firmly. His parting words were spoken with mock sincerity for the guard's benefit.

"Tell everyone else in here to behave better in the future and not to run afoul of the law."

With that parting shot they left and I hurried back to Thies. We immediately checked the fence and agreed that the spot was well chosen. It was 14 September and the nights were dark, perfect for our purpose, so we completed our preparations which included a scheme to short-circuit both the search lights and the illumination of the fence. Primed and ready to escape in less than twenty-four hours, we were instead roused at 4 a.m. the next morning together with the rest of the camp. From the assembly, some two hundred of us were chosen and bundled into a train of freight cars that began a slow crawl south across the border and on toward Hamburg.

* * *

The man who is tenacious of purpose in a rightful cause is not shaken from his firm resolve by the frenzy of his fellow citizens clamoring for what is wrong, or by the tyrant's threatening countenance.

Horace

In the late summer of 1944, the pressure of Allied armies driving into France from the invasion beaches coincided with catastrophic defeats and huge Wehrmacht losses on the Eastern Front. Despite the bleak situation, Hitler still maintained his hold on power as head of both state and armed forces. His strength had been founded at the outset on a great deal of genuine support. The population had been swayed at the elections in 1932 and 1933 by flattery and glorification of Germanness, and by appeals to traditionally strong national loyalties. There had been pressure as well. The SA street brawlers had served their purpose of intimidation, and loss of career opportunities was certain in all walks of life for those who failed to cooperate with the party.

A decade later, pressure and coercion had become predominant. Himmler's SS and SD, assisted by numerous other shadowy agencies, monitored unceasingly the civilian population and struck mercilessly at any murmur of discontent. Whatever the motivation in the heart of each citizen, there was never any possibility of widespread growth or concealment of opposition to the regime.

The German officer of World War Two cooperated with the Nazi system for reasons as varied as those of the civilian citizen: ideological commitment, unit cohesion, concern for subordinates, desire for decorations and promotion, avarice,[94] simple fear of defeat. And the ubiquitous menace of Himmler's spies hovered over soldier and civilian alike. Wherever dedication lacked in the lower ranks, the leadership enforced obedience and discipline with a system of military justice best described as terror. An average of 5,000 executions per year for an estimated wartime total of 30,000[95] throw a revealing light on one reason for the solidity of German soldiery.

The attempts that nevertheless took place to remove Hitler testify that there will always be some individuals strong enough both to refuse temptation and to disdain being cowed. The earlier mentioned attempts did not come to public knowledge at the time they occurred, but in July of 1944 a very small group of high-ranking officers carried out a plot that could not be concealed from the public. The group centered on Lt. Colonel Klaus Philip Schenk, Count von Stauffenberg. Born to an old, distinguished South German family, von Stauffenberg was possessed of a brilliant, inquisitive mind. At the age of 19, he entered the army as an officer cadet in the Bamberger Cavalry Regiment, the famed *Bamberger Reiter*.

After several abortive tries von Stauffenberg on 20 July attended a meeting in Hitler's Rastenburg headquarters to which he brought a bomb in his briefcase. Just before detonation, Hitler changed his position in the room and thereby survived the explosion.

The failure of von Stauffenberg's bomb to exterminate Hitler unleashed a massacre of members of the officer corps, the aristocracy, and conservatives of the old regime. Drumhead trials and "people's courts" meted out summary justice to Germans who had known nothing of the plot and whose culpability was based on nothing more than guilt by association. Hitler ordered the plotters to be "strung up like cattle," and so they were. In an orgy of torture and killings, the secret police organizations shot, hanged and tortured to death virtually all of Germany's actual and potential opposition to the regime,[96] filming the goriest executions for Hitler's enjoyment.

Chapter 46   September 1944

*The belief in a supernatural source of evil
is not necessary; men alone are quite capable
of every wickedness.*

Joseph Conrad

Thies and I stood between two slop buckets at the freight car's steel door when the train finally came to a halt. The trip from Frøslev had taken two days, most of the time spent idly at remote sidings in the countryside. We had seen neither food nor water, as the freight car had stayed bolted shut, and the tin cans serving as slop buckets had been long overflowing. Reacquaintance with hunger and thirst had told us that we had become indurated to neither by our brief ordeal in Vestre Fængsel. As we were to find out, one never becomes used to being hungry. Never, never, never. With a dull screech the door slid open, and after a quick glance out our eyes met. We had arrived at Neuengamme concentration camp.

We descended from the filth of the car. As our small Danish column trudged through the gate in the electric fence, I could not help thinking of Dante's admonition *All hope abandon, ye who enter here!* We walked to one of the low, ugly buildings where we were ordered to undress for showering. Our clothes went into a large barrel while personal belongings, money and wristwatches went into a smaller one. Then we proceeded into the building, showered briefly without soap in tepid water and filed out the other side of the building where a Kapo sheared the hair off our heads with a dull manual clipper and told us to get dressed, pointing to a pile of rags on the ground. The Kapos were prisoners working in staff functions, and the name is an acronym formed from the word *Kameradschaftspolizei*, the term itself a morbid joke as they were brutal killers, drawn from the criminal elements among the inmates.

There is something strange, alienating and demeaning in being shorn of one's hair. People are hardly recognizable as the upper part of their heads appear, like great, white maggots, for the first time in their adult lives. Looking around at each other we gamely cracked a few feeble jokes about our new and glabrous appearances, unwilling to admit that the bastards were getting to us, but as we picked through the rag pile, wet and already miserable, we secretly longed for our warm and comfortable clothes on the other side of the building and wished for some kind of headcover to hide our nakedness.

Thies was savagely expostulating on the irony in trying to delouse Danes, of whom not one percent had ever seen a flea or a louse, but I began vaguely to perceive that the exercise had a purpose altogether different from cleanliness or hygiene. It was the first step in a process of methodical dehumanization, of converting us from ordinary healthy citizens into creatures merely caricatures of humanity, the subhumans of which Hitler was babbling and which the super-race could eliminate without qualms, indeed with feelings of doing virtuous work with a good conscience, as one might have when ridding society of vermin.

We were marked as political prisoners by red triangles sewn to our rag coats, so that we were to that extent identifiable on sight. We later learned that other colors indicated other categories: green for common criminals, black for asocial individuals, brown for gypsies, yellow for Jews, the digits 175 for homosexuals, and so forth. As we moved on to our assigned block, a one-story wooden barracks building, we saw what further changes a few weeks or months wrought in the prison population. Starvation and illness added grotesque touches to the appearances, as some of the inmates deteriorated physically and mentally to a state the guards contemptuously called *Mussulman*, a shadowy state of dwindling life in which the victim as a walking skeleton has crossed the borderline between ravenous and good-as-dead. Thies and I realized that we were looking at facsimiles of ourselves, seeing what we were destined to become sometime in the not too distant future, unless we got out or the war ended. It was clear to us that a concentration camp was designed as an ultimate destination. The intent was for us to succumb to illness, hunger or summary execution, whereupon we would disappear into some unmarked grave or otherwise be disposed of as just so much rubbish. In effect, we had been consigned to oblivion.

It is difficult to describe a concentration camp. The physical conditions can be readily related: the double fences of electrified, barbed wire, the squalid barracks separated by internal fences of barbed wire, the filth, the tiny ration of low-grade food. What cannot be communicated is the atmosphere, the mood of the place, the pervasive fear generated by the imminence of gruesome death.

Neuengamme contained about ten thousand prisoners.[97] Breakfast was thin ersatz coffee. The one and only daily meal was dished out in late afternoon and consisted of a chunk of bread, heavily laced with sawdust,[98] and a bowl of "soup," actually salty water with pieces of boiled turnip. Unless an inmate had been assigned to an *Arbeitskommando,* a work group, the day was spent in idleness, but no one was allowed to go inside the barracks block. Everyone had to stand outside on the dirt which became a filthy muck when it rained, as it did most of the time, because fall was underway. In the evening the inmates had to stand endlessly at muster in the central square, being counted and recounted, usually in the rain, and at night sleep was interrupted by compulsory trips to the large air raid shelters, when Allied bombers unloaded their cargo on nearby Hamburg. We soon realized that these trips had nothing to do with concern for our safety; they served as harassment by depriving us of some of the sleep for which our exhausted bodies cried out. When the sirens sounded their grim ululations, prisoners thronged in and out of the shelters in a solid mass of humanity with Kapos running on top of the mass, stepping on heads and shoulders and with their clubs raining blows onto this living carpet in futile attempts to hurry things along.

On our second day, a Polish woman from the smaller, separate female section of the camp was hanged in a public ceremony. She had a baby, probably from being raped by the SS, and in her desperate effort to keep the infant alive she had committed the ultimate crime of stealing a piece of bread. Caught, she was promptly hanged in a gallows on the edge of the square. The baby was strung up beside her in a bag. By the following morning the bag had stopped moving, presumably because exposure had completed the work of starvation. The irremediable horror of such scenes made a deep impression on the newly arrived, but with the adaptability under stress that humans possess, or perhaps in an instinctive attempt at psychologic defense, we soon became inured to the ways of the camp.

Shortly after our arrival a contingent of newcomers marched into an enclosure within shouting distance of ours. They looked somehow familiar and had been permitted to wear their own clothes. They turned out to be a group of Danish police who, incredibly, were reluctant to talk with us, as they considered us criminals.[99]

The SS guards were visible mainly at the camp's perimeter, manning the towers, gates and nearby administrative barracks. From time to time one would enter our block which then had to spring to attention. It happened shortly after our arrival, one morning before we were ordered outside for the day. A guard appeared in the doorway, looked around as we came to instant attention, and began a slow stroll down the center aisle between the barrack's two rows of bunks. There was dead silence in the building, broken only by the clicks of his heels against the floor boards. In his hat was the silver eagle with a swastika in its talons, on his collar patch gleamed the jagged silver runes of the SS. As he moved down the row, the black uniform seemed like death itself approaching. We sensed that he was angling for an opening, just a flicker of a cause, to unleash the unbridled cruelty savored by the sadist, and we kept a posture of rigid attention at the foot of our bunks, everyone looking down or straight ahead to avoid meeting his glance, lest he might read in our eyes a hint of our thoughts.

He stopped in front of a middle-aged school teacher and pointed to the dirty blanket on his bunk which had been rolled up but was lying slightly askew. The schoolteacher understood the hissed command and quickly bent to adjust the bundle. As he did so, the cane came down in a lightning slash across his back, and as his reflex caused him to jerk upright, the guard hit him across the face, crushing his lips and breaking his front teeth. The incident took but three or four seconds, and the guard immediately continued his stroll at the same un-hurried pace.

Thies and I had managed to get adjoining bunks and every evening discussed our situation in whispers after dark. It was clear to us how the camp system itself helped establish the SS attitude. As starvation and cold reduced the inmates to a state of desperation and despair in which the survival instinct gradually sup-planted civilized human emotions, the SS could with contempt point to the "subhuman" behavior of their victims and slaughter them without compunc-tion.

We resolved rather to die of hunger than to let down our civilization and vowed to get through our predicament by making ourselves into a "unit of two," assuring each other – and ourselves – that it would more than double our chances of survival. By sticking together and looking out for each other as we had been used to doing as saboteurs, the two of us would stand a far better chance of coping than one man alone. Survival clearly would be furthered more by determined mutual support than by attempts at individual preserva-tion. Rumor had it that *Arbeitskommandos* were chosen from time to time, and we decided to grab any chance to change scenery, but to stay together at all costs.

In our whispered exchange we also discovered, odd as it may sound, that we never before had come close to realizing the merit of our cause. The full scope of horror that Nazism was perpetrating was only now being borne in on us.

Our whispered strategy talks always ended on an optimistic note, and then we reverted to talk about food, our favorite and inexhaustible topic, discussing and planning in elaborate detail meals we would consume together with our fami-lies on such and such a happy future occasion. In our hungry state food talk never failed to generate pleasure and excitement. It is a miracle that our diges-tive juices did not eat right through our stomach walls.

"The Americans have crossed the Rhine!"

The news was passed on excitedly, but later on we realized that such "news" was deliberately released by the Germans only to arouse hope followed by sub-sequent deeper despair. A simple *Nervenkrieg*, psychologic warfare.

The rumor about Arbeitskommandos proved true, however. After two weeks of hellish existence in Neuengamme about half of the Danish prisoners were one morning assigned to a work group of some fifteen hundred men and shoved into freight cars which started rumbling northwards, back in the direc-

290

tion from which we had recently come. Thies and I got ourselves included, and two days later our train arrived in Husum.

* * *

The advance of a Russian army is something that Westerners cannot imagine ...

Hasso von Manteufel

The reality of the concentration camps was one reflection of the Nazi attitude toward those they considered enemies or racial inferiors. In the East this German contempt for the suffering of others, or the outright sadism, was demonstrated particularly by the SS *Sonderkommandos* and *Einsatzgruppen* as well as the Wehrmacht soldiers who dutifully followed orders. But the mindless viciousness of German fighting methods turned out not to be the expedient Hitler had hoped would bring quick victory. Instead, it was a costly mistake that infuriated Germany's adversaries and appalled the world at large. In Russia, German excesses imbued the simple Soviet soldier with a wrathful determination that helped forge the Red Army into a fearsome fighting force.

Three years after the Germans had wantonly challenged the Russian bear, the Red Army had despite its losses become the largest land force ever to take the field in battle in all of recorded history.   Enhanced with material support from the Western Allies, this immense army was the angry host that in the summer of 1944 had expelled the German invader from Soviet territory and was now pushing into Poland. Toward the end of July the Red Army slowed its advance in the approaches to Warsaw and paused on the Vistula River across from the city. The Polish exile government in London was eager to have the Polish underground army, the AK (Armie Krajowa) take control of the capital before the arrival of the Soviets and ordered the AK in the city to rise against the Germans. The poorly equipped insurgents rose and fought bravely, hoping for outside help. Disliking the Poles fully as much as Hitler did, Stalin refused to send aid and also refused to facilitate delivery of help by British and American long-distance air operations.

The Germans put the uprising down with a barbarity equalled only at the destruction of the Ghetto one year earlier, simultaneously razing the city on Hitler's orders. In September Russian units started crossing the Vistula, and Stalin lifted his veto on letting the Americans use Soviet airfields in a support effort, but there was nobody left to help in Warsaw. Stalin had succeeded in having the Germans annihilate the AK for him.

In the West, Eisenhower's forces had cleared France, Belgium and parts of The Netherlands and had advanced to the Rhine. In this desperate situation the Nazis still single-mindedly pursued, as a holy quest, the mass murder of those they considered undesirable: Jews and "subhumans." Transports to death camps had everywhere top priority, ahead of military needs, in the rush of taking these hapless innocents to their destruction.

Chapter 47   October 1944

And be these juggling fiends no more believed,
That palter with us in a double sense;
That keep the word of promise to our ear
And break it to our hope.

Shakespeare

Our column, four abreast, comprised only about 300 prisoners. The main body had as usual marched off to the tank ditches north of town, but we had been detached and were led through Husum itself, straight toward the harbor. This was our first opportunity to get a close look at the town and its inhabitants, and we felt some excitement at seeing real, ordinary people, and at having them see us! We expected ... we weren't quite sure what, but maybe a handout of a slice of bread, or some cast-off clothing, or maybe just a sympathetic glance or a consoling comment, ... anyway, SOMETHING! But as we shuffled along, the street was empty of traffic, the doors fronting on the sidewalks, closed. Behind a couple of store windows a few faces could be seen peering out. Otherwise, we attracted no more attention than one of the cats out for a morning stroll.

"Can you believe this? The people here might as well be SS for all the interest they show in us." The comment, pure indignation, came from Valdemar Sørensen, the tall stonemason of my Ribe group and one of the most upright people I have ever known.

"I can't imagine a column of poor bastards like us being trooped through a Danish town, and people paying no attention," said Niels Christensen, as he tried to spot some of the elusive locals. "Do they really not give a damn?"

We were still discussing what we thought of as strange behavior when we arrived at the harbor. The SS guards formed us into two human chains, stretching across the harbor square from a small coastal schooner moored at the quay.

The vessel held a cargo of red brick which we were to unload, and shortly the bricks passed from hand to hand, four at a time, making two stacks slowly take shape at the far side of the square.

Located on the west coast of Schleswig, the northernmost German province which abuts the Danish border, the small port town of Husum created as dreary a backdrop for a concentration camp as mind could imagine. Enclosed in a rectangle of double fences of barbed wire, the camp consisted of nine old, dilapidated barracks buildings, two kitchen barracks and four toilet sheds, actually just shed roofs over open ditches with a pole to perch on. Outside the fence stood four guard towers, one in each corner, and a couple of guard buildings. Our arrival crammed the camp with miserable inmates to almost five times its nominal capacity of four hundred.

It was well into fall, and cold rain pelted our paltry rags as we sloshed through endless mud in our daily labor. The task for which our work group had been taken here from Neuengamme was to dig V-shaped trenches, five meters wide and three meters deep, as defense against tanks. It was a Wehrmacht project code named *Frieserwall*, Frisian Wall, intended to defend against an Allied invasion on this part of the North Sea coast. Nobody could guess why, for the invasion in Normandy seemed already to have succeeded, but the orders stood.

The ground we were attacking with spades and shovels, half of them bent or broken, was the bluish-grey marsh silt I knew well from the beaches near Ribe, only some sixty miles farther north. Deposited over centuries of tidal action, it is firmly packed and hard to dig by hand, an exhausting task under the best of circumstances.

Exposure and illness had right away begun to thin our ranks, aided by the grim effects of starvation. Of all the ways man has devised to kill his fellow man, simple starvation must be among the most painful, particularly if you start with a healthy young body, for the process then becomes protracted. In the concentration camp setting, eventual death was caused by the onslaught of numerous illnesses – some of them hitherto unknown in Western medical annals – brought on by debility from prolonged hunger. To our physical agony was added frustration and anguish from the certain knowledge that our misery and approaching death could be avoided, easily and immediately, by something as simple as a bit of food, something we knew to be readily available in our nearby homeland. In a minor way our predicament was compounded by our general ignorance of nutrition, a subject about which we knew pitifully little. One of the Danish inmates, a captain in the border gendarmerie, collected worms, nightcrawlers, and walked around with them in his pocket for several days, trying to get up his nerve to eat them but hesitating because he thought they might be nutritionally harmful. On a couple of occasions we had access to potato peels and some raw turnips, but did not take advantage of the opportunity, because we thought the stuff indigestible. We noticed that Russian inmates ate those things, but reasoned naïvely that their stomachs probably were used to such fare, while ours were not. Little did we know that potato peels had been black-marketed during the California gold rush, when the forty-niners discovered the beneficial effects of chewing on them.

After a few weeks, our largely liquid diet had begun to cause some serious stomach disorders. Thies did not contract it severely, but I had two bouts with dysentery and could feel my strength sapped each time. The infections were promoted by overcrowding, as two prisoners were squeezed into each bunk at night. For a week I shared a bunk with Vilhelm Nellemose, a navy captain of forty-six, whose face had been disfigured in an accidental explosion on the Danish cruiser, *Gejser*, some twenty years earlier. Patching him up, the surgeons had used two strips from his scalp to replace his eyebrows which had been destroyed. They functioned quite well, the scalp strips, but they never quite understood their new rôle and continued to grow hair of a length suitable for their former location. I helped Nellemose keep the wayward hair out of his eyes by trimming his bushy growth with some flint flakes we picked up during our digging. Besides holding a navy commission he was also president of the prestigious International Council for the Exploration of the Sea which was based in Copenhagen. We had long discussions about our after-the-war plans and resolved to become partners and pursue Nellemose's already flourishing business venture of manufacturing stylish women's shoes from the skins of plaice, the red-spotted North Sea flounder served in Belgium and Paris as *sole meunière*. The shortage of traditional materials had led Nellemose to test the tough fish hides, and they became an immediate success.

But one morning his ravaged body failed to move, as the Kapos' yells roused us to another day of agony. His eyes seemed to stare straight at me, and there was a slight, sardonic smile on his face, as if his powerful spirit yet lingered to defy our tormentors.

As replacement, another "old" bunkmate moved in with me, a teacher of fifty-four by the name of Aage Rosenkjær. He was quite depressed and had actually given up hope despite the fact that his dysentery was only slight, and such was the interdependence between our physical and mental states that despair was tantamount to suicide. I remonstrated with him to summon up his determination to see this ordeal through, but the psychologic impact of the camp experience had affected him with such depression that he actually wished to sweep the whole dreadful world from his sight by the simple act of ending his life. After a week of our cohabitation, he too died quietly during the night.

Being a carpenter, Viggo Hansen had been put to work making caskets, crude boxes of rough pine board, into which the bodies of the night's dead were shoved unceremoniously every morning. In the beginning of our six weeks in Husum his work was light, but the death rate escalated quickly, and Viggo soon found himself unable to meet the demand, even though orders were issued to cram two bodies into each box. The problem was solved in characteristic SS fashion: Viggo was ordered to make four boxes, each large enough to hold three corpses. Each morning the boxes were loaded with the night's dead, transported to the cemetery, and emptied into a large hole, thence to be returned for reuse. Once or twice, two trips were required in one morning.

Corporal punishment for minor or imagined infractions was a favorite SS pastime. One of the guards took a dislike to me and on one occasion allotted me twenty lashes in front of the ranks. As administered by the SS, caning hurt like hell. Each stroke was like a touch of red-hot iron, but as the cane fell on my skinny posterior it became a matter of immense urgency not to cry out. To endure it stoically was the only satisfaction an inmate could attain, and the victim's countrymen among the onlookers always watched anxiously lest a whimper should escape him to sully their national pride. Why this should be so, I don't know. The reasons must be deeply buried in the psyche of maleness. But I clamped my jaw shut and tried to blot out all awareness of the present, as the pain surged through my body in searing waves. No sound escaped me, and when it was over, I walked stiffly back to my place in the line with the spectators' silent approval.

A few minor events had enlivened the dreary camp routine. One took place on a Sunday evening as we filed out of the barracks to muster for counting. The Kapos did their usual running around, shouting to hurry the inmates and lunging randomly with their truncheons at the hindmost. The camp commander was an SS Untersturmführer by the name of Hans Griem, a window glazier in civilian life, who featured himself a marksman with the pistol. A few days earlier he had put a bullet in the heart of a Russian, boasting afterward about his "wunderbarer Schuss." He was also a chronic alcoholic and that evening somewhat more drunk than usual. Standing in the middle of the dirt street between the barracks, feet well apart and arms akimbo, he watched the activity while swaying slightly, his small, piggish eyes bloodshot from the effects of his holiday schnapps intake. Impatient with our lack of speed in getting out and onto the parade ground, he suddenly pulled his P-38 from its holster and fired two shots at the nearest barracks to speed things along. The 9mm bullets went easily through the wood wall, one wounding a Pole in the forearm while the other lodged in the groin of a Dutch inmate.

Among the Danish prisoners was a young physician by the name of Paul Thygesen who had become camp doctor of sorts after the camp received its allotment of medical supplies: a pair of scissors, a small knife and some gauze bandages, actually ersatz gauze, made of paper. The Reich had deemed this adequate for two thousand inmates, half of whom were seriously ill. Later that night, Poul removed the bullet with a knife sterilized in the flames of a stove's firebox after Thies had honed it on a piece of stone. The prisoner recovered.[100]

Another incident occurred a few days after the shooting. While laboring at our task of ditching in the infernal, clayey mud of the North Sea marsh, we heard the heavy drone of a lone bomber approaching above the low, iron-grey overcast. After a few moments, it mingled with the snarl of a Messerschmitt rising from a nearby aerodrome to meet the intruder. Seconds later, two bursts of machine gun fire punctuated by the tunk-tunk-tunk of a 20mm cannon reverberated through the cloud as we waited, digging mechanically but with all our attention directed skyward. Then an airplane wing suddenly came spiraling down like a falling leaf, the German cross clearly visible on it, and almost simultaneously a parachute with a man dangling below broke from the overcast, obviously the fighter pilot. A ragged cheer rose from the prisoners, causing the guards to lash into the ranks in a furious effort to still the derisive jubilation.

Thies and I were well aware that our physical condition was deteriorating, and that we were becoming both physically and mentally less and less capable of attempting a break for freedom. When we returned in the evening and saw the barracks come into view under the slowly ascending smoke from the stoves, the temptation to drop onto a bunk and let sleep – truly the brother of death – bring oblivion was almost irresistible. Ever after, the cozy smell of wood smoke would recall to my memory those evenings, as we clustered shivering around the small black cast-iron monster, trying to coax a bit of warmth from it with a few wet sticks gathered on the column's way home from work. It was nearly impossible to summon the mental energy to plan a getaway. Nevertheless, we discussed endlessly every conceivable opportunity to escape, for the tantalizing proximity of the Danish border beckoned us to do so. So far we had been stymied, however, by the problem of cutting through the perimeter fence without any kind of tool.

On the far side of the square the brick stacks had risen in neat rectangles to almost six feet, while Thies and I had patiently worked our way to the shipboard end of our chain and on into the hold where the brick stacks were shrinking. With Thies keeping an eye on the nearest guard who was posted on deck above the open hatch, I made an inconspicuous stroll to the door of the engine room where a boy of about sixteen was working on the ancient power plant. Among the tools on the floor beside him lay a pair of pliers with half a jaw broken off. Throwing caution to the winds, I pointed to the broken pliers and asked him quietly if I could have them to repair my shoes.

Our eyes met. In an instant of silent rapport we both knew that I didn't intend to repair shoes; we also both knew that a word to the SS guard on deck could have caused my being beaten to death, then and there. After a moment, he shrugged and turned back to his work. *Hitler, you failed to get this boy on your side.* I snatched the pliers and tucked them in my pocket.

Two hours later we wearily trudged through town, this time ignoring the local citizens as they ignored us. Our column had as usual divided itself, the members of each nationality clustering for mutual support and ease of communication. Close to the edge of town a large dog, a German shorthaired pointer, came tearing out of a doorway, barking furiously at the passing inmates, and disappeared snarling and barking into a section of the column consisting of Russian prisoners. The barking ended abruptly in a yelp, and the animal never reappeared. At the evening meal one of our blockmates reported that the Russian block was feasting on dog meat, roasted on the stove, and Thies cracked a few jokes about the risks of barking up wrong trees, but we were too preoccupied with escape plans to pay attention.

The rain was slanting in sheets as we crept on our bellies through the cold mud to the camp perimeter between two guard towers. At the fence I fumbled for a few interminable minutes with the broken pliers, while Thies' voice from the darkness behind me urged me to hurry. At last I succeeded in cutting the two lowest strands of barbed wire, and we got back to our barracks, soaked to the skin. Our plan was to short-circuit the search lights on the following night and then make our break across the cleared strip outside the fence. As we were getting back in our bunks, all hell broke loose in one of the neighboring blocks but we decided not to investigate.

The next day we discovered the cause. As bad luck would have it, five other prisoners had planned a break the same night and made their own attempt to short out the lights. The circuit board was at one end of a block filled with Russians, and when a Pole from the other escape group tried to pry open the electric locker, the Russians woke and raised an alarm, thinking thieves had entered their domain. The Pole had beaten a hasty retreat, but the SS had gotten wind of something being afoot and made a careful inspection of the fence. When we came back to camp in the evening, our hole had been found and repaired. This was the first time anyone had tried to escape from the Husum camp, and the guards' increased vigilance ruled out any immediate repeat attempt.

* * *

The Slavs are to work for us. Insofar as we
don't need them, they may die.

Martin Bormann

Our puzzlement at the indifference of the local people when our miserable column trudged through the streets of Husum indicated the chasm by which Germans had separated themselves in behavior and outlook from Scandinavians, a condition of which I only gradually became aware during my stay in Germany. War affects people in many ways, few of them positive, and long before the outbreak of World War Two, the German populace had been systematically conditioned to accept and participate in organizing their nation and the rest of Europe according to Nazi concepts. By 1944 they had endured eleven years of Nazism. Starting immediately after the takeover, streams of rabid propaganda had eructed from government, party cadres and all manner of public agencies,

298

lecturing citizens on the inferiority of Slavs and the evils of Jews, leading them toward concluding that the world would be better off without these groups and hardening their attitudes to become generally merciless toward enemies, internal and external.

After the outbreak of war, letters from soldiers, often with photographs, described in vivid detail mass killings in the East. Hitler himself repeatedly boasted of keeping his promise to render Germany *judenrein*, free of Jews, and if more direct influence were needed to affect civilian attitudes, the masses of Zwangsarbeiter, slave laborers freighted into the country, brought brutality tangibly to the average citizen, literally to the doorstep of the German home.

Wretchedly fed and housed, constantly hounded and mistreated, cruelly punished for minor or imaginary offenses, these slave laborers were ubiquitous in wartime Germany, their treatment graduated according to alleged racial status: Western Europeans had the best chances of survival; the Soviet workers were treated worst and suffered horrible death rates. Nazi authorities worried constantly about the prospect of introducing inferior bloodlines by German women having sexual relations with the foreigners, and public hangings of offenders became a common spectacle as in medieval times. The daily practice of exploiting these unfortunate human beings everywhere in the economy demonstrated and legitimized to German civilians their own mastery and their perceived right to use "inferior" people as they saw fit, accountable to nobody.

Started in 1939 with prisoners from the Polish campaign, the forced labor program had grown massively, taking in about a million each of French and Soviet prisoners. The Soviet contingent was the remnants of five million captured Red Army soldiers of whom three million had been murdered or starved to death, one million impressed as auxiliaries with the German army. Another four to five million individuals had been randomly rounded up in occupied territories, mostly in the Soviet Union. After Italy's exit from the war, hundreds of thousands of its soldiers and many thousands of workers were forcibly dispatched to work in Germany.

Administering this huge labor pool of seven to eight million persons required a vast bureaucracy of its own. In 1942 Fritz Saukel[101] had been appointed Reich Plenipotentiary for Manpower, and under him innumerable agencies had sprung into being, each fiercely engaging in jurisdictional infighting to claim the largest possible turf for itself. After five years of war, this bureaucracy, the SS and branches of the military had all acquired vested interests in the programs to manage, exploit and when needed, exterminate the slave laborers. Such work offered good prospects of reward and promotion, and the persecution of unarmed civilians did not carry any of the onerous risks attending service at the Front.

Master race status, standing on the top rung of the Nazi racial hierarchy, entailed benefits that were amply obvious to people surrounded by cold and starving foreign workers. When pondering the New Order, a citizen of Germany could hardly assess its merits without being influenced by his own vantage point in the setup. However, mere practical advantage fails to explain how millions of ordinary Germans could set aside all of civilization's restraints and accept, or even engage in, simple murder. The state of the victims, dirty, ill-clad, foreign-looking, thieving (in desperation) in the case of *Ostarbeiter*, workers from the East, and physically or mentally unattractive in the case of handicapped Germans, may have gone some way toward persuading ordinary German citizens to steel themselves against their humane inclinations, but it seems insufficient.[102]

Chapter 48   December 1944

Glück auf!

German miner's Good-bye

Thies and I were standing in the second floor of the lift tower that squatted over what we perceived to be a mine shaft, although neither of us had seen anything like it before. Our group of about seventy or eighty clustered around the iron grid work surrounding a large square hole in the floor, some eighteen feet on the side, below which could be seen the gaping mouth of the mine. For the last few minutes the heavy double steel ropes in the middle of the hole had been moving upward at high speed, passing over a large wheel at the top of the tower structure and disappearing somewhere, evidently hoisting up an elevator. Judging from the speed of the steel ropes and the time they had already been tearing by, the elevator must be coming from very far down. This was a new experience.

Toward the end of November, sufficient tank traps had been dug to satisfy the Wehrmacht planners, and the Husum camp had been evacuated, but not all of us got to leave. When boarding the dirty and bitterly cold railroad cattle cars, we left behind in sixteen rows of unmarked graves three hundred of those who had entered the camp with us two months earlier. In our steel coffins we began to rattle south toward Neuengamme, and Thies and I took stock of the situation. There was not enough room to lie down, but we squeezed into a corner and sat down on the filthy floor so as not to expend precious energy on needless standing. We had long since learned that two bodies in contact – side to side or back to back – lose heat more slowly than they do singly, so we sat pressed side to side with our knees tucked under our chins, occasionally fending off a collapsing fellow traveler. Two air raids interrupted our snail's pace the first day, and each time the freight sat for long hours, abandoned by locomotive engineer and SS guards. The planes were after bigger game, so they posed no threat, but the delay without food or water was hard enough.

The second day dawned with a clear sky, and by mid-morning another raid brought us to a stop. Shortly, a faint drone announced the oncoming aircraft, and through the cracks around the bolted steel doors we saw an unforgettable sight unfold above us. The bombers were very high, striating the deep blue sky with their vapor trails. At the head of each thin white line, a plane could be seen as a tiny silvery point, as formation after formation of aerial might bore down toward Hamburg in what seemed like endless succession. It was our first glimpse of Allied fighting power and we thought it awe inspiring. Breathtaking. Sheer beauty in the raw! For the moment misery and nagging hunger were forgotten as we grinned at each other in ecstatic joy. We counted more than eight hundred planes; this could not fail to beat the Germans, and we should see their defeat if only we could stay alive long enough! In the evening our train disgorged its human debris in Neuengamme, and it was apparent that the two-day trip itself had further depleted our ranks. In our car alone, three had succumbed during the ordeal.

Our second stay in Neuengamme lasted two weeks during which time the Danish prisoners each received a small food parcel from the Red Cross in Copenhagen. The parcels had all been cut open by the SS and rifled for certain items, but even so they were nothing less than a life-saving miracle. They still contained a flannel shirt, a package of oats, a jar of Ovaltine, a chunk of salami and some cigarettes. We became instantly the envy of the camp as we lugged around the small cardboard boxes with their precious contents. During the night a Russian prisoner with a sharp knife tunneled through the bottom of Thies' bunk, through the mattress and into the box cradled in his arms, extracting half its content before we discovered the theft in progress. A confused scuffle ensued in the dark, but we failed to recover the lost items. After the incident we decided to pool our remaining resources and keep them in pockets and pouches strapped to our bodies.

Over two months had passed since we had our heads shaved upon our first arrival in Neuengamme, and our hair had grown just enough so that we could now be given the "autobahn" to mark us as seasoned prisoners. This was done by running a pair of clippers from the middle of the forehead across the dome of the skull and down the middle of the back of the neck, making a two-inch, close-cropped strip named after the German superhighways. When the hair grows, such a strip remains clearly visible, serving the purpose of making a man readily noticeable and identifiable as a *Häftling*, a concentration camp inmate, should he ever escape.

A few days later we were asked at muster about our occupations, and long lists were prepared in good bureaucratic fashion. Thies and I reported ourselves identically as machinists and were both chosen with about one hundred others for another *Arbeitskommando* that was shipped off the following day. This time the train rattled south, away from Denmark. We went across rivers, through cities, over farmland and through forests, then more rivers, cities, farmland, forests. Being used to a small country that one could bike across in a day and a night, we had a sinking feeling, a sensation of being swallowed up in the vastness of unknown enemy territory. Even if we escaped from the camp for which we were headed, we would now have untold miles of hostile land between us and home.

The trip southward took three days and two nights, again without food, so we were truly weak when we arrived at our destination, a small village in Thuringia, Wansleben-am-See. The transport was shunted onto a rusty spur that led directly into the Wansleben concentration camp which, as we later found out, was an *Arbeitslager*, a work camp, as well as an *Aussenlager*, or satellite camp of Buchenwald.[103] The camp was actually an old mining operation, comprising the elevator tower characteristic of a deep-shaft mine as well as some brick buildings of which one proclaimed itself to be Chlorkaliumfabrik Wansleben. After unloading the corpses of those who had died during the trip, we received a small bread ration and were assigned bunks on the second floor of a gloomy brick-and-concrete structure that was drafty and suffused with bone-chilling cold and dampness.

An hour later we were issued new clothing, for we had now become part of an industrial enterprise, one of those classified as essential to war production and thus entitled to a consignment of slave labor. The clothes were striped prisoner uniforms of a coarse, burlap-like material that would offer neither comfort nor protection against the elements. Still, the change of clothes was an improvement of sorts. We had tried to glean some scrap of news about the state of the war, but nobody knew anything. It was as if the winter had frozen the fronts into immobility.

"Do you suppose all of them have gone into hibernation?" Thies sounded disgusted.

"Maybe no news is good news," I suggested, but neither of us thought so.

On this, our first morning after our arrival, we had been marched to the lift tower and stood shivering here for half an hour in the predawn darkness.

The motion of the steel ropes slowed and the elevator hove into view, a huge box, partly open on the sides so it could be entered from any direction. Herded into the box our group crammed it to overflow capacity, as it was only intended for forty miners at a time. A bell rang somewhere, and we started moving down, slowly. Then we went into what felt like a free fall into the bowels of the earth.

Being flatlanders, as all Danes are, Thies and I knew absolutely nothing about mines or mining, so we were intensely curious. During the descent we discovered to our surprise and delight that the temperature rose, reaching a comfortable twenty-eight degrees Celsius by the time we disembarked fifteen hundred meters down. We looked around in amazement, finding ourselves in a vast hall hewn out of solid rock. It was well illuminated by overhead mercury lights, and on the floor were rows of tool machines, chiefly lathes and milling machines, all working and giving us the impression of having stepped into Vulcan's cave.

* * *

Now we stand on the threshold of Germany ... This is no moment to slacken.

Winston Churchill

The absence of news that we lamented in Wansleben was a reflection of the actual situation in the last months of 1944. The German lines were holding in the East, where the Soviet offensives had ground to a halt. The Red Army made some minor reinforcements of its bridgeheads across the Vistula and Narev Rivers at Warsaw, had penetrated in the North to Gumbinnen in East Prussia, and south of the Carpathians had pushed as far as Budapest. Now it must temporarily focus its efforts on preparations for a final thrust at the heart of the Nazi beast: Berlin.

In the West, operations had tapered off in the late fall. Paris had been liberated in August and General de Gaulle arrived and proclaimed a provisional French government. As Winston Churchill had been the rallying point in Britain's hour of need, so Charles de Gaulle had emerged in the course of his London exile to become leader of the French *Résistance* and of the Free French forces scattered throughout the remnants of France's colonial empire. Virtually unknown when he made his first radio broadcast to the French people in June of 1940, de Gaulle came to symbolize the indomitable spirit of his nation that neither defeat nor subjugation could wholly eradicate.

After the liberation of Paris, Eisenhower's staff had confidently believed the German armies effectively beaten, but the perception in Allied headquarters of a Germany tottering to its knees in defeat was false. Hitler retained his iron grip on leadership and decision making, ordered extreme mobilization of manpower resources and accelerated work on new weapons to turn the tide of war.

In September, the first V-2 ballistic rockets were launched against London where they caused extensive damage and killed over 15,000 people, but they never could deliver the death-blow of which Hitler dreamed. The one real threat Germany was still able to mount was conventional: land forces equipped with the latest and most powerful armor. In the fall Hitler set about a last try to recoup by that means.

Allied analysts perceived, correctly, that any major German offensive would be a waste of resources without any realistic chance of success. This led them to disregard, mistakenly, that Hitler might try nonetheless.

Chapter 49   Christmas 1944

Who going through the vale of misery use it
for a well ... they will go from strength
to strength.

Psalm 84

I walked to the washroom to clean the sores on my feet, silently cursing the fact
that my instep was so high and my shoe size so far off the average. My footwear
had been a problem all along, and the leftovers from dead prisoners provided
few scraps that would fit me. A pair of worn-out galoshes tied with string had
served me after a fashion through the mud of the Husum tank traps, but by the
time of our arrival at the mine they were coming apart, irreparably. The only replacement I had been able to obtain was a pair of wooden clogs of unimaginable origin. They were large enough, but without the cushioning intermediacy
of any socks their unyielding material quickly chafed a sore across the instep of
my feet. Over the following weeks Thies and I engaged in a contest of morbid
jokes, as I gradually whittled away the tops of the clogs with the result that the
areas covered with sores slowly enlarged toward my toes. One effect of starvation is that the body takes much time in healing itself. I remembered that Paul
Thygesen, our Danish physician in Husum, had called it "reduced vitality of the
tissue." My insteps had stayed a bloody mess for weeks but seemed at long last to
be slowly healing. Painful and unpleasant, but not life-threatening.

Tonight was New Years Eve, nearly midnight; almost everyone was asleep. I
missed being able to talk to Thies; he had been moved to a different building,
separated from mine by a fence, so that we saw each other only as chance would
allow. I tried a water tap and it produced a trickle. I was in luck. Most of the time
there was no water pressure, so that the feces piled up in the rows of toilets lining both sides of the room. I put my left foot under the tap. The trickle felt
good.

In the days after our arrival we had pieced together a general picture of our situation from our own observations as well as scraps of information obtained from others. The Wansleben mine itself was part of a vast system comprising hundreds of kilometers of tunnels built over centuries at many levels. When going up or down, the elevator passed gallery after gallery, many of them abandoned long ago, from which arched passageways led into the blackness of old tunnels. We had been taken to one of Germany's most productive mining regions whence miners of the Mansfelder Bergbau had furnished the Reich ore and minerals for generations. As Allied bombers made city life above ground ever more untenable in Germany's industrial centers, some of the arms manufacturers sought refuge for their production facilities in these ready-made catacombs, eminently safe under a mile-thick blanket of rock and soil. The plant of which we had become a small part produced under the aegis of the Armaments Inspectorate, the *WiRüAmt,* the hydraulic mechanism retracting the landing gear on one of the Fokker aircraft. The machines together with German technicians had been brought from Leipzig, Dresden and Halle, but the workers were *Fremdarbeiter,* foreign forced labor, plus concentration camp inmates. The foreign workers, mostly Poles, lived in nearby barracks and were only slightly better off than we.

The German employees were glum, and although they applied themselves with tenacity, there was a mood of hopelessness about them. The war was obviously lost, but it was a serious offense even to hint at such an eventuality. On the contrary, the obdurate struggle of the dying Reich had to be portrayed in a way believed to infuse and maintain hope.

The Polish workers were a sullen lot and not particularly skilled. Thies had been teamed with two of them for bench assembly work, and his consummate mechanical skills enabled him to accomplish in ten minutes what took the two Poles more than an hour. He described with contempt their clumsiness and lack of ability in one of his unique comments: "They can't poke a stick into a turd without ruining both." He got along very well with them, however, and gladly throttled back on his own speed to match theirs.

The workers' lack of skill and motivation kept the mine plant's output low and its percentage of rejects must have caused no end of embarrassment to the people responsible. The workday was twelve hours, and I was initially assigned to clerical work, trying to keep materials flowing to the production line. It turned out to be easy to sabotage this flow by selectively losing a few requisitions, and the already slow-moving line almost stalled. Nobody could diagnose the trouble, but some of us were moved elsewhere, and I ended up on a punishment detail blasting out new halls and passageways to expand the layout of the plant.

There were six of us in the blasting group, under the supervision of a wily old German miner. The routine called for drilling three-inch diameter holes about ten feet into the rock, after which our *Meister* would fill them with explosive charges and plug them. Then we would all retreat a respectful distance, fervently hoping the detonation would not bring the roof down as an added bonus. After each explosion came the labor of loading the loosened debris into small rail cars for removal, and the process started all over. Similar work on the surface would surely have killed us in the course of the winter, but in the mine we were protected against the pitiless cold. Geothermal heat – the slow emission of heat energy from radioactive decay in the Earth's molten interior – kept the mine at its steady and comfortable temperature summer and winter.

My twenty-fifth birthday had passed unnoticed in November, but we had engaged in mock discussions about how to celebrate Thies' thirtieth which was coming up in January. The period between our birthdays was punctuated by Christmas and New Year. On Christmas Eve, the focal point of celebration in Denmark as well as in Germany, the underground factory was shut down, but in order not to waste available labor the concentration camp segment of the work force was ordered out to haul bricks. Owing to the incessant Allied bombing, piles of rubble had sprouted wherever buildings clustered, and with their propensity for ant-like activity, German authorities constantly felt a need to move thousands of bricks hither or thither. It was natural, therefore, on that Christmas Eve to have a long, single file of prisoners move endlessly from one end of the camp to the other, each man carrying six bricks.

It was bitterly cold, and Thies and I critically eyed each other as we shivered in the striped uniforms we had been issued, silently assessing what strength and endurance the other had left. Thies had lost a great deal of weight. His six-foot frame was just that, a frame, and he bravely dead-panned a comment about being able to walk through a picket fence by turning sideways. Two inches shorter but more heavily built than Thies, I had lost proportionately less, but my dysentery continued to linger, and almost constant diarrhea had made me permanently tired. We found a piece of wire in the rubble and from it fashioned each a sling, a simple loop to put around the neck to support the bricks instead of spending precious arm muscle energy to support them while carrying. It cut the actual labor drastically, and we could now indulge in a favorite pastime, discussing what to do after the war, how best to visit suitable punishment on the Nazis, and what to have for dinner on various commemorative occasions after we got out. Being able to speak our native tongue and to indulge in lighthearted cursing of our jailers worked like a restorative tonic, lifting weeks of depression from our minds. The labor continued until darkness drove us back to the dormitory building, where the daily bread ration was issued. It was exactly the same meagre size as usual. Only the change to cold and clammy outdoor work marked the day as being different from any other.

I finished washing my feet and sat down on one of the toilets, waiting for them to dry. Today, New Year's, the plant had worked a normal shift, but now in the evening the German personnel was celebrating in their own quarters. In the deep stillness their voices echoed faintly through the ventilation shaft, suddenly joining in an old drinking song –

Trink, trink, Brüderlein trink
Lass doch die Sorgen zu Haus'
Meide den Kummer und meide den Schmerz
Dann wird das Leben ein Schertz ...

I wondered how much *Schertz* their lives would contain in the year to come.

* * *

The well-kept secret of what had been going
on behind the German scene was largely
undiscovered or misunderstood by Allied
Intelligence and so not anticipated by
Allied commanders.

British Official History

Two hundred and fifty miles west of the Wansleben mine in the wintry gloom on the Eiffel side of the Ardennes, German commanders were anxiously check-ing weather reports. The weather gods obliged, and under a protective canopy of cloud and fog three armies of armor and infantry surged out of the dense forest, crashing through the Front in a dozen places as the Americans reeled back in surprise and shock.

Even with the advantage of the total surprise achieved by the Germans, Hitler's last offensive had no chance of reaching its objective. Only a fourth of the minimum fuel supply was available, and the panzers were unable to seize the American stocks on which they had counted. The drive stalled, having created a huge bulge in the Allied line that prompted Churchill to coin the name: the Battle of the Bulge.

Sepp Dietrich, one of Hitler's most loyal followers, put his assessment in re-alistic terms before the battle:

> All Hitler wants me to do is cross a river, capture
> Brussels, and then go on to take Antwerp. And all this in
> the worst time of the year, through the Ardennes when the
> snow is waist deep ... and with reformed divisions made
> up chiefly of kids and old men.[104]

Both sides fought with intensity. The Germans made use of infiltrators in U.S. uniforms of whom most were caught and summarily executed by firing squads in accordance with international rules. At the village of Malmedy the SS 1st

308

Panzer Division committed one of the atrocities which had been its routine on the Eastern Front by massacring a large number of American prisoners. The consequent outrage of the American troops added to the fury of the contest.

By the middle of January the Front had been restored. The Ardennes offensive – often referred to as Hitler's last gamble – had gained the Germans a little time at great cost but had won no ground back at all.

Chapter 50   February 1945

*The strongest of all warriors are these
two – Time and Patience.*

Tolstoi

My *Stubendienst* came hurrying down the aisle between the rows of bunks and stopped at mine. It was a Sunday morning and it looked like we might not work today, and I wondered what he could have on his mind. He was a usually phlegmatic Belgian who carried out his duties with the air of presumed authority befitting someone in charge of the dormitory's miscellaneous routine tasks such as delousing and periodic recutting of the autobahn stripe across each prisoner's skull.

"Is your name Skov?" He pronounced it "Skoff", but no matter.

"Yes."

"There is a parcel for you in the office, *Croix Rouge*, I think."

A Red Cross parcel for me? In this God-forsaken place with only three Danes among some fifteen hundred prisoners? The *Stubendienst* nodded as he repeated the magnificent news, trying to make it sound as if he had personally helped bring it about.

"I will go with you and speak to the guard at the fence."

His voice had suddenly become polite, if not outright ingratiating. The contents of a Red Cross parcel was spoken about with much respect but also without much first-hand knowledge. So far as I knew, fewer than half a dozen parcels had reached this camp up to now; the Poles and Russians had no tie-in with the Red Cross, and the French, Italian and other branches of that organization looked after their countrymen with less efficiency and diligence than the Scandinavians did.

I got out of the bunk and went with him.

Our daily grind had not changed in the course of the winter. After more than a month on the punishment detail, I had gotten back to less strenuous duty in the office, this time filing shop orders. While I had been drilling and blasting and loading rubble, Thies had spent his time more constructively. He was doing bench assembly work which gave him access to metalworking tools, and he had used this opportunity to make knives for both of us. With superb craftsmanship bordering on actual artistry, he made the blades out of high quality carbon steel. The handles were fashioned of brass sheets, spaced and riveted to allow the blades to fold neatly. They were honed to a fine edge and could actually be used for shaving, although we had no need for this feature. In all our time in camp we never had a shave, nor did we need any. Our bodies seemed to have entered a state of semi-hibernation, the better to endure the starvation regimen. Our hair, beard and fingernails grew hardly at all, and bodily secretions had been reduced as if our anatomy jealously hoarded each and every calorie in its possession.

The folding-blade feature made the knives easier to hide, an important attribute, because the SS guards were pathologically afraid of knives in the hands of prisoners and frequently mounted impromptu searches and shakedowns. Losing one's life over a knife might seem a bad bargain, but we cheerfully accepted the risk in return for the convenience of having this tool that has been so basic to human activity since the beginning of mankind. In this context the SS feared particularly the Russian prisoners, as if in subconscious expectation that the endless atrocities they inflicted on the Soviet nation were bound eventually to engender a reckoning.

The Russians on their part were a diverse and interesting lot, but it was difficult to communicate with them, for our only common language was German which they spoke poorly. They spent much of their time hunting for tobacco, of which minute amounts entered the camp through the forced laborers and the German personnel. Whenever a fragment of a cigarette was obtained, a small group of three or four would smoke it greedily, always in a homemade, wooden holder to allow every last shred to be converted to smoke. After using a holder for a few weeks, during which time the wood absorbed some tobacco juice, its owner would carefully whittle it into tiny chips, roll the chips into a scrap of newspaper to form a crude cigarette, and smoke that!

Besides Thies and me there was one other Danish prisoner in the camp. His name was Benjamin Mørch, 23 years old, the son of a Copenhagen importer of French tool machinery. The family had lived in France where Benjamin had learned the language fluently. He was severely affected by depression and preferred to hang out with the Frenchmen who numbered about forty, occasionally gleaning a bit of news gossip from that source. Even starvation conditions could not quite subdue Gallic loquacity, and as a group the French inmates managed to gather a fair amount of worthwhile intelligence by chatting with the outside work force which contained many of their compatriots.

The most impressive prisoner I had encountered was a German from the Rheinland. He was one of the sect called Jehovah's Witnesses and had come into possession of a small Bible – it was hard to imagine how – and he was living proof that mind indeed can triumph over matter. Surrounded by squalor and despair, he appeared relatively healthy, serene, and unconcerned with anything except spreading God's word. He was the only prisoner I ever saw share his starvation ration with someone else. We had some lengthy discussions on spiritual matters, and he read me copious extracts from the holy book while caressing it lovingly, but in the end I concluded that I simply lacked faith, let alone the burning, all-pervading kind that makes saints sing at the stake or a concentration camp inmate suffer deprivation with no apparent ill effects.

We had no reliable news about the war, but rumor had the Russians approaching us through the Balkans. German newspaper reports carried by the foreign workers repeatedly accused the Russians of raping old women, something the German propaganda apparatus seized and harped upon as subhuman behavior. Thies and I thought it hilariously funny that Goebbels, the Propaganda Minister, would have us believe that the Red Army with an unlimited supply of young German women at hand should elect to rape grandmothers. However, the important fact was that the end must be near.

The SS clerk in the office handed me the parcel. Even he appeared awed by the occasion. The small cardboard box had been torn open and rifled in transit, or perhaps right here in this office, but there was still plenty left to make this a tremendous windfall. Back in the dormitory, I dove into my bunk and made a quick survey of the contents while thinking about the best way to protect the goodies. There was slightly more in the parcel than I could unobtrusively carry on me, but not more than the two of us could after I shared it with Thies, as was my intent. The *Stubendienst* had solicitously offered to keep the items in what he claimed to be the greater safety of his small office, but I gave him a cigarette from my parcel and sent him away with polite thanks.

Instead, I set out to visit Thies, something I had not been able to do before. A cigarette bought me transit across the yard to his dormitory, and his face changed from surprise to delight as he saw what I carried under my arm. In the shelter of his bunk we divided the treasures: a one-pound piece of bacon, a pack of sliced dark rye bread, a pound of cheese, a pound of lard, a package of oats, a jar of Ovaltine, and a quantity of cigarettes. We realized that most of the cigarettes had been stolen, but there were still nine packs left, each containing ten. Despite the starvation around us, tobacco was by far the most valuable commodity to possess. Any number of prisoners would kill for a good smoke. We split our supply evenly, and Thies looked at me as he lit one of his with unimaginable pleasure.

"You know, Niels, we have both been going downhill rapidly toward the point where a man can neither fart nor beat a drum, but if we consume this stuff slowly, it'll give us a new lease on life. Our patience has been rewarded."

He leaned back against the headboard and with his eyes half closed watched the smoke curling upward from the glowing North State.

"I wonder if a parcel for me is stuck in the mail somewhere."

312

***

Anger is a short madness.

Horace

As we later ascertained, Goebbels' stories about Soviet soldiers indulging in free-for-all rape were not exaggerated, although our doubt about grandmothers being at greatest peril may have been right. In January the Russians opened their winter offensive. In the early phase Zhukov thrust as intended to the Oder River east of Berlin, but the Germans hauled in their remnants of armored units from the west, forcing a slowing and build-up on Zhukov's Front during February.

Farther north where the Hanseatic League in the Middle Ages made Königsberg and other Baltic ports into great cities, the region had for eight hundred years been the eastern outpost of German language and culture. The Red Army's arrival provoked a stampede of refugees as two million East Prussians poured from homes and farms in a panicky exodus, when the suppressed knowledge of what their nation had perpetrated, both in Russia and toward Russian slave laborers in the Reich, suddenly burst upon their consciousness.

After cessation of hostilities I had occasion to interrogate many of these refugees and formed a picture of the rapid Red Army advance which was characterized by frenzy and savagery. Seeing German prosperity to be far superior to his own, and realizing that these wealthy Germans had come to Russia to steal his meagre possessions, enraged the Soviet soldier as much as the inflicted atrocities. The soldier in many cases reacted with raping and killing, and where terror-stricken refugee columns clogged the snowbound roads, racing tank spearheads would grind them to a bloody smear of humans and horses, carts and belongings. Avengers had arrived on German soil.

In February the three leaders of the Allies had met again, this time at Yalta in the Crimea. In the Yalta negotiations the Poles became the great losers and undeservedly so. They had fought since September 1939, fielding an exile army that stood fourth in size among those opposing Hitler. Under Soviet pressure the Allies shifted their country westward, the Soviets keeping Eastern Poland, while they received German territory in compensation. Against these concessions to the Soviets the Western Powers obtained recognition of American and British predominance in Greece, Italy, France and The Low Countries.

A minor topic in the discussions was that of repatriation of prisoners of war and other categories of people uprooted and displaced by the war. Many Soviet citizens feared for their lives and would not willingly return to their homeland. Although averse to forced repatriation, the British and Americans were con-

313

cerned about getting back their own prisoners of war, liberated in Germany by the Red Army. In the end both nations committed to returning all Soviet citizens against Soviet assurances of prompt return of Western nationals.[105]

Chapter 51   April 1945

I am escaped with the skin of my teeth.

Job 19:20

Lined up on the *Appelplatz*, all the Wansleben inmates were being counted one last time. The *Stubendiensts* walked along the rows and handed each man a tin can of preserved food, something we had never received before. Apparently the meager stores were being emptied rather than left to the enemy. The guards were dressed in what they had of battle gear, which was not much. They were mostly older men who had been drafted at one of the last scrapings of the German barrel of manpower. Their uniforms looked worn and second hand, and they lacked helmets, wearing only ordinary cloth caps. Half of them carried infantry rifles, not a good firearm for the task at hand, but the rest had Schmeisser submachine guns.

The camp commander barked an order, and our long column, six abreast, started moving through the open gate, out onto the road beyond which we had never seen the landscape before. Thies and I walked near the head of the column, observing the surroundings carefully in the fading light of the April afternoon, while the barbed wire fences disappeared behind us.

The previous day the camp commander had received orders to eliminate the camp by killing the prisoners and evacuating the German personnel. Higher authority must have decided that the enemy was about to arrive, though which enemy was uncertain. The order had posed a practical problem, for the guards did not have enough ammunition for any such wholesale slaughter. Under stress to solve the problem, the SS with customary German resourcefulness hit on a more imaginative solution: if the elevator cables were removed from the mine shaft we could all be dumped into that ample hole with firm assurance that a one-mile free fall would accomplish the mission. They ordered the cables removed.

Fortunately, our camp's *Lagerälteste,* the senior or head prisoner who performed some administrative functions, was a shrewd old German who divined the intent behind removing the cables. A small-town mayor in the pre-Hitler period, he was a tall man in his late fifties, endowed with a commanding personality. Even the SS reckoned him to be worth listening to, and he managed to talk them out of the free-fall solution by invoking the specter of certain retribution by the approaching Allies. The commander was swayed to the alternative of evacuating everyone, and in the late afternoon of this 12th day of April, we marched out.

The order to kill had been the last communication reaching the camp, and the guard detachment had been left in limbo since then, having received no instructions, no information of any kind. Consequently, nobody knew where we should be going. Nobody knew where the battlefronts were. All that was known was that the Russians were coming somewhere from the east, the Americans somewhere from the west. Our column shuffled along into the approaching darkness, somewhere in between.

The narrow country road was utterly deserted. Near the camp we had seen a *Schlepper,* a one-cylinder tractor, pulling two large trailers which now served the stuttering economy as make-do transport, but otherwise road and countryside were empty and gloomy, foreboding almost palpable in the air. After a couple of hours of marching, the column had lengthened noticeably and now stretched over more than half a mile of road. We walked four and five abreast in what one might describe as controlled disorder, the strongest prisoners toward the head, the weaker receding toward the column's tail. On each side walked the guards. They had started out with intervals of a dozen yards or so, but due to stretching of the column they were now some forty yards apart, with a dozen or so clustered at each end. Prisoners too weak to keep up were summarily shot by the tail guards.

A couple of times, prisoners had broken from the column and run into the darkness, only to be cut down by a short burst from the nearest guard's Schmeisser. Despite the lack of success thus demonstrated before us, we decided to use this simple, direct method to get away, for we were far too weak to take out a guard, even though they were old men, "dangling dicks" in Thies' contemptuous description. But we devised an improvement. By estimating the time it took a guard from the moment of seeing an escape attempt to get the gun off his shoulder, click off the safe and fire, we would know when to drop when our turn came. Thies and I worked our way slowly back and forth through the column to survey the situation, on the way collecting Benjamin for whom we felt responsible; it was obvious that we now had our best chance to escape since our earlier plans to do so had been preempted in Frøslev. Benjamin wanted us to jump in different directions from the column, but we told him rudely to shut up, which he did.

The camp commandant had apparently chosen a route to avoid forest, of which this area in any event had little, but the night was fairly dark with clouds obscuring the starry sky most of the time. Over the next half hour, two more prisoners broke from the column, and we timed the delay before firing to be ten to twelve steps at our current walking speed. We opted to go for the lower figure. A bit farther along we had on our left a field sloping slightly away from the road and covered with knee-high, dry grass. The three of us walked up close behind the nearest guard, so that the next one back who would be the one to see us run would be at maximum distance. When the sky seemed as dark as we could hope for, we took each other by the hand for support, Benjamin in the middle, and started to run, counting: one ... two ... three ... four ... five ... six ... seven ... eight ... nine ... DOWN. Within less than a second of hitting the ground we heard a Schmeisser cough a short burst and *sensed* the bullets just overhead. Not bad shooting, for an old guy. On the other hand, we had not exactly put forth an Olympic dash, so we were still close to the column, very close. It seemed to take forever before they all dragged by and we heard the noise fade in the distance. Then we got up, spied the big dipper through a rift in the clouds and began walking in a westerly direction, stumbling in the dark on the uneven ground but making headway across unknown, open countryside. We were free.

The thrill of freedom almost immediately gave way to the discomfort of the night's bitter cold. In central Europe April nights are cold, quite cold. We needed protection from the weather, we needed to get warm and to rest. Above all, we needed to hide, for when daylight came, we could hardly hope to avoid discovery in the open fields, and our striped uniforms plus the autobahn on our heads would instantly give us away. Any civilian was obligated to capture or kill us, and troops of young boys from the *Hitlerjugend* were used to search for downed airmen and escaped prisoners. The little fiends were both capable and bloodthirsty, and in our weak condition we would be easy prey.

After a while, the dark outline of a small village loomed ahead, and we closed in on the nearest farm, warily lest a dog should hear us. It was a very large, square structure with all its doors closed tight. Cautiously we searched for a suitably discreet entrance and finally tested a very small door in what looked like the barn section. It was hasped from the inside, but we pried it open, squeezed in, closed it carefully behind us and climbed a ladder to the hayloft above. The loft was huge but contained only a few piles of old, moldy and unattractive hay; we burrowed into it to try to escape the cold and by lying close together to stop our bodies from shivering uncontrollably. We were thoroughly miserable. Our precarious freedom brought no feelings of elation as counterweight to the penetrating cold and discomfort which kept us from sleeping despite our physical exhaustion.

At daybreak light began to trickle in, and we noticed that some of the roof tiles were glass, dimly illuminating our hideout. We decided to move to the western end of the loft to be able to observe the surrounding terrain in that direction, for we hoped the Americans would be coming from there. The move entailed traversing a stretch where the loft floor was missing to allow hay wagons from below to unload their cargo directly up into storage. The gap was bridged by a narrow plank from which the roof stringers could be reached to serve as a handhold. Benjamin crossed first and went on to our chosen spot, but when Thies and I were both on the plank, a door opened just below us and a soldier entered with a heavy machine gun which he started to disassemble and clean. Caught in the most awkward position imaginable – balancing on the plank immediately above him – we stood still as if chiseled in stone, afraid that the slightest motion might cause a straw to float down and make him glance up and see us twelve feet above. The soldier went about his task slowly and methodically, cleaning and oiling all the parts and then reassembling his weapon. From my own experience, I knew that the job must have taken about twenty minutes, but it seemed an eternity with our emaciated bodies screaming to be released from their frozen posture.

At long last, the machine gunner finished and left, and we could move on and take up position at the end of the loft, where a glass roof tile allowed us view toward the west. A narrow road leading by our farm traversed a slight depression in the landscape and disappeared out of sight over the next rise. Taking turns as lookouts we kept our eyes fixed on that rise and settled down to wait. We still carried the tins we had been issued before leaving the mine. They were unlabeled, so we cut them open with our knives and examined the contents. It was some kind of gristly meat which we ate without trying to make any closer identification. Then we took turns at resting, with one of us keeping lookout and making sure the others did not fall asleep and snore.

"Hey, they're coming!"

Benjamin's excited whisper aroused us and we crowded around the glass tile, all trying to see out at the same time. A column of six tanks had come into view and was crawling down the far slope of the depression. The tan-colored monsters were followed by a small, funny looking, four-wheeled vehicle, altogether a procession looking like nothing we had ever seen before. From somewhere below us a *Panzerfaust,* the German equivalent of the bazooka, let go with a CRRUMP, its grenade glancing off the lead tank's turret. The column reacted by fanning out and accelerating toward us with two of the tanks' machine guns chattering, but after their Parthian shot, the Germans beat a hasty retreat out the other end of the village. Moments later, one of the tanks shouldered its way around the corner of our barn, a white star on its hull. We decided it must be American and jumped out to hail the crew. In the open hatch of the tank a gum-chewing head appeared.

"Well, lookit them poor bastards." The sergeant's comment was to his crew climbing out as he looked us over sympathetically, and I started to practice my English for the first time in my life.

318

The Americans of this small reconnaissance column, the first we had ever seen, were a novelty in more ways than one. In Denmark our only source of news from the Allied side had been from the BBC in London. The British gave good coverage from all the battlefronts, but the listener could be forgiven for gaining the impression that the fight against Nazism was being waged – if not exclusively at least overwhelmingly – by the British empire. That is not to say that I can in any way fault the Brits for being one-sided. When it mattered most to the survival of Western civilization, Britain *did* stand alone, and for a long time they carried on alone, and they prevailed. Winston Churchill never wavered.

We on our part were not particularly noteworthy to the American GIs. They had long since become accustomed to seeing DPs, displaced persons, of more than a dozen different nationalities and categories: forced laborers, German refugees, escaped prisoners, deserters in civilian garb, officials trying to evade time and place of reckoning, war criminals, concentration camp inmates, POWs ... the list was a long one.

The small column stayed only long enough for the GIs to have a quick meal from the rations they carried, washing it down with Niersteiner of local supply. Some of them had gone straight for the farm's wine cellar, giving us the first of many proofs that the frontline troops were well acquainted with the common German wines, each man indulging his particular preference. They shared some of their rations with us, and as we fiddled awkwardly with the unfamiliar little cans and other packing material, we exulted in tasting our first decent food since leaving Frøslev seven months ago. Remounting their tanks half an hour later, the GIs advised us to head for Eisleben where a U.S. military headquarters was being set up. Then they pushed on at a brisk pace, out of the village in the direction the fleeing Germans had taken. The procession was being led by the small, funny-looking vehicle – I now knew that it was called a jeep. We were again on our own.

As the last tank departed in the fading light, the village suddenly looked much less friendly. Germans were nowhere to be seen, prudently staying indoors, out of sight, but we were well aware that our situation was still precarious. The "Front" was many miles deep, a continuously changing, confused area in which opposing forces, POWs, stragglers and deserters roamed unpredictably. German military discipline was beginning to break down here and there. Some units were capitulating to the Americans and British, while others with fanatic zeal blew up bridges and overpasses to render every road, highway and rail line impassable to the advancing enemy. Yet other thousands quietly discarded their uniforms, donned stolen civilian clothes and tried to disappear into the throngs of refugees in towns and cities.

As for us, we were still easily identifiable as escaped *Häftlinge*, essentially defenseless, but it took us only moments to decide on an aggressive initiative as being most likely to succeed. It was urgent to show no hint of hesitation, so we marched with firm step to the largest farm in the village and demanded with haughty impatience to speak with the owner. We were informed that his name was Haase, and that he had recently been drafted with the rank of major; but his wife was there, a graying, middle-aged woman who eyed us suspiciously but also with a detectable trace of fear. Her thin, faded lips were turned down at the corners in what looked like a permanent expression of sour unfriendliness, and she was accompanied by her mother-in-law who was grossly overweight – a rare sight at the time. The latter's appearance triggered a mumbled remark from Thies that it would be faster to jump over her than to walk around, his standard comment about such individuals. Suppressing a laugh which would have impaired our little charade, I informed Frau Haase with an air of arrogant condescension that the American military authorities had appointed me supervisor of this village for the time being, and that I had chosen this farm for my administrative headquarters. Now, to get organized there were a few things I wanted done without delay. First, close the farm up tight and observe the blackout. Second, no one was to enter or leave the premises without my permission. Third, all inhabitants of the farm were to go to their quarters immediately and stay there until 9 a.m., at which time there would be muster in the yard for everyone.

The woman actually looked vastly relieved at being subject to such eminent authority, and the orders were carried out speedily. In this regimented society everyone always expected to be ordered around, and obedience was second nature. Then I sent the older woman to her room and ordered Frau Haase to bring a lantern, paper and pencil, and conduct us on an inspection tour of the premises. Starting at the main entrance our little procession made a clockwise circuit of the complete establishment, first the woman, lighting the way with a flickering kerosene lantern, explaining and answering questions, then Thies and I conversing earnestly in Danish but posing questions in German and lacing our progress with several offhand asides in German about the imminent arrival of American occupation troops the following day. Last came Benjamin who was beginning to look almost cheerful as he was taking notes for the benefit of our imaginary military authorities.

The farm was an enormous affair, very unlike the ones we were familiar with from Denmark. Laid out in a square, it enclosed a spacious, stone-paved yard one hundred and sixty feet on the side. The buildings were a full two stories high, plus attic space and some cellars, the corners constructed of hewn granite blocks with connecting walls of stone rubble, partially covered with cement plaster. We had taken over not just a farm but a small fortress. It looked to be of late 17th or early 18th century vintage, and while slightly larger and more prosperous, it was in style and layout representative of the rest of the village. It provided habitat for one hundred and fifty-four persons, the woman reported, about three-fourths of them Polish workers, the rest indigenous including some bombed-out German refugees from Leipzig and Halle. Almost all were women, with some children and old men as well.

Our inspection tour took over half an hour and revealed that the farm was functioning passably well with its present ragtag work force. Only four horses and a few cows remained in the stables but ample supplies of feed and seed grain had been produced and hoarded. In the main building the owner's bedroom was unoccupied, as his wife had moved in with her mother-in-law in the latter's smaller quarters which were easier to heat in the winter months.

I ordered the beds made up in the master bedroom and sent the woman away with strict orders to keep the curfew. When she had disappeared out of earshot we looked at each other and burst into happy, uproarious laughter.

Then we headed for the kitchen.

The kitchen was a sizable affair, containing numerous counters, cabinets and sinks. At one end, a large wood-fired cook stove protruded in peninsular fashion, its embers streaming delicious warmth through the room. Pots and pans hung suspended from the ceiling and off to one side, and the air was redolent with the fragrances of food. We located the spacious and well-stocked pantry, grabbed some bread, cheese and sausage and looked around while eating. A container of fermented milk attracted our attention and provided the next course. Bowls and spoons in hand, we kept exploring and found a smoke room containing some legs of mutton and half a pig. The room was about ten by twelve feet in size and was somehow supplied with cold smoke, and we marveled at the thoughtfulness of having our bacon thus ready. Thies set about slicing with a large carving knife and started frying bacon and eggs, while I surveyed the culinary domain further, turning up some jars of pickled beets, some fresh milk, liverwurst, blood sausage, lard and butter.

Then we sat down and ate it all, complimenting each other on the fine composition of the menu which, we agreed, actually far surpassed anything we had fantasized about in camp. None of us had heard of the special diets doctors recommend when bringing people from near starvation back onto normal food intake. For us, however, ignorance turned out to be bliss. There were no ill effects whatever. Our food intake seemed simply to explode into energy. As we applied ourselves to the unaccustomed task of chewing real, wholesome food, Thies looked at me pensively.

"At this time yesterday," he said, "we could neither fart nor beat a drum, but look at us now: we can easily take on half the remaining Wehrmacht."

I had to agree. We were undergoing nothing less than a miraculous recovery and physical transformation, wrought by the simplest of all medicaments: some real food.

After the meal was finished and we had time to ponder the situation, we began to wonder about the farm's abundance of food. It had to be unusual, even for a wealthy farmer. Back in the bedrooms we decided to search the owner's adjoining office-lounge, a beautifully panelled room with numerous clothes closets. The mystery momentarily deepened as we uncovered drawers full of Cuban cigars, cocoa, cognac, and other products unobtainable even on the black market. Then his personal papers in a desk drawer provided the answer. Major Haase had been the area's *Ortsbauernführer*, the Nazi official heading the party's local farmer organization. No wonder he had escaped the draft until a few months ago, and this also explained his high army rank. Reflecting on the ebb and flow of the fortunes of war, Thies and I lit two of his Cuban cigars. Then we looked at each other, grinning with delight at our present situation, and went back to the kitchen to make some cocoa.

After cocoa and a substantial snack we heated water on the stove, threw our striped clothes and our shoes in the fire, washed ourselves, and checked each other for lice, an easy task as we were still almost bald.

We returned to the bedrooms and with much merriment chose underwear, clothes and footwear from our host's bulging closets. Only a pair of black uniform boots proved large enough to accommodate my big feet, and I combined them with a pair of riding pants, a Loden jacket and a cap, the selection making me resemble, Thies assured me, a specimen of landed gentry with party connections. Thies settled on a brown suit that fit rather loosely on his spare frame, a trench coat and a felt hat, looking for all the world like a poorly disguised Gestapo agent. We had to prod Benjamin, who first refused to put on clothes from a Nazi closet, but at length he opted for a more informal outfit of black wool pants, navy sweater and a beret, acquiring the appearance of a French navy seaman on shore leave. We had found no weapons and felt suddenly naked without guns, so we fetched some vicious looking knives from the kitchen, locked and barricaded the bedroom doors, checked the heavy shutters and went to bed.

In the deep silence we could hear the intermittent murmur of distant artillery, and we contemplated for a minute our good luck that morning in not having a straw drop on the machine gunner twelve feet below us.

* * *

If the war is to be lost, the nation will also perish.
... There is no need to consider the basis of a most
primitive existence any longer. The nation will have
proved itself the weaker, and the future will belong
exclusively to the stronger Eastern nation. Those who
remain alive after the battles are over are in any case
only inferior persons, since the best have fallen.

Adolf Hitler, March 1945

After the Ardennes offensive the Western Allies had no illusions about lack of German determination to fight on to the bitter end, however pointlessly. Eisenhower therefore proceeded to reduce the remaining German forces west of the West Wall fortifications. The Rhine barrier was vaulted by the 9th Armored

Division's successful rush of a bridge at Remagen, when the retreating Germans fumbled its destruction.

Eisenhower directed Montgomery with his British and Canadian armies through Holland to take the German ports on the North Sea and Baltic coasts and seal off Denmark. They succeeded in doing this only a small jump ahead of the Soviets who were pressing forward from the east. British forces drove into Lubeck twelve hours before the Russians could get there, sealing off Denmark and saving that country from becoming part of the Eastern Europe that was to languish under Soviet hegemony for almost half a century.

The main thrust under Bradley was directed east toward Erfurt-Leipzig-Dresden, well south of Berlin. A southern branch became the troops we encountered near Eisleben. Knowing that Berlin was in the occupation zone intended for the Russians, Eisenhower thereby deliberately left the city to the Red Army, infuriating the British but with firm American backing. On 25 April, Americans and Russians met at Torgau on the upper Elbe.

Part IV

Return to Sanity

World War: Aftermath

Chapter 52   April 1945

In war nothing is impossible, provided you use audacity.

George Patton

"I agree with you that we ought to get out of here while we have them all confused."

Thies stated his opinion with low-key emphasis at the end of our discussion. We had weighed various courses of action, while Benjamin was organizing a committee meeting of sorts in the yard. He was coming out of his depression to some degree and was willing at least to talk to the Germans.

Our sleep, uninterrupted and in real beds, had been wonderfully restorative. We felt strength and energy flowing back into our bodies, the concentration camp that ended only the night before last seemed but a bad dream. We ate a hearty breakfast in the kitchen, banishing the women temporarily from that domain, and at nine sharp inspected the sorry collection of German refugees and Polish laborers currently inhabiting the farm. We had left Benjamin to designate four of them to represent the whole group and to meet with them to hear their grievances. This was what he was doing at the moment, and through the open window we could hear bits of their conversation, all of which pertained to food. The fat mother-in-law had been in charge of the planning and cooking and apparently had thrived at the expense of everyone else. When confronted with the accusation she denied it shrilly and vehemently, but her fear and guilty conscience were evident. Benjamin admonished her sternly to do better in the future and relegated food planning and cooking to the four plus the mother-in-law. In a matter of minutes, they were practicing budding culinary democracy.

Thies and I had discussed what we perceived to be our options and had concluded that the Haase farm had sufficiently served our purposes. It was time to move on. In the large stable we found an old man who claimed to be in charge of the animals, a few cows and four draft horses. I sent a grateful thought to my boyhood's equestrian pursuits as I selected the two sturdiest of the beasts, pointed to a four-wheel wagon in an adjoining shed, and told the old stable hand to harness them and hitch them up. We returned to the kitchen where the women had resumed their cooking, and admonished the owner's wife to carry on in our absence, as we were going to the U.S. headquarters in Eisleben for a conference. Shortly, we rumbled out of the yard and down the narrow road where the tanks had appeared the previous day.

The weather was cloudy and we soon came to both road forks and crossroads, all with their signs removed, so that we ended up thoroughly lost, having only a faint wind to give us any hint of direction. A farmer searching for turnips in a nearby field responded sulkily to our inquiry about the road to Eisleben, suspicious when seeing draft-age men in civilian garb. We had our heads well covered to conceal the telltale autobahn marking us as escapees, and Thies patted his coat pocket menacingly, hinting at the presence of a gun. The man yielded with a surly grimace, pointing to the road straight ahead. We could hear cannon fire from time to time, but it sounded like coming from several directions, merely telling us that we were in a combat zone. Shortly, an American military ambulance came tearing down the road toward us. It stopped in response to our hail, and the driver told us that Eisleben was a few miles distant, "that-a-way."

We continued on the narrow road which offered no view of the more distant landscape, so we could not get any overall impression of our surroundings. After a while a car came zig-zagging backwards toward us and nearly rammed into our horses. The driver got out and hailed us, somewhat unsteadily. He turned out to be a GI who had fallen behind his outfit due to a delay in a wine cellar. He had succeeded in liberating the car, a small DKW, but could not make the unfamiliar gearshift change out of reverse, hence the backward dash to catch up with his buddies.

"I can drive you to your company."

My offer made good sense and he accepted eagerly. His name was Len, and we found his platoon after some searching, got out of the car and were immediately bombarded with questions. I listened to Len's explanations, trying to follow the rapid exchange, then he turned to me.

"You'd better get the hell out of here. Do you want the car?" He sounded anxious to get rid of it.

"Sure," I said breezily, and thereby acquired my first automobile.

When I got back to the others, Thies sold horses and carriage to the nearest farmer, and the three of us continued toward Eisleben in the DKW.

A small, very picturesque city of sixty thousand people, Eisleben was known chiefly for being the birthplace of Martin Luther. It had suffered little war damage, because absence of industry had made it an unimportant target, and it was in any event so far east in the Reich as to place it on the margin of Allied bombing range.

328

The author and Thies in American uniforms in Eisleben, three weeks after their escape from the Wansleben concentration camp.

329

We arrived in the afternoon, and American forces had driven in from the opposite side just before noon. U.S. Military Government Detachment 34 had already moved into Hotel *Goldener Löwe* and was in the process of taking charge of the city. Troops were moving about everywhere, and at first glance bedlam seemed to reign, but on closer scrutiny the process was purposeful and orderly enough. Germans kept out of the way, staying indoors.

At the hotel we found a young officer struggling to make himself understood in issuing orders to the German personnel about rooms, mess facilities, office space, supply storage and a myriad other items. Despite his German name, 2nd Lt. Spiegel spoke only a few words of the language, and the local citizenry spoke virtually no English, a result of long neglect of foreign language instruction during the xenophobia encouraged by the Nazi regime. My offer to interpret was immediately accepted, and I spent the rest of the day with him, as we crisscrossed the city from the hotel to city hall, hospital, railroad station, police station, courthouse, waterworks and miscellaneous other public agencies. The American rapidly fired orders right and left: instructed prominent officials to be in his office in the morning, ordered smaller fry to carry on in their functions, and made notes of problems: fuel needed at the power station, medical supplies for the hospital wing he had requisitioned for the U.S. Army, and so forth. My English held up fairly well, but my school vocabulary had frequent holes.

"Niels, ask the chief physician how many vacant beds the hospital has ..."

"Yes ... uh ... what does 'vacant' mean?"

But the job got done quickly enough. While we were thus occupied with Military Government, Benjamin had found an empty truck convoy destined for Paris, and he departed with it in the evening, desperate to get out of Germany. Thies and I encouraged him to go, hoping he could more easily regain mental stability in France where he knew a number of people. We had little news about the broader picture of the war but felt perfectly at ease in our current situation. We learned that President Roosevelt had died the day before and sensed the momentous importance of losing him, yet hardly turned from what we were doing to contemplate or discuss the event. Among soldiers at war interest vanishes in anything unrelated to the task immediately at hand.

As we sat down to a late meal in the hotel's dining room-cum-mess hall, Spiegel eyed me thoughtfully, and at length suggested that a U.S. uniform would improve my appearance. I agreed readily and made sure that Thies also be so equipped. Spiegel assigned us a room in the hotel, and the following morning we metamorphosed to become U.S. Army volunteers, uniformed and armed. The DKW had disappeared during the night, probably retrieved by the owner, and Thies chided me for being so careless with our belongings.

Thies understood some English, but his speaking vocabulary never exceeded about three dozen words. His taciturn, low-key demeanor made up for this shortcoming, and he made friends with everyone in the detachment by being a superlative listener. A heavy smoker, he also took great delight in the unlimited availability of cigarettes. Soldiers at war take to smoking with a vengeance, per-

Cpl. Stanley Hajduk of Detroit, Michigan, who served with U. S. Military Government Detachment 34 in Eisleben. Tireless when traveling with Thies in pursuit of Nazi war criminals, he also accompanied the author and Thies on their first drive to Denmark after the German surrender.

haps driven by physical yearning for the nicotine but more likely for deep psychological reasons. Lighting a cigarette implies that a man is well in control of the situation at hand. Uncertainty and even fear are suppressed, while self-confidence asserts itself as he slowly takes a deep drag and nonchalantly flicks away the match, or closes the lighter with a meaningful click. Exhausted fighters in all armies, from the battlefields of Europe to remote South Sea islands, sought and received succor and hope by this simple expedient. The notion was reinforced and perhaps owed its origin to American movies of the prewar era. The leading actors, heroes and villains alike, could always be relied upon to light up at crucial points, when deep thought or impending action needed emphasis. When Clark Gable in *Gone with the Wind* lit up a cigar and with a grin charmed the Yankee officers, the audience knew that he was in control of the situation. Perfect control. And when Humphrey Bogart and a horde of supporting actors chain-smoked their way through *Casablanca*, the audience was well satisfied that each scene was pregnant with danger, seen and unseen.

In a world suspecting no ill effects from smoking, the enjoyment of tobacco was looked upon as innocent, even wholesome. Thies favored Phillip Morris and always kept one of the elegant brown packs handy, but the army offered four other brands: Chesterfield, Lucky Strike, Camel and Raleigh. How Raleigh got included in this select company was a mystery, for nobody liked the brand. Army stores kept regular cartons of ten 20-packs, but a tiny pack of four cigarettes was thoughtfully included in each C-ration so that no soldier ever needed to be without.

Detachment 34 of Military Government was commanded by Captain Oliver C. Kuntzleman, a tall, easygoing career officer who sported an ivory-handled .45 revolver in the style of George Patton and communicated in a slow, nasal drawl that belied a quick and incisive mind. He was a competent administrator, and his outfit functioned effectively from the day of its arrival. The immediate Allied aim in occupied German territory was one of denazification, i.e. implementing a program to clear Nazi leaders out of positions of authority, bringing to justice those guilty of war crimes, and preparing the country for the kind of democracy that so far in its history had failed to flourish. It was an undertaking in which the Allies were motivated not by a desire for revenge but rather by everyone's long-term interest in not leaving a major Western nation to flounder outside the pale of democracy. One night after a few drinks, Kuntzleman put the Allied position more succinctly.

"This time, Niels, they're going to get democracy, if we have to ram it down their fuckin' throats."

"Do you think it can be made to work here?"

He thought for a moment before answering.

"Hard to tell. Political stability takes time to achieve, but we have to try. In that regard we are different from both the Russkies and the Limeys."

"How is that?"

"Well, you see, the Russians got into this because they were attacked. So they had to fight, and now that they have won, that's the end. They don't give a damn what happens here so long as the Krauts can't threaten them. The Limeys had treaty obligations to fulfill, and once they got in, Churchill wouldn't settle for less than complete victory. But America – now, that's different. We weren't attacked, and we could have turned our back and ignored the whole fracas in Europe. When Roosevelt got us in, it was for the sake of principle. We don't want a damn dictatorship in the middle of Europe. Civilized, advanced countries ought to be democratic, otherwise they become problems down the road. So, having won the war doesn't close the case for us. We have to make sure that these bastards are set straight. You see, then, we have to weed out the bad eggs, at least some of them, and try to put people in charge who can get Germany turned around."

Cpl. Ralph Kentebuck of Logansport, Indiana, who served with the U.S. Military Government Detachment 34 in Eisleben. He frequently traveled with the author, tracking down Nazi officials who tried to hide and disappear in the general chaos following the war's ending.

"And the Russians aren't going to help, for they don't even know what democracy is, but what about the British?"

"Oh, they'll go along with us, but the war has worn them out. It's really up to us to get the job done." Kuntzleman paused and took a swig of beer. "The way I see it, the Nazis you haul in every day will at least be out of circulation for a while. It shows we mean business, and it gives the people we move into leading positions some reassurance. They've been cowed for so long, they're afraid of being in charge."[106]

Our talk drifted to other topics, but his comments had given me a slant on the American position that I had not understood till then. American war aims really *were* different from those of the other Allies. The others had been fighting for their lives, for national survival, America had not. I could not help thinking how the Danes had been unwilling to fight, even for national survival. And these Americans were willing to shed their blood motivated by principle, not by fear or aggressive desire.

American determination not withstanding, cleansing the German body politic to reestablish civilized conditions was no quick or simple task. All German organizations, regardless of their original purpose – technical, agricultural, civic, commercial, cultural, sportive, labor, etc. – had become politically led and corrupted to serve the ends of the Nazi party. After Hitler's takeover, ubiquitous Nazi tentacles had been ramified and solidified by placing politically-appointed functionaries at every level and in every sphere of German society. To purge the country of Nazism, the occupying powers set about arresting such officials above certain ranks in the hierarchy, and the American Military Government had arrived with lengthy and precise lists in order to carry out this sweep of the civil administration. The lists defined the so-called "automatic arrests," people whose high positions *ipso facto* made them corespondents for Nazi crimes. But one thing was to know whom to arrest; something else was to find them in the remains of devastated cities and the general chaos of a war still being fought.

By virtue of our first-hand experience and language proficiency – not to mention motivation – Thies and I were ideally suited to this task, and we went to it with a vengeance. Working as a team to start with, we left after breakfast with a jeep and driver, returning to headquarters when we could cram no more prisoners into the back of the vehicle; but after two days we split our forces and took off each with a jeep and driver to cover more ground. Our *modus operandi* was simple enough and in principle depended on the fear of an eventual reckoning that most German people had built up, perhaps subconsciously, during the Hitler years. When operating in the cities, we laid stress on the awesome consequences, largely imaginary, of obstructing in any way the Allies' just pursuit of Nazi culprits. When searching in the countryside, we picked up in each village the first man we saw, told him solemnly that he was under arrest, and that he was now on his way to prison, "because we know you are the Ortsbauernführer here and things look bad for you."

"Oh, no, no, you have me confused with Heinrich Jung who lives in that farm behind the church!"

After collecting Heinrich and letting our first man go, the charade would continue, and with our new prisoner's cooperation, easily gained, we could flush other automatic arrests, both local people and with luck some not native to the village but temporarily there as refugees.

It was fascinating to see the braggarts and strutting supermen of yesterday reduced to whimpering nonentities, pleading their innocence of any share in or responsibility for twelve years of calculated mayhem. And the change from arrogant dominance to abject submission occurred practically from one day to the next. Only once did I encounter resistance to arrest. The man in question had led a *Hitlerjugend* troop in search of a downed American pilot. They had found him lying in a field with his leg broken, sustained in landing by parachute. The troop leader took a small spade from one of the boys and hacked the disabled American to death with it while the troop looked on.

The trail took me to the city of Halle. In the course of searching for the murderer I picked up three automatic arrests and late in the afternoon obtained what looked like a conclusive lead from a *Blockwart*, while my driver, Ralph Kentebuck, was keeping an eye on our catch. I returned to the jeep where Ralph was smoking while the three Nazis watched, glum and worried. My talk with the *Blockwart* had pinpointed that our man was holed up at a certain address, and that he was armed. We decided to get rid of the three prisoners before continuing our pursuit and returned to Eisleben.

In the morning we were back early and located the address. It was an apartment house of which half had been blown away by a blockbuster bomb. Although one side of the building was a scar of gaping holes, rooms ripped open, the wound had proven less than mortal, for the rest of the structure was inhabited and stood, precariously, four stories high. A family in a ground floor apartment indicated that our prey might be on the third floor, the apartment on the left. We mounted the stairs and I positioned Ralph on the landing between the second and third floors. He had brought a carbine for the occasion; normally we carried only our 45ers. With my 45er cocked I knocked on the door and stepped aside, a habit ingrained from the underground. There was no sound from the inside. I knocked again, hard, and stepped aside. A man's voice called out.

"Wer ist da?"

This was not unusual, and I gave my usual gruff reply with commanding emphasis.

"Amerikanische Polizei. Öffnen!"

What happened next took only a couple of seconds. Three shots crashed through the door, the door was flung open, and a man bolted out, crouched. Two bullets from my 45er spun him half around, and he dropped sideways with a thud on the down stairway, sliding slowly head first the last few steps to the landing where Ralph stood, the carbine in his hands following the body's descent until it came to a stop, almost touching the muzzle.

"Jesus fuckin' Christ!"

Ralph let out the expletive with his eyes glued to the body and a rapidly spreading pool of blood. Then he continued, with his voice expressing utter disbelief.

"The guy's fuckin' dead." After a moment he added, "An' the sonuvabitch tried to kill us!"

I was only half listening to the comments, mentally recording my own reactions. One of my bullets had caught him in the shoulder, the other had torn through his chest, killing him instantly. The 45er is devastating at such short range. The German's gun lay on the landing outside the apartment, a Walther P-38. I picked it up and kept it. We checked his identity; he was our man all right. And he was the only noteworthy exception to an otherwise surprisingly nonviolent process.[107]

At each arrest we routinely searched the premises for weapons, Nazi documents, pictures, regalia and the like. Just as routinely, we also liberated cameras, binoculars, portable typewriters, daggers, medals and other interesting items, making sure that each member of our detachment had a good collection of Nazi memorabilia for his eventual return home. Among military personnel there was a brisk and never-ending trade in souvenirs of all kinds, fueled by the typical GI's insatiable desire to acquire exotic trinkets to take back from his adventures abroad.[108] Besides, frontline troops always indulge in some looting, regardless of nationality. It is simply not realistic to expect a combat soldier not to do so. If a guy just tried to kill you, it is contrary to human nature that you in the next breath should respect his property rights. There were of course strict rules against any such goings-on, and "lootin' is verboten" was mouthed as a standard joke whenever stuff was swapped or traded, but the activity could not be suppressed, much less eliminated. On balance, the actual looting perpetrated by Western Allied troops was minuscule compared with that of the Russians, let alone the systematic, government-sponsored plunder by the Germans in the lands they had occupied. But it is a simple fact that looting was common. It is part and parcel of war.

The Western Allies had a better record in regard to rape. I never learned of any instance of rape by American troops, maybe because of the severity of punishment, but probably more because there were plenty of willing young women. In contrast, the Russians got a deservedly bad reputation on this score, possibly because of a more lenient attitude by their military authorities. Lord Alanbrook, Chief of Imperial General Staff during the war, mentions in his memoirs that he discussed with General MacArthur a case in which a Russian commander actually issued orders that in his sector every woman between the ages sixteen and sixty was to be raped twice by Russian soldiery as an example of the superiority of the Russian race.[109]

One of Military Government's published orders stipulated that all firearms in the possession of civilians be surrendered for destruction. A flood of guns immediately inundated the collection points, and from this mass we picked and liberated half a dozen shotguns, all collectors' items, including some antique Spanish models. I also confiscated a 9mm Mauser rifle, a forerunner of the Wehrmacht infantry rifle, when I searched the home of one Nazi official. The man claimed he had "forgotten" to turn it in when the collection was ordered. It looked like a good hunting gun for large game, and I decided to keep it.

Planning to get married when he got back home, Thies also equipped himself with a sizeable hopechest filled with all manner of linen, items that for years had been off store shelves but which Nazi coffers yielded up readily. When I suggested that kitchen utensils might also please his bride-to-be, he collected a generous quantity of those as well. On one trip we found a large military tractor left by the roadside by a German artillery company. Thies sang its praises when he examined it and immediately proposed that we take it to Denmark. When I pointed out the difficulties involved, he settled reluctantly for selling it on the spot to a nearby farmer, deriving some consolation from that transaction.

On the morning of 1 May, we were readying our jeeps for the day's hunt, when Spiegel emerged from his office with the news that Hitler had died at his headquarters in Berlin, an apparent suicide. We paused only a moment, speculating whether the remnants of the Wehrmacht would fight on, then we jumped into our jeeps and roared off. Our own point of momentous transition had occurred during the night of our escape. Now there was work to do, and history was moving nicely with us again playing our small parts in the process. But a few days later we heard that Admiral Dönitz, Hitler's designated successor, had decided on unconditional capitulation which Eisenhower accepted in a Rheims schoolhouse. Now we paused to consider. Could we get word to our families that we were alive and well? Telephones were not functioning, but Capt. Kuntzleman agreed to let us borrow a jeep and make a private dash to Denmark provided we were back within six days. Two hours later, just after dinner, we sped out of Eisleben with our driver, Stanley Hajduk.

* * *

Mors ultima ratio.
[Death is the final accounting]

Anon.

While Thies and I exerted ourselves in denazification, death throes convulsed the last remnant of Nazi Germany only a hundred miles to the northeast. Fifty-five feet under the Chancellery Garden close to the Reichstag building, a small clique of top Nazi leaders spent the last days of the Third Reich in the comparative comfort of the Führer Bunker. Hitler had entered his final headquarters in January and emerged briefly on only two occasions. In rapidly declining health, afflicted by Parkinson's disease and affected by addictive drugs his quack physician had been prescribing since the bomb plot, his mind was gradually distancing itself from reality, as he ordered decimated or nonexistent divisions to perform impossible feats of arms.

Since the attempt on his life the previous July, he had grown distrustful of everyone and was unable to control his terrible temper. In this state he issued a directive which if it had been carried out as intended would have turned all of Germany into a wasteland. The order specified destruction before the advancing enemy of all industrial plants, power generating facilities, gasworks, waterworks, food stores and clothing stores; all railway and communication installations, bridges, waterways, ships, freight cars and locomotives.

The swift advance of enemy forces and the efforts of Albert Speer and a number of army officers prevented most of the destruction. The Führer's intent of having his nation perish with him in a blood-drenched Armageddon was to some extent thwarted.

At a Stavka conference in the Kremlin Stalin laid down a final line separating two Russian thrusts against Berlin, one under Konev and one under Zhukov, placing the Reichstag and Hitler's bunker inside Zhukov's sector. Having masterminded most Red Army strategy since the Germans stood before Moscow, Zhukov was to be the conqueror of Berlin. With tenacity the German garrison

337

still held a ten-mile east-west strip of the inner city, defended by some Wehrmacht remnants, Volkssturm and Hitlerjugend units mixed with shreds of foreign fanatics, Frenchmen of the Charlemagne Division, Walloons and Balts, whom the chaotic fighting had thrown together in a last stand. This motley was no match for the Red Army onslaught. On 29 April Russian guns were demolishing the Reich Chancellery itself.

In the bunker below, Hitler in the early morning hours married Eva Braun, his mistress of 12 years. He then dictated his "political testament," a diatribe blaming the officer corps for losing the war and enjoining continued fight against international Jewry. He dismissed Speer for failing to carry out his scorched-earth order and expelled Göring and Himmler from the Nazi party. Göring had incurred his wrath by prematurely suggesting his succession, Himmler had sent peace feelers to the Allies through the Swedish Count Folke Bernadotte. After lunch on the 30th, Hitler and his bride retired to his private quarters where they took cyanide, and Hitler simultaneously shot himself.[110] Hitler's valet and an orderly assisted by Bormann carried the bodies up to the garden, placed them in a shell crater and ignited them with gasoline. Later Goebbels and his family committed suicide, and the rest of the entourage fled the bunker.

On 2 May General Hans Weidling, commandant of the Berlin garrison, surrendered to the Russians. From Chuikov's headquarters he sent out his capitulation signal, and at 3 p.m. the guns fell silent.

Though Germany's fate was less than the ultimate Armageddon, Hitler got his wish for a bloody ending to the Third Reich. Aside from prolonging for a few days the lives of some top leaders, the Battle for Berlin was symbolic, serving no military purpose, for the outcome was preordained. It cost the heaviest toll suffered by the Red Army in any battle except the great encirclements and captures in 1941.[111] Around 125,000 Berliners died as the tanks of assault troops crashed through houses and yards, followed by a crazed, revenge-seeking mob of released prisoners and slave laborers bent on killing Germans, any Germans.

The Russians were hell-bent on taking Berlin, and Churchill and his military staff also yearned to posses this emblem of Nazi power. In America, few sensible people – certainly very few soldiers – will quarrel with Eisenhower's sober decision not to expend thousands of Allied lives to capture the place. Leave it to the Red Army who paid so dearly for it. Eisenhower's southern thrust gained a different advantage, this one political, as it put two-fifths of the area intended for Russian occupation under American control by the time of the surrender. This was a move from which Thies and I came to benefit greatly.

Chapter 53

May 1945

Breathes there a man, with soul so dead,
Who never to himself hath said,
This is my own, my native land!
Whose heart hath ne'er within him burned
As home his footsteps he hath turned
From wandering on a foreign Strand!

Sir Walter Scott

Our headlights lit up the road ahead as we bounced along on another detour, for Stan had scraped the hooding off the lenses. No need for blacking out now that the war was over. The night air was cold, but our field jackets and gloves kept the chill at bay. Comfortable but too excited to sleep, I sat next to Stan whose turn it was at the wheel, contemplating our speed of travel and estimating when we could be on home ground.

The military jeep was a marvelous vehicle: reliable, surefooted and well-balanced, even with a heavily loaded trailer. We were carrying twenty-two jerricans of gasoline plus as much Nazi loot as the trailer's steel box could hold, and we drove without stop, taking three-hour turns at the wheel with one man dozing in the back, comfortably resting on Thies' linen pile. The highway running north and west toward Braunschweig was in poor condition, and the U.S. Army had built and marked several long detours for the benefit of military convoys, for the retreating Germans had systematically destroyed their own bridges at river crossings and intersections. This night the roads were deserted. We had lost our way twice, both times in forested areas, and had to backtrack and find the detour markings with the aid of flashlights. Near Wolfenbüttel we encountered an army roadblock, but a jeep with three U.S. soldiers was nowhere subject to scrutiny. At a curve in the road south of Hannover, someone took a shot at us as we streaked by, probably a sniper from some diehard Wehrmacht rem-

De to danske Sabotører, „Thies" (tv.) og „Aage", fotograferet i Gaar deres amerikanske *jeep* foran *Nationaltidende.*

Thies and the author in their jeep in front of the Copenhagen daily Nationaltidende upon their return two days after the German surrender.

nant. We saw the muzzle flash, and the bullet nicked the tubular steel frame of our windshield, but we didn't stop to argue. A bit farther on, our headlights showed another roadblock and we slowed to a halt. This one was British, and we were delayed for an hour. A sergeant offered us tea which we sipped, while his platoon cleared a section of road ahead of snipers. A few more miles of detour, and we got onto the autobahn toward Hamburg, part of the superhighway system Hitler had constructed in the 1930s. In those days it had been an object of national pride and international envy and had been pointed out as one of Nazism's accomplishments, eliminating unemployment and building the country's infrastructure. Not mentioned at the time was the obvious strategic value in wartime of these concrete ribbons, as they allowed swift east-west movement of armies across the face of Germany. Now they were in worse condition than the regular highway, potholed and broken and fragmented by countless detours.

As the jeep hurtled north, the surrounding countryside showed no glimmer of light anywhere. Aside from the blackout, electric power had ceased to be, making the gloom absolute in this devastated land. At daybreak we pushed into Hamburg. Army bulldozers had cleared a passage through the rubble, just wide enough for one vehicle to pass. Heaps of debris alternated with empty shells of houses looming beside what used to be streets, but nowhere could any dwelling be seen still useable for human habitation. A lone light pole remained standing at an intersection, its wires hanging like limp spaghetti into the broken mass below. The narrow thoroughfare crossed a small square, buried under six feet of building fragments. Off to our left, a statue of a man on horseback protruded above the litter, a mute, ineffectual guardian. The dawn was calm, and a light smoke mixed with the smell of carbolic acid hung over the area. The bustling city I remembered seeing in my boyhood had been converted to a silent, stinking graveyard by the ravages of aerial bombing. Staying on the autobahn as much as possible, we sped on northward to Eckernförde and Schleswig and already sensed ourselves on native soil in these ancient towns that had been within the Danish kingdom from Viking times until Bismarck's troops took them in 1864. It elated us enormously to know that we were again on home ground, and in conversation broken by surges in the jeep's noise level we marvelled at discovering in ourselves a territoriality of which we had been unaware.

We reached the border at Krusaa and tarried for a moment to chat with the British soldiers manning the frontier crossing. Under a shed roof outside the guard building lay an enormous pile of stuff: clothing, food, implements, sacks of money, bicycles, leather goods, anything light enough to be carried. It was loot which German soldiers now trickling across the border had attempted to take along home to the Vaterland. The border troops had confiscated the lot. After five years of systematic looting, the final German contingent was made to leave Denmark empty-handed.

A young steel-helmeted civilian with a red-white-and-blue armband and a submachine gun slung decoratively over his shoulder strolled over to our jeep, and Thies eyed him curiously, finally asking in Danish the question that puzzled both of us.

"Who the hell are you?"

The young civilian came smartly to attention.

"I'm a *Frihedskæmper* (freedom fighter)."

We looked at each other in silent disbelief and finally burst into laughter. I put the jeep in gear and as we drove off, Thies turned with a parting shot.

"Where the hell were you at this time last year when we needed you?"

The spring sun revealed the lovely countryside along the Jutland east coast where groves of beeches stood nakedly silhouetted against the blue sky, ready to burst into green. We laughed happily, assuring each other that not all of our beech forests had gone up in generator smoke to fuel Wehrmacht vehicles.[112] We stopped at a bakery in Haderslev and tried to buy *wienerbrød*, the incomparable pastries which – we assured Stan – could only be had in Denmark, but at the sight of our uniforms the baker refused payment and presented us with a large bagful, fresh out of the oven. From the store I telephoned ahead to D.S.B., the Danish State Railways, in Nyborg and learned that the next Big Belt ferry was scheduled to leave in less than an hour. Informed that an American Army jeep with important personnel was enroute from the border, the D.S.B. authorities readily agreed to hold the ship until our arrival. We raced on across the island of Funen and onto the big vessel that had been standing by patiently in its dock for half an hour, loaded with two trains but no other motor vehicles.

As we sat down in the elegant first-class salon and ordered lunch, Stan slowly hefted a glass of Carlsberg beer, balancing it on the fingertips of his right hand. Studying its froth thoughtfully, he finally made a quiet comment.

"I don't know how you bastards do it but ... Kee-rist ... I wish my old man could see me now."

We all laughed and toasted to a memorable trip. After the meal we suddenly realized that we had not carried money for a long time and had no means of paying our check, but the ferry personnel waved aside our excuses, insisting that the Danish State Railways would be more than pleased to make it gratuitous. As we left the salon, they were firmly declining money from some civilian travelers who had been plying us with questions during the meal and who were now vying for the privilege of picking up the tab. We began to sense the strength of an apparent euphoria buoying up the country. The day before, Field Marshal Montgomery had presented himself to King Christian and been received by one million Copenhagen inhabitants delirious with joy. Thanks to the British thrust northwards to liberate and occupy Denmark before the Russians could get there.[113] Wherever an Allied uniform was to be seen, people competed for an opportunity to show their gratitude.

When we landed in Korsør, Thies succeeded in making a telephone call to his home, telling his mother that we were both alive, shortly arriving, and to call my mother and let her know. Our hearts singing, we streaked across Zealand on an empty highway, every hill and curve familiar and friendly, through Roskilde with its cathedral's green copper spires gleaming in the spring sun, on through the Copenhagen suburbs where flags fluttered from gardens and balconies, and on to the apartment block on Frederiksborgvej where my mother lived. I bolted up the stairs, but she was already halfway down to meet me. The sound of the jeep's engine echoed from the buildings as Thies and Stan drove away. I was home.

Our stay in Copenhagen was short and hectic. During the last year of the war the trickle of Danes seeking refuge in Sweden had swelled greatly, and with Swedish approval and cooperation they had organized and trained an infantry force that became known as The Brigade, fully armed and poised to make a fighting return. The Swedes, however, maintained scrupulous neutrality to the bitter end and did not release this contingent until the day of the German surrender. The Danes thereby completed a perfect record of official military non-contribution to bringing down the Nazi scourge, and the Swedes rounded out

On the city hall steps Carlo Thomsen (Thies) and his bride, Cordia, board the jeep after taking their wedding vows before the mayor of Copenhagen.

their record of neutrality, leaning toward accommodation of the Nazis. The Brigade had nevertheless received a hero's welcome upon its return two days before our arrival and was performing useful service by maintaining order during the confused first days of peace, when many local people declared open season on collaborators. My mother told me that Ole Kuhlman and my sister Angla were both members of The Brigade and that they were married. The Gestapo had tried to arrest Ole but he had eluded them and escaped to Sweden. While waiting in a small coastal village for passage across the Sound, he and my sister had been married by the local parson with only witnesses present. My sister's wedding gown had been lovely camouflaged parachute silk. After hearing of my arrest, the seamstress had brought the finished dress to Angla, refusing to charge anything for sewing it. Mother had heard nothing from the Germans since my being exported to Neuengamme, but during my imprisonment and the interrogation period in Copenhagen, our apartment had been searched minutely. This had uncovered my store of explosives in their hiding place inside the old piano. The Gestapo agents had carted away, triumphantly, not just the explosives but the piano as well, and it was never recovered, thus terminating my musical career.

I had Stan bring the jeep and started to comb the city for further news. Torben Halkjær had been arrested by the Gestapo shortly after he and Hanne had walked into the lion's den to visit me in Frøslev, and he had later perished in the

343

This picture was taken when the author passed through Hamburg immediately following the German surrender. Like most cities of the Reich, Hamburg suffered incredible destruction from aerial bombardment.

Porta Westphalia concentration camp. Aage Schoch had been arrested by the Gestapo in September but had succeeded in confusing the interrogators about his actual involvement. Niels Jørgensen had returned alive, was convalescing, and now thought about writing a book to record an inside view of the concentration camps for a posterity bound to deem it unbelievable. Not all of the others from the *Hjemmefronten* group had made it back. Birger Mouritzen had succumbed in Porta Westphalia, and Erik Westh had died in the Bergen-Belsen camp. On the positive side, I found Aage Kjellerup and Alfred Sander alive and well, both in Brigade uniforms. They were still spoiling to fight and cursed the Swedes for having denied them the opportunity. Erik Hansen had succeeded in getting from Sweden to England where he had joined the British Special Forces. He now wore the uniform of a British lieutenant and worked in an Allied headquarters in Copenhagen which had been set up in Dagmarhus, the building that formerly had housed the Gestapo.

While I rushed around town gathering news in bits and pieces, Thies had been trying to arrange getting married, but his efforts were frustrated by city hall which required four days to process so weighty a matter. The wedding had assumed great urgency in the minds of both Thies and his intended bride, which caused Stan and and me to speed to city hall. The capital was ruled by a council of three mayors, and I went to the chambers of the chief mayor where

344

my American uniform again magically opened all doors. The mayor, a small pleasant man of great vitality, listened with sympathy and issued a few instructions on the phone with the result that Thies and Cordia were married the same afternoon. We drove our trusty jeep up the wide steps of the city hall where the ceremony was performed, and carried the happy couple away on a very brief honeymoon.

My inquiries revealed that Ellen Quistgaard was in Washington, working as secretary to Henrik Kauffmann, the Danish ambassador. Kauffmann had during the war been recognized by the American government as Denmark's true representative although the government in Copenhagen had issued an indictment against him as a traitor. Acting on his own initiative, Kauffmann had represented his country in a most admirable way, among many other important actions concluding an agreement with the United States to establish air bases in Greenland.

On the evening before our departure I located Hanne. She pleaded without hesitation to go with us to Eisleben to be able to observe Germany in defeat. As we had room in the jeep after unloading our loot, I gladly consented.

We left Copenhagen early in the morning and drove west across Zealand with a redolent sunrise behind us. The bright spring light revealed how much the landscape had changed from what we had observed five days earlier. Far different from maple and alder, the beech forest has its own rhythm, its own ritual. First the forest floor clothes itself in a shift of anemones, flowers so fragile that they cannot survive in a vase even for an hour. When the anemones are at their peak, the beech leaves unfold, changing the forest aspect from silvery brown to a delicate light green, and it happens virtually overnight. This annual spring miracle is an event to which everyone looks forward eagerly, for it marks even more than the equinox the changeover to balmy spring from winter darkness. It always occurs in the middle of May, varying but a day or two from year to year, and people rush to cut a few beech branches, although their leaves are almost as short-lived as the anemones. As the jeep roared west, we sat silently, each with his own thoughts. We had been favored by luck and fate to survive hardships and perils until on this lovely spring morning we could turn our minds from the madness of war.

I was savoring childhood memories of cutting beech bouquets in spring forests. Life was a delight again. The Nazi holocaust was past, the threat to civilization extirpated. The world was at peace. From what I had observed and learned during the six war years it had become clear to me that although the two warring sides objectively speaking may have appeared to differ little, as they did their best to kill the largest possible number of their opponents, the German nation under Hitler had in this war indisputably represented Evil, and had done so with uncivilized abandon, even with enthusiasm. The Allies had been reluctant entrants into the conflict, but had under duress represented Good, much to their enduring credit.

I also felt in my bones that I had never been in doubt about the war's eventual outcome. Why this should be so puzzled me, as the jeep zoomed along in the morning light, until I realized that I had some basic conviction that Good is inherently superior to Evil. Moreover, it had to be more satisfying to exert oneself on the side of Good. I wondered whether my attitude in this regard was instilled in me by exposure to religion. That might well be the case, although I was by conviction an agnostic and considered religion to be at best delusionary, at worst egocentricity and vanity on mankind's part.

We rolled onto the ferry and had lunch in the 1st Class restaurant on the top deck. Still preoccupied with sorting out the war's rights and wrongs I solicited Thies' view of the relative merits of the belligerents. He replied that he had not thought about it beyond the simple fact that the Krauts were assholes who needed and deserved to be stepped on. Hard.

Thies' approach to abstract questions was, as always, direct and ingenuous; while reassuring, it offered no analytical support. As we drove on, I kept pondering, groping for a philosophy, some personal ethic unconnected to religion. Coming up with no satisfactory answers, I realized how skewed, incomplete and wanting my education had been so far, and I resolved to remedy at least some of my shortcomings. Then I realized with a rush of excitement that I was contemplating my future in a way that had become lost in recent years, while the Damocles sword of war hung over our existence night and day. My prospective future now stretched indefinitely ahead, barring accidents, holding unlimited promise and potential. Throughout the occupation period, daily problems demanding full attention and absolute concentration had forced us to ignore longer range concerns. There had been neither time nor energy to spare from the demands of immediate survival. Those years were past.

We made our return trip through Ribe to check whether the group there had come through alive. It had, but Kjær and Prahl were gravely ill with tuberculosis, and Valdemar Sørensen's health was also impaired. Toward the end of the war, Valdemar had been sent with an *Arbeitskommando* to a camp producing storage batteries for the U-boat fleet. His work consisted of filling the battery frames with a clay-lead mixture, then adding the acid prior to loading the electric charge. The work was extremely debilitating due to the high toxicity of the lead mixture, and the inmates worked largely unprotected, because gloves and aprons were either badly torn or not available at all. Average life expectancy on this assignment was only seventy-one days, but the German collapse had fortunately precluded Valdemar from testing this statistic. After only two weeks of making U-boat batteries, he had been collected together with other Scandinavian prisoners in his locality by a Swedish Red Cross unit touring the collapsing Reich and taken straight home.[114] Sigurd Laursen was alive and well and greeted us in his gun shop.

Life in Ribe appeared unaltered. Bathed in the spring sun, the town like an old person's face showed the traces of time's passing. How strange it seemed that soldiers should have come from far corners of the earth to defeat the ancient German foe menacing her from the south, while the town could not bestir itself to any serious effort, only a handful of young men being willing to take up the challenge.

While we were having a quick meal at my grandparents' apartment, my old friend, Østbirk of the criminal police, dropped in to give me with a big smile a special present: an envelope containing copies of the official police photographs taken by the crime technical squad from Kolding after Ribe Autoværksted had been thoroughly destroyed by fire two years before. He had correctly surmised that it was my doing and had kept the photos, confident that I would come back alive.

Our return trip was uneventful except for a minor incident. On the autobahn south of Hamburg signs diverted us onto a long detour that took us through several villages and some forest. It was so poorly marked that we got lost but after further driving managed to find our way back to the autobahn where we continued, thinking we had passed the point of obstruction that caused the detour. It was late afternoon, visibility was getting poor, and I was driving, pushing the jeep to its best performance. The highway's concrete wound through a landscape of gently rolling hills, and we had passed one crest and were speeding down the mile-long decline of the next valley in which we were to cross a small river. As we rushed toward the low point, we all simultaneously saw the road ahead broken by a black chasm where the bridge should be. My foot hit the brake at the same time as my two companions screamed "Stop!!" with all the urgency only fear can compel. The jeep slued through a half-turn with the trailer skidding drunkenly behind and came to rest facing in the opposite direction from which we had been traveling, the trailer twisted at a crazy angle that strained even the massive, drop-forged hitch. We were less than fifteen feet from the edge and could look down on the river's dark water thirty feet below. The near-accident taught us never to depart from and forgo the security of a detour.

We arrived in Eisleben after an absence of six days and seven nights. As agreed.

* * *

Since the Russian winter offensive started the exodus of refugees from Germany's eastern regions, millions had been pouring westward. With the Allied armies converging from east and west, the pressure became ever more intense, as civilians were joined by soldiers, all frantically fleeing the Red Army to reach the British or American occupation zones, the borders of which had prematurely become public knowledge. In this initial panic flight from the east as many as one million Germans may have died from hardship and deprivation in the bitter winter conditions.

Appointed Hitler's successor, Dönitz ordered all U-boats to return to port and tried together with Jodl and other general staff officers to arrange a surrender to the Western Allies. Eisenhower ordered all such attempts categorically rebuffed, as the Allies had agreed not to make any separate peace. Finally abandoning hope of obtaining conditions of any kind, Jodl with Dönitz' authorization on 7 May signed the surrender, total and unconditional on behalf of Germany, at Eisenhower's headquarters in Rheims. It was accepted by Bedell-Smith who signed for the Allies, with the Russian and French representatives signing as witnesses. Two days later the Russians and Germans signed the surrender instrument in Berlin.

Chapter 54   June 1945

Now to what higher object can any mortal aspire
than to … discourage and abolish tyranny
and vice?

John Adams

Captain Kuntzleman leaned back in his chair and eyed me reflectively.

"Niels, in four days we'll be pulling out of this town."

"Out? Why?"

"It seems our President and some other bigwigs have decided to give this area to the Russkies. Furthermore, Detachment 34 will be broken up and the pieces attached to other parts of our administrative setup. Now, if you and your buddy want to keep on doing what you've been doing here, I can easily find you another outfit to work with, but I thought you might like to return and finish your schooling. Why don't you think about it and let me know tomorrow."

In the evening Thies and I discussed our prospects over a couple of cans of beer. It was the end of June. After our quick visit home we had continued our manhunt of automatic arrests with renewed vigor. The losses among friends we had known so well spurred us on, turning our roundup of Nazis into a personal vendetta. We had spent long hours following the tentacles of Nazidom that everywhere penetrated the German nation, and we had used evenings to compare notes, checking if the trails we had covered during the day were converging or crossing at some point. Our efforts had paid off. Between us we had put 224 Nazis behind bars and one in the cemetery, not a bad result we thought. However, going to work with a new outfit had little appeal; besides, Thies was not unwilling to return to married life. Finishing our beer, we decided to go home.

This time our transportation would not be by jeep. Shortly after our return

```
                    HEADQUARTERS
              MILITARY GOVERNMENT DET 34
                     EISLEBEN

                                              2 June 45


          L E T T E R   O F   C O M M E N D A T I O N


To Whom it may Concern :


     Niels Skov has been in the employ of this detachment for a period
of one and one half months, and during that time has served faithfully
and well. His knowledge of Germans and the German language, and his
understanding of the Nazi mind has made him of great value in the loc-
ation and capture of many "war criminals".


     As commander of this detachment, I commend Niels Skov for his faith-
ful and untiring service to Military Government Detachment 34 during the
early period of the occupation of Germany.




                                        OLIVER C. KUNTZLEMAN
                                        Capt.            AUS
                                        Commanding
```

The letter acknowledging the author's service to U.S. Military Government in Eisleben, Germany, during the initial stages of American occupation. Thies received a similar letter.

from Denmark, Thies hatched a bright idea which we had promptly acted upon. It was quite simple. Why not locate and examine the official lists of motor vehicle registrations in the local area and use that information to find and liberate the best Nazi-owned civilian automobiles? They would serve to take us home, as we would have to leave our service jeeps behind. An inquiry revealed that the registration lists were kept in the office of the *Landrat*, the approximate German equivalent of a county auditor. He was a jovial bureaucrat by the name of Meissner who had been our source of information on other occasions, useful and willing to help us in our Nazi hunt. He had been appointed to his present position by the U.S. Military Government based on his personal record as a socialist during the Weimar period and having had no Nazi involvement later. We perused the registration lists while Meissner tried politely to stifle a chuckle, realizing what we were after, and he agreeably pointed out some of the party members among the vehicle owners.

350

As expected, we found that most of the larger cars had been requisitioned years earlier by the German military, but a number of fine vehicles were still sitting on blocks in garages here and there. We decided to liberate one each to take back to Denmark. Thies selected a small four-cylinder Mercedes. The records listed it as "Typ 170V Schwingachswagen 1.7 liter," and I chose a convertible BMW displaying the lovely, flowing lines of 1939.[115] Using his magic touch with all things mechanical, Thies soon had both vehicles purring, and in the following weeks we had loaded them methodically with more high-quality Nazi loot.

While we were thus occupied, Hanne had busied herself elsewhere and had started an affair with a French liaison officer who visited our detachment. It took me totally aback when I found out. Hanne and I had been acquainted for only a couple of days before my arrest, but during my prison time in Copenhagen our brief relationship had loomed large in my solitude, and after our reunion we had decided to consider ourselves engaged. Furious, I set out to find her and the Frenchman, but on the way Thies had intercepted me and dragged me off for a heart-to-heart talk. He started by encapsulating his message in one of his characteristic sentences.

"You are my best friend, so I have to tell you this straight: Hanne is a nymphomaniac I wouldn't touch with another man's dick on a flag pole."

Momentarily stunned, I havered my temper. Could Thies be right? Some minor incidents that had puzzled me suddenly fell into place. Slowly, I realized that Thies indeed was right. I also realized that I wasn't in love with Hanne and that only my vanity had been injured. At the end of our talk, I decided to continue with what we were doing and let Hanne go her sexy way. When I told her so, she left our outfit the same day, with the Frenchman. Only later did it occur to me that Hanne was functioning in a mode in which I had been operating for some time myself.[116]

The early summer morning was crisp and clear. Starlings nesting under the eaves of hotel *Goldener Löwe* were busily feeding their young; several cocks were crowing in the neighborhood as if announcing distant warnings to stay out of their territory. I was standing in the yard, leaning on my BMW while waiting for Thies to say good-bye to some of the guys in the mess hall. My car was loaded so full that only the driver's seat was free, and Thies' little Mercedes parked beside me was crammed even more. So this was good-bye to Eisleben where we had savored the first weeks of freedom after the concentration camps. The town reminded me of Wernigerode where I had visited with my family a dozen years earlier, but it was devoid of the aggressive energy of the Hitler years. In the interim, the German nation had bled away the flower of its youth. How long would it take to recover? And what would be the attitude of the next generation?

Ralph Kentebuck came out of the door to the hotel kitchen. He was slightly unsteady, for we had discovered a quantity of mint liqueur in the basement of the liquor store next door and had liberated a few cases last night. It was sweet and sticky stuff, but with a thirty-five percent alcohol content it had been an instant hit with Detachment 34. Ralph pumped my hand, searching for an appropriate good-bye statement.

"Fuckin' shame you're leaving."

He looked at the cars and with a sudden inspiration unbuttoned his pants.

"Hey, this is for good luck on your way home."

He proceeded to piss on each of the wheels on the BMW and went on to the Mercedes, managing only three before running dry. As he was buttoning his pants, Captain Kuntzleman emerged from his office just as Thies came out from the mess hall. He handed each of us an envelope.

"Here, a letter of commendation for each of you. Sorry to see you go, but you are doing the right thing, I'm sure."

We thanked him and shook hands, jumped in our cars and were off. As we drove through the portal of the inn onto the street, I wondered if we would ever see Eisleben again.

* * *

We have learned from hard experiences that stronger, more efficient, more rigorous world institutions must be created to preserve peace and to forestall the causes of future wars.

Winston Churchill

From the time when the Normandy invasion had established the Anglo-American forces firmly on the continent, Allied planners had increasingly concerned themselves with postwar political problems. Everyone desired to avoid future war, particularly among the major powers. The idea has come up many times over the centuries, predictably after some bloody conflict had torn an irreplaceable segment of youth from the nations involved. Having seen the Wilson administration's hopes for the League of Nations dashed by America's withdrawal into isolationism, Roosevelt felt compelled to use America's now immensely swelled power and prestige to create a more effective world organization.

At a meeting in August 1944 at a Georgetown estate, Dumbarton Oaks, delegates from the U.S., Britain, the Soviet Union and China had found themselves far apart on several important questions. The Soviet Union insisted on unanimity among the four major powers on all decisions, effectively allowing any one of the four to veto any proposed action. Another point of disagreement surfaced when the Americans insisted that in settlement of a dispute, the parties involved in the dispute should abstain from voting. The Soviet Union categorically refused any such procedure, making it clear that it would not allow the possibility of being outvoted. It also insisted on having sixteen votes in the General Assembly, one for each of its constituent republics. The Dumbarton Oaks group adjourned in October with disappointing results.

At the Yalta meeting a compromise was reached, allowing the Soviet Union two additional votes, one each for the Ukraine and Belorussia, and settling the unanimity question by upholding the veto power as the Soviet Union insisted. On this basis the Allies proceeded to a founding conference, hosted by the U.S. in San Francisco and organized by a fifty-nation steering committee. Two months of intense debate produced the new organization's charter, providing for a General Assembly of all members and a Security Council of five, U.S.A., U.S.S.R., Britain, France and China. The debates made it ever more apparent that the totalitarian Soviet state was basically unable to accept the rules and principles by which democratic states can function in concert. An impasse was reached over a Soviet demand that the five-power veto should apply even to discussion or consideration of a question brought to the Security Council. The smaller states rebelled against this possibility of being muzzled by a major power, and they were backed by the United States. President Truman who had ascended to the presidency after Roosevelt's death stood firm. In the end Stalin backed down, and the Charter of the United Nations was signed in June of 1945. In the closing plenary session the Soviet delegation still insisted on a number of attachments to the record, stating Soviet reservations and disagreement.

Despite the difficulties, the United Nations was born amid euphoria and optimism, but it was becoming increasingly clear that countries with traditions of democracy and popularly elected governments could cooperate with totalitarian ones only under conditions of extreme external pressure. This had been the case during the exigency of war, when both sides accepted compromises against their better judgment. It did not last when the pressure was off. Stalin was worried about being "ganged up on." Roosevelt[117] had worried about principles of Anglo-American justice and fair procedure. The two were incompatible.

Chapter 55   August 1945

*There are few things that can bind two individuals
more closely than to be intimately connected in a
vast, prolonged struggle against overwhelming odds,
and to emerge on top.*

Alanbrooke

"Are you complaining because our countrymen are mad at the Krauts?" Thies
looked at me quizzically across the desk.

"I'm saying it makes no sense to blame women and children for the misdeeds
of Hitler and his henchmen."

We were sitting in the principal's office at Sct. Jørgens Gymnasium where I was
temporarily carrying out my duties as administrator of refugee camp #17. While
we were Hitler's prisoners, Denmark had become a reluctant host to large numbers of German refugees, women and children evacuated from the ruined cities
of the Reich in the final months of the war. After our return from Germany we
had been asked to take charge of two of the improvised camps, each housing a
few hundred of these unfortunate victims of their Führer's war. Thies was busy
repairing his mother-in-law's house and had turned down the request. Having
nothing more constructive to do, I took on the task for about a month at a Copenhagen high school and occupied myself making the impromptu quarters
livable and securing rations and minimal medical care for the temporary occupants. To my surprise the Danes were distinctly hostile to the refugees, so much
so that I was moved to write an article in *Nationaltidende,* taking issue with the attitude and the resulting treatment. A deluge of personal letters from the
paper's readers showed to my dismay that more than half of the writers were eager to take their anger and resentment of the Nazis out on the refugees. So far
as I could judge, many of the people who had been docilely passive rather than

actively resisting the occupation now turned out to be the ones most vocal and greedy for revenge.

The German occupation troops had quietly disappeared from the country. When armistice was announced, the soldiers found themselves in the untenable position of unwelcome guests in a hostile land, members of a crumbling army. In such circumstances the soldier's typical reaction is to want to head for home by any means at his disposal. This rarely meant motorized or rail transport, of which little was functional and available, and as the internal structure of the once proud Wehrmacht broke down, the soldiers fell back on the simplest expedient at hand and started hiking for home. In small groups, or even singly, grim-faced men set out on their own on the last trek of their ill-fated war, to quit the lands where they had never been wanted.

At their hurried departure, and with a natural desire to travel light, the Germans left behind all manner of impedimenta, from office equipment to guns and armored vehicles, and these abandoned goods created an unprecedented opportunity for bold enterprise. Considered the ablest traders in the North, Danes have no particular need to be larcenous, but the combination of wartime shortage and unguarded property of which rightful ownership was at best doubtful proved to be an irresistible temptation. What started as a process of picking up a souvenir or two rapidly developed into a sport of impressive scope, as resistance people and ordinary citizenry happily tried to secure their personal compensation for five years of hardship and damages inflicted by the invaders. Public authorities were temporarily missing or replaced ad hoc by resistance groups, and the resulting fluid situation, quite without precedent in anyone's memory or experience, invited the process and allayed moral qualms. Thus to acquire "ownerless" goods immediately became known as *rulle*, to roll (something), and numberless items from binoculars to typewriters were "rolled" from the abandoned Wehrmacht quarters into citizens' possession. One particularly ambitious Brigade member managed to sidetrack and unload an entire railroad car of German supplies. Thies and I looked on with amusement, having already engaged in looting on a much more select and profitable scale. We pointed out to each other that the fine natural ability for personal enrichment which had come into full flower with the Vikings evidently had remained a latent Danish trait, nurtured from time immemorial due to the country's location at the crossroads of ancient trade routes.

Besides looking after my German wards, minor medical problems of my own had claimed my attention, a new experience as my adult life hitherto had been without sickness. In order to repair some of the effects of the concentration camp period, I spent a good deal of time with my dentist, a woman who had taken care of my teeth since my childhood. Her work used to consist of a quick annual check that had revealed a total of three small cavities by my twenty-fourth birthday; but when Dr. Inger Fledelius first looked into my mouth after my German interlude, she wept. The damage wreaked by the lack of vitamins, minerals and proper nourishment was extensive, and my teeth had become so soft that she hardly needed a drill to shape their numerous cavities for filling. They fortunately seemed to be regaining their customary hardness, but the damage caused during the period of starvation diet could not be undone, only repaired.

Our discussion today was prompted in part by the fact that the return of peace found Denmark in 1945 very different from the gentle and peaceful country in which we had grown up. War does strange things, and inevitably brutalizes both individuals and nations, even those who are merely spectators, and the occupation experience had certainly altered Danish society. Particularly the last occupation year had wrought profound change in Danish attitudes, a fact of which Thies and I were keenly aware, for it was this change that had saved us from execution in the summer of 1944. The long, slow process of kindling sabotage had set the example that in the end galvanized and determined ordinary citizens to take action that, fortuitously for us, culminated in the people's general strike while we were in prison.

"Perhaps so," Thies admitted, "but don't forget that we wanted people to get good and mad at the Germans, and a year ago it saved our necks that they were."

"That was then, this is now. The war is over."

Thies chuckled.

"I don't know much about changing public opinion, but I'm sure it takes more time than you're willing to give. If it took four years to make the Danes angry, it may take four to calm them down again."

"Anger is legitimate, and God knows there's plenty of reason for that, but taking it out on women and children ... ? It isn't in the Danish traditions."

"Listen, nothing has been in any Danish tradition since the Krauts came here. What you need is some female company to get your mind off social issues."

Thies was rarely circumspect. His approach to life was direct, and he was a great believer in sex as a cure-all.

The café was quietly elegant, the hushed voices of a few patrons barely audible. Copenhagen did not have such profusion of restaurants as throng the street corners and squares of Paris, but the choice offered something for every taste and occasion. This one was perfect for a tête-à-tête, and its soothing ambience visibly calmed my companion. She took a sip of her coffee, looked at me, and continued to relate the unhappy tale of her breaking marriage, while I pondered how this had somehow become a concern of mine.

I had left the administration of the refugee camp after putting it in good order and had spent two weeks vacationing on the north coast of Zealand with the remnants of the old Ribe group, Viggo, Valdemar, Aage and Niels, plus wives and girlfriends. Kjær and Prahl were too ill. After my return to Copenhagen I had been invited to a party at the home of an old friend, John Andersen, and had gladly accepted. When I arrived at John's apartment, the party was well

While serving sa administrator of a camp for German refugees in Copenhagen in the summer of 1945, the author got briefly embroiled in a public discussion about the treatment of the refugees, largely women and children of whom many were undernourished and afflicted with sundry diseases.

underway, several couples dancing to phonograph music in the living room, while others were standing around a table in the parlor, balancing drinks while snacking on choice delicacies. When John let me in, he waved a hand at the crowd.

"I think you know some of the people here, but I want to introduce you to a visitor."

He led me across the dance floor to intercept a couple on the other side, dismissed the man with an apology and turned to the woman.

"Aase, this is Niels, the man I told you about this morning. Niels, this is my sister, Aase. She is one of the wholes. As you know, I'm only a half."

John was referring to their Jewish ancestry. Their mother was Jewish, had three children by her first husband, a Jew by the name of Cohn. After being widowed early, she had two children by her second husband, a Gentile by the name of Andersen. John was one of the "halves" and had stayed underground in Denmark after the German attempt to apprehend the Jews in 1943. I had always liked his cool courage in defying the German threat and admired his business acumen. Owner of two delicatessen stores, he was in the process of starting a factory he called UG to make various deli supplies, and it was already rated a success.

John left us in order to attend to host duties, and I looked at Aase with what must have been obvious admiration. Tall and slender, her features and proportions were what most women could only dream of but never attain. She had a slight suntan, no doubt acquired on the beach, and for a moment I wondered what she might look like in a bathing suit. At the introduction I noticed the light brown of her eyes had a hint of green that contrasted with her jet-black hair. Very exotic in a Danish setting. I had met John's other siblings, all attractive individuals, but Aase was far more than attractive. At thirty, she was strikingly beautiful.

"So you are the one John has been telling me about. He thinks very highly of you." She spoke high Danish without a trace of the flat Copenhagen accent, her voice low and pleasant.

"And I of him. He stayed put and worked against the Germans when other Jews sensibly took refuge in Sweden."

"But you fought the Nazis when you could have been sitting out the war, and you're not even Jewish."

"Why should being Jewish make a difference?"

"Oh, we are really the ones Hitler was after. Gentiles like yourself actually elicit the Germans' respect in a racial sense." She was obviously well informed and aware of the Nazi ideas. We stood for a moment, unabashedly sizing each other up. Then she said, impulsively, "Let's dance."

She walked to a table to put her drink down, and I followed, watching her from behind. The image that came to mind was that of a purebred racehorse: perfection in every move. The phonograph was blaring out a tango when she put her drink down and turned, and I put my arm around her. She looked at me with a smile that made the rest of the world's women fade into pale, insubstantial shadows, and we danced most of the evening away. She did not seem to mind being monopolized, and I was in seventh heaven. I learned that she was married to a furniture manufacturer in Aarhus, but I gathered also that her presence in Copenhagen had been prompted by marital troubles as much as by desire to visit her brother.

John was only two years older than I but already had substantial income, and the sundry branches of his family were of economic means far beyond the circles with which I had been acquainted. Rationing and scarcity during the war years had been great economic levelers, blotting out differences in personal wealth by making money inconsequential, but with peace and availability of goods, money was regaining its normal rôle, reminding individuals of their fi-

358

nancial limitations and firmly marking the lines of economic class structure. Although selective looting in Germany had made my own circumstances momentarily comfortable, I sensed the gulf separating the average middle class from the relatively few who are not compelled constantly to adjust plans and actions to economic capacity. I had seen John frequently after my return, and associating and interacting with the Andersen and Cohn families had been educational, making me realize the advantages of private entrepreneurship as compared with working for someone else. I had made a mental note to become my own boss and gain financial independence as soon as possible.

Our initial meeting had led to an affair that probably accelerated the breakdown of her marriage, and in this café with impeccable decorum I was now being confronted with the consequences. Aase's lips trembled uncontrollably every time she uttered the word "divorce," and I began to realize why she was so profoundly upset. Her background and upbringing entailed a close-knit family that stayed together at any cost, and she was blaming herself rather than her alcoholic and abusive husband for the impasse. My own childhood had been different. The prospect of divorce held no dread. People make mistakes, and in my philosophy it was better to correct them than to live with them. Besides, in her case there were no children involved.

She wore a white summer dress, simple but elegant, no jewelry except a filigree gold necklace with a jade pendant that matched the green in her eyes. She was telling me about her difficulties in finding a job, something her education had not prepared her for, but her sheer, delicate beauty made it hard to concentrate on what she was saying. She was describing an interview for a position as receptionist at an international corporation, and I visualized her presence in the hushed atmosphere of the entrance to a world-class corporate headquarters. Surely, clients would throng the place just to get a glimpse of her. She paused a moment and sipped her coffee. Then her next sentence jolted me to rapt attention.

"Niels, do you think we could have a future together?"

For a few moments, I was speechless. This incredibly lovely woman, cultured in the extreme, with exquisite taste, intelligent ... sophisticated ... affectionate ... I could not think of sufficient superlatives even to begin to describe her desirability. And she was actually inviting me to marry her! Would I like to marry her? Would I indeed!

Then the reality of my own situation crowded into my reluctant consciousness, covering the vision of a deliriously happy future like a wet blanket. Who was I? A poor engineering student with a year of studies still to go. My former classmates had long since graduated, while I had spent my time dodging the Gestapo, playing slave laborer in various concentration camps, or chasing Nazis. I had no lack of confidence in my eventual success, but it would be years in the future. Moreover, it would take my full and undivided attention and concentration. The world was not about to knock on my door. I'd have to batter my way up. I just felt it in my bones! Perhaps most important, I had never really contemplated marriage, and the attendant responsibility loomed immense. The thought actually made me panicky. Any way I looked at it, I wasn't remotely ready for that step.

"Aase, I'm a penniless nobody, not even at the start of my career. It will be years before I can amount to anything. And you are already accustomed to a certain level of luxury."

She smiled. "Penniless perhaps, but you aren't a nobody. And as for luxury, I don't need it."

She was aware of my lowly status and was willing to share it. Was it a possibility after all? Then I pictured the two of us in a cheap flat, she trying to make ends meet, I trying to concentrate on studying. And suppose I flunked out of Teknikum's uncompromising study curriculum because marriage diverted my attention? I would be washed out, a pitiful failure relegated to marginal jobs, never accepted in the company of competent people.

"Aase, you know the old Danish saying that one cannot live on love and spring water alone. Good folk wisdom. Poverty is not romantic."

The streetcar lurched through a curve on Østerbrogade. At the rear entrance I was hanging on to a handhold while trying to scan an afternoon newspaper on my way to see Thies. As I was jostled by the late afternoon rush of people going home from work, a headline had aroused my curiosity: POWERFUL NEW AMERICAN BOMB. The paper reported that the Americans had dropped a new type of bomb on Hiroshima in Japan, erasing the city's center with one single explosion. The new weapon was called an atom bomb.

I scanned the article but my mind tended to turn to the present and personal. My meeting with Aase a week ago had ended on a strained note. I had not seen her since, and I missed her. I knew she was depressed, and it bothered me that I could do nothing about it. I corrected myself: nothing that I was willing to do. But our discussion had taught me something about myself. While in prison awaiting execution I had resolved never to let mundane things bother me again, if I got out alive, and I now discovered that I could look at matters of this kind in that perspective. Things might go wrong, might be unfortunate or annoying, but with the Gestapo experience fresh in mind I could not get really upset or unhappy by anything. After all, I was alive and free, and the world was a wonderful place. I tried unsuccessfully to make Aase see that problems of our own making were not worth getting really unhappy about, but she was unable, or unwilling, to adopt my perspective. She was depressed, actually devastated, by her personal situation despite my efforts.

I had spent some days in Ribe but got along poorly with the resistance group now in charge of the town, all of them newcomers since we were on the scene. At one point, it came to an outright confrontation, when I stripped the tires off an abandoned German military car and put them on my BMW, something the newcomers felt was infringement on their prerogatives. They actually tried to

360

charge me with theft. Fed up, I had left town and gone back to Copenhagen to see how Thies was getting along in married bliss.

When I sat down with Thies, we discussed the atom bomb news briefly without thinking much about it one way or another. We were simply pleased that the new invention was in American hands. I threw the paper on the table with one last comment.

"This is one time in history when might *is* right."

Thies nodded. "And I'm not surprised the Americans could manage such a scientific feat. You know how all our equipment in Eisleben was absolutely perfect, made for the job. We were mighty impressed with the Krauts' equipment when we first saw it here five years ago, but remember also how much of it was just civilian stuff, Opel trucks given a coat of camouflage paint. By comparison, all our matériel was made for military use. Can you imagine fielding an Opel moving van against a General Motors six-by-six?"

Then he brought out another newspaper and handed it to me.

"Look at that item on page 6. Maybe Randschau will get what he has coming to him! What do you think?"

The notice contained a list of traitors who had been arrested and might be executed, the upshot of a determined pursuit of collaborators, informers, and all manner of henchmen recruited by the German occupation authorities and used to carry out their dirty work. Prior to the war, Denmark had for generations recoiled from capital punishment, looking upon this penalty as downright uncivilized; but popular furor aroused by German excesses was such that a capital punishment statute had been passed, made retroactive to the beginning of the occupation, and was now being enforced.[118] In justifying the legislation the Minister of Justice had observed that the legislative organs had been unable to function during the occupation period, and that the legislative process ultimately must rest on a generally-held sense of justice. Not to punish severely the serious and unprecedented crimes committed with German connivance would be a greater affront to people's sense of justice than making the legislation retroactive.[119]

There was a brief description of the crimes committed by each of the ones on the list. Johannes Konrad Randschau had during interrogation stabbed one victim in the thigh, puncturing an artery so that the prisoner bled to death.

I shook my head in reply to Thies' question.

"I'm not going to shed any tears. The world would be better off without him. But do you realize that a few years ago neither of us would have taken such a cavalier attitude about a human life?"

"True, but the whole country has changed."

And indeed it had.

In the summer of 1945 Denmark was trying to regain its equilibrium and composure as a sovereign nation. Its rôle during the war had been fully as inglorious as that of France, but on the strength of early resistance by a few and be-lated resistance by many more, both countries assumed themselves into the honorable company of the victors. One of the prerogatives of victors is that of writing history – the final and official version – and both countries' contributions to the Allied cause therefore look quite respectable in today's history books.

This particular summer was a time of political turmoil with the miscellaneous groups comprising the resistance movement challenging the reestablishment of political authority by elected officials who had been temporarily disenfranchised. In the aftermath of the upheaval, the old establishment uneasily groped for a return to normalcy, which it interpreted to mean that it should again be in charge. A power struggle had arisen between the politicians of the prewar era and the resistance movement spawned by the occupation, with the former eventually gaining the upper hand, due to its greater adeptness in political maneuvering. Neither Thies nor I took any interest in these squabbles, and with more than a trace of arrogance we declined donning armbands, when they were proffered us. We had both of us been active from the beginning of the occupation, and while we were now grateful that the mass of our countrymen had shown their will to resist during the crucial July days of 1944, we looked on the bulk of the official resistance people as Johnnies-come-lately.

We rarely discussed domestic politics. My preoccupation with that subject during my teenage years had evaporated, replaced by indifference toward the political events now evolving. Thies' attitude mirrored mine, best described as being cool toward the squabbling factions. It was not a matter of underrating the importance of what was taking place, but rather a lack of patience with the political give-and-take on which democracy thrives. The result was that we had both stayed completely out of the ongoing fracas. Instead, we kept our U.S. uniforms handy, for in those first months they were still endowed with magical power.

"What it comes down to," I said, "is that our personal war isn't quite over yet."

"What it comes down to," said Thies, " is that I'm tired of sitting home with my ass puckered up, and so are you, when we could still be useful down there."

By "down there" he meant Germany, of course. It was after midnight, and we had been talking through the evening, swapping news and comparing recent experiences, and in the end we concluded that the exigencies of war had affected us in ways that made us what Thies described as "temporarily restless." Ill at ease with celebration of victory, neither of us had simmered down enough to be content with studying or working eight hours a day. The war was over, but we had as individuals not yet made the transition from war to peace.

"Let's go back to Germany," I suggested, and Thies added, "Yes, and let's catch some more Nazis."

* * *

362

MacArthur reconquered the Philippines in the summer of 1945 and the American war machine turned on Japan itself. So far, the Pacific war had been unique, not just in strategy and tactics, but in the novel use of forces and in the proportions of forces committed. The U.S. Pacific Fleet had swelled explosively by the spring of 1945.[120] In battle it had reduced to impotence the Imperial Japanese Navy whose few remaining units stayed in harbor for lack of fuel. At the same time the Pacific war had been small in terms of manpower committed. Some 450,000 men had been posted to Southeast Asia and the Pacific, less than one-fiftieth of the Allied ground troops engaged to subdue Germany.

This was about to change, for the impending invasion of Japan was going to be a fight to the bloody finish, dwarfing anything yet seen in the Pacific theater, and most of Japan's army was intact, had in fact not yet seen combat but was well trained and equipped. The Japanese would be able to field more than two million men for the defense of the home islands where the emperor resided and where every warrior could be expected to fight with fanatic abandon.

In the last part of July the Allies met in the German city of Potsdam, their last wartime meeting. They agreed on a declaration that called for a Japanese surrender but also gave assurances about Japan's future. While at Potsdam, Truman received word that a test at Alamogordo in New Mexico had confirmed that the atom bomb could work. Possession of the bomb eclipsed any American desire for Soviet involvement in the war against Japan, and Truman and Churchill decided that the weapon should be used forthwith. The Americans hurried to make the bomb operational to try to end the war before the Soviets could become involved.[121]

The Potsdam Declaration was issued on 26 July. On the 30th, the Japanese Prime Minister, Admiral Suzuki, gave a press conference at which his answer appeared ambiguous and temporizing, a not unusual occurrence in Japanese diplomacy. On 6 August, an atom bomb dropped from a B-29 obliterated the central section of Hiroshima. On 9 August, another atom bomb fell on Nagasaki, a civilian port.

The world had entered the atomic age but it would take time before people began to fathom the ramifications of mankind's taking atomic power into its scientific inventory, and into its armory. Even in Japan, the impact of being an atomic target did not immediately register in the higher circles of government. The death toll at Hiroshima was no greater than that suffered from massive B-29 attacks in March, and the government was preoccupied with the question of ending the war without jeopardizing the Emperor's position. A decision was finally reached at an Imperial Council meeting, when Emperor Hirohito himself ordered acceptance of a surrender.

On the battleship *Missouri,* anchored in Tokyo Bay, MacArthur on 28 August formally accepted the surrender from the Japanese Foreign Minister, the Chief of Staff and the Chief of Naval Operations. The signing ceremony on the battleship's deck was witnessed by representatives of Britain, the Soviet Union, France, China, Australia, New Zealand and Canada. The signing completed, MacArthur in a radio broadcast echoed throughout the world made the announcement to the American people:

> ... Today the guns are silent. A great tragedy has
> ended. A great victory has been won. The skies no longer
> rain death – the seas bear only commerce – men everywhere
> walk upright in the sunlight. The entire world is quietly
> at peace ...

World War Two was over.

Chapter 56   September 1945

Now two punctilious envoys, Thine and Mine,
Embroil the earth about a fancied line;
And, dwelling much on right and much on wrong,
Prove how the right is chiefly with the strong.

Boileau-Despréaux

Noises from the yard woke me early. Sunlight was streaming through the small window, and the blue snout of my .45er peeked out from under my pillow where I had put it the night before. Holstering it, I rolled out of bed and glanced down into the yard below. The noises came from a recalcitrant cow two of the farm women were trying to hitch to a two-wheel wagon, the kind portrayed in van Gogh's paintings and noticeably different from anything ever used in Denmark. Thies was shaving at the pump with his soap and other paraphernalia spread out on the edge of a large water trough.

The small farmstead which had served as our quarters for the night was run by four middle-aged women who had sulkily yielded to my order and made the tiny loft room available when we arrived. Their attitude had suddenly changed when the two of us dined on a couple of C-rations and I gave them one. They had spent an hour marvelling at the contents and had made coffee on the Nescafé, very thin but emitting the fragrance for which they had been yearning since the war began. We had noticed that they used oxen as draft animals, something that to our knowledge had not been seen in Denmark since the nineteenth century. When we quizzed them about it, they told us that it was not due to the momentary deprivation of war but that it was commonly done that way in their region. To our further surprise, the "oxen" were brought in for milking in the evening, and we had marvelled at the incongruity of a society launching predatory aggressive war with Messerschmitts and Tiger tanks while plowing the home fields with cows.

Breaking the routine of hunting Nazis, the Counter Intelligence team spent weekends on sports and sightseeing. This photograph was taken on a trip through Austria. The car, a convertible Wanderer, was one of several "liberated" vehicles formerly owned by Nazi officials.

It was four days since we had discussed our situation in Thies' home and decided to go back to Germany. The next day I had sold my BMW to my friend John Andersen for ten thousand kroner and put the money in the bank. Thies and I donned our U.S. uniforms and John drove us to the border in his new acquisition, gushing praise at its speed and acceleration; after parting, we set our course south, hitchhiking on military vehicles. Rides were easy to get, and at night we stayed and ate at military quarters for transient personnel. Our route became rather circuitous and took us through unfamiliar towns and countryside. In the golden sun of late summer we rumbled south into the German heartland in the back of a British weapons carrier, again observing the devastation everywhere and wondering how the country would ever rebuild itself. I recalled some telling figures from our work with Military Government: 754 sunken barges blocking Rhine traffic; 885 destroyed railroad bridges paralyzing rail transport. And that was just in the American sector. As yet we had no figures on civilian housing destroyed, but the count clearly ran into the millions of units. Neither of us could visualize any meaningful recovery in our lifetimes. The Nazis' vision of being a superrace ruling Europe from the Atlantic to the Urals and bringing German culture and Hitler's New Order to the lands in between

366

had failed to become reality. Their army, citizenry and social sinews had strained mightily to carry out the conquests, but in the end the entelechy of Nazism had proven unequal to the task. Germany in defeat was a humbled empire, her bridges awash in the river beds, her autobahns chewed to pieces by heavy tank treads, her people scrabbling to survive.

As a first step in preventing German resurgence, the Allies had parceled the former Reich into four zones, American, British, French and Russian. Since Eisleben was now in the Russian zone, we decided to aim for the heart of the American zone, staying well away from the Russians. Their innate secretiveness and paranoia made it cumbersome even for Allied military personnel to travel into their domain, whereas the boundaries between the other three Allied zones existed only on paper, and we could move freely across them. Already, Stalin was sealing up his western border, creating what Churchill two years later so aptly dubbed the Iron Curtain.[122]

We went first to Heidelberg. It was in the American zone and had suffered little damage aside from having the bridges across the Neckar River destroyed by the retreating Wehrmacht. Not finding any military outfit to our liking, we left the town and went north toward Frankfurt am Main. Rather than taking the autobahn, we chose the Bergstrasse, a parallel road a bit farther east that is known for its equable microclimate and boasts numerous palm trees. Dating back to Roman days when it was known as *strata montana*, the Bergstrasse runs alongside the rift valley on the Upper Rhine on the western slope of the Odenwald region and passes through some picturesque villages. One of these is Bensheim where we had arrived the previous night and had parted with the truck we were riding, when it had to turn east, off the Bergstrasse. We had randomly chosen the small farm where the four women were performing all of the chores in the absence of their menfolk.

We left after breakfast, to the apparent regret of the women, to whom we had meant diversion besides being a heaven-sent source of Nescafé. A passing six-by-six offered a lift, and we rumbled north through countryside that in peacetime would have had great tourist appeal. Our driver who turned out to be from Georgia never tired of singing the praises of his home state; an hour later we reached his destination, a U.S. Army motor pool close to the *Hauptbahnhof*, the main railroad station in Frankfurt am Main.

The station was thronged with people, mostly German soldiers and many of them wounded, who with haggard faces were looking for transportation in the general direction of their home, hoping they still had one. Others were desperately searching for their families or trying to ascertain if they still had any. Ragged children, some in cut-down Wehrmacht uniforms, followed a parent or other adult, or just wandered aimlessly in search of food. At long and random intervals, a train would leave, crammed with humanity.

We found Frankfurt heavily damaged, but the I. G. Farben Company had been spared, so that its office complex now could serve as military occupation headquarters for the American zone. The building was modern and still ele-

The remnants of the bridge carrying the autobahn superhighway across the Werra River. This bridge like hundreds of others was destroyed by the retreating Germans to stem the advance of the Allied armies.

gant. It was served by a novel system of one-person elevators, small platforms that moved continuously while passengers singly stepped on or off, holding on to a steel bar during the lift. Thies joked about what might happen at the top when the little platform changed direction from up to down. Did it collapse and squish a tardy rider? Neither of us tried to find out.

While Thies went in search of coffee and doughnuts I made some inquiries and was advised that a Counter Intelligence Corps team with offices in Hofheim needed people with our particular talents. Over coffee and doughnuts at a U.S.O. counter we located the place on a map, a village situated in the Taunus, west of Frankfurt.

"It looks small, which is good," Thies opined, "for we sure don't want to stay in this city. What does Counter Intelligence mean, anyway?"

"I don't know and didn't want to ask. Just nodded sagely when it was mentioned. Shall we take a chance and go find that outfit?"

"Sure, why not?"

Thies helped himself to another doughnut from the tray on the counter, and we set out to find the village of Hofheim.

"I'll tell you, Niels, of all the rotten things Hitler did, there was one thing he did that was all right. He suppressed the Jews and got them out of all positions of influence."

Ben's voice was getting thick and slightly unsteady, effects of the after-dinner champagne.

"He did a lot more than that. He killed even more of them than other concentration camp inmates. There was a whole murder program. Haven't you read the reports?" Pieces of information, carefully kept secret by the Nazis, had begun to trickle into our office.

"Well, he may have been too rough, but I still say he was on the right track."

"What in the world makes you say that?"

"Well, you probably don't have many in Denmark, but I'll tell you, we have plenty of Yids in the States, and they always worm themselves into top positions, even in banking. My father is vice president of the State Street Trust in Boston, and he sees plenty of them. Damn unattractive people."

It was New Year's Eve, and my outfit, Counter Intelligence Corps Detachment 970/11 Team B, was celebrating the coming of 1946 with a party to which each of us had invited a current girlfriend. Team B operated in the Höchst area and had selected billets with great care. The large villa in the wooded setting of the Taunus foothills had belonged to a high-ranking party official, and its second floor easily accommodated in separate bedrooms the twelve members of our team. On the main floor was an ample dining room, where we had just finished dinner, and a spacious lounge/music room with a grand piano where we were now sipping our drinks, while Special Agent Bill Collins played some Chopin waltzes. The lounge had French doors opening onto a tiled terrace overlooking the garden. The villa's basement held a wine cellar, and the house was surrounded by a park-like garden with two glass-enclosed greenhouses.

Three German women kept the large kitchen spotless. At the outset, they had struggled without much success to produce palatable meals from our military rations but after a few weeks had abandoned their attempts and quietly traded some of the rations for fresh produce, eggs, milk, etc. As our supply man thoughtfully drew our full rations from each of two divisional centers, there was plenty to trade, with enough left over to pay the women with food besides money, making their families the best fed in the nearby village. To keep our wine cellar stocked, we periodically dispatched a six-by-six to the French zone which straddled some of Germany's best wine producing regions, and it returned loaded with Sekt, Rüdesheimer and Niersteiner. Not a bad setup. In fact, we were living like a conquering army in the Roman mold, for the occupation forces were still the combat troops of a few months ago who treated the Germans in the rough manner due a vanquished enemy.

All around us the Taunus countryside and low, forested mountains teemed with game, as the region had effectively been a refuge bereft of hunters for five years. In the evening, we often went hunting by jeep after dark, driving cross-country through the fields. When a hare appeared in the headlight beams, it was an easy target for a carbine, and the jeep was so quickly loaded with long-eared twelve-pounders that we sometimes used our .45 side arms, combining hunting and target practice. As the distance from jeep to hare usually was about

fifty feet, even our .45's sufficed to fill the vehicle. One night we ran out of ammunition as a wounded hare was trying to escape. My companion grabbed a
wrench for want of a better weapon and pursued his prey across the field while
I followed, keeping them both in the headlights. He succeeded in the end and
returned, puffing from the exertion of the chase. As he flung his quarry onto
the pile, he muttered that there would be no point in relating this story back
home. Who'd ever believe it?

We used the game as payment for civilian services. Each of us had tailor bills
for ski clothes or riding pants, shoemaker bills for handmade boots and other
footwear, mechanic bills for maintenance of our civilian cars, and so on. With
money of no real value, as there was little or nothing to buy on the civilian market, we paid with cigarettes or game, both of which were readily available to us
and prized by the Germans. On the Frankfurt black market, cigarettes rather
than currency had become the basic medium of exchange.

The CIC team was commanded by 2nd Lieutenant Darrell D. Drolsum, addressed by everyone as D.D. It comprised a disparate group of individuals of
whom I worked closest with special agent Benjamin R. Vaughan, a Bostonian
and Brown University graduate who had just started law school when he was
drafted. We pooled our talents productively. I brought in the Nazis and Ben
wrote up the paperwork. When the captive's military records showed service in
the East, I helped Ben with interrogation, as I was interested to find out about
German activities there. Thies had been similarly paired off with another agent,
when we first arrived but had found his English insufficient for the CIC requirements. Besides, the language difficulties added to his pangs of conscience at
having left Cordia during her pregnancy, and after two weeks he had decided to
go back home. We liberated a car for him and loaded it with enough gasoline
for the return trip.

I had my own conscience pangs to contend with whenever I thought of Aase,
which was frequently. My immediate decision not to consider marriage did not
hold up well under reexamination. With patience I was able to build a good
case for ending bachelorhood and embarking on marriage, and I felt my earlier firm resolve to be weakening.

Throughout the fall, I had been doing essentially the same work as previously in Eisleben, but life with the intelligence team had certain advantages. In
contrast to the rest of the military establishment, Counter Intelligence operated with vast discretionary power. This enabled us on weekends to write out travel orders for each other, throw a ten-in-one ration in the trunk, and take off to
skate in Bavaria, or trade food for jewelry at Idar-Oberstein's semiprecious gem
center, or sightsee in Strassbourg. One weekend D.D. and I had visited Nuremberg where a military tribunal was trying such of the top Nazis as the Allies had
managed to catch alive. We watched briefly the sorry lot of fallen supermen,
found the proceedings dull and headed for the ski slopes instead.

On other weekends we just stayed home to hunt or ride in the Taunus. Of
our various leisure activities, Ben and I preferred horseback riding and spent

A typical party during the first occupation year. This one was largely Air Force pilots who enjoyed somewhat of an elite position among the troops. As always, there was an abundance of Fräuleins eager to take part. The author is on the far right.

many hours in the saddle. We had found a riding stable at the Kronberg Castle north of Frankfurt, also frequented by Eisenhower whom we saw quite often. The general was always immaculately attired and a fair horseman, in the casual Western style. He preferred the forest trails, rarely with more than one or two companions and sometimes alone.

Weekends at home usually entailed evening dances to the tunes of our well-worn phonograph records.[123] There was no shortage of female companionship for weekend trips or other activities, for Germany was positively packed with sex-starved women. The war had seriously reduced the number of men in our age group, and most of the survivors were still in POW camps. I wanted to perfect my German and was making strides in doing so with the aid of two sisters, Giselinde and Irmtrud Thöne, daughters of a Bad Soden dentist. The girls were well-educated, spoke High German elegantly and *Frankfurterisch* engagingly, and they patiently groomed my language on weekday evenings and on weekend trips. Giggi, at sixteen the youngest, was artistically gifted and produced a colorful stream of doodles that could have elicited the envy of the best cartoonist. I particularly treasured an illustrated map of Denmark she gave me for my 26th birthday.

On this New Year's Eve, Irmtrud was my party companion. A willowy brunette of nineteen, she had for this occasion dressed with meticulous care in a pale green frock embroidered with tiny flowers, no doubt Giggi's handiwork. I knew the girls made their own clothes, materials probably scavenged from somewhere or purchased on the black market. Irmtrud's soft brown eyes tended to sparkle when she got animated, as she was right now, talking to D.D. a few feet away. She reminded me of a younger version of Aase.

Bill came to the end of his Chopin repertoire and reached for his drink on top of the piano, when a persistent knocking on the French glass doors caught our attention. D.D. opened and found our gardener, Hofer, standing on the terrace hat in hand, puffing heavily and pouring forth a stream of information in the local dialect. Walking home to his village, Hofer had found an injured American soldier lying by the wayside. They had been unable to communicate, but the man obviously was in need of help, so Hofer had run all the way back to alert us. Enjoying his momentary importance, he once again assured us that the soldier – possibly an officer, he couldn't tell in the dark – was in need of immediate help. D.D. turned to me.

"Niels, you and I had better look into this, and Ben, you come along too. I think we are the most sober ones here right now. Let's get our coats."

Ben and I nodded and ran upstairs to get dressed for a frosty trip in an open jeep. A few moments later, we were on our way with Hofer in the back as guide. Shortly, our headlights revealed the object of our trip. It turned out to be an American airman, a fighter pilot, who mistakenly had jumped from a transport plane when the bailout warning signal malfunctioned. With the honed reflexes of a combat pilot, he had departed the transport instantly, though unnecessarily, and fractured an ankle landing on the frozen field a few yards from the road. He had been on his way to the States to be discharged, and I have never heard more virulent or sincere blasphemies in the English tongue than those he produced at having his trip home thus cancelled. My modest store of American profanities increased by leaps and bounds.

We loaded him into the jeep, gave Hofer the parachute as a present, and set off for an Army hospital in Königstein. At the hospital a young doctor took over our ward, who interrupted his stream of blasphemies only briefly to thank us, and we returned to our party, feeling like Good Samaritans.

Back at the villa, we settled down to midnight snacks and more champagne. Ben leaned toward me.

"Niels, did you notice that doctor at the hospital?"

"Sure. We were lucky to find someone on duty."

"Well, yes, but let me tell you this: he was Jewish."

"So?"

"So, you see how we find them everywhere. Damn unattractive people!"

I thought about the helpful young intern and never felt more keenly my need to improve and expand my ability to communicate in English. One thing is to translate and use simple everyday statements. Something else is to explore questions in the realms of ethics or philosophy, such as those raised by Ben Vaughan. That was as yet utterly beyond me.

The morning sky was clouded as I drove through the village of Hofheim, heading east, and half an hour later I was on the autobahn, driving north. It was just after the vernal equinox, and I was leaving CIC, leaving Germany, going home. And this time I was determined to finish my education and start a career. The world was waiting, impatiently, I felt sure. The tires of my big Wanderer were humming a quiet tune against the concrete, punctuated by the staccato rattle of endless potholes, while I thought of my six months with Counter Intelligence.

I had departed Team B with regrets and also with gratitude, for the experience had been instructive in many ways. There had been some turnover in the Team, as members were rotated back to the States for discharge. D.D. had left shortly after New Years, his job taken over by Captain Forbes E. Jordan, a redheaded attorney of Irish ancestry who managed operations efficiently and reined in some of D.D.'s freewheeling practices.

Ben Vaughan was due to leave any day. Despite our being poles apart on the Jewish question, we had formed a firm friendship in the course of our CIC work. Ben had given me some preliminary insights into the grandeur and contradictions of the United States, a world so obviously and profoundly different from that of Europe. Our equestrian pursuits had continued through the winter and intensified after we had switched stables in January, when I had discovered a better place on one of my Nazi-tracking trips.

It happened on a crisply sunny winter day when I was routinely checking various leads to party members, among them a certain von Richter, whose address was Rettershof near the tiny village of Fischbach in the Taunus. As my jeep bounced down a narrow forest road, I saw for the first time Rettershof, a lovely little castle nestled in the Taunus forest. Von Richter turned out to be an old baron, owner of the castle, and at 70 beyond the age group of party membership with which we were concerned. As my inquiries later revealed, he was one of the few who had joined under pressure in order to be able to keep his estate. The castle had been closed since the war broke out, and the von Richters had taken up residence in the adjacent *Hofgut* farm. An aristocrat of the bluest blood, he looked at seventy as if he had just stepped out of the Kaiser's court. He was a horseman *par excellence*, and before the war Rettershof had contained a riding school where he taught horsemanship to upper-class young ladies from all over Europe. His wife, a beautiful woman in her midfifties, combined the looks and virtues with which only storybook aristocracy is expected to be endowed. They had lost one son in Russia, but their other son, Hubertus, had returned alive. The Rettershof stables still held seven fine horses, and a large tat-

Hofgut Rettershof im Taunus was an elegant Damenreitschule, a riding academy for young ladies of European upper society and aristocracy, in the 1930s when this picture was taken.

tersall was situated on the grounds. Taking advantage of our CIC privilege our team had without wasting time put **OFF LIMITS** signs around the entire estate, and throughout the winter we used the indoor riding facilities to full advantage without having to share them with other military personnel.

The baron was also a lifelong hunter and a raconteur of note who could endlessly relate stories of hunting feats past. His estate bordered on the Taunus hunting preserve of the Opel automobile clan, and we also posted this hunting

Baron and Baroness von Richter on horseback in the Taunus near the Rettershof castle, spring 1946. The Baroness is riding sidesaddle which was still preferred by some ladies at the time.

ground OFF LIMITS to keep overeager GIs with Thompson submachine guns from shooting up the area. Under the baron's guidance we had a series of hunting excursions and bagged deer and elk. Our M-1 with diopter sight proved to be an excellent hunting rifle for large game, and I was lucky enough also to shoot a wild boar, the only one our team got, for they are shy and fast and difficult even to catch a glimpse of. The Germans were delighted with the large windfall of meat, and at a dinner in the Baron's quarters we tasted both venison and wild boar steak. In the course of the winter I came to count the baron, his wife, son and daughter as friends. Shortly before my departure, von Richter had insisted on arranging a jumping competition to measure our progress under his tutelage. Prior to the event, he spent hours in the tattersall with Ben and me to improve our horsemanship and gave us numerous pointers to perfect our style. When one of us came cantering to the end of the rink and turned to face the hurdle, he would habitually shout, "Vorwärts, aber FESTE!" as the rider urged his mount straight for the jump. The competition came to include six riders, four from Team B and two German teenagers. I was lucky to become the winner, and the baron offered me a choice of prizes: a painting of the Taunus landscape or a small bronze copy of a classic horse sculpture. To my later regret, I chose the latter.

A detour – the sixth so far – took me off the autobahn's concrete and onto a succession of back roads. Repairing the war damage, much of it self-inflicted, had not gotten under way. The civilian economy appeared still to be in shock.

375

This was an extremely long detour, taking me north and east as far as I could determine, one stretch running for miles along the Werra River and passing under the broken concrete ribbon of the autobahn, dangling high above. The massive columns that used to carry it across the river had defied destruction by Wehrmacht engineers and still stood on the opposite shore, pointing aimlessly skyward, deprived of purpose. By noon I had passed Kassel, and a cold rain had started to fall as I pressed on into the British occupation zone. This was no place to stop for meals or fuel. British Army cooking could spoil even the high-quality American food supplies, and their motor pool procedures were slow and cumbersome. No matter. I had loaded the trunk and back seat with eleven jerricans of gasoline and plenty of rations to see me through to Denmark. The car I was driving, a 1939 Wanderer sedan, was my latest acquisition. Most of the winter I had used a 1937 Wanderer, a convertible with red leather upholstery, but had traded it for the later model sedan in the expectation of getting a better price for it at home. That should pay for my remaining studies.

Toward the end of the winter I had run into Hanne in Frankfurt. From bits of information floating my way I knew that her liaison with the Frenchman had been short-lived but had been followed by numerous others, as she used her natural attributes effectively. We had dinner in Hofheim and a long chat. She was looking chic in an American uniform, was driving a liberated Adler, and functioned officially as interpreter for some headquarters. She stayed the night in my CIC billet, and we parted with no hard feelings.

In my CIC work I had brought in a total of 178 Nazis, driving just under twenty-six thousand miles in pursuit of them. What had compelled me to call a halt was my desire to enroll for my senior year in engineering school, and the semester was scheduled to begin early in April. Having been out of touch since parting with Thies the previous fall – civilian communications were still dysfunctional – I was also eager to catch up on news from home.

It was close to midnight, and my odometer tallied almost eight hundred kilometers when I drove through Hamburg and continued north. Those detours sure added to the mileage. Since Thies and I had made that first dash home almost one year earlier, the countryside had not changed its appearance of devastation, but the brigands and diehards of Wehrmacht fragments had long since disappeared. There was no traffic aside from a few British convoys of lorries, great beasts on four huge wheels, with one large center headlight without dimmer. Instead, the driver switched it off when converging on another vehicle, turning it back on for split-second peeks at the road ahead and usually blinding any oncoming driver in the process. I had learned to squint, fixing on the right side of the road which alternated between pitch darkness and garish illumination. It was like bearing down on a flash photographer who kept snapping pictures. Miraculously, no collisions.

I stopped on a deserted road near Itzehoe, curled up in an army blanket on the front seat, and went to sleep instantly. Three hours later, the pain of distort-

The author's sister, Angla Kuhlman, escaped to Sweden and as a nurse joined the "Lotte" corps, auxiliaries attached to the Danish Brigade.

ing my body woke me. I ate a cold ration and washed it down with a can of beer instead of the coffee I yearned for. The rain had stopped, and I drove on into a gray dawn.

In the early afternoon I reached my mother's apartment, and in a happy torrent of words we exchanged summaries of our respective news of the last half-year's events. Svend Jacob Kjær had died from aftereffects of the concentration camp. Our family was well, and my sister Angla had given birth to a daughter. Cordia and Thies were fine, still expecting their first child.

My mother went to the kitchen to make coffee. Good idea, for I had difficulty staying awake. I could hear her voice as she kept chatting and telling minor news she happened to remember, but it was difficult to concentrate on what she said. Suddenly, I felt an overwhelming urge to see Aase. Had she moved to Copenhagen? If so, her name would not be in the phone book yet, so I'd have to call John and ask him. I dialed his number, and at the second ring John's voice answered.

I skipped preliminaries: "This is Niels. I just came home and would like to get together with you so we can catch up on news. But first I want to ask you if Aase has moved to Copenhagen, and if so, what's her phone number?"

There was a pause. Maybe John was trying to remember, or maybe he was looking up her number. Then he spoke again, and my blood froze.

"Aase committed suicide a week after you left with Thies."

* * *

That four great nations, flushed with victory and stung with injury, stay the hand of vengeance and voluntarily submit their captive enemies to the judgment of the law is one of the most significant tributes that Power has ever paid to Reason.

Justice Robert H. Jackson,
opening the Nuremberg Trial

When D.D. and I were observing history in the making at the Nuremberg Trial, our short attention span was typical of soldiers on active duty, but it was not widely shared by people in general. Both in Europe and elsewhere in the world there was strong public interest in the proceedings.

Well before the war in Europe ended, the Allies had discussed what to do with the Nazis after surrender. Churchill suggested summary execution of major war criminals; Stalin, only half in jest, proposed that 50,000 German general staff officers be shot (a number far exceeding what had ever been on the general staff). Joseph Pulitzer, an American publisher, urged the shooting of 1,500,000 Nazis. However, when time came for a reckoning, the victors wisely eschewed summary punishment. Under American prodding they set up an international tribunal to indict and to mete out punishment to those deemed responsible for starting the war and for perpetrating atrocities. Such retribution was also intended as a warning to future national leaders. The London Agreement, signed on 8 August 1945, established the tribunal, outlined its jurisdiction, and stipulated four counts of crimes for which German leaders could be tried.[124]

The tribunal was composed of members from America, Britain, France and the Soviet Union. Of these, the British certainly had every right to membership, having fought the Germans from beginning to end. The Americans were in a morally strong position as well, as they had entered war against Japan after having been attacked at Pearl Harbor and had joined the war against Germany after the latter had opened hostilities. It is difficult to justify inclusion of the French who after their initial defeat had collaborated with and fought on the side of the Germans against the Allies on numerous occasions. The Soviet representatives were ill at ease, and understandably so. Their country had made the German campaign in Poland possible by the German-Soviet nonaggression pact and under its secret codicil had committed aggression and usurpation of Polish territory.

Half a century later it sounds unbelievable that the Tribunal could have been ignorant about the Holocaust, the systematic mass murder of Europe's Jews, but it had in fact almost no information about it. The judges listened in stunned silence, as the prosecution presented a mountain of evidence to document the numerous ways in which mass murder had been carried out. One witness, a construction manager by the name of Friedrich Gräbe who had worked for the German Army in occupied Ukraine, submitted an affidavit that read in part:

> Thereupon I drove to the site ... and saw near it great
> mounds of earth, about 30 meters long and 2 meters high.
> Several trucks stood in front of the mounds. Armed
> Ukrainian militia drove the people off the trucks under the
> supervision of an SS-man. The militia acted as guards on
> the trucks and drove them to and from the pit. All these
> people had the regulation yellow patches on the front and
> back of their clothes, and thus could be recognized as Jews
> ... Now I heard rifle shots in quick succession, from
> behind one of the earth mounds. The people who had got off
> the trucks – men, women, and children of all ages – had to
> undress upon the order of an SS-man, who carried a riding
> or dog whip. They had to put down their clothes in fixed
> places, sorted according to shoes, top clothing and
> underclothing. I saw a heap of shoes of about 800 to 1000
> pairs, great piles of underlinen and clothing. Without
> screaming or weeping these people undressed, stood around
> in family groups, kissed each other, said farewells and
> waited for a sign from another SS-man, who stood near the
> pit, also with a whip in his hand. During the 15 minutes I
> stood near the pit I heard no complaint or plea for mercy .
> ... I walked around the mound and found myself confronted
> by a tremendous grave. People were closely wedged together
> and lying on top of each other so that only their heads
> were visible. Nearly all had blood running over their
> shoulders from their heads. Some of the people shot were
> still moving. Some were lifting their arms and turning
> their heads to show that they were still alive. The pit
> was already 2/3 full. I estimated that it contained about
> 1000 people. I looked for the man who did the shooting.
> He was an SS-man, who sat at the edge of the narrow end of
> the pit, his feet dangling into the pit. He had a tommy
> gun on his knees and was smoking a cigarette. The people,
> completely naked, went down some steps which were cut in
> the clay wall of the pit[125] and clambered over the heads of
> the people lying there, to the place where the SS-man
> directed them. They lay down in front of the dead or
> injured people; some caressed those who were still alive
> and spoke to them in a low voice. Then I heard a series of
> shots. I looked into the pit and saw that the bodies were

twitching or the heads lying already motionless on top of the bodies that lay before them. Blood was running from their necks. I was surprised that I was not ordered away, but I saw that there were two or three postmen in uniform nearby ...[126]

The secrecy that had enabled the Germans to keep the world from knowing about the Holocaust equally shrouded the scope and nature of the concentration camps until American and British troops overran the first of these establishments in April of 1945 and Life Magazine brought pictorial documentation to an incredulous public.

The judges had to contend with problems that would have sorely tried a Solomon. The definition of aggressive war as resort to violence to alter the international status quo ran counter to Soviet ideology which aimed to liberate proletarians worldwide by revolutionary means. The Russians nevertheless went along, but Soviet actions in Poland, Finland and Bulgaria clearly fell into the aggressive war category. And only days before Japan's surrender, when Japanese diplomats were begging the Soviet Union to arrange termination of their war with America, Stalin had instead ordered an attack on Japan, had seized possession of the islands in the Kurile group and for good measure seized four more strategically desirable islands, renaming them the "Lesser Kuriles."

The first Nuremberg trial ended in October of 1946. Twenty-two top leaders were indicted of whom only twenty-one were physically present; Martin Bormann could not be found. Twelve were condemned to death: Bormann (in absentia), Frank, Frick, Göring, Jodl, Kaltenbrunner, Keitel, Ribbentrop, Rosenberg, Saukel, and Seyss-Inquart. Seven received prison sentences: Dönitz, Funk, Hess, Neurath, Räder, Schirach, and Speer. Three were acquitted: Fritzsche, Papen, and Schacht.

Although never previously outlawed, the taking and execution of hostages figured prominently in the final indictment. (It was declared legal in one of the later trials.) The Germans were charged with murdering in the Katyn Forest in Poland 925 Polish officers, a figure that was raised to 11,000 on Russian insistence. A widespread belief that the massacre actually had been perpetrated by the Soviets caused a storm of objections in the United States, and the charge was quietly dropped.[127] The unprecedented ferocity of the conflict at Hitler's insistence on indiscriminate and savage extermination impelled the judges to pose questions to establish guidelines for the future. A brilliant young New York attorney, Telford Taylor, served as assistant prosecutor in the first Nuremberg trial and as chief prosecutor in the subsequent trials. In setting the stage for the prosecution, he discussed the position of career officers when military practices and politics are at odds:

The military defendants will perhaps argue that they are pure technicians. This amounts to saying that military men are ... above and beyond the legal and moral requirements that apply to others, incapable of exercising moral judgment on their own behalf ... Such is not the view of the United States. The prosecution here representing the United States believe that the profession of arms is a distinguished profession. We believe that the practice of that profession by its leaders calls for the highest degree of integrity and moral wisdom no less than for technical skill. We believe that, in consulting and planning with the leaders in other fields of national activity, the military leaders must act in accordance with international law and the dictates of the public conscience.[128]

The Nuremberg proceedings generated numerous comments from American officers, many of whom profoundly respected the German officer corps and were ignorant about the excesses of which it was manifestly guilty. After the end of the war in the Pacific, no such latent sympathy was shown toward the Japanese adversary. MacArthur convened a court of five regular U.S. Army generals to try General Tomoyuki Yamashita whose troops had massacred many Filipino civilians. Yamashita was judged guilty and executed despite lack of evidence that he had ordered or even known about the massacres.[129]

Whatever shortcomings the trial exhibited, it was conducted with decorum and achieved justice of sorts. On the background of the enormity of Nazi crimes, few people will find the punishment severe. Still, having victors sit in judgment of the vanquished was not a model to be emulated. The peoples who had suffered German occupation, Belgians, Czechs, Danes, Dutch, French, Greek, Norwegians, Poles, Soviets and Yugoslavs, dealt with their own traitors and criminals, and did so more harshly than the Nuremberg Tribunal. Even Germany's former allies, Bulgaria, Finland, Hungary, Italy and Romania, were permitted to conduct their own trials, and they generally did so with efficiency and fairness. In Hungary a number of "people's courts" operating under supervision of a multiparty parliament sentenced to death 476 defendants of whom 189 were executed, including four who had served as prime ministers.

Germany had a clear statute against murder, and German military regulations also ruled out murder. Surprisingly, these were never modified or overruled by any Nazi decree, and they were never qualified as to race, religion or nationality. Had Germany been allowed to conduct its own trials, perhaps under a person such as Konrad Adenauer, a respected lawyer with strong anti-Nazi credentials, far more criminals would undoubtedly have been brought to task, including many in the various murder programs. But at the time, international mood was too inflamed by the Nazi excesses to trust Germany to purge itself.

The General Assembly of the United Nations lent its weight to the principles established by the Tribunal's charter and judgment by unanimously affirming both.[130]

Chapter 57 May 1946-May 1947

Pin on your wings, give me your hand
Let's rise to sunny sky.
Abandon things of fettered land
Slip earthly bonds – and fly.

The minister's voice echoed from the stone arches of the Frederiksborg Castle church as he intoned the old christening ritual. The baby cradled in my right arm squirmed slightly but had otherwise behaved admirably until the point where he spoke the key words, "and your name shall be Inge-Lotte Kuhlman."[131] Here the minister dipped his fingers in the font and sprinkled a few drops of water on the unsuspecting infant. The affront of this symbolic but shocking baptism brought forth an outraged yell that competed favorably for the attention of the small gathering and caused the man of God to hasten to the end of the short ceremony. This met with approval from the audience, for among irreverent Danes – the overwhelming majority – attendance at church ceremony is not a favorite pastime, evidenced by the saying that you must visit the church four times in your life: at your christening, confirmation, wedding and burial, but out of these you need to walk there yourself only twice.

After returning to Denmark I had found myself continuing a process of read-justing to peacetime life. I had moved back in with my mother, enrolled at the Teknikum and buckled down to study. I had sold the Wanderer for fifteen thousand kroner, and reverted to a trusty bicycle. A car was unnecessary and in any event would have been sheer profligacy for a student to possess. Together with revenue from selling all the other liberated goods, it allowed me to pay off a small student loan I had taken out three years earlier, with a nice bank balance left over. I could face the rest of my technical studies without monetary concerns. That Wanderer, by the way, was the finest car I have owned, before or since; the manufacturer was one of four comprising the *Autounion*, a German automobile cartel of prewar fame.[132]

Readjusting to peaceful living, I maintained close contact with Thies, for our experiences had been almost identical and our needs and attitudes so similar that either of us could bring up a matter and expect instant understanding by the other. Besides talking with Thies I was tying up a number of loose ends in my life, most of them left over from the resistance period, others created more recently. Among the former, getting my engineering degree was by far the most pressing. Among the latter was the baptizing of my niece which had been put off till my return from Germany. The baby was born on 1 December 1945, and the parents wanted me to be her godfather. The christening had therefore been planned for the spring after my return, and it was now being held in Hillerød, home town of Ole's family. In conformity with Danish custom this entailed a brief church ceremony followed by a family get-together.

Having recovered his composure after the interruption, the minister finished the ritual and retired to his study to make out the baptismal certificate which in Denmark serves a function equivalent to that of a U.S. birth certificate. I handed Inge-Lotte back to her mother while we filed out into the afternoon sunshine to embark upon the other segment of the name-giving affair, an elegant dinner at Ole's parental home. In fulfilling my rôle as godfather I was obliged to hold the baby during the key part of the church ceremony and also to give the main speech at the subsequent dinner.

The meal was in the traditional Danish style, starting with a small slice of dark rye bread with *sild* (marinated herring) and onions, chased by several drams of aquavit and strong lager beer. Then came large trays of *smørrebrød,* open-face sandwiches with shrimp in pyramid, beef tartar with raw egg yolk and capers, grilled cod roe, smoked eel with shirred egg, liver paté with pickled beets and *sky* (jellied consommé), *rullepølse* (pressed sausage) with fresh horseradish, *gravlaks* (lightly-smoked salmon) with dill, and many, many other delicacies to gladden the heart and titillate the palate. After this introduction came the warm dish, veal fricassee, with good French wine, followed by dessert and Madeira. Then it was time for strong coffee and cognac or whiskey.

I chose to speak as soon as the *smørrebrød* appeared in order to open the floor for others who might want to say a few words. To gain the guests' attention, I struck a note on my wineglass and was rewarded with expectant silence. All went well, for I had prepared my remarks carefully, giving proper recognition to the various family members, some of whom on Ole's side had come from as far away as Sweden for the occasion. This released other speeches, most of which were made during the early part of the meal when minds were still sober and people were better able to appreciate sparkling wit, but after the formalities had been properly taken care of, everyone loosened up a bit, helped by the good meal and the percipient choice of wines.

Toward the end there was singing at which Swedes and Danes tried to outdo each other for good patriotic reasons, and the party wound up by late evening with everyone agreeing that the family needed more babies born so there

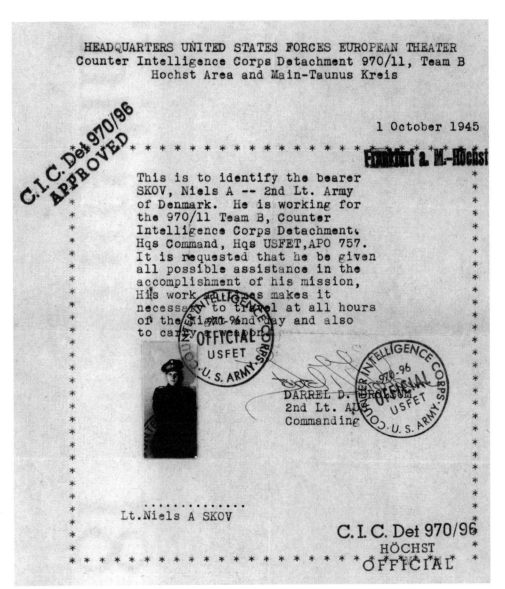

HEADQUARTERS UNITED STATES FORCES EUROPEAN THEATER
Counter Intelligence Corps Detachment 970/11, Team B
Hochst Area and Main-Taunus Kreis

1 October 1945

Frankfurt a. M.-Höchst

This is to identify the bearer
SKOV, Niels A -- 2nd Lt. Army
of Denmark. He is working for
the 970/11 Team B, Counter
Intelligence Corps Detachment,
Hqs Command, Hqs USFET, APO 757.
It is requested that he be given
all possible assistance in the
accomplishment of his mission,
His work requires makes it
necessary to travel at all hours
of the night and day and also
to carry a weapon.

DARREL D. DROLSUM
2nd Lt. AUS
Commanding

Lt.Niels A SKOV

C.I.C. Det 970/96
HÖCHST
OFFICIAL

Improvised IDs such as this one issued by Lt. Drolsum, CIC Team commander, enabled the author to travel throughout the Western occupation zones of Germany. Being stopped or questioned was rare, as the Western Allies ran their occupation administration on a loose rein, but the Russians kept their sector sealed and inaccessible from the outset.

would be occasions to get together more often. Then we parted, giving each other generous and firm assurances that we would do our best to see that this be accomplished as soon as possible.

* * *

This letter acknowledges the author's service with the U.S. Counter Intelligence Corps in Hofheim, Germany, during the early phase of the Allies' deNazification program. The letter served to establish the author's identity and explain his absence abroad to the Danish authorities whose stamp in the lower left corner states that food ration coupons have been issued to him.

We came in at just the right altitude and speed. When we crossed the boundary of Kastrup's grass landing strip I cut the power and flared out, feeling the plane lose flying speed and settle the last few inches to touchdown. A perfect three-point landing. Morian nodded his approval.

"OK, you're on your own. Go solo!"

He shouted to be heard above the engine noise and signaled me to taxi to the office hut where he swung himself to the ground, closed the door behind him and waved me off. My big moment was at hand.

I taxied to the downwind end of the field, slowly, to have time to review in my mind the proper routine. Once in place, I fixed my eyes on the control tower and waited. A minute later one of the two controllers came out onto the tower's iron balcony, aimed a light gun at me, and I saw the green signal light up. Cleared for takeoff!

I gunned the Cirrus engine, causing the little plane to lurch ahead, almost leap into the air and magically soar skyward, relieved of the load of the instructor. I was airborne. Alone!

All through the occupation years, my dream of getting to England and joining the Royal Air Force had remained unfulfilled. The reasons for staying put just a little longer had always seemed compelling, until the choice was no longer mine. As a result I felt cheated for never having earned my wings, not to mention any glory, and in the summer of 1946 I resolved to remedy at least the former shortcoming. It could not, alas, be rectified in Spitfires; less would have to do.

A small flying school had just been set up at Kastrup, the airfield serving Copenhagen, by J.H.F "Morian" Hansen, a Danish motorcycle bum who happened to be dirt-track racing in England when the war broke out. Morian promptly enlisted in the RAF, easily earned his wings, and in the course of combat flew more than a dozen types, from Lancasters to Spitfires. By war's end he was the RAF's most decorated foreigner.[133] He had a natural affinity for engines and was a superb pilot, particularly when sober. In his capacity of flying school operator he spent his time in equal amounts on flying, drinking and chasing any and every female within reach. I learned early to be alert when drinking with him, as his favorite practical joke was to test his companions' sense of taste by surreptitiously pissing in their beer while they were dancing or otherwise distracted.

Morian was stationed in the British zone in northern Germany when the war ended. Showing both foresight and presence of mind, he combed every airfield in the area and succeeded in locating a Messerschmitt *Taifun*, civilian forerunner of the formidable ME-109 fighter. After loading a spare engine into it, Morian liberated both by flying the *Taifun* to Denmark, where he stashed it in a barn. Needless to say, I was green with envy.

The thought of bringing a plane home had, I hasten to note, also occurred to Thies and me, but since neither of us could fly and ground transport of a aircraft would have been too cumbersome, we were unable to pull it off. Using the *Taifun* as collateral, Morian had borrowed money to purchase two Danish-built KZ-3 aircraft for primary instruction and started his school, where I began my training in July with him as instructor.

Flying was every bit as exciting and enjoyable as I had imagined. In these early postwar days while tourism and mass air travel were still in the future, the Kastrup airport was a sleepy grass-covered field with a small control tower and a cozy little terminal building housing *Hammers* restaurant. We did most of our flying within sight of the field, but it was in any event impossible to get lost. Immediately after takeoff, one had a panoramic view of Copenhagen and the attached island of Amager where Kastrup was located. Across the Sound to the east lay Sweden with the city of Malmö rising in the distance. To the north and west the view trailed off into the pleasant countryside of Zealand.

Outstanding skill in a given field often fails to go hand in hand with ability to teach that skill, and Morian notably lacked the patience to teach. Consequently, he left most of the instruction to two former Danish Air Force pilots, and that worked out fine. Morian's career struck me as intriguing in the extreme, and I was forcibly struck by the totally different sets of human attributes demanded by nations at war as opposed to those at peace. Unflinching courage, natural flying talent and steady nerve in the face of danger had justly earned Morian all his medals, but these inborn qualities weighed but lightly in a society where peace reigned, and he never seemed to be at ease in the management function needed at the flying school.

Flying lessons constituted my chief recreation in the summer of 1946. My last year of engineering school was proving exciting but filled with so much work that free time was considered a luxury. My studies had twice been interrupted, each time for two years, so it required concentration to catch up, but it was enjoyable because our school work had reached an advanced level. In our experimental laboratory the Teknikum institute had acquired a BMW radial engine from a German fighter aircraft. It was strictly state-of-the-art, designed with water injection to produce a very short but substantially increased power surge to be expended in aerial combat. Suspended from an overhead I beam in the center of our lab, BMW's last contribution to the Luftwaffe had inspired me to select for my thesis project the design of a light aircraft engine on which I had embarked with all my energy. The calculations were done by hand or slide rule, and the drawings had to be in India ink and to exacting standards. I slid back into my old routine of continuing each Saturday's studies with an all-night work session until Sunday morning bird song sounded from the rooftops. Over the weeks and months this helped bring the many design details and elaborate drawings into being.

These first moments of flying alone summed up the total joy of living, as I climbed to six thousand feet on a westerly course. Below lay the south part of the Copenhagen harbor complex with the city to the right. A steamer was heading through the harbor channel, probably bound for some Baltic port. Out of sight from the airfield I did a series of lazy eights, trying to keep my altitude locked on six thousand. Then I returned to Kastrup to buy the customary round of beer at the flying school. Though still needing to reach the thirty hours of total flying time required before my license test, I was a pilot.

* * *

The procession wound through the town three abreast, blocking the narrow street to other traffic. I walked between Aage and Thies, close behind the hearse. None of us had taken part in a funeral before, and we were unprepared for the agonizing slowness, dictated by the walking ability of the oldest and most infirm of the participants. The distance from the cathedral to the old graveyard in the south end of town we could easily have covered in ten minutes, even at this pace, but the last resting place for our old comrade was to be in the newer cemetery on the east side, well beyond the railroad station, probably at least half an hour from the church. To make a sad occasion even more dreary, it was starting to rain, a cold, insistent drizzle announcing the onset of autumn.

Two days ago word had come from Ribe that Prahl had died, finally succumbing to a virulent tuberculosis, contracted while in concentration camp. At thirty-two he had been the oldest member of the CB group, and at his death he left his wife with three small children. As we followed him under the rainy sky, I felt more depressed than at any time after my return. My thoughts drifted back to that initial meeting, when I recruited the Ribe group after Aage's departure for Sweden. Johannes Prahl and Svend Jacob Kjær had both been there, and now both were dead from the same cause. Svend Jacob had succumbed while I was hunting Nazis for the C.I.C. Both men had been courageous and cheerful, the best of resistance fighters, and had it not been for my carelessness, they might never have been caught.

The hearse turned from the street through the cemetery gates and halted at the gaping hole in the black soil. We pulled the coffin from the small sea of flowers surrounding it, carried it through the mud to the hole, and lowered it awkwardly to the bottom. Someone tried to shield the minister with an umbrella while he spoke the words committing Prahl to eternity ... "ashes to ashes ... dust to dust ..."

After the burial, the three of us commiserated in our hotel room over a bottle of whiskey. We realized to our amazement that none of us had come to grips with the awesome majesty of death before. Although Thies and I had seen death as daily routine in the concentration camps, our instincts had in that setting blotted out sympathy and pity, replacing such civilized feelings with simple concentration on personal survival. The same applied to the killing in the course of combat or when pitted against an adversary where the choice is to kill or be killed. Now, readjusting to peace, we had to face in proper perspective how serious is the finality of losing life. It is something one should never be called upon to cause, directly or indirectly, for another human being.

We tried in vain to decide whether what little damage we had managed to inflict on the Germans could possibly have been worth the dreadful price paid in lives. As night and booze dwindled away, we concluded that there was no satisfactory answer to that question. The Nornes that spin out our fates had granted the three of us the luck to come away alive. They had cut the threads of Kjær and Prahl and so many others who died of illness, giving their lives less gloriously but just as generously as those who died in battle.

* * *

The idyllic airfield at Lucerne, Switzerland, consisted of a strip of luscious meadow. As it was rarely used, a shepherd was allowed to graze his sheep on the runway. In this picture the sheep are being shooed off the field to permit an early morning takeoff. Mt. Pilatus can be seen in the background.

The Auster was grinding its way north at two thousand feet above the concrete ribbon of the autobahn. The airspeed indicator showed ninety-six knots, yet we were making good no more than sixty in ground speed. That headwind must be freshening. For the tenth time I recalculated in my head our ETA for Frankfurt. We should be able to make it just before dark, but the wintry overcast just above me told a different story. Daylight was slipping away.

Elizabeth Ziegler who was sitting next to me was enjoying herself hugely. First time in an airplane, private trip, piloted by her boyfriend. There would be plenty to talk about when she got back to Frankfurt. Elizabeth was Swiss, at the moment a civilian employee of the U.S. Army. We had first met at a dance at Rettershof when I worked with C.I.C., and since then our relationship had been an on-again-off-again affair. Yesterday I had flown from Copenhagen to visit her in her home town of Basel, and we had gone to Luzerne and stayed at a picturesque *Gasthaus*. Last night after our arrival, the airfield – a grass strip in the shadow of towering Mt. Pilatus – had been invaded by a flock of sheep, penned in by moveable fences and happily grazing the field itself. This morning our takeoff had been delayed while we located the shepherd and had him move the sheep sufficiently to allow us a bit of runway. Then we had to stop in Basel to get some stuff Elizabeth wanted to take back to Frankfurt. When we finally got off in the afternoon, it was later than I would have liked.

She had been watching the landscape below, but now she detached her wristwatch and set it. I saw her twiddle the hands a full hour forward. Hey! It suddenly dawned on me why daylight seemed to fade prematurely. I had forgotten to allow for Swiss time being an hour behind German and Scandinavian. Damn! There was no way we could get to Frankfurt and land in daylight. The Auster had neither instrument lights nor exterior lights for navigation and landing. Besides, I was not licensed to fly at night and had never tried to. Adding insult to injury, it was clearly my own fault. There was no excuse. I had simply been careless, thinking more about having fun with Elizabeth than about minding my pilot duties. And my flying record so far had been flawless. Well, almost flawless. How utterly embarrassing it would be to crack up the plane by attempting to land it in the dark.

I pushed the throttle all the way forward, but the Auster gained just two more knots.

After getting my pilot's license in the late summer I had naturally been eager to put my new skill to use, and I was bored with buzzing around Kastrup. I suggested to John Andersen that we make a flying visit to Paris, something to which he had agreed without hesitation. We purchased the requisite charts, RAF's excellent series in scale 1:500,000, and rented a KZ-3 from Morian. The Danish-built two-seater was a fine primary trainer, but when viewed with long range cruising in mind, it was somewhat frugally equipped. Engine instruments consisted of tachometer and fuel gauge, while turn-and-bank and altimeter served flying needs. The only navigational equipment was a small magnetic compass. We had no radio and received takeoff and landing clearances by light signals from the tower, if the airfield had one.

As we were about to take off, John asked without betraying undue concern whether I thought we could find Hamburg and its airfield, our first stop. Without letting on that I had myself been wondering about that, I replied that we probably could, and added reassuringly that we would soon find out.

Flying on the compass heading and following our progress on the chart, a navigational method known as dead reckoning, we saw Hamburg's rubble heaps right on time and managed to locate the Fühlsbüttel airfield as well. After all, an airfield is a pretty big item and not too difficult to spot in clear weather. As no civilian air traffic existed as yet, all sizeable airfields in occupied Germany were in military hands, and we landed on the interlocking steel mats that served as runways on all of these, left over from combat operations. The local RAF squadron obligingly filled our tank, at no charge of course, and we flew on to Le Bourget outside Paris, again hitting our goal squarely, thanks to our little magnetic compass and careful ground contact. Le Bourget allowed only radio-equipped aircraft, but we kept circling the field until the control tower finally gave us a green light to get us out of the sky.

A cab driver took us to an inexpensive hotel of his choosing which turned out to be *Hotel du Théatre*, a tiny family enterprise in rue Chéroi just off Boulevard des Batignolles, where we arrived in late afternoon. Its seven rooms were clustered around a spiral staircase, two of the rooms opening onto the stairs without any landing, as if long ago the builder just cut out the doorways as an afterthought. The stairs were covered in red velvet and the peripheral bannister was brass, polished to a high gloss. Everything was conspicuously clean, kept so by madame and monsieur and their seventeen-year-old daughter, Madeleine, who to our consternation carried our bags up to our rooms. Our Scandinavian upbringing made us recoil at having a woman carry a man's baggage, but as we learned in time, most of Europe had no such qualms.

It was our first time in Paris, and we came with all the anticipation of children entering a fairyland. To Scandinavians of our generation Paris had always beckoned as the city of light, the cultural heart of the continent, a place for romantic strolls along boulevards crowded with sidewalk cafés, ultimate setting for racy adventures with dark-eyed ladies. We were not disappointed, for the city's majestic beauty easily outweighed all the lingering reminders of wartime deprivation. We spent two delightful days taking in the sights and exploring a few museums and numerous bistros, finding out that nice girls were much harder to catch than at home. We returned to Copenhagen without mishap and learned afterwards that ours was the first private flight out of Denmark after World War Two. John had been so inspired by the evident ease of flying that he enrolled to take instruction with Morian, and a few months later obtained his own flying license.

Back in Copenhagen I dug into my studies with a vengeance but at intervals went flying and always enjoyed it immensely. Nothing so completely dominates a person's attention, blotting out all other concerns, as navigating the limitless reaches of the atmosphere. In the course of fall and winter I logged a number of long distance trips, renting the aircraft from *Sportsflyveklubben*, a sports flying club of which I had become a member. The club owned two planes, both Austers of the type *Autocrat*, 3-seaters with flaps, a feature missing on the KZ-3, and one of them which I came to prefer was equipped with a long-range belly tank. The military version of this type, identical in every respect, had served as spotter and liaison plane in the British army during the war. The Auster handled beautifully, would spin and recover easily, and was like the KZ-3 equipped with a control stick rather the clumsy yoke used on larger craft. Having been confined at home for five years, people were travel hungry, so I had no difficulty finding friends willing to share the cost of long-distance flying. With Alfred Sander and his father I made a trip to Paris and Nimes, and with John Andersen and another friend one to Barcelona.

After John had obtained his own license we had rented two planes and made a spectacular trip to Brussels, managing to do some crude formation flying despite our inability to communicate without radios. John had invited his fiancée, Erna, and I took a lady friend by the name of Astrid. A divorcée with a daughter of eight, she was a former model who now owned a designer firm producing upscale ladies wear for the Copenhagen market. I liked her a great deal. Besides the kind of looks that make men sit up and take instant notice, she had a sense of humor, an incisive mind and deft business talent.

The Brussels trip turned out an animated affair from the moment of our arrival. On our way to the city by taxi I instructed the driver to find us a small hotel, but my one year of high school French had left me a lot short of fluency. The message did not get across, or the driver possibly had his own agenda. We ended up in three double rooms at a large and expensive downtown hotel where they insisted on assigning our two female travelers to one and the rest of us to the two other rooms. This took place with much hilarity on our part, not shared by the staid hotel personnel whose opinions of Danish morals suffered severely. Out of sight of the front desk, we made our own sleeping arrangements.

Always on the lookout for new delicatessen ideas, John insisted on investigating the Belgian phenomenon – unfamiliar to us – of selling French fried potatoes from pushcarts. After sampling several, supplemented with apéritifs at a sidewalk restaurant, we dined on *moules marinière* with lots of wine. In Denmark wine and other spirits were taxed very heavily, so that French and Belgian prices looked to us like bargains, hard to pass up.

After the Brussels trip, I flew with Angla and Ole to the south of France, where we went to see the annual bullfight in Nimes. On our way back we landed at the tiny village of Tallard, high in the French Alps. The airfield manager turned out to be the village grocer who came out on his bicycle and cleared the little hangar of cattle, informing us that no airplane had landed there since before the war. The village folks had taken to using it as a cow stable, having seen no fliers for seven years.

Then my mother and I had a memorable trip to Switzerland, where we strolled agog among the bulging stores in this untouched haven of peace and prosperity. At our return, an accident at the Kastrup airport provided a grim reminder that flying safety requires more than simple piloting skills. When we landed, smoking wreckage at the end of the runway marked the site of a disaster that had taken place less than an hour earlier. A Danish airliner, a DC-3 converted from military use, had crashed on takeoff.[134] Among the passengers who all perished were Grace Moore, American soprano of Hollywood fame, the Crown Prince of Sweden, and Gerda Neuman, talented star of Danish musical shows who with her brother Ulrik had delighted audiences until their escape to Sweden when the Germans went after the Danish Jews.

In the course of all this flying I had become good at dead-reckoning navigation and had never experienced any difficulty in finding my way. Weather was
not a peril, for I usually stayed below the overcast. A couple of times I did get
caught above but simply went down through by carefully gliding a straight
course – no turns when flying blind with only a turn-and-bank indicator – and
hoping the cloud would not be all the way to the ground. My luck held, but my
attitude had become far too nonchalant. On one trip, when I flew with Aage
and a girlfriend to Nimes, we did not have all the charts needed for the route
segment south from Paris. We ended up using a postcard with a three-by-four
inch picture of France to guide us to our destination on the Mediterranean
coast. Crossing the Auvergne plateau we had doubt about our exact position
but resolved it by flying low over a railroad line, very low, and reading a station
sign: Clermont-Ferrand.

The reason for my nonchalance was simply that after years of playing cat-and-
mouse with the Germans, risks in connection with flying seemed minor, if not
downright trivial.

All this went through my mind as we left Karlsruhe behind and continued
under a lowering ceiling, and I realized ruefully that my fine record just might
owe more to luck than to skill and foresight. I had been gradually descending to
stay clear of the overcast and was only six hundred feet above the wintry landscape. It was still easy enough to follow the autobahn which ran straight north
toward Frankfurt, and I could see the farms below me clearly, for the ground
was powdered with just a touch of snow. The fields were plowed and frozen, and
it took little imagination to visualize what the plane would look like, if an emergency landing were attempted on one of those. It would be like setting down on
a giant, coarse grindstone.

I was beginning to feel trapped. There is something unsettling, even chilling,
about getting caught aloft in the dark without the means to land. I estimated at
least another hour's flying time to Frankfurt. It would definitely be dark by then.

We were coming up on Heidelberg and I remembered from my Nazi-hunting
travels that it had a small airfield used for American observer and liaison
planes. I made a quick decision to try to find it, rolled into a right turn and
made a circuit over the city, failing to locate it. I thought the field was on the
southwest side and made another circuit, again without success. Below me the
few cars in the streets had their lights on. That decided me to put down, right
then! A railroad line ran through the city, sunk down so that street traffic could
pass level across the bridges leading over it. Along the tracks was what seemed
like a flat narrow stretch between two bridges. I wrenched the plane around in
a sharp turn, came down with full flaps, almost touching the first bridge, narrowly avoided a huge pile of scrap metal, actually airplane debris from the war,
touched down and came to a stop before the second bridge.

My passenger was happily unworried, an endearing quality of nonpilot companions, as I pretended the incident to be almost routine. I pulled the plane

The author's Auster aircraft refueling on Hamburg's Fühlsbüttel airport. The perforated, interlocking steel mats served as standard surface material to repair bomb damage on airports taken by the advancing Allies.

clear of the tracks and climbed up the embankment to the street. When I turned to look back, the plane was already invisible in the darkness.

We slept at the airfield installation where the USAAF personnel explained that they had heard me and had turned the lights on along the field's grass landing strip, but too late. We became the objects of immediate and keen interest, Elizabeth in particular, for our visit was a welcome distraction in their unexciting daily routine. In the morning they took us to the plane in a jeep. We were followed by a heater truck with a large hot-air hose which the driver connected to the airscoops on the Auster's cowling. After fifteen minutes of warmup, I propstarted the engine without difficulty. Then there was some lively betting whether I would be able to clear the second bridge at takeoff. Actually, this presented no problem, for the Auster climbs better than the L-3. We taxied to the first bridge, gunned the engine and lifted off about halfway to the second bridge. I held it a few inches above ground almost to the bridge, then pulled up steeply to disappoint the ones betting against me.

We 'flew on over to the Rettershof where Maus, von Richter's daughter, was preparing to get married. As a wedding present, I had bought in Switzerland a meatgrinder, the bride's most urgent desire, for such consumer goods were still unavailable in Germany. Circling above the castle, I dropped the well-padded package into the courtyard.

My fellow students at the Teknikum would undoubtedly have been dumbfounded at the thought of buzzing around Europe on weekends and holidays, but my habit of avoiding chitchat about personal affairs made it easy to maintain privacy. I realized dimly that my flying was a release, a compensation for imprisonment. The idea of being able to get airborne and go anywhere – *anywhere* – was effectively restoring in me the mental balance we associate with living in freedom.[135]

That my mental balance should be in need of adjustment had occurred to me only after Aase's suicide. When I left and went back to Germany with Thies, it must have seemed like forsaking her in favor of fighting a private war against the Nazis. And in a sense it was. After returning, I had spent long nights reproaching myself for not having seen the depth of her despair, nor having understood that simplistic satisfaction with merely being alive was something to which only those are privy who have been in prolonged danger of losing the privilege of life itself. In our discussions Thies and I had come to recognize that the war had changed us, and that some of the changes would prove permanent.

* * *

Thies put two bottles of Tuborg on the table, opened them and handed me one with a quiet "Skaal!" We drank, and I put my bottle down.

"This morning I received my immigration visa from the American consulate."

Thies leaned back in his chair, allowing no hint of expression on his face.

"When will you be leaving?"

"There's an East Asiatic Co. ship, the *Jutlandia*, leaving on the first of July. It still has a couple of berths available."

We sat for a minute, each in his own thoughts. In many previous talks we had arrived at an understanding about the future and made a decision to face it together. This May evening, the future had moved closer and was staring us in the face. My die was cast.

The winter of '47 had for me been a time for decisions and planning, and the pressure of studying for finals had not kept me from pondering what to do next. When weighing my options, I was aware of a tendency to search for excitement and challenge, an inclination possibly resulting from the activities of the occupation years and something I was still inclined to indulge. Although Thies and I had settled into the humdrum of peace, the prospect of building an engineering career in Copenhagen and fitting myself into a nine-to-five routine did not have great appeal. My travel in Europe had made me adept at getting around on my own in foreign lands, speaking with people of other nationalities and overcoming the kind of obstacles and problems not encountered within one's own borders. I had seen a little of the world, and my appetite had been whetted. Engineering training was useful anywhere, so that occupational constraints would not confine me to making my living in Denmark. Moreover, having done what I could for my country in her hour of trial, I felt no obligation to stay and apply my life's work there.

While I was cogitating about my future, a letter from Ben Vaughan had arrived in April and settled the matter. Ben had been discharged and was back home in Melrose, a suburb of Boston, and he offered to be my sponsor, should I want to emigrate. At the end he posed the question: did I want to emigrate to America? Putting the letter down, it had taken but a moment to decide. I wanted to.

My mind made up about emigrating, I had gone to see Thies. Our collaborative existence had been a day-to-day venture, and our preoccupation with staying alive had focused our mental energies on the here and now to the exclusion of thoughtful reflection. But on that April evening we discussed the war in an overall sense and our rôle in it, for we wished to put the period behind us and get on with our lives. We both felt that inordinate luck had seen us through, and that the prospect of a long life ahead was something we should plan to make the most of.

In the two years since the German collapse evidence had built a detailed picture of the sacrifices the Western world had made to defeat Nazism. The brunt had been borne by the belligerent Allies, but the occupied countries, particularly Poland, had yielded active resistance rather than the acquiescence or collaboration the Germans had needed and hoped for. For this resistance the Poles and others had paid a heavy price in blood and treasure. Thies and I found that we had come to identical conclusions about the rôle Denmark had played in the five war years. It had been ignominious.[136]

We came to this view from entirely different backgrounds. A product of the middle class, I had as a teenager held a romantic respect for things military, a leaning toward conservative and reactionary ideas, and a supercilious disdain for political dissent. My attitude toward Nazism had been tolerant, bordering on admiration. Only as an adult could I reject their insidious claim to racial superiority, their silly Kantian and Hegelian metaphysical ideas, their primitive claptrap about German destiny and Teutonic *Blut und Erde*, sacred blood and soil. Thies on the other hand had come from a working-class environment steeped in social democracy. But Social Democrat politicians had been instrumental in bringing Denmark to a state of disarmament that had dictated abject surrender, and as political representatives they had lost some respect during the occupation period. With a unionized worker's instinctive distrust of all manner of military establishment, and with outright contempt for German heel-clicking discipline, he had neither inclination nor wish to explore Nazi ideas but had recognized them as unDanish and their propagation as something to be resisted. Consequently, our respective attitudes toward politics had converged, mine from the right of the political spectrum, Thies' from the left, to a common position best described as being not very interested.

Most of our friends and acquaintances seemed to be reliving the war, interminably talking about what they did, or could have done, or might have done. I had no wish to recount the past, and neither did Thies, so we had both dodged various requests to relate in detail our sabotage and other resistance work. We felt that, as a topic for conversation, a person's war experience ranks with one's minor personal ailments in the sense of being notably boring to the rest of the world. Moreover, our accomplishments in the war did not even merit mention in the same breath with those of people like Morian Hansen and many others. We resolved, therefore, not to talk about or even to think about the war and the concentration camps.[137] Instead, we would direct our energies toward positive ends, first and foremost our own lives ahead, for we both considered World War Two to be history. Moreover, we felt that our mental readjustment from war to peace had been accomplished. It had been a matter of returning to sanity.

Thies had been as well impressed as I was by our experience with Americans and also liked the prospect of going to the States, but he and Cordia now had a one-year-old daughter who curtailed his mobility compared with mine. He had suggested that I go, get settled, and send him word when to follow. And that is how we had left it.

Our bottles were nearly empty. We had reviewed our sketchy plans, were pleased with their simplicity, and thought their potential for opportunity and success unlimited. Thies emptied his bottle and put it on the table.

"I figure it will take me about a year to save enough money to get us to the States. Do you think you'll have your feet on the ground by then?"

"I don't see why not."

Listening to my own voice, I felt momentarily reassured. Then I realized that I didn't know what I was talking about.

* * *

Our wealth is often a snare to ourselves, and always a temptation to others.

Caleb Colton

The end of the occupation found Denmark a profoundly changed country, not least in the economic realm. Whereas absence of real hardship had made most people, including myself, feel the experience interesting and challenging rather than painful, this was in part because the nation was consuming its accumulated resources. As members of one of the world's most prosperous nations, individual Danes were able to stretch personal belongings of clothing, footwear, linen, furniture, household items, bicycles, and so forth to last out the five-year interlude in which few or no replacements were available. Food, housing and medical services were husbanded by the government to serve the citizens equally, on a basis of need. Conditions remained perfectly tolerable, and certainly far better than in most of the other countries under German occupation, despite a tightening vise of pressure by the occupiers to drain the country's economic lifeblood into the Nazi war machine.

Denmark's prewar economy had never been aimed at self-sufficiency but was totally dependent on export/import trade in free-market conditions. Under occupation the country found itself shackled to the German economy without access to its traditional markets. Beyond construction of air bases and employment of some Danish workers in Germany,[138] the Germans initially were unsure whether they needed to maintain Denmark's economy to support their war efforts, but the advantages in doing so soon became apparent.[139] Totally dependent on fuel imports, the Danes had little choice, and an economic tug-of-war ensued, heavily weighted in Germany's favor.

A clearings account was set up in *Nationalbanken*, the Danish National Bank, to record all export/import transactions, and the balance of payments showed steadily rising Danish credits, so that by 1945 an amount of 3 billion kroner was owed by Germany. In addition a *Værnemagtskonto*, a Wehrmacht account, was set up against which the occupying troops could draw for payrolls, supplies, facilities and fortifications. By 1945 this account showed 5 billion kroner owed by Germany. Food for the occupying troops was recorded on the clearings account as exports, because the Germans insisted on maintaining the fiction of the official claim that the Wehrmacht was supplied from the motherland. Danish regulations governing National Bank transactions mandated publishing of weekly totals. As the Germans did not want to reveal the cost of the occupation to the Danish public, the Wehrmacht account was merged with certain others under the heading Miscellaneous Debitors.

Despite the systematic exploitation during the occupation years, the Danish economy recovered quickly when peace returned. The country easily reestablished its position among the world's twenty richest countries per capita.[140] Vigorous German efforts to recruit Danish volunteers for their fighting forces resulted in creation in 1941 of a military unit, *Frikorps Danmark*, totalling about 1,000 men. In 1943 another unit, *Schalburgkorpset*, was set up, totalling between 500 and 600 men. It was used to retaliate with terror and murder against Danish resistance. In addition, the Germans drafted into the Wehrmacht Danish citizens born before 1920 in the zone of southern Jutland which in that year voted itself back to Denmark in the aftermath of World War One. In total, some 7,000 Danes took up arms on behalf of the Third Reich in World War Two, most of them by compulsion.

Chapter 58   July 1947

If a man does not keep pace with his companions,
perhaps it is because he hears a different
drummer. Let him step to the music which he
hears, however measured or far away.

Thoreau

M/S *Jutlandia* nosed its way slowly toward Ellis Island. The gentle motion drawn from the Atlantic swell ceased, and in a whisper of land breeze the fetid stench from the great harbor overwhelmed the sea air. Daylight was almost gone, calling forth a myriad of city lights on the shore which was now embracing us on three sides. Ahead, I saw for the first time the Statue of Liberty holding high her torch on the background of the magnificent Manhattan skyline. Alone on deck I wondered vaguely what my fellow passengers all might be doing that was more important than watching our arrival in New York. Oh well, they were mostly middle-aged Danish-Americans returning from a long-delayed visit to the old country.

My application to the U.S. Consulate in Copenhagen had been approved in only three months. In the meantime had I graduated cum laude, and on 1 July 1947 I left Copenhagen aboard the *Jutlandia*, bound for New York.

My friends threw a gay farewell party in my cabin, toasting to my luck and happiness, many of them wishing they could go themselves. The old Mr. Sander, Alfred's father, had made me a pillow of eighteen kinds of seal skin for a going-away present in memory of our flying trip to Paris. When we took the last sip of champagne at the call for visitors to go ashore, I suddenly felt that our ways were parting in a profoundly final manner. We would certainly keep in touch, and I might see them again, but henceforth I would be marching to a different drummer, toward different goals. Only with Thies was my parting different. We shook hands in the firm conviction that our paths would only momentarily diverge, that we had yet untold adventures ahead of us as a team.

Financially solvent, I left without debt of any kind, my ticket to New York paid, seventy-eight dollars in my pocket, two suitcases, boundless energy and optimism.

The trip, my first sea voyage, had been pleasant enough. A freighter with accommodations for 76 passengers, *Jutlandia* offered a respectable level of comfort. I shared a double stateroom with a middle-aged man, originally from Copenhagen but after thirty years in New York a naturalized American citizen. We had bunk beds of which I resided in the upper, we enjoyed daylight through a port hole and had a private bathroom with salt water shower. Our meals – excellent in my opinion – were served in the large dining room, where my roommate and I shared our table with a family from Detroit, a couple with two teenage daughters.

Our ship took the route north around Scotland, skirting just south of Cape Farewell, then past the Grand Banks and along the North American coast. In summer the warm waters of the Gulf Stream interact with cold air from the high latitudes to create fog, and we churned along day after day enveloped in the gray vapors and seeing neither horizon nor other vessels. Unaffected by the lack of visibility, shipboard life was congenial enough. We played deck games for prizes, or lounged in the deck chairs swathed in blankets. At 5 p.m., shipboard time, the bar opened, a tiny cabin off the main deck where Scotch could be had at $1.50 a bottle and the bartender would put the purchaser's name on the bottle and keep it in readiness. Fortunately, several of the passengers were accompanied by their grown children, so that lively night life had developed after a few days, and I had experienced my first Fourth of July celebration with a great party, complete with fireworks on the aft deck.

The rattle of the anchor chain through the hawsehole broke my reverie. The ship was turning slowly into the wind and becoming motionless in the current of the outgoing tide, as we lay securely anchored offshore. I was still standing at the railing, taking in the impressions in the soft warm summer night, trying to imagine what my existence would be like in this huge, unfamiliar country. I felt alone. Worse, I felt inept by not having any idea where or how to put my skills and energy to use. But then I thought of the millions of others who had stood as I was standing now, only far less prepared, many not even speaking any English. And here was I: young, healthy, strong, well-educated, and speaking the language. There would be no excuse for failure, another depressing thought.

From the nearby shore came the faint murmur of the city at night. Above me loomed the towering bulk of the Statue of Liberty, like a huge mountain I now felt compelled to climb.

* * *

I don't know how others have made the crucial decision to leave their place of origin and emigrate. It should be obvious to anyone that our upbringing, education and cultural heritage all shape us to live our lives in the society of our birth, not to play the rôle of stranger in a foreign land. Nevertheless, I gave not even passing thought to the adaptation that would be required to make my particular background mesh with the needs and demands of an alien country, and I suspect few immigrants do. Nothing prepares one for being an immigrant, and neither does anything lead one even to contemplate any problem beyond the obvious one of language. Besides, in the glow of hopeful expectation, the mind balks at analytical reflection.

Still, as I am writing this with the benefit of long hindsight, I am puzzled by the swiftness of both decision and execution. I was Danish to the core. I knew better than most my nation's history, its songs and legends, language and literature, its customs, mores, and jokes. I knew and understood the poetry that could bring tears to my countrymen's eyes, or smiles to their lips. I had been ready to die for my country's cause, without regrets, yet I was now ready to leave with no thought of looking back.

There have been emigrants leaving the United States as well as immigrants arriving to stay. The former have been fewer, but a number of them noteworthy, some of them Black. I will venture a guess that their decisions to forsake America were more carefully weighed and thought through than mine to leave Denmark. I was forcibly reminded of this group when reading a news item in The Wall Street Journal that James Baldwin had died in St. Paul de Vence in France. One of our greatest contemporary authors, he took many years ago the step of turning his back on America and making France his adopted country. A generation earlier Josephine Baker had done the same. Both of them received in time the order of the *Légion d'Honneur*, gaining abroad the respect and recognition their native America had been too bigoted to give. But in the spring of 1947 I had only the faintest inkling about racial prejudice in America. The U.S. image in my mind was positive only, and I made my decision with neither confusion nor fatuity.

Europeans today look upon America with mixed emotions. Our record in international affairs has not always been one to elicit respect. But to Europeans of the immediate postwar period, the United States of America was the promised land, epitomizing excitement, opportunity, accomplishment and success, a nation deserving of our gratitude as well as our admiration. To some of us with long memories it still is, shortcomings notwithstanding.

* * *

Thies never joined me in the United States. Shortly after the war, he fell victim to cancer and after radical surgery was reduced to a painful shadow existence until his death in 1985. Aage Kjellerup lived a full and happy life, became an avid bridge player in his later years and died of cancer in 1995. Erik Hansen and

Alfred Sander returned to their respective careers. Both live in retirement in Copenhagen as of this writing. Also living in retirement is Valdemar Sørensen, last survivor of the Ribe group. I never saw Ellen Quistgaard after she left for Sweden in the winter of 1944. She worked for several years as a member of the Danish embassy staff in Washington and later took up a university teaching career in Copenhagen. Never remarried, she died in 1989. On a business trip to Copenhagen thirty years after the war, I saw Gurli Lyngesen. Still a stunningly beautiful woman, she owned another beauty salon. I never saw Hanne Schlederman after our chance meeting in Hofheim. My inquiries revealed that she died in Singapore in the 1970s. Niels Jørgensen regained his health after his stint in concentration camps and became advertising manager of Phillips in Copenhagen. He died in 1994, afflicted by Alzheimer's disease. When I checked on Morian Hansen in 1991, I found him driving a cab in a Copenhagen suburb. He could look back on a steadily declining career since his zenith at the end of the war. But at 86, he was the same Morian--hell-may-care, indomitable.

Chapter 59　　　　　　Summer 1983

Older men declare war. But it is youth that must fight and die. And it is youth who must inherit the tribulation, the sorrow, and the triumphs that are the aftermath of war.

Herbert Hoover

When driving through the entrance, leaving behind the Normandy *bocage* with its cozy fields and stately medieval farms, I was struck by being surrounded with impeccable neatness. The small administration building set back from the parking area was in the local style of architecture, immaculately maintained. The path led across manicured lawns and through a thin screen of trees, each trimmed to perfection.

Beyond the screen the horizon came into view, the dark blue water of the Channel meeting the light blue summer sky. Then I saw the crosses. They were set with absolute precision in the pattern that gives an observer the illusion of always being at the focal point, no matter where he stands. As if the dead insist on their own geometry, the rows radiated in all directions out of sight.

I was in the Normandy American Cemetery and Memorial. It is situated on a cliff plateau high above the beach and commands a spectacular view to the sea, the coast of Sussex visible as a faint line in the far distance. This is the resting place for 9,386 Americans who lost their lives on the beaches below the cliff, giving the invading Allied armies their first foothold in France. Of the headstones, 307 mark the graves of Unknowns whose remains could not be identified, and in a Garden of the Missing are inscribed the names of another 1,557 whose bodies were never recovered, perhaps lost at sea during the attack.

Slightly above the cemetery stands the memorial, a semi-circular colonnade with a loggia at each end. I walked up the sandstone pavement to the platform half enclosed by the colonnade; in its center stands a 22-foot bronze sculpture,

Spirit of American Youth, depicting a young man rising out of the crest of a wave. It is the most poignant and beautiful piece of sculpture I have ever seen, devoid of bombast and posturing, humble in its serene tribute of eternal gratitude. To my surprise, tears kept rolling down my face, uncontrollably, making me turn embarrassedly away from Diane and my 13-year-old son, Joshua. After all, it was thirty-nine years since the last shot had been fired here. But then, time had stopped for these nine thousand. While I had been sitting uselessly in Gestapo's prison in Copenhagen, these guys had fought the war for me, and given their lives to win it.

How can one ever repay a young man for giving up his life for you? I left filled with two emotions. One was a feeling of compelling obligation to strive to improve the human condition which these contemporaries of my youth had striven to preserve before being violently cut off. At the same time I felt grateful that they had been able to die in combat, capable of exerting themselves to the last with all the strength and abandon of youth, rather than perishing in filth and misery from nameless disease in a prison camp.

Epilogue

Denmark's response to the historically unprecedented German attack and occupation in World War Two was shaped by a pervading unwillingness to even
contemplate going to war. This antiwar attitude was more than an expedient
excuse for not joining in a possibly pointless blood bath, as World War One was
felt to have been. It was a common belief – an article of faith really – that the
country's forces would always be too small for serious defense against a major
power. Added to this defeatism was the conviction that serious international
problems in any event should not be settled through violence. It added up to an
attitude with roots in the Danish *persona* as friendly and easy-going.[141]

These Danish convictions may have been arguably defensible from a moral
or idealist standpoint, but they were initially inimical to resistance, and even after public opinion swung to support sabotage, the number of people actively involved was pitifully small. Although a reader of official Danish accounts, or a visitor to the Freedom Museum in Copenhagen, may gain the impression that the
Danes did their share to defeat Nazism, the reality was different. When Thies
and I drove back into Denmark in May of 1945, some 35,000 Freedom Fighters
with armbands and submachine guns were everywhere in evidence, and the
Danish Brigade had arrived from Sweden, well trained and equipped. However,
neither group saw action against German forces, and trigger-happy latecomers
contented themselves with rounding up a number of local collaborators and informers.

This postfact show of force, much publicized and photographed and fondly
remembered by the participants, was quite disproportionate to the actual resistance during the first four of the five occupation years. I do not know how
many were actively risking their lives at the time we played hide-and-seek with
the Gestapo in the spring of 1944. Nobody does. A rough statistical calculation
based on official records leads me to a number of about sixty. Jørgen Hæstrup,
the eminent historian on Danish and other European resistance, mentioned a
figure of fifty,[142] and Aage Trommer who has researched important segments of
the resistance in depth ventured a guess of one hundred.[143] Wherever the truth
may lie, the figure is small. If one adds the military people who radioed intelli-

gence to England on ship movements through the Sound and kept busy organizing the "Underground Army" that never saw action, the number would of course be higher. A more respectable contribution was made by Danish merchant marine sailors who were on the high seas when the occupation started, six thousand of whom entered Allied service despite instructions from home to seek neutral harbor. A few overseas Danes volunteered and fought with the Allies; ninety-six joined the Royal Air Force, twenty-six of whom were lost. Still, the Danish contribution was small.

With the impatience of youth, I equated the Danish refusal to resist with simple cowardice, but subsequent events, particularly the widespread popular unrest that culminated in *Folkestrejken*, the People's Strike in the summer of 1944, proved otherwise, when the population rose in furious indignation over German duplicity, battling the Wehrmacht empty handed and without prospect of succor from abroad. The Danes were not cowards. I was wrong. They just were not attuned to violence.

Looking at the overall picture of civilian resistance to German occupation in Europe, two questions present themselves which have been touched only in passing by historical and other writings about the period. The first is whether European resistance movements contributed to the Allied war effort to the extent of shortening the war. In 1940 the British professed to believe that they could do so, and in a memo dated 19 August to the British War Cabinet Hugh Dalton even suggested that "subversion should be clearly recognized by all three fighting services as another, independent Service."[144] Although resistance was never recognized as such a "4th arm", Churchill trumpeted his exhortation to set Europe ablaze with popular resistance to the Nazi usurpers. But the hope that a thousand small wounds, a thousand obstacles to war production, would materially help to bring down the German war machine was never realistic. The leadership was grasping at straws in Britain's darkest hour, when they fought alone with stubborn courage, while realizing that they could never beat Germany unaided.

What finally brought the Nazi beast to bay was the attrition in German military manpower. Simply stated, it was necessary to kill huge numbers of German soldiers in order to terminate the war. In the four years following the attack on the Soviet Union, that came about. More than four million German servicemen died, a depletion too drastic to enable German continuance of hostilities. Seventy-five percent of these German losses occurred on the Eastern Front at the hands of the Red Army, supported by Soviet guerillas at great cost. In the vastness of the Soviet Union resistance by guerillas claimed many German lives both directly in partisan transactions and indirectly as partisans enhanced the Red Army's fighting power. By comparison, resistance movements in the occupied Western countries drained very little blood from Wehrmacht ranks; the Danish Resistance, none.

While militarily unimportant, resistance in the occupied countries did have a psychological effect, both on occupier and occupied. Such tangibles as underground newssheets or visibly sabotaged railroads and factories had a depressing effect on the occupation authorities and correspondingly infused with hope the people chafing under the Nazi yoke. Reported in the Allied press, they also stimulated those who bore the burden of fighting and sent a message to neutrals. And in both its physical and psychological manifestations, popular resistance contributed to the special nature and depth of World War Two. Moreover, the concept and practice of this form of warfare proved infectious. Numerous revolutionary and liberatory movements in the postwar world have taken their cues from the anti-Nazi fighters, often with startling success. That latter-day terrorists have done the same is an unsavory but perhaps expectable corollary.

The second question is this: What drives people to active resistance? What makes ordinary citizens risk their lives in an unequal struggle, when passivity offers a better chance of riding out the storm of war and surviving? To a young person it was thought-provoking to watch how fellow citizens reacted when confronting life-and-death issues. In an occupation situation people tend to ponder and discuss certain matters, practical as well as philosophical, that in peace rarely receive attention. If the discussions are carried on in underground newssheets, these are a first step toward action. Taking up active resistance should not be compared with taking up arms as a soldier which is an almost automatic occurrence, although it may only happen once in a person's lifetime, if at all. Cultural norms, societal pressures and legal compulsion combine to rule out noncompliance. When the call goes out, draft dodging is rare in Western nations. In contrast, it is an altogether different matter to join an insurgent group, not to mention going it alone. The above factors that make the regular soldier's induction a routine procedure will tend to prevent the prospective insurgent from joining a band of what are, technically, outlaws.

Most people will conclude that the sensible thing is to accommodate, resign oneself, yield to pressure, opt for survival through passivity, or oblige the occupiers out of fear.[145] Arguments in favor of passivity and collaboration come readily to mind and can be advanced regretfully so as not to invite accusations of deserting the cause of freedom or admitting that fear is the motivator. But when resistance becomes seen as fighting against evil, it takes on other dimensions, not measurable by cost/benefit calculation. Some individuals will gradually adopt a different view and say that living, as distinct from surviving, acquires its value from taking risks and making sacrifices that make life itself richer and more desirable, though possibly shortening it as well. Can such individuals be predicted or identified in advance? As earlier mentioned, I was notably unable to do so. Rather, I was repeatedly baffled by acquaintances acting in ways – positive or negative – contrary to my expectation. This may have been due to my own immaturity and lack of psychologic insight, or perhaps to the motivating factors being so deeply rooted in the person's character as to be hidden from an observer. That leaves an investigator with the task of distilling commonalities and other clues from individual case histories such as the foregoing or from statistical treatment of larger groups.[146]

Finally, a number of people, without soul searching, simply enjoyed the thrill of doing something nominally illegal and demonstrably dangerous but morally defensible. Peacetime does not offer such opportunity.

The return of peace leaves those who did resist and survived with a simple question: Was it worth it? Was it worth the loss of precious lives before German firing squads, or the loss of lives or health in the filth and misery of concentration camps? Thies and Aage and I discussed that question at length several times, in the end concluding merely that we would do it all over again, should the need arise. Our attitude must be typical, for I have never encountered any other old saboteur who regretted his or her resistance work. It leads me to believe that gratification of both personal and national self-respect – not tangible results toward victory – does justify the sacrifices. What the dead would say we cannot know.

In practical terms, Danish government officials, diplomats and foreign service personnel were able to parlay the resistance efforts into acceptance by the Allies of Denmark as a friendly nation and as a sponsor of the United Nations founding conference in San Francisco. They also embellished the official history of the period, making it into something later generations need not be ashamed of. If it rests partly on myth, what segment of history doesn't?

Notes

1. Actually, I have one such document, a small book by Lorenz Nissen, *Meine Wege und Umwege zur Kirche* (Altona, Germany: J. Hammerich, 1826). Lorenz Nissen was my paternal great-great-great-great-great-grandfather who rose from a peasant background to become a minister of the church. His little book was intended to guide others to the church and salvation, and although I treasure it, I wish he had instead told more about his daily life. And of my other great-great-great-great-great-grandfathers (there may be sixty-three of them) I have no record.
2. See bibliography.
3. The hill was an ancient burial mound. It had been excavated by the National Museum and the scar was visible, appearing somewhat like an entrance and lending further credibility to the story. Here is the story of *The Little Green Man*, as he told it to me: Many many years ago, over on Jutland's west coast, there was a small town called Ribe, and outside that small town was an even smaller village called Høm. In Høm lived, many many years ago, a poor peasant with his wife. They were very very poor, so much so that frequently they even lacked money to buy food. In consequence of this deplorable condition the peasant woman every week on Wednesday walked on her foot all the way to Ribe with two large baskets in a yoke over her shoulders. In Ribe she went straight to the main street, called *Storegade,* and there to the store of the friendly, fat baker Kharkov. In the store the pale, pasty-faced baker's girl gave the peasant woman bread and whipped-cream pastry from the day before, which the nice, fat baker Kharkow could not sell because it was too old. The woman put these baked goods in her baskets and walked on her foot all the way back to the village of Høm where she sold the bread and whipped-cream pastry from the day before to the peasants in the village, thereby earning a few øre with which to augment her family's income.

   This was all very well, but on the way from Ribe to Høm the road led by a hill in which there lived a terrible troll who occasionally would grab people, innocent passers-by, as they passed by his hill. Fortunately the woman was lucky and nothing happened to her, but then one Wednesday when she was on her way back from Ribe to Høm with her two baskets full of bread and whipped-cream cake from the day before, a rainshower came up and induced the woman to take a short-cut across a field, quite close by the troll's hill. She was plenty worried that he might come out and get her, but things seemed to go all right so far, until suddenly: **RROWRR!!** The huge troll came tearing out, grabbed the woman and took her and her baskets into the hill with him. She cried and begged for her life: Please let me go home, Mr. Troll! .. but no, nothing doing. He said: No, you have to stay here and keep my hill clean and cook for me and that's that! So the poor woman stayed, for she had no other choice. Every day after breakfast the troll would leave the hill and go out into the surrounding fields where he would steal potatoes and turnips from the farmers' crops, but before he left he would roll a big boulder against the door so the woman could not escape.

Well, after about a year the woman had a son whom she called Hans. Hans grew up to be a big, strong boy, unusually big and strong, the apple of his mother's eye, and he and his mother were always plotting how to escape from the troll's hill. It was not possible however, for the boulder was too heavy for them to move, and the troll always rolled it against the door before leaving. But as Hans got to be twelve years old, he was a strong boy, a very strong boy, and one evening he said to his mother: Tomorrow we try! The next morning after breakfast the troll left, having rolled the boulder against the door. When his steps died away, Hans and his mother both put their shoulders against the door, pushed and PUSHED ... and suddenly the boulder toppled BLLRMM ... BLLRMM ... down the hill and the door sprang open. Hans and his mother took each other by the hand and ran as fast as they could across the fields all the way to Høm. The peasant said: Hmm..that trip took a long while! He was otherwise glad to have his wife back, but he said: This boy of yours, we can't afford to feed him! Hans said: Don't worry, just give me some sandwiches and a strong stick, and I'll make my way through the world! As said, so done. The woman made a pack of sandwiches, but when the peasant brought Hans a stick, he swung it once and it broke like a match. The peasant then brought him one of oak, but even that broke like a match when Hans swung it. The peasant then took him to the blacksmith who forged Hans a stick of iron. Hans swung it and said: That's for me! Then he shook hands with the peasant, kissed his mother good-bye, took his pack and his stick and went out into the wide world.

Hans walked for quite a while, and by now it was getting close to lunch time. As he walked past Seem plantation, he noticed a man felling trees, and he stopped for a moment to watch. This was no ordinary tree feller. He did not use an axe, nor a saw. Instead, he walked up to a tree, threw his arms around it, and yanked it right out of the ground. He was so terribly strong! Hans looked on and then said: "That's mighty hard work, but I guess it must be well paid?" "No," said the tree feller, "that's just the pity of it, I get paid very little." "Then, why do it?" said Hans. "Why don't you come with me? I have a pack of sandwiches, and the two of us will easily make our way through the world!" "Good idea," said the tree feller, and he went to get his coat that was hanging nearby on a low branch, and the two went off together. After a while, they came to a stone crusher who crushed stones with which to repair the road, and they stopped for a moment to watch. This was no ordinary stone crusher, for he did not use a mallet or sledge for his work. Instead, he took one large stone in each hand, flung them together so the fragments flew, and they turned into gravel. "That's mighty hard work," said Hans, "but I guess you must get paid well?" "No, that's just the pity of it," said the stone crusher, "I actually get paid very little." "Then why do it?" said Hans. "Why don't you come with the tree feller and me, for I have a pack of sandwiches, and the three of us will easily make our way through the world." "Good idea," said the stone crusher and went to fetch his coat which was lying on a pile of gravel nearby. The three went on together, and as they walked shared the sandwiches Hans' mother had made. They were hungry, and the sandwiches tasted good.

Toward evening they approached Gelsbro forest and the road took them straight into the forest where soon it was quite dark, but they walked on till they saw up ahead a tiny light gleaming. As they got closer it turned out to be a candle in a window of a small hut. Hans knocked on the door, and when no one answered, he opened the door and they walked in. The room was quite empty except that in the middle of the floor stood a table beautifully set for three, with a white tablecloth, silver and crystal glasses, and all the fine dishes your heart could desire. There was

412

roast goose and stewed red cabbage, lamb fricassee and good red wine, fresh rye bread and Gorgonzola cheese, enough to tempt the palate of a king. Hans said, "Well, it would be a pity to let this fine food get cold, so we had better eat." As said, so done. They sat down and ate everything.

When the meal was finished they again searched the room to find a clue to who lived here, but all they found was a trap door in the floor in a corner of the room. They opened it. Below a dark shaft led down, they knew not where, and a large, strong basket hung on a stout rope. Hans jumped into the basket and told the others to let him down, and so they did. The shaft was pitch dark, but as Hans got farther and farther down, it began to lighten a bit, and suddenly the basket with Hans aboard landed in a beautiful, sunny garden. It was absolutely delightful: flowers everywhere, trees casting gentle shade, birds singing, a white marble fountain gushing water in the center, and beyond the fountain a splendid castle lifting its slender spires toward the blue sky. Hans strode around the fountain and up the broad marble stairway to the castle and into the entrance hall. There he looked around, but not a soul could be seen anywhere. He noticed, however, that in the wall hung a small silver whistle on a golden nail. Hans took it down, examined it, and finally put it to his lips and blew ... pwuiiiittt!! And presto, right out of the floor jumped a little green man. He took off his hat and bowed deeply to Hans, saying "Master, what do you bid me?" "Who are you?" asked Hans. "I am the Little Green Man" replied the little green man, "what do you bid me?" "Tell me who lives here," said Hans. "Oh, it is a terrible story," said the little green man, "here used to live the king and the queen with their daughter, the princess, but a dreadful dragon came one day and ate everyone except the princess, whom it now keeps prisoner in the back room." "Then I had better go and rescue her," said Hans. "No, no!" cried the little green man, "for it is a dreadful dragon and it will immediately eat you too!" "We'll see about that," said Hans. Then he marched right through the castle until he came to the back room, and he could immediately see that this was indeed where the dragon was, for evil-smelling, acrid smoke curled out from under the door. Hans took a good grip on his iron stick, then he kicked the door open and ... RROOOOWR!! The dragon jumped right at him, smoke and fire belching from its throat, but Hans swung his stick once: WHAP! ... twice: WHAP!! and the dragon fell dead with a broken neck. The princess rushed out and threw her arms around Hans' neck, crying "Thank you, thank you, Hans, my hero!" Hans took her out in the garden so she could wash her face in the fountain and freshen up a bit after her ordeal. Then they walked over to where the basket was hanging, and Hans lifted her into it and yanked on the rope. His two comrades above started hoisting it, and it disappeared out of sight, but soon after, it came back down. Hans was about to step into it, but suddenly he got a premonition, and instead he threw in his iron stick and yanked on the rope. The basket was hoisted up quite a ways, but suddenly the people above let go of the rope and the basket came crashing down. It would have killed Hans, had he been aboard! Hans realized that his comrades must be too evil at heart to be entrusted with a princess, and he sat pondering for a spell. Then he went over to the where the basket lay and took a good grip on the rope dangling from above, and then he started to climb up the rope. It was hard work, hand over hand, dark in the shaft all around him, but he had tenacity and slowly gained way upward! At long, long last he got hold of the edge of the floor in the little hut and wearily pulled himself up into the room. For fully ten minutes he lay gasping to catch his breath; then he got up and went outside, but neither the princess nor his two treacherous companions could be seen anywhere. He stood there, deep in thought with his hands thrust into his pockets, and suddenly he felt his fingers touching the little silver whistle. He pulled it out, put it to his lips and blew ... pwuiiiittt!! And presto, right out of the floor jumped the little green man. He took off his hat and bowed deeply to Hans, saying "Master, what do you bid me?" Hans said to him, "I need a horse!" The little green man snapped his fingers and lo, there stood a fine charger, its saddle and bridle inlaid with silver. Hans jumped into the saddle and galloped down the dark path. Horse and rider swiftly raced through the dark forest, and finally, up ahead Hans spied the two culprits dragging the princess between them. As Hans bore down on them they turned to fight, but Hans swung his iron stick once: Whap! and the tree feller was down! Then Whap!! and the stone crusher was done for. The princess threw herself around Hans' neck and cried, "Oh Hans, you saved me again!" But Hans just said, "Shucks, any time, fair princess." Then he scooped her up and put her in the saddle in front of him, and together they rode away and lived happily ever after.

4. Op, op dovne krop   (Up, up lazy bones
   Ellers pisker jeg dig op   Otherwise I'll whip you up
   Boller vil jeg have   Sugar buns I want
   I min lille mave.   In my little stomach.)

5. William L. Shirer, *The Rise and Fall of the Third Reich* (New York: Simon and Schuster, 1960), p. 122.

6. Ronald Lewin, *Ultra Goes to War* (New York: McGraw-Hill, 1978), p. 30.

7. Her slibes knive   (Knife sharpening here
   Her slibes sakse   Scissor sharpening here
   Sakse og knive slibes   Scissor and knife sharpening here
   :Her er: Skærslipperen.   :Here is: the knifegrinder.)
   :Sild er godt: (:Herring is good:
   Store ferske sild er godt   Large, fresh herring is good
   Tre pund for halvtres øre!   Three pounds for fifty øre.)

8. *I Skoven skulle være Gilde* (Forest Party), *Dengang jeg drog Afsted* (Marching off to War), *Kejseren af Kinesiens Land* (The Emperor of China), *Vinden er saa Føjelig* (The Breeze is Agreeable), *Tingelingelater Tinsoldater* (Ding-dong Tinsoldiers), *Hønsefødder og Gulerødder* (Hens' Feet and Carrots), *Fra Tyskland uddrog en Flok Spillemænd* (Musicians came from Germany), *Per Nilen har trukket sin Jolle i Land* (Per Nilen Dragged his Boat Ashore), *Storken sidder paa Bondens Tag* (The Stork is Perched on the Farmer's Roof) ...

9. It is interesting to note that people in the border areas of Schleswig-Holstein can be easily identified as being of Danish or German origin based on ethnologic evidence. See Claus Eskildsen, *Dansk Grænselære* (Copenhagen: C. A. Reitzels Forlag, Axel Sandal, 1939).

10. A clear and concise description of Hitler's accession to the chancellorship is given by Henry Ashby Turner in his book *Hitler's Thirty Days to Power: January 1933* (New York: Addison Wesley, 1997).

11. Shirer, p. 117-118.

12. Donde's theme song:
    Saa ska' vi altsaa te'et igen   (So, here we go again
    Nu spiller Donde og hans mænd,   Here play Donde and his men
    Lad unge hjerter slaa i takt   Let young hearts beat in sync
    mens dansen gaar   while dancing
    Med fuld musik fra   With rousing music from
    København og Kalundborg   Copenhagen and Kalundborg
    Lad ung og gammel, søster, bror   Let young and old, sister, brother
    Kun nynne med i blandet kor   Just sing along in happy chorus
    Lad pigen danse med sin ven   Let the girl dance with her friend
    Saa ska' vi altsaa te'et igen!   So, here we go again!)

13. Ball-point pens, later to be scattered like chaff to the farthest corners of the world, were still in the future.

414

14. The other two were *Livjægerkorpset* and *Akademisk Skyttekorps.*

15. Claiming credibility from a description of the early Teutonic tribes by the Roman writer Tacitus, the idea of a pure racial strain, rich in martial virility, emanating from the Hercynian forest, has since the Middle Ages intermittently attracted public attention and agitated some German scholars. Certain passages in Tacitus' *Germania* were eagerly embraced by scholars and used by the Nazis to demonstrate that the Third Reich inhabitants were martial by nature. For example: "You will not so readily persuade them to plough the land and wait for the year's returns as to challenge the enemy and earn wounds: Besides, it seems limp and slack to get with the sweating of your brow what you can gain with the shedding of your blood." Tacitus, p. 285.

16. For the purpose of "authenticating" the racial origins, Himmler already in 1935 set up a special section of the SS labeled *Ahnenerbe*, roughly translatable as Ancestral Heritage, to uncover the origins of the German race. In the inimitable manner of the Nazis, the "racial scientists" stood the research on its head by claiming their thesis of racial superiority as axiom and accepting only supportive evidence. In his book *Das "Ahnenerbe" der SS 1935-1945* (Stuttgart: Deutsche Verlags-Anstalt, 1974), Michael H. Kater gives a thorough description of this undertaking that owed its existence to a pursuit of Hitler's racial ideas, twisted by Himmler's bizarre personality. It also shows the Nazi regime as less of a monolith than a confused arena of multiple institutional forces enmeshed in an unending struggle for power.

17. The reason for Stalin's delay may have been the fact that the Soviet Union was engaged in a campaign against Japanese forces in Mongolia – an undeclared war in fact – where a young general, Georgi Zhukov, was distinguishing himself. See Alvin D. Coox, *Nomonhan: Japan against Russia, 1939* (Stanford, California: Stanford University Press, 1985).

18. For a good, concise description of the fortifications and their eventual fate, see Anthony Kemp, *The Maginot Line: Myth and Reality* (New York: Military Heritage Press, 1988).

19. Swedish ore shipments on the order of ten million tons annually were essential to the German war industry. Alan S. Milward, *Die Deutsche Kriegswirtschaft 1939-1945* (Stuttgart: Deutsche Verlagsanstalt, 1966), p. 47.

20. Besides maintaining a brisk pace of ore delivery, the Swedes were supportive in many other matters as well.

21. It was just as well that surrender was not to be. Hitler's plans, unknown outside a small top-level Nazi group, involved virtual annihilation of the British as a nation: forcible permanent removal of all males between seventeen and forty-five to labor camps on the continent, and the thorough and systematic looting of the country. It is clear, however, that Churchill was one of the few who understood Hitler's overall aims, as revealed in an interview with Chicago Daily News reporter Edgar Ansel Mowrer. In the course of their conversation, Churchill said: "Make no mistake: the position of the United States will, if Great Britain goes under, be one of dire jeopardy ... if he (Hitler) got us down, he would go for you at once." The statements were promptly suppressed by Brendan Bracken, British Minister for Information. See Martin Gilbert, *The Churchill War Papers, Vol. 2: Never Surrender, May 1940-December 1940* (New York: Norton, 1995), pp. 532-33.

22. William Manchester *The Last Lion* (Boston: Little, Brown and Company, 1988) gives more details. Only fragments of Churchill's oration could be perceived at the time in Denmark, as the Germans jammed the BBC news broadcasts, but the gist of the message came through to some of us.

23. It is remarkable, yet often overlooked, that the British leadership in the summer of 1940 was well aware that beating Germany was for reasons of demography and industrial capacity simply not a possibility for Britain alone.

24. In contemporary usage the term euthanasia refers to "mercy killing," i.e. painlessly ending the life of a terminally ill person at his or her request. The Nazis used the term in referring to their policy which, however, was based on premises different from that of mercy. First, the decision to terminate a life was taken by an official body rather than by the patient or the patient's family. Second, the criterion was not the patient's welfare (avoidance of pain) but whether the patient's life was judged of value to the community. In this form the idea predated the Nazis, having been raised by two German professors, Karl Binding and Alfred Hoche, in the 1920s. They suggested that Germany should divest itself of *Ballastexistenzen*, living burdens, to speed national revival after World War One.

25. Henry Friedlander gives a thorough description of the murder programs in his book *The Origins of Nazi Genocide: From Euthanasia to the Final Solution* (Chapel Hill, North Carolina: University of North Carolina Press, 1995).

26. In the Danish army each company numbered its soldiers by height, so that the tallest in the battalion's fourth company became designated as #401, proceeding to the shortest who would receive the highest number. When in basic training in Odense, I was #412 in Fourth Company. We were addressed only by number and knew each other by number, rarely bothering to learn names. The Danish dragoons used a different system, naming the individual for the village from which he came. My great-grandfather thus became known as Tarp, a local place name.

27. Stalin had refused to believe warnings from both Churchill and Roosevelt that the attack was imminent, and the Russians paid dearly for their dictator's innate distrust of capitalist statesmen.

28. John Keegan, *The Second World War* (New York: Viking Penguin, 1989), p. 186.

29. The Führer's boast proved premature, though no more so than the assessment by the American General Staff who in July had advised U.S. newspaper editors that the collapse of the Soviet Union was only a matter of a few weeks. In August, 1941, he revealed certain other plans, as follows, to the Danish envoy, O. C. Mohr, in Berlin: "We can no longer permit Germans to emigrate to America. On the other hand, we must draw Norwegians, Swedes, Danes and Dutchmen into our eastern regions. They will be citizens of the German Reich. These German settlers will live on spacious, beautiful farms. The German soldiers will be quartered in impressive buildings, rulers in palaces ..." Henning Tjørnehøj *Rigets bedste mænd* (Copenhagen: Gyldendal, 1990), p. 177.

30. Among those unable to judge the progress of the war was Charles Lindberg who fourteen years earlier had dazzled the world by making the first transatlantic west-to-east flight. He had naively swallowed Nazi propaganda, accepting in 1938 from Hitler the "Service Cross of the German Eagle with Star." He now condemned Britain for having encouraged the smaller nations to fight against hopeless odds. President Roosevelt took a more realistic view of the situation and in October made a decision of fateful consequence to this and all future wars, as he issued an order to attempt production of an atom bomb. But this immense new project was to remain shrouded in complete secrecy for another four years.

31. The Japanese expected the attack and the American naval losses to break American morale and resign the U.S. public to acceptance of Japanese conquests in Southeast Asia. Instead, it changed in a heartbeat the lingering mood of isolationism.

32. The military consequences of this order excited postwar debate already at the Nuremberg Trial with some German staff officers asserting that it may have prevented German collapse at certain points in the Front. Overall, however, it proved costly in German lives.

33. In his book *The Life and Death of Adolf Hitler* (New York: Praeger Publishers, Inc., 1973), pp. 460-61, Robert Payne relates how Göring tells the following about the POW camps: "After having eaten everything possible, including the soles of their

boots, they began to eat each other, and what is more serious, have eaten a German sentinel." It is the kind of story Göring liked to share with Hitler, who would slap his thigh and burst into a fit of giggles.

34. Sigurd Laursen also provided some money by altering and selling certain matériel for us such as military bicycles we had stolen from the Wehrmacht.

35. Gerhard L. Weinberg, *A World At Arms* (New York: Cambridge University Press, 1994), pp. 329-30.

36. Legend has it that young maidens are particularly at peril from the elfin king. Legend further informs us that his back is only a hollow cavity, so that a girl easily can unveil his identity by viewing him from behind.

37. Speer, a gifted young architect and devoted follower of Hitler, raised output by fifty percent in the first six months after taking over. See Alan S. Milward, *Die Deutsche Kriegswirtschaft 1939-1945* (Stuttgart: Deutsche Verlags-Anstalt, 1966).

38. As we had no confidence that the Danish military leadership would be any less dilatory than it had been at the German attack in 1940, we planned to take one platoon with two machine guns and make a dash for Ribe on our own cognizance. If the invasion should come after our discharge, we would do it on our own. The scheme was ambitious though militarily sound.

39. Certain targets in Britain were protected by barrage balloons, whose steel anchoring cable discouraged low-level attack by enemy bombers. When encountered in Denmark, the German authorities declared the balloons to be military property and forbade civilians to touch them, but this was ignored in the privacy of the countryside.

40. In German the piece is entitled *Was kann der Sigismund dafür dass er so schön ist.*

41. The original *Lilli Marlene* was actually sung by the Norwegian Lale Andersson, but most of the soldiers did not know that.

42. People used the coins as symbolic jewelry by tying a narrow silk ribbon through the holes in one 5-øre, one 2-øre and two 1-øre coins, carrying the polished coins on the lapel (all these coins had a hole in the center). The sum of nine indicated the date, and the number of coins the month of the German invasion in 1940.

43. In October he issued his infamous top secret Commando Order. It stipulated that captured enemy special forces be immediately executed, in flagrant violation of the Geneva Convention. As a result a number of British and American prisoners were killed in cold blood. Shirer, p. 955.

44. In the unequal contest, Stroop's official count came to 56,065 people killed. Shirer, p. 978.

45. The code later became simplified by including at the end of each newscast a sentence ostensibly sending greetings to some girls. It would typically run: "Tonight we have special greetings to Gudrun, Lise, Sylvia, Mette, Anna, Karen, Marie ..." The list, new every night, would comprise more than a dozen girls' names. The name selected as code for our drop had been established by courier, and this system allowed the announcer to alert several groups in different locations.

46. The raid was carried out by Otto Skorzeny, an SS Standartenführer known as "Hitler's Commando."

47. The handover was deservedly criticized in a secret communication from the British to the Danish admiralty. Jørgen Hæstrup, *European Resistance Movements, 1939-1945: A Complete History* (Westport, Connecticut: Mechler Publishing, 1981).

48. Niels Alkil, *Besættelsestidens Fakta: Dokumentarisk Haandbog* (Copenhagen: J. H. Schultz Forlag, 1945).

49. Jørgen Hæstrup, ed., *Besættelsens Hvem-Hvad-Hvor* (Copenhagen: Politikens Forlag, 1963), pp. 91-92.

50. Dalton, Hugh. *The Fateful Years: Memoirs 1931-1945.* (London: Frederick Muller Ltd.), 1957. p. 7.

51. American fliers also became actively engaged. The USAF lost 135 airmen in operations over Denmark.

52. The incident took place when Molotov was negotiating with Ribbentrop questions arising from friction between Germany and the Soviet Union after the partition of Poland. Carrying on the discussions after RAF bombers had forced the negotiators to move to an air raid shelter, the Germans insisted that Britain was effectively beaten. Molotov replied, "If that is so, why are we in this shelter, and whose are these bombs which fall?" Shirer, p. 809.

53. More correctly: Nelholts Maskinfabrik in Ørnegade, which made the Ruko hardware.

54. Prior to Pearl Harbor, conventional wisdom in the American military held the Japanese to be imitators whose slanted eyes prevented them from becoming proficient pilots.The lightning Japanese conquests and the painful experience of the Guadalcanal campaign restored a measure of balance in the American assessment of the Japanese. A deeper understanding and appreciation of cultural differences – conspicuously lacking not just in the United States but elsewhere in Western culture – eventually gained inroads. The process was greatly aided by Ruth Benedict's seminal anthropological research, briefly reported in her book, *The Crysanthemum and the Sword* (Cambridge, Massachusetts: The Riverside Press, 1946).

55. The other members with whom Thies and I were in touch at the time were Knud Axelholm, Otto Cortzen, Jørgen Danzer, Anders Georg, Per Markussen, Carl Johan Meyer, Birger Mouritzen, Kaj Nyholm, Hans Jørgen Olsen, Henning Vagn Petersen, Erik Sundø, Holger Søderberg, Erik Westh, and Jørgen Zacho. Several of these men were destined for substantial positions in government or industry which, coupled with Niels Jørgensen's professional expertise, accounted for the newssheet's success.

56. We collected ten pistols and a good deal of ammunition from the actress Ellen Gottschalck whose son, an officer in the Royal Guard, before going to Sweden had deposited them in a cellar under an Amager villa belonging to a manufacturer by the name of Knudsen. We later used the cellar for the contents of a railroad car from Amagerbanen, a private rail line. The car had been loaded with Danish army rifles, model 1889, and was destined for Germany, but we sidetracked it with the help of a yard assistant. On another occasion the Germans had confiscated an automatic Eickhoff printing press from a printer, Erik Rasmussen, in Studiestræde. It had been put on a truck for transport, and while the guards were leisurely having lunch, the truck was left standing at the short end of Studiestræde. I held up and removed the driver while Thies took the press to a garage in Blaagaardsgade.

57. Actually, the Anglo-American cooperation had already begun in the early fall of 1940 with the Tizard Mission which arranged an exchange of the two countries' technical secrets. Historically unprecedented, it redounded to immense mutual advantage. See David Zimmerman, *Top Secret Exchange. The Tizard Mission and the Scientific War,* (Montreal: McGill University Press, 1996).

58. By stating these points as war aims, America in effect was taking an important step toward active involvement in the war. Unless attacked, a democracy cannot go to war without strong and stated reasons. The declaration became known as the Atlantic Charter.

59. In total the United States alone delivered during the war to Russia 22,000 aircraft, 12,000 tanks, 2,000 locomotives, 2.7 million tons of gasoline, 13 million pairs of boots, and tens of millions of rations; but the item that perhaps most enhanced the Red Army's tactical potency as a fighting force was 500,000 General Motors six-by-six trucks that gave it a hitherto unknown mobility.

60. Eric Hobsbawm gives a more profound analysis of the differences in his book *The Age of Extremes*, p. 132: "Yet European Fascism ... belonged essentially to the era of

democracy and the common man, while the very concept of a 'movement' of mass mobilization for novel, indeed for would-be revolutionary purposes, behind self-selected leaders, made no sense in Hirohito's Japan. The Prussian army and tradition, rather than Hitler, fitted their view of the world. In short, despite the similarities with German national socialism, Japan was not fascist."

61. Wary of the "Jewish problem" before and during the early part of the war, the Swedes had come around to granting shelter to Jewish refugees who reached their shores. Swedish relief efforts also got underway. For a well-documented account of the Swedish record, see Steven Koblik, *The Stones Cry Out: Sweden's Response to the Persecution of the Jews*, (New York: Holocaust Library, 1988).

62. Børge Outze had arranged for the boat through a man by the name of Erling Kjær.

63. Whereas religious persecution has been a common affliction of Jewish life within Christian communities, the onset of *racial* persecution has been located in the period of the Spanish Inquisition by Benzion Netanyahu in his book *The Origins of the Inquisition in Fifteenth Century Spain* (New York: Random House, 1995). Under pressure, some 100,000 Spanish Jews had converted to Christianity by the early fifteenth century. Many of these *conversos* advanced to high posts in the royal governments of Aragon and Castile and in city administrations, positions from which they had been barred as Jews. The Christian establishment's resentment of the *conversos'* success caused some cities by midcentury to enact statutes to exclude the *conversos* based on a requirement of "blood purity" (in Spanish *limpieza de sangre*). Proposed as doctrine, the idea was to disqualify people of Jewish "impure" blood, which by extension included the *conversos*.

64. Incredibly, Hitler permitted a number of Jews to remain on active duty in the Wehrmacht, actually thousands of men of Jewish descent, what the Nazis contemptuously called *Mischlinge*, mongrels, as well as many they termed "full Jews." Ongoing research by Yale historian Bryan Riggs has uncovered a 1944 German army personnel document listing 77 high-ranking officers "of mixed Jewish race or married to a Jew." The list includes two generals, eight lieutenant generals, five major generals, and 23 colonels. Hitler personally excepted all 77 on the list from a 1935 law barring anyone with a Jewish grandparent from becoming an officer.

65. Weinberg, pp. 472-73.

66. Børge Rosenbaum became well known in the U.S. as an entertainer under the name Victor Borge.

67. For more information, see Samuel Abrahamsen, *Norway's Response to the Holocaust: A Historical Perspective* (Washington, D.C.: Holocaust Library, 1991).

68. For a succinct description of the Freedom Council, see Aage Trommer, "Scandinavia and the Turn of the Tide," in *Scandinavia During the Second World War*, ed. by Henrik S. Nissen (Minneapolis, Minn.: The University of Minnesota Press, 1983).

69. This was a significant step in gaining for the resistance movement both respectability and acceptance. The Freedom Council later obtained recognition by the Allies as an underground government.

70. Niels Jørgensen was also critical of the Freedom Council's presuming to speak on behalf of all Danish resistance, as he considered the Council to have insufficiently diverse composition. For details on this, see Jon Vedel, "Opposition til Danmarks Frihedsråd 1943/44," in *Historisk Tidsskrift* (Copenhagen: Gyldendal, 1983), Bind 83.

71. It was in the nature of sabotage that realization and success of a particular action usually depended on 1) the appearance of some unforeseeable opportunity and 2) who was on hand to take part.

72. See Peter Calvocoressi, Guy Wint and John Pritchard *Total War* (London: Viking, 1972) pp. 413-25.

73. For a detailed discussion of the deception scheme, see Lewin, pp. 309-14.

74. Niels Christensen, Viggo Hansen, Jens Carl Jepsen, Svend Jacob Kjær, Johannes Prahl and Valdemar Sørensen. They were men I had known for years, though not well, but Aage, who knew them very well from growing up with them and working with them in the auxiliary police service, composed the list and assured me of their reliability.

75. The arrival of the American P-51 "Mustang" vastly boosted the Allied fighter strength.

76. Besides the one in Hovgaardsgade we also had one on Sdr. Fasanvej and another in the Østerbro district.

77. Earlier we had met with members of the *Frie Danske* organization to discuss the proposed "sabotage stop" but had failed to agree.

78. Code named *Magic* this capability conferred upon the Allies the same advantage vis-à-vis the Japanese as they enjoyed vis-à-vis the Germans by means of Ultra.

79. This was revealed in the inquiry following the Japanese attack. Roberta Wohlstetter in her classic analysis of the 39 volumes of hearing transcript has stated flatly:

    "Not only did we know in advance how the Japanese ambassadors in Washington were advised and how much they were instructed to say, but we also were listening to top secret messages on the Tokyo-Berlin and the Tokyo-Rome circuits ... The signals lay scattered in a number of different agencies; some were decoded, some were not; some travelled through rapid channels of communication, some were blocked by technical or procedural delays; some never reached a center of decision. For complete details, see Roberta Wohlstetter, *Pearl Harbor: Warning and Decision* (Stanford, California: Stanford University Press, 1962).

80. Lynn Crost, *Honor by Fire: Japanese Americans at War in Europe & the Pacific* (Novato, California: Presidio Press, 1994).

81. Randschau later told me how they made the arrest. On each of the four street corners forming the intersection two agents were posted. Marquart approached me head on, and two agents came up from behind. Counting the driver, the team thus came to twelve men. This may seem profligate with manpower, but if the target person (I in this case) were to break away and run, at least two of the street corner agents would have a close if not clear shot at him as he ran down any street.

82. A Brazilian expeditionary corps fought in Italy alongside American forces. German U-boat and raider predation on Brazilian shipping had driven the country to take that ultimate step, the only Latin American country to do so.

83. See Arthur Bryant *The Turn of the Tide* (Garden City, New York: Doubleday & Company, 1957). The Alanbrooke diaries detail the unsuccessful British efforts to enlist Turkey's participation with the Allies.

84. In many other matters the Swedes were supportive as well. They built fishing craft for the German Navy, intended for minesweeping; chartered small tankers to refuel U-boats; cooperated with the German Navy in laying an anti-submarine net in the Sound; and provided transit and rail transportation for German troop movements. The transit was of particular help to the German military and the volume was large. In the fifteen months from July 1940, Swedish railways carried a daily load of 1,800 soldiers and weapons, and 75,000 tons of military supplies across Swedish territory. Henry Denham provides a thorough insight into Swedish preferences in his book *Inside the Nazi Ring* (London: John Murray Ltd., 1984).

85. For all of the effort Sweden expended to please the Nazis, the German High Command in December, 1942, issued orders to draft an invasion plan to occupy the country. General Rudolf Bamler prepared the plan which involved an attack from Norway where three extra divisions would be available. The operation was never implemented, and the Swedes had no inkling of the possibility until it came to light after the war.

86. Known in Danish as a *Lommebog*, this carried besides a calendar miscellaneous use-

ful information such as weights and measures, a map of Denmark, opening hours of government offices, national flags, income tax rates, etc.

87. Sigurd Laursen continued to do useful resistance work through the rest of the war. Oscar Førsting was an older man to whom I sent a few diary records for safekeeping from time to time. Vilspang was a foreman in Ole Kuhlman's father's locomotive shop in Frederikssund. My contact with him was largely for newssheet distribution. He actually built in the locomotive shop an armored car on an old truck body and took it into action at the time of the German surrender by shooting up a group of HIPO, an auxiliary terrorist force the Germans had recruited from Danish prison populations during the last months of the war. They were holed up on one of the Zealand north shore bathing beaches in a sumnmer cottage belonging to a collaborator. The armored car made short work of the cottage which got somewhat perforated and blood splattered in the process, but it was still serviceable. It was in that cottage I spent a week with the remnants of the Ribe group later in the summer. The armored car is now standing outside Frihedsmuseet, the Liberation Museum, in Copenhagen.

88. The V-1, V for *Vergeltungswaffe* (Retaliation Weapon) was a flying bomb powered by a pulse jet. The first was launched on 13 June 1944 and landed near Gravesend in England. Some of the British fighters, notably the Hurricanes, were fast enough to catch these bombs in flight and bring them down with cannon fire or by deflecting the bomb's stubby wing with the fighter's wingtip, sending it spinning to the ground before reaching the target. In this manner the Royal Air Force brought down 1,771 of the bombs. The rest landed on London and elsewhere.

89. A Total of 10,492 were sent against London before the Allies overran the launching sites. Of these, only 2,419 reached their target, see Calvocoressi, p. 556.

90. It was, however, followed by some supergun development in Britain in the 1980s, one of the monsters being shipped to Iraq during the Gulf War.

91. Descendants of these appeared forty years later in the Near East, used by the Turks against the Kurds, and one was used in a Japanese subway attack by a terrorist group in 1995.

92. Another fundamental question was how fission could be slowed during manufacture to keep the process under control. The Germans recognized the isotope of "heavy water" as usable for this purpose and had by occupation of Norway incidentally gained possession of the world's only large facility capable of producing it. The Norwegian plant was sabotaged in a series of Allied actions in 1943.

93. Niels Jørgensen, ed., *Fem Aars Kamp for Friheden* (Copenhagen: Alfred G. Hassings Forlag, 1966), VI, pp. 8-9.

94. As supplementary lien on their loyalty, Hitler during the war instituted an enormous, secret program of systematic bribery involving virtually all officers at the highest command levels. The most enthusiastic of his followers, people such as Guderian, Schörner, Model, or Dönitz, could also expect rewards in the form of estates, conveniently stolen in occupied lands. Weinberg, p. 455.

95. Weinberg, p. 466.

96. For details of the assassination plot see Payne, pp. 513-17. A first-rate account of German resistance to the Nazis is written by Joachim Fest in his book *Plotting Hitler's Death: The Story of the German Resistance* (New York: Henry Holt & Company, Inc., 1996).

97. Neuengamme's population stayed fairly steady at about 10,000 inmates throughout the war with an average death rate of 50 per day, making the life expectancy in the camp a mere 200 days.

98. In order to save flour the bread contained a generous admixture of sawdust filler which, of course, is without nutritional value to a human body.

99. Some of them did indulge in some shouted exchange of information, but their

leader told them, "Snak ikke med de forbrydere." (Don't speak with those criminals.) One of our number, police chief Simoni from Varde, furiously identified himself and cursed them roundly and at length.

100. Paul Thygesen survived his ordeal in Germany, later to become chief surgeon at Gentofte General Hospital near Copenhagen.

101. Telford Taylor, *The Anatomy of the Nuremberg Trials* (Boston: Little, Brown, 1992), pp. 427-431.

102. Some speculation about this question has been raised by Christopher R. Browning in his book *Ordinary Men: Police Battalion 101 and the Final Solution in Poland* (London, Harper-Collins, 1992) and Daniel Goldhagen, *Hitler's Willing Executioners* (New York, Alfred A. Knopf, 1996).

103. The concentration camp system comprised 52 main camps with 1202 satellite camps scattered throughout Germany and her eastern neighbors. Map 6 shows a few of the main camps plus Wansleben and Husum, the latter a satellite of Neuengamme. For a summary of the several categories of camps and the number in each category, see Gudrun Schwarz, *Die nationalsozialistichen Lager* (Frankfurt-am-Main, Campus Verlag, 1990).

104. Keegan, p. 441.

105. The very complex problem of prisoner repatriation is well exposed by Denis Hills in his book *Tyrants and Mountains* (London, John Murray, Ltd., 1992).

106. Eisenhower describes some of the denazification program in his book *Crusade in Europe* (Garden City, New York: Doubleday, 1948), p. 434.

107. Shortly afterward, Thies in a similar situation also had to resort to shooting. The outcome was not fatal to the scoundrel who was wounded in the leg. We decided to keep to ourselves any incident involving shooting, as we had previously done in the underground. We both found it distasteful to dwell on bloodshed and thought it anyway peripheral to our success or failure in catching the people we were after.

108. Nazi emblems and decorations were popular, as well as the innumerable medals struck to commemorate particular events. The more discerning observer could find quite intrigueing memorabilia, some of historical interest. Major Anton Panowicz of the 1104 Combat Engineer Group showed me the telephone directory from Hitler's Bad Nauheim headquarters. Its twenty-eight typewritten pages contained a few dozen listings, ranging from SS Reichsführer Himmler to such mundane ones as whom to call in the village in case of water damage.

109. Lord Alanbrook mentions this in his memoirs, see Arthur Bryant, *Triumph in the West,* (London: Collins, 1959), p. 508.

110. Shirer, p. 1133.

111. The Russians lost 304,000 killed, wounded and missing. See Keegan, p. 533.

112. The Germans reserved their gasoline for military vehicles and aircraft, operating most civilian vehicles by means of gasgenerators. These were cylindrical vessels, resembling a domestic water heater, in which pieces of wood were burned in incomplete combustion. The gas produced by this process contained sufficient carbonmonoxide plus traces of other hydrocarbons to fuel a reciprocating engine, although with reduced power output. The economy of occupied Europe kept its transportation system functioning by such German resourcefulness and toward the end of the war even the Wehrmacht had to resort to generator gas for some of its vehicles. Certain hardwoods such as beech were particularly suitable for the gas generators. See Niels A. Skov and Mark L. Papworth, *The Pegasus Unit* (Tacoma, Washington: Mercury Press, 1976), and F. Jantsch, *Fahrzeuggeneratoren* (Berlin: Joh. Kasper & Co., 1943).

113. The country narrowly escaped Russian occupation except for the island of Bornholm in the Baltic. At the time, the Danish public was unaware of the enormous political implications of the timely British arrival and would almost as happily have re-

ceived Russian liberators, but the subsequent experience of the Bornholmers and their protracted difficulties in expelling the Russians occupiers shortly became an object lesson.

114. Valdemar Sørensen was to suffer severe headaches for several years while his body slowly purged itself of lead.

115. Thies' choice was a model that later became a true collector's item. The style of my BMW made later postwar designs look like packing crates by comparison.

116. My problem, not uncommon, was later neatly encapsulated by Piet Hein in one of his Grooks: The errors hardest to condone in other people are one's own.

117. In later assessments of Roosevelt's dealings with Stalin it is often forgotten that cultural differences were poorly understood or appreciated by Western statesmen of the World War Two era. Research into cultural behavior is largely a postwar phenomenon. Ruth Benedict's study of the Japanese was an early eye-opener and proved valuable to MacArthur in his work in Japan.

118. An amendment to Denmark's mandatory sentencing law, Straffeloven, was passed on 1 June 1945. See Ditlev Tamm, *Retsopgøret efter besættelsen* (Viborg, Denmark: Nørhaven Bogtrykkeri, 1985) p. 267.

119. In the short period the statute was in force, 78 traitors were sentenced to death. Of these, 46 were executed by firing squad before the Danes recovered their equilibrium. The Danish authorities took great pains to carry out the executions discreetly and in a civilized manner, if that term can apply to any killing. The first took place in January, 1946, the last in July of 1950, more than five years after the liberation. See Ditlev Tamm, pp. 323, 335.

120. The U.S. Pacific Fleet comprised by the spring of 1945 a dozen battleships, fifty aircraft carriers, fifty cruisers, three hundred destroyers, and two hundred submarines. It was by itself the largest navy ever floated in all of history, and its 3,000-plane air force was also the largest.

121. Charles Mee gives a detailed discussion of these proceedings in his book *Meeting at Potsdam* (New York: M. Evans & Company, Inc., 1975).

122. In the 1980s I found to my surprise that none of my college students knew what the term iron curtain actually refers to, neither its theatrical origin nor its modern geopolitical connotation.

123. Our favorites: *You've got to Accentuate the Positive* and *Starliner.*

124. The four counts named were: 1) Planning, preparing, initiating, or waging wars of aggression; 2. Participating in a common plan to accomplish any of the foregoing; 3. War crimes, a broad category that included murder, ill-treatment and deportation of civilians in occupied territories to slave labor camps in Germany; crimes against prisoners of war; killing of hostages; the plunder or wanton destruction of cities, towns, and villages, and devastation not justified by military necessity; 4. Crimes against humanity, a new idea, applying to inhuman acts committed against civilians before or during the war on political, racial, and religious grounds.

125. The report here quoted from a Ukraine massacre should not lead anyone to the conclusion that Jews typically went to their death in this manner without fighting. Despite forbidding handicaps, the Jews fought bravely at the destruction of the Warsaw Ghetto, and many others resisted and succeeded in joining underground movements in Western Europe of guerilla bands in Poland and the Eastern Soviet areas. See also Calvocoressi, pp. 255-260.

126. Taylor, pp. 244-46.

127. In one of its last acts before collapsing, the Soviet Union forty-five years later confessed to having murdered 15,000 officers in the Katyn massacre and elsewhere in Poland.

128. Taylor, p. 252.

129. Taylor, p. 239.

130. On the General Assembly's request the International Law Commission formulated on this basis seven principles which have become part of the body of international law. See Calvocoressi, p. 575.

131. Inge was Ole's mother's name and Lotte was the universal name for female service personnel in the Finnish armed forces, later also used in the Danish Brigade where my sister and Ole had both served.

132. The Wanderer was never produced again after the war; in fact only one of the four companies rose from the destruction, the Deutsche Kraftwagen Werke, which produced the DKW. In the 1930s, the DKW was Europe's lowest-priced car, parts of the body made from plywood, and in Germany it was nicknamed the "pat-pat" from the distinctive stutter of its two-cycle engine. Its descendant today is sold as the Audi, last remnant of the famed cartel. The name Audi is an acronym drawn from the old cartel, Auto Union Deutscher Industrie.

133. Morian Hansen's decorations include the following: Distinguished Flying Cross, George Medal, 1939-1945 Star, Air Crew over Europe Star, France-Germany-Holland Rosette, Burma Star, Medal of Defense for England.

134. The cause of the crash was unusual. The DC-3s' elevators tended to flap in the wind when the aircraft were parked. In order to prevent this, wood wedges were inserted while the aircraft were waiting at the terminal. The wedges were supposed to be removed before departure, and it was moreover one of the pilot's duties to ascertain free movement of the controls during pre-flight checkout. Neither action was taken in this case, and the ill-fated plane took off with the wedges inserted and the elevators immobilized. The plane became airborne but stalled, crashed back onto the runway and exploded.

135. I think it fair to say that anyone who had been seriously involved in resisting the Germans was permanently affected by the experience in some way. The effects were not invariably negative, some individuals merely having become more assertive or decisive, while others were bizarre and seemingly shaped by opportunity and circumstance. In one such case, one of the Ribe group had landed a job as mail carrier on a rural route southwest of town. Some time later, large piles of undelivered mail was discovered in his basement, where he had dumped it on days when he did not feel like making the bike trip to the outlying villages. The discovery caused much hilarity in the old saboteur group, although the postal service took a dimmer view. When quizzed about it, he told me, "Niels, what I liked best about doing sabotage was that we did it against the strictest orders of the authorities. Now, when the postal service gave me detailed instructions about how to organize my route and delivery, telling me every call to make, every step to take, something in me just rebelled."

136. Most Danish historians of the period take a more charitable view of their country's performance. One notable exception is Aage Trommer, whose painstaking research led him to a different conclusion. He alludes to Danish sabotage during the occupation as being of very little military consequence though serving as "an alibi for the nation." Aage Trommer, *Myte og sandhed i besættelseshistorien* (Copenhagen: Gyldendal, 1974), p. 72. My own experience compels me to concur with Trommer.

137. Except for reminiscing with Thies at long intervals, I carried out that resolve until my college lectures more than thirty years later occasionally touched upon World War Two, by then just distant history that played itself out long before my students were born.

138. Despite the Danish government's misgivings lest Danish workers become nazified during their stay in Germany, some 40,000 took employment south of the border in 1941. *See, Fem Års Kamp for Friheden,* vol. 3. The Danish government need not have worried, however. The workers found little to attract them to Nazi ideas. Recruitment tapered off in step with Allied bombing of German industrial sites and ended with the devastation of Hamburg in 1943.

139. Danish exports of foodstuffs provided rations for 8.2 million Germans for most of the war. Keegan, p. 283.

140. J. Bradford De Long, "Productivity Growth, Convergence, and Welfare: Comment," *The American Economic Review*, Vol. 78, No. 5 (December 1988), pp. 1140-41.

141. It should be noted that all the countries eventually involved, certainly all the democracies, were reluctant to go to war. But even the French, pushed far enough, were willing to fight. Most Danes were not.

142. Personal communication, 4-13-1995.

143. Personal communication, 4-13-1995. Trommer assessed the extent and effects of railroad sabotage in Denmark, among other research projects.

144. Dalton, p. 9.

145. Even the British were not averse to accommodation in certain situations. For a description of British attitudes in the German-occupied Channel Islands, see Mardeleine Bunting, *The Model Occupation: The Channel Islands Under German Rule, 1940-45* (New York: Harper Collins, 1995).

146. In May 1995 I had occasion to spend some time with a group of old Danish Resistance fighters unveiling a memorial at Arlington National Cemetery. I was forcibly struck by a number of similar traits among us, going beyond superficial features. To my knowledge no systematic study has been done of such groups, although it might prove informative.

Bibliography

Abrahamsen, Samuel. *Norway's Response to the Holocaust: A Historical Perspective.* Washington, D.C.: Holocaust Library, 1991.

Alkil, Niels. *Besættelsestidens Fakta: Dokumentarisk Haandbog.* Copenhagen: J.H. Schultz Forlag, 1945.

Benedict, Ruth. *The Chrysanthemum and the Sword.* Cambridge, Massachusetts: The Riverside Press, 1946.

Bruun, Hans S. *Paa Dødsmarch Gennem Hitlers Tyskland.* Copenhagen: Nationalmuseet, 1976.

Bryant, Arthur. *The Turn of the Tide: A History of the War Years Based on the Diaries of Field-Marshal Lord Alanbrooke, Chief of the Imperial General Staff.* Garden City, New York: Doubleday & Company, 1957.

Bryant, Arthur. *Triumph in the West 1943-1946.* London: Collins, 1959.

Bunting, Mardeleine. *The Model Occupation: The Channel Islands Under German Rule, 1940-45.* New York: HarperCollins, 1995.

Butler, James Ramsay Montagu, Gwyer, J. M. A. and Ehrman, John. *Grand Strategy.* United Kingdom military series, vol. 5. London: H.M.Stationery Office, 1956.

Calvocoressi, Peter; Wint, Guy and Pritchard, John. *Total War.* 2d. ed. New York: Pantheon Books, 1989.

Coox, Alvin D. Nomonhan: *Japan Against Russia, 1939.* Stanford, California: Stanford University Press, 1985.

Crost, Lynn. *Honor by Fire: Japanese Americans at War in Europe & the Pacific.* Novato, California: Presidio Press, 1994.

Dalton, Hugh. *The Fateful Years: Memoirs 1931-1945.* London: Frederick Muller Ltd., 1957.

De Long, J. Bradford. »Productivity Growth, Convergence, and Welfare: Comment.« The American Economic Review, Vol. 78, no. 5, (December 1988).

Denham, Henry. *Inside the Nazi Ring.* London: John Murray Ltd., 1984.

Eisenhower, Dwight D. *Crusade in Europe.* Garden City, New York: Doubleday & Company, 1948.

Eskildsen, Claus. *Dansk Grænselære.* Copenhagen: C.A. Reitzels Forlag, Axel Sandal, 1939.

Fest, Joachim. *Plotting Hitler's Death: The Story of the German Resistance.* New York: Henry Holt & Company, Inc., 1996.

Fleron, Kate. *Kvinder i Modstandskampen.* Odense, Denmark: Forlaget Sirius, Andelsbogtrykkeriet i Odense, 1964.

Foot, M. R. D. *SOE in France.* London: H.M. Stationery Office, 1968.

Friedlander, Henry. *The Origin of Nazi Genocide: From Euthanasia to the Final Solution.* Chapel Hill, North Carolina: University of North Carolina Press, 1995.

Gilbert, Martin. *The Churchill War Papers, Vol. II: Never Surrender,* May 1940-December 1940. New York: W. W. Norton & Company, 1995.

Goldhagen, Daniel Jonah. *Hitler's Willing Executioners.* New York, Alfred A. Knopf, 1996.

Hein, Piet. *Grooks 4.* Garden City, New York: Doubleday and Company, Inc., 1973.

Hilderbrand, Robert C. *Dumbarton Oaks: The Origins of the United Nations and the Search for Postwar Security.* Chapel Hill, North Carolina: The University of North Carolina Press, 1990.

Hills, Denis. *Tyrants and Mountains: A Reckless Life.* London: John Murray Ltd., 1992.

Hitler, Adolf. *Mein Kampf.* Munich: Zentralverlag der NSDAP, 1938.

Hobsbawm, Eric, *The Age of Extremes,* New York: Pantheon Books, 1994.

Hong, Nathaniel. »The Illegal Press in German-Occupied Denmark April 1940-August 1943.« (unpublished Ph.D. thesis, University of Washington)

Hæstrup, Jørgen. *Hemmelig Alliance.* Copenhagen: Traning og Appels Forlag, 1959.

Hæstrup, Jørgen. *Besættelsens Hvem-Hvad-Hvor.* Copenhagen: Politikens Forlag, 1963.

Hæstrup, Jørgen. *European Resistance Movements, 1939-1945: A Complete History.* Westport, Connecticut: Meckler Publishing, 1981.

James, Robert Rhodes (ed.). *Churchill Speaks, Winston S. Churchill in Peace and War Collected Speeches, 1897-1963.* New York: Chelsea House, 1980.

Jantsch, F. *Fahrzeuggeneratoren.* Berlin: Joh. Kasper & Co, 1943.

Jørgensen, Niels. *Paa det Tyske Slavemarked.* Copenhagen: Stig Vendelkærs Forlag, 1964.

Jørgensen, Niels (ed.). *Fem Års Kamp for Friheden.* Copenhagen: Alfred G. Hassings Forlag A/S, 1966.

Keegan, John. *The Second World War.* New York: Viking Penguin, 1989.

Kemp, Anthony. *The Maginot Line: Myth and Reality.* New York: Military Heritage Press, 1988.

Koblik, Steven *Sweden's Development from Poverty to Affluence, 1750-1970* Minneapolis, Minnesota: The University of Minnesota Press, 1975.

Koblik, Steven *The Stones Cry Out: Sweden's Response to the Persecution of the Jews 1933-1945.* New York: Holocaust Library, 1988.

Kühnrich, Heinz. *Der Partisanenkrieg in Europa 1939-1945.* Stuttgart: Dietz, 1968.

Liddell Hart, Basil Henry, Sir. *History of the Second World War.* New York, Putnam, 1971.

Manchester, William. *American Caesar.* Boston: Little, Brown and Company, 1978.

Manchester, William. *The Glory and the Dream, Volume One.* Boston: Little, Brown and Company, 1974.

Manchester, William. *The Last Lion: Winston Spencer Churchill Alone 1932-1940.* Boston: Little, Brown and Company, 1988.

Mee, Charles L., Jr. *Meeting at Potsdam.* New York: M. Evans & Company, Inc., 1975.

Milward, Alan S. *Die Deutsche Kriegswirtschaft 1939-1945.* Stuttgart: Deutsche Verlags-Anstalt, 1966.

Netanyahu, B. *The Origins of the Inquisition in Fifteenth Century Spain.* New York: Random House, 1995.

Nissen, Henrik S. (ed.). *Scandinavia During the Second World War.* Minneapolis, Minn: The University of Minnesota Press, 1983.

Noakes, J. and Pridham, G. *Nazism: A History in Documents and Eyewitness Accounts, 1919-1945, Vol. 2.* New York: Schocken Books, 1988.

Payne, Robert. *The Life and Death of Adolf Hitler.* New York: Praeger Publishers, Inc., 1973.

Pitt, Barrie. *The Military History of World War Two.* New York: The Military Press, 1986.

Rosholt, Malcolm. *Flight in the China Air Space 1910-1950.* Amherst, Wisconsin: Palmer Publications, Inc., 1984.

Russell, Ruth B. *A History of the United Nations Charter.* Menasha, Wisconsin: The George Banta Company, Inc., 1958.

Schwarz, Gudrun. *Die nationalsozialistischen Lager.* Frankfurt-am-Main, Campus Verlag, 1990.

Skov, Niels A. and Papworth, Mark L. *The Pegasus Unit.* Tacoma, Washington: Mercury Press, 1976.

428

Stevenson, William. *A Man Called Intrepid.* New York: Harcourt Brace, 1964.Jovanovich, 1976.

Sykes, Christopher. *Tormented Loyalty: The Story of a German Aristocrat Who Defied Hitler.* New York: Harper & Row, 1969.

Tacitus *Dialogues Agricola Germania.* Cambridge, Massachusetts: Harvard University Press, 1963.

Tamm, Ditlev. *Retsopgøret efter besættelsen.* Viborg, Denmark: Nørhaven Bogtrykkeri, 1985.

Taylor, Telford. *The Anatomy of the Nuremberg Trials.* New York: Little, Brown, 1992.

»The United Nations Conference on International Organization.« Department of State. Publication 2490, Conference Series 83. Washington, D.C.: United States Government Printing Office, 1946.

Thygesen, Paul. *Læge i Tyske Koncentrationslejre.* Copenhagen: Stig Vendelkærs Forlag, 1945.

Tjørnehøj, Henning. *Rigets bedste mænd.* Copenhagen: Gyldendal, 1990.

Trommer, Aage. *Jernbanesabotagen i Danmark under den anden verdenskrig.* Odense, Denmark: Andelsbogtrykkeriet, 1971.

Trommer, Aage. *Myte og sandhed i besættelseshistorien.* Copenhagen: Gyldendal, 1971.

Turner, Henry Ashby, Jr. *Hitler's Thirty Days to Power: January 1933.* New York: Addison-Wesley, 1997.

Urban, Wincenty. *Droga krzyzowa Archidiecezji Lwowskiej, w latach II wojny swiatowej, 1939-1945.* Wroclaw, Poland: Semper Fidelis, 1983.

Vedel, Jon. »Opposition til Danmarks Frihedsråd 1943/44.« Copenhagen: Historisk Tidsskrift Bind 83, 1983.

Weinberg, Gerhard L. *A World at Arms.* New York: Cambridge University Press, 1994.

Wohlstetter, Roberta. *Pearl Harbor: Warning and Decision.* Stanford, California: Stanford University Press, 1962.

Zimmerman, David. *Top Secret Exchange. The Tizard Mission and the Scientific War.* Montreal: McGill University Press, 1996.

Map 1. Europe in 1924

Map 2. Denmark, principal Railroads

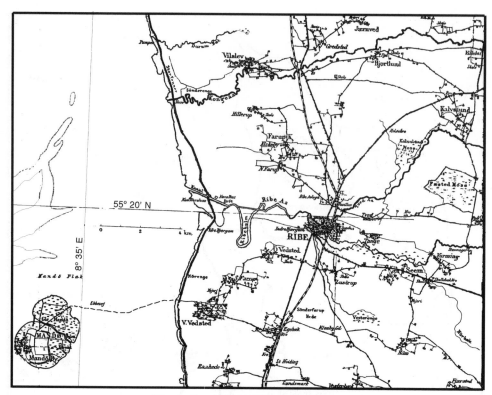

Map 3. The Ribe Area

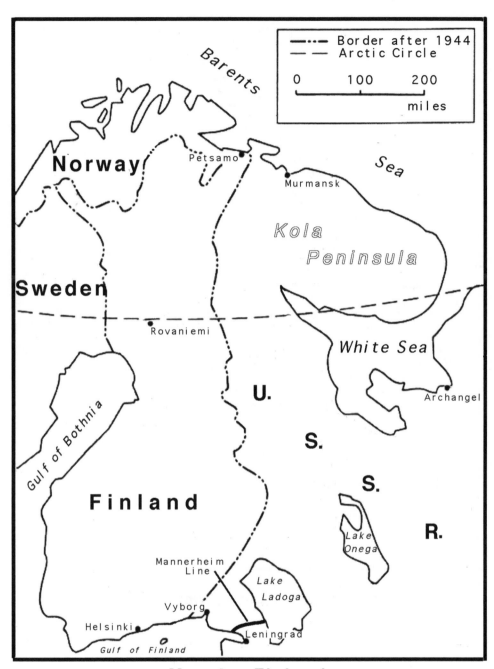

Map 4. Finland

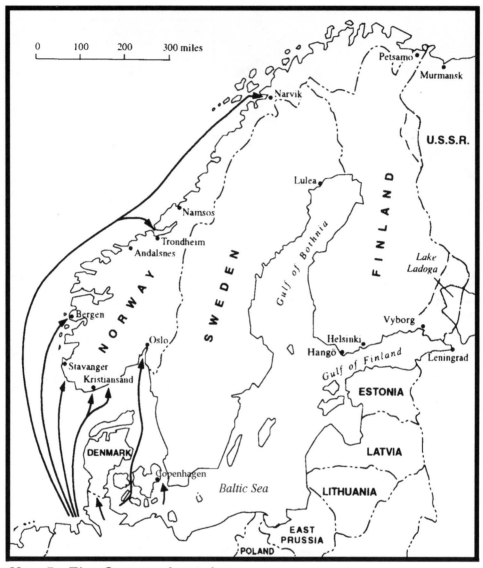

**Map 5. The German Invasion
of Denmark and Norway**

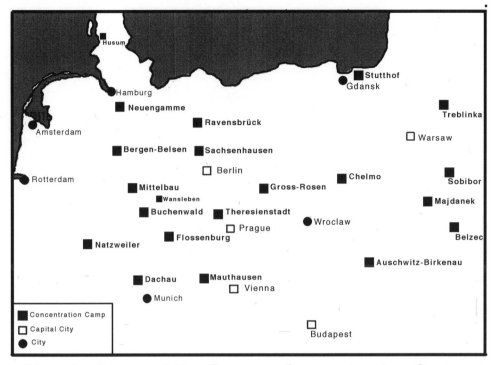

Map 6. Some of the German Concentration Camps